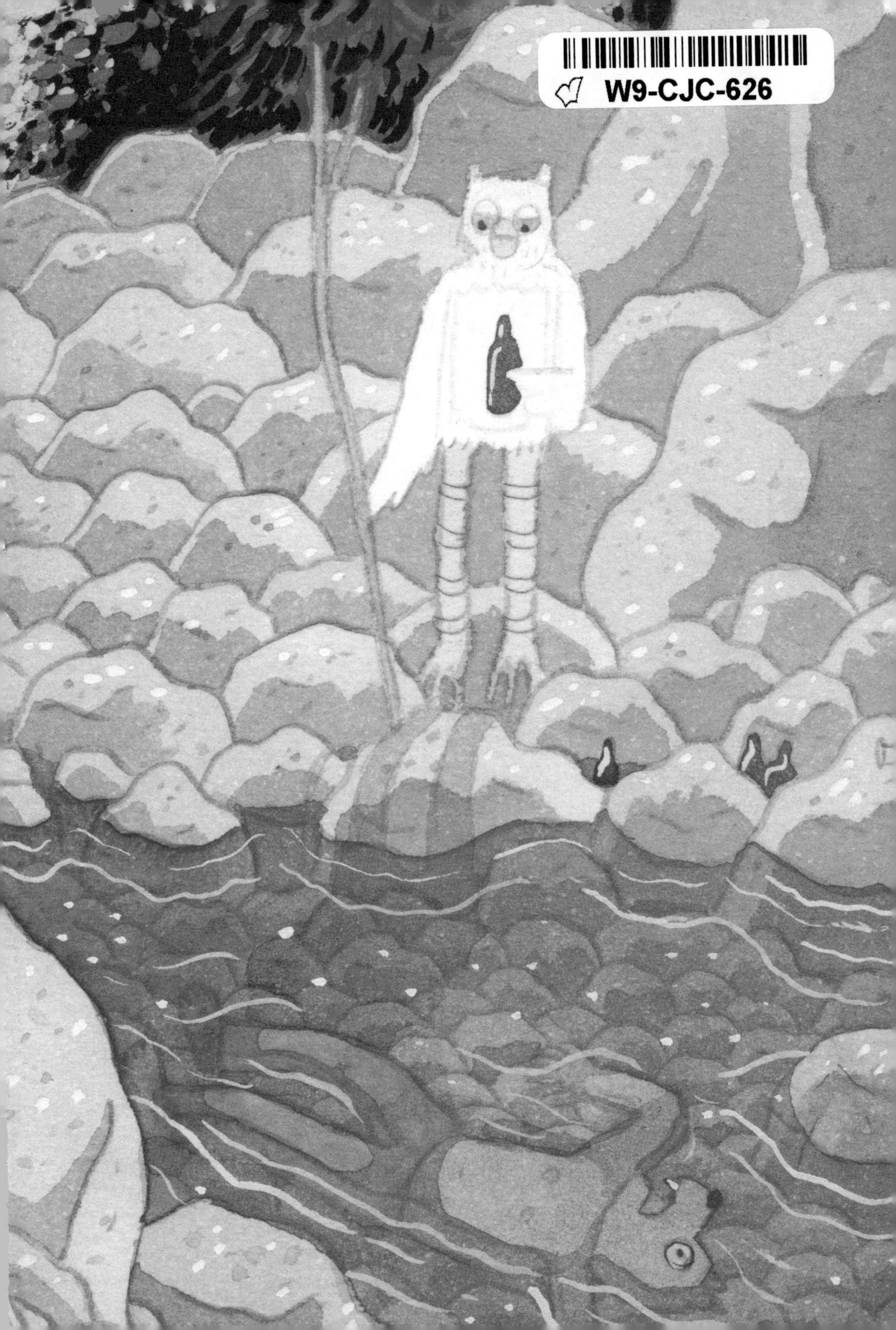

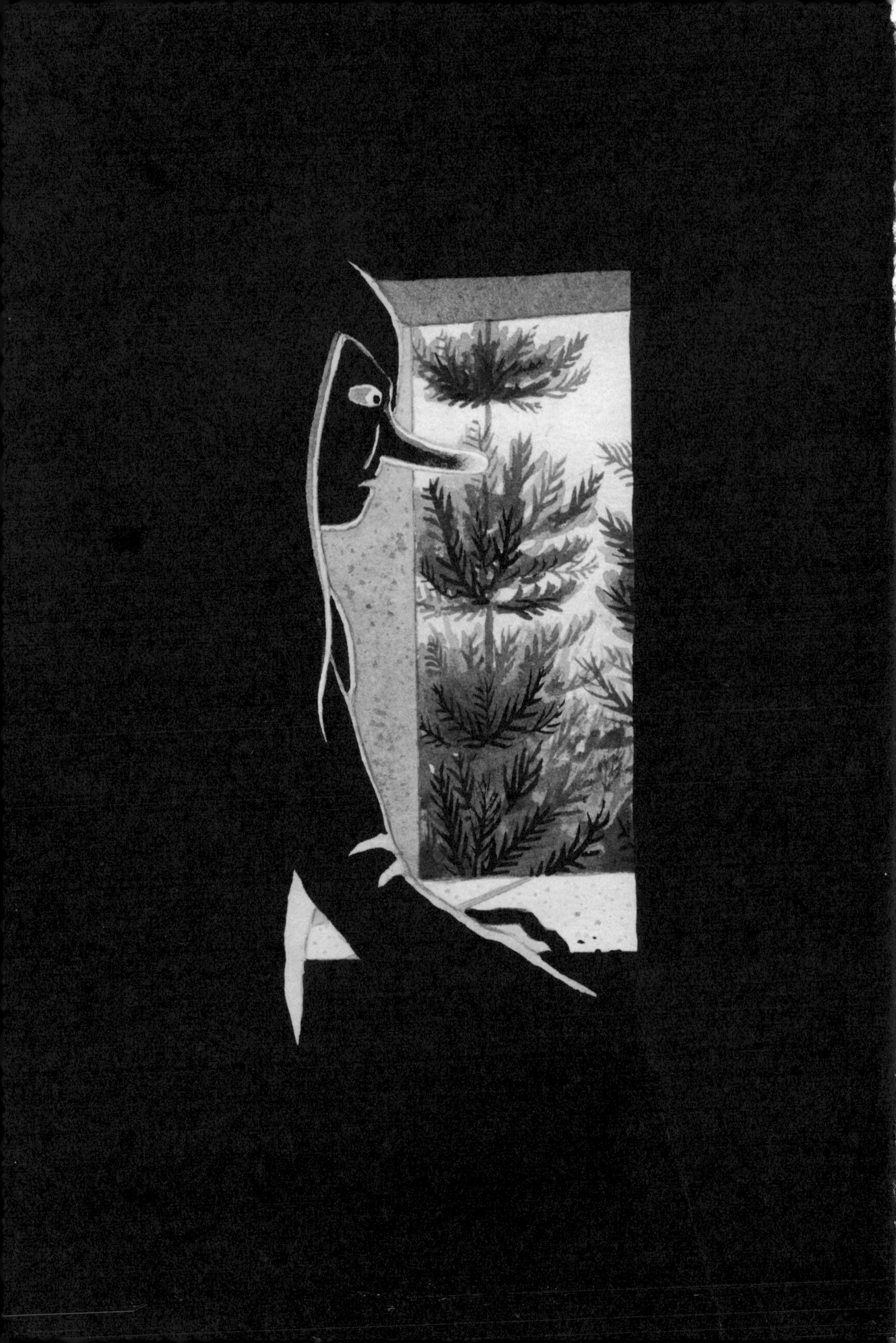

FANTAGRAPHICS BOOKS
SEATTLE, WA, USA

SCENE SELECTION:

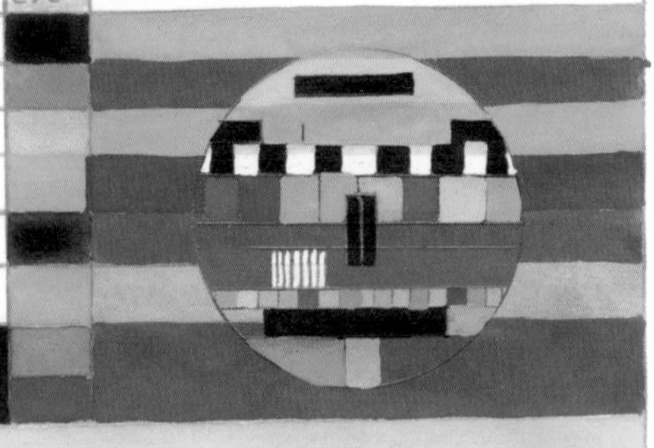

EDITOR AND ASSOCIATE PUBLISHER: ERIC REYNOLDS
BOOK DESIGN: SIMON HANSELMANN
PRODUCTION: PAUL BARESH
PUBLISHER: GARY GROTH

FANTAGRAPHICS BOOKS, INC
SEATTLE, WASHINGTON, USA

ISBN 978-1-60699-743-7
FIRST EDITION: SEPTEMBER 2014 / THIRD PRINTING: JULY 2015
PRINTED IN SINGAPORE

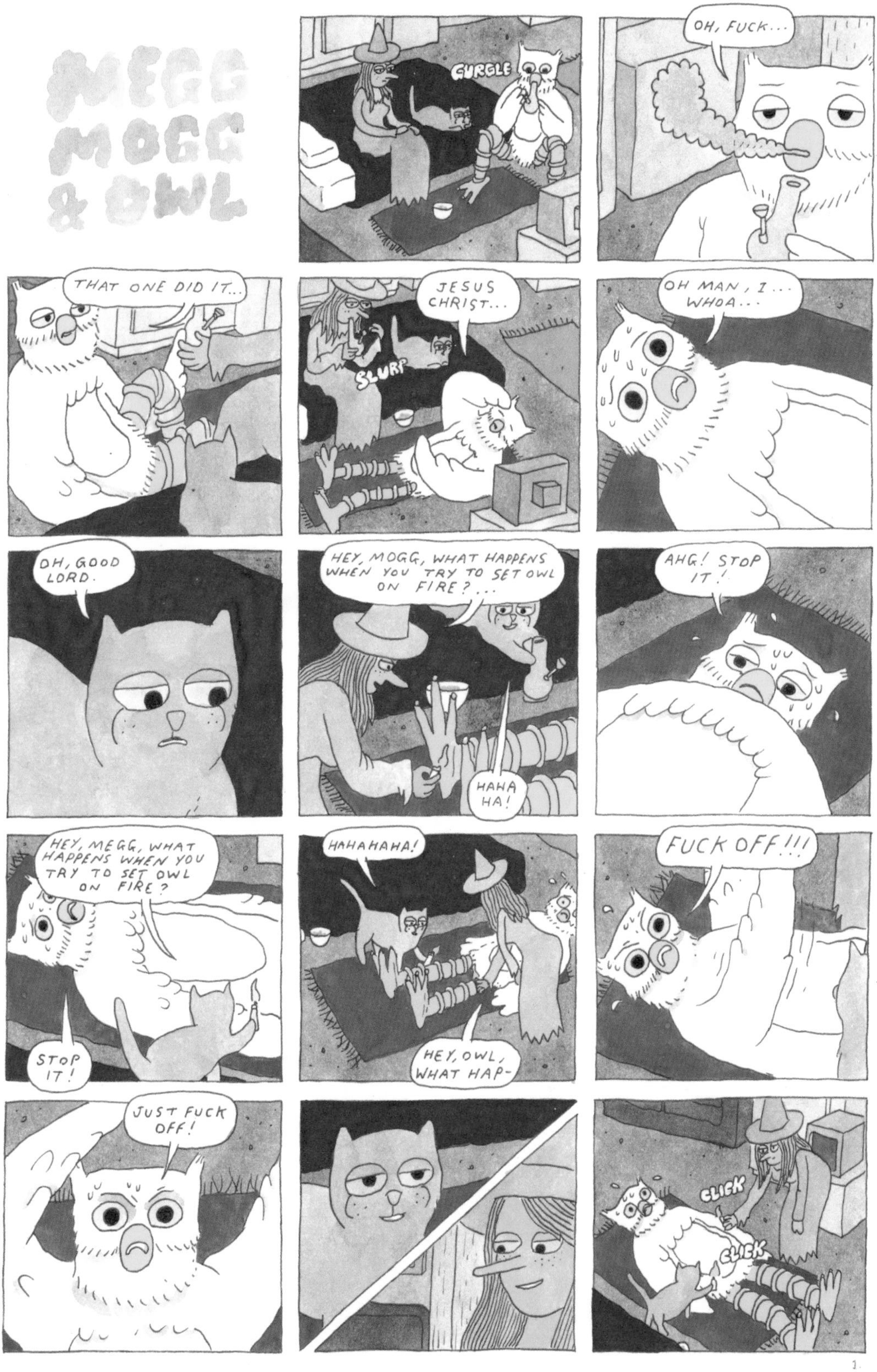
MEGG MOGG & OWL
GURGLE
OH, FUCK...
THAT ONE DID IT...
JESUS CHRIST...
SLURP
OH MAN, I... WHOA...
OH, GOOD LORD.
HEY, MOGG, WHAT HAPPENS WHEN YOU TRY TO SET OWL ON FIRE?...
HAHA HA!
AHG! STOP IT!
HEY, MEGG, WHAT HAPPENS WHEN YOU TRY TO SET OWL ON FIRE?
STOP IT!
HAHAHAHA!
HEY, OWL, WHAT HAP-
FUCK OFF!!!
JUST FUCK OFF!
CLICK
CLICK

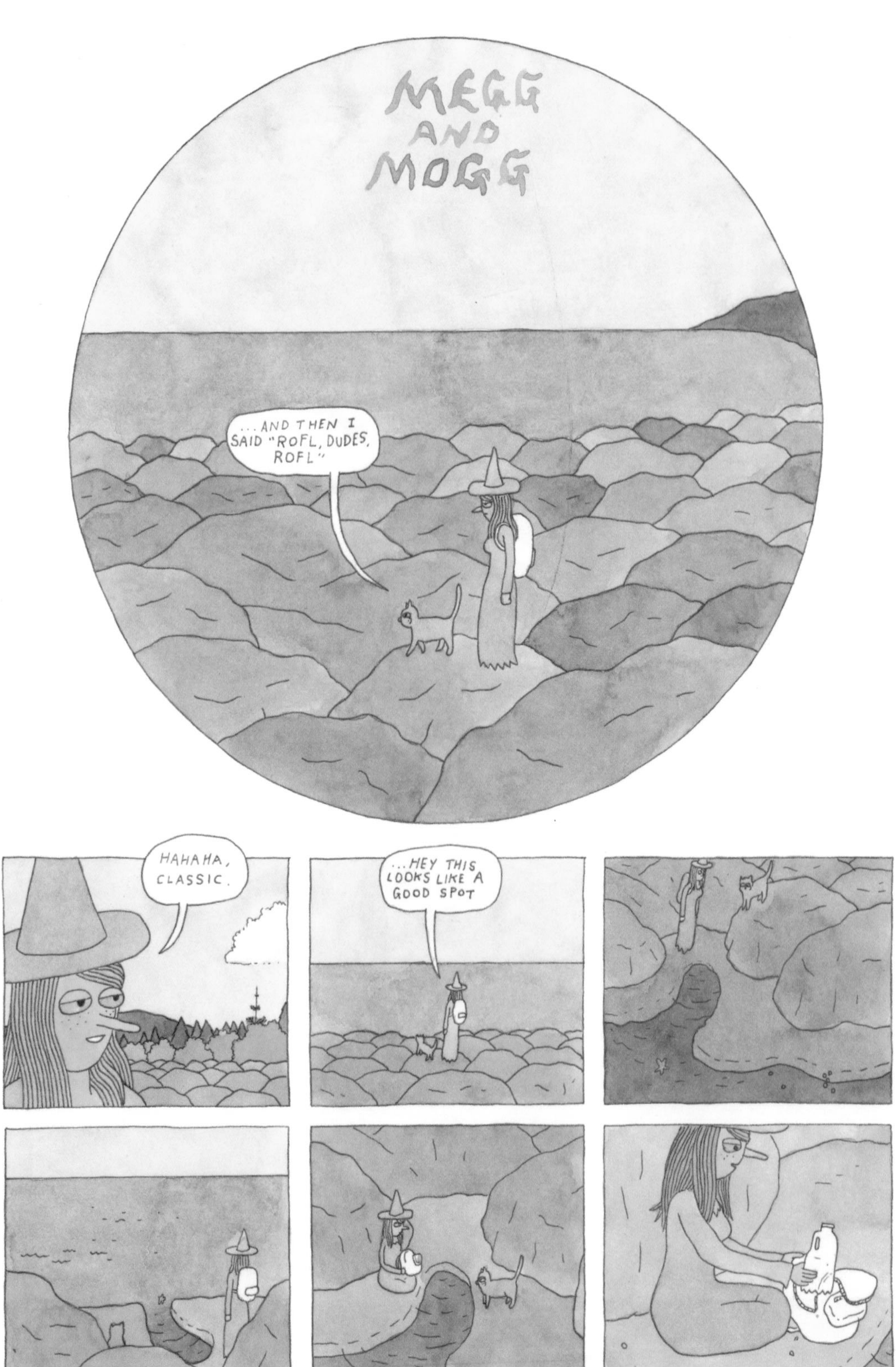
MEGG AND MOGG
...AND THEN I SAID "ROFL, DUDES, ROFL"
HAHAHA, CLASSIC.
...HEY THIS LOOKS LIKE A GOOD SPOT

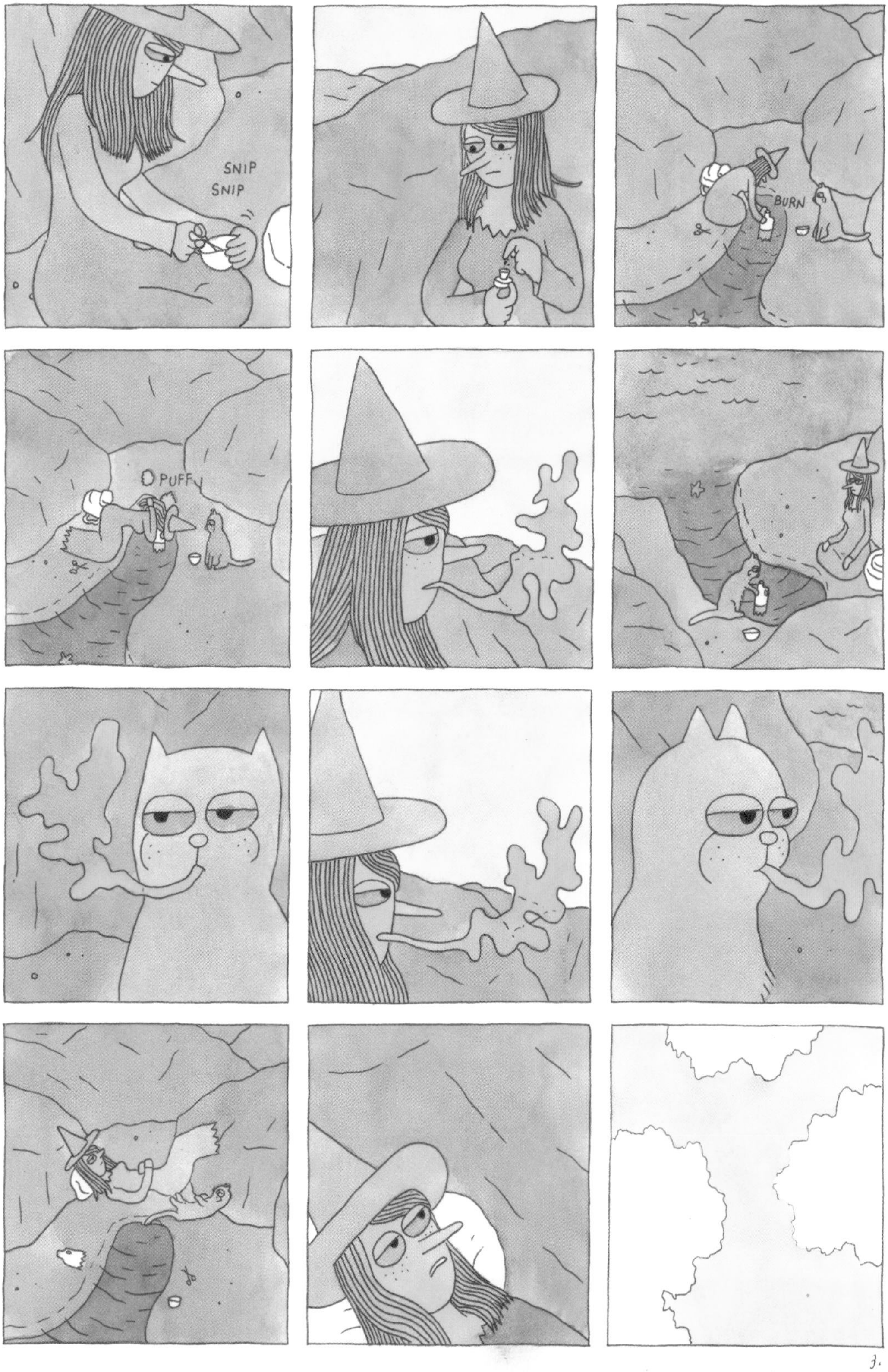
SNIP
SNIP
BURN
PUFF

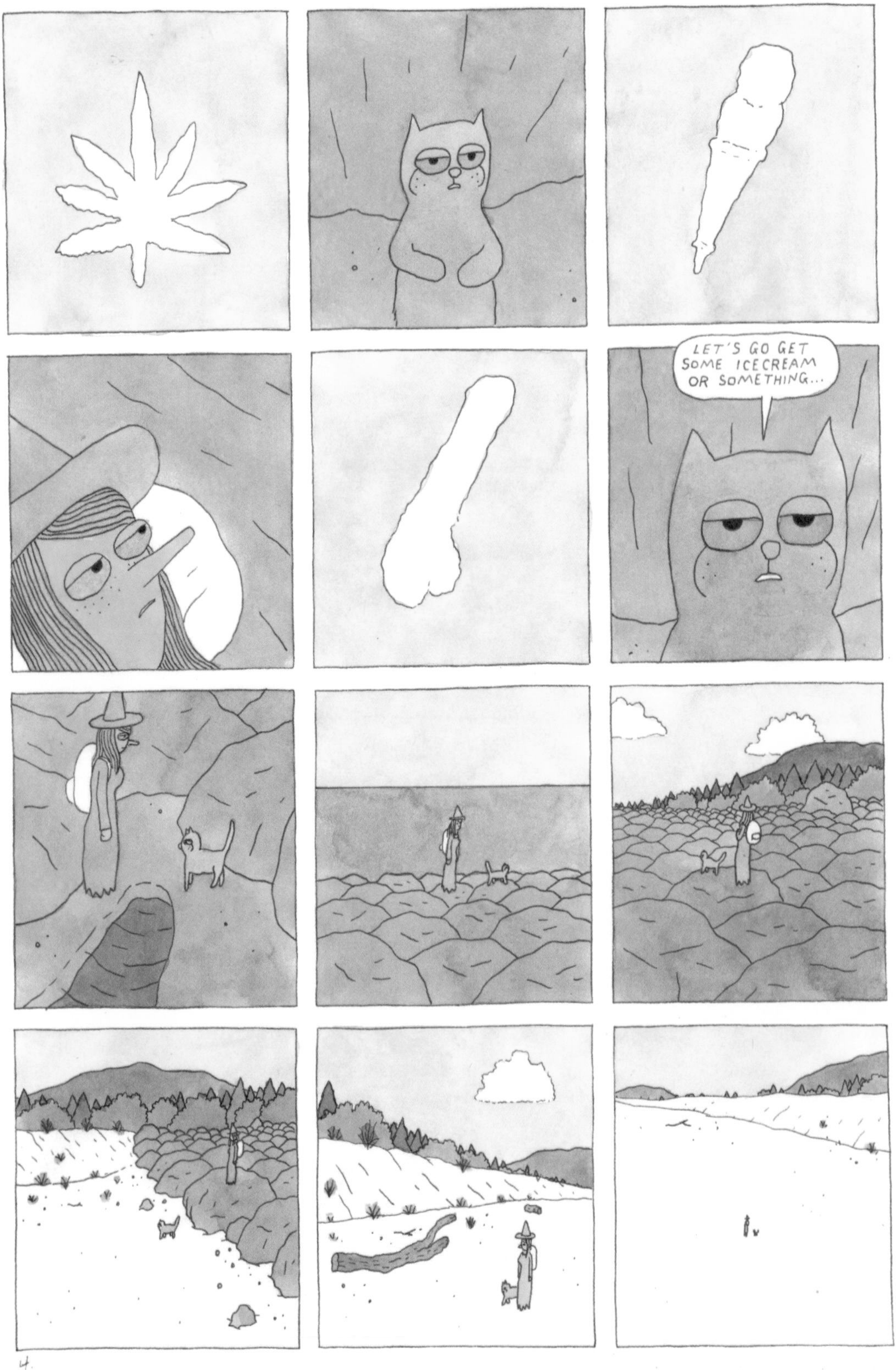
LET'S GO GET SOME ICECREAM OR SOMETHING...

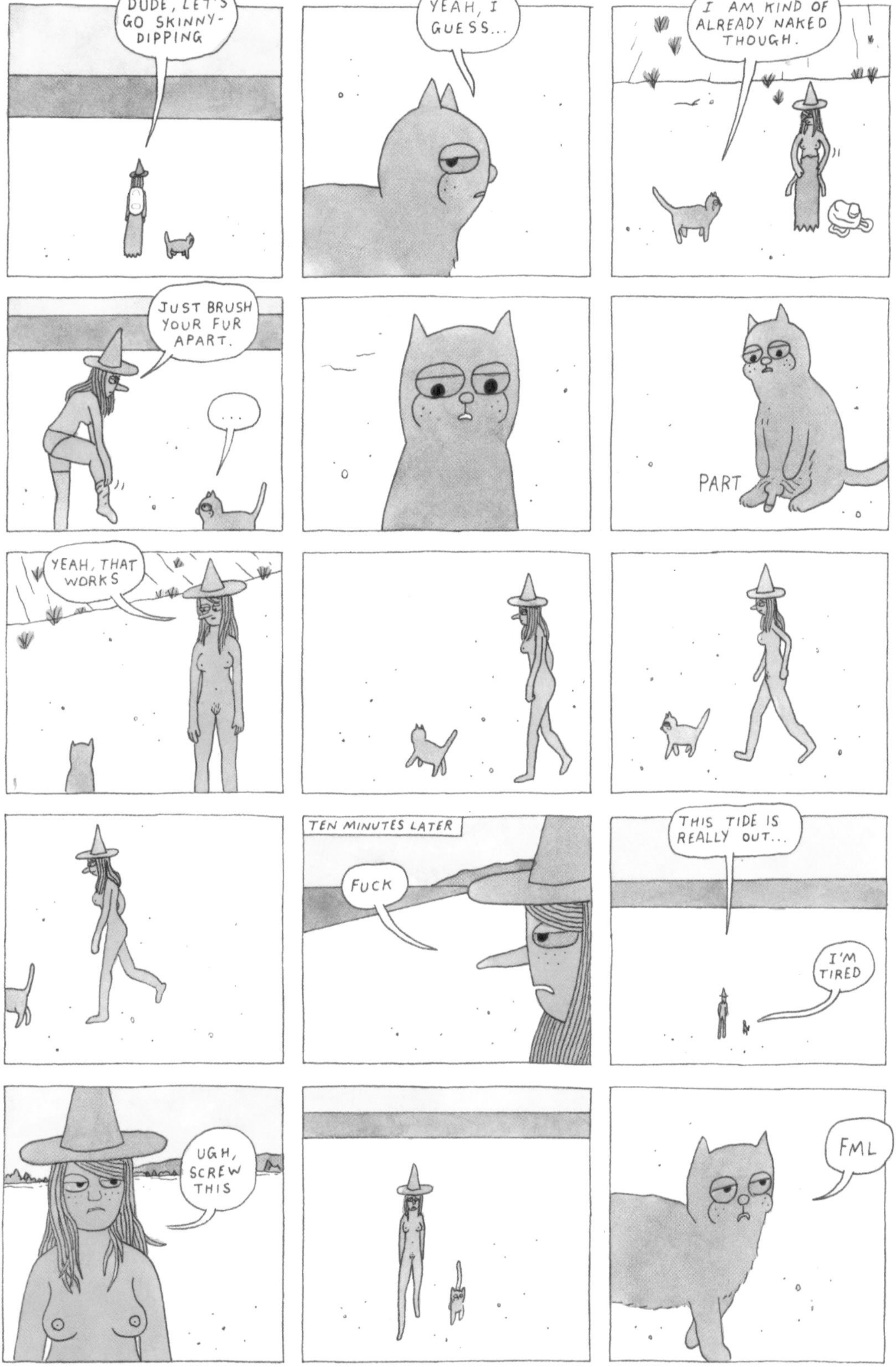
DUDE, LET'S GO SKINNY-DIPPING
YEAH, I GUESS...
I AM KIND OF ALREADY NAKED THOUGH.
JUST BRUSH YOUR FUR APART.
...
PART
YEAH, THAT WORKS
TEN MINUTES LATER
FUCK
THIS TIDE IS REALLY OUT...
I'M TIRED
UGH, SCREW THIS
FML

MEGG AND MOGG

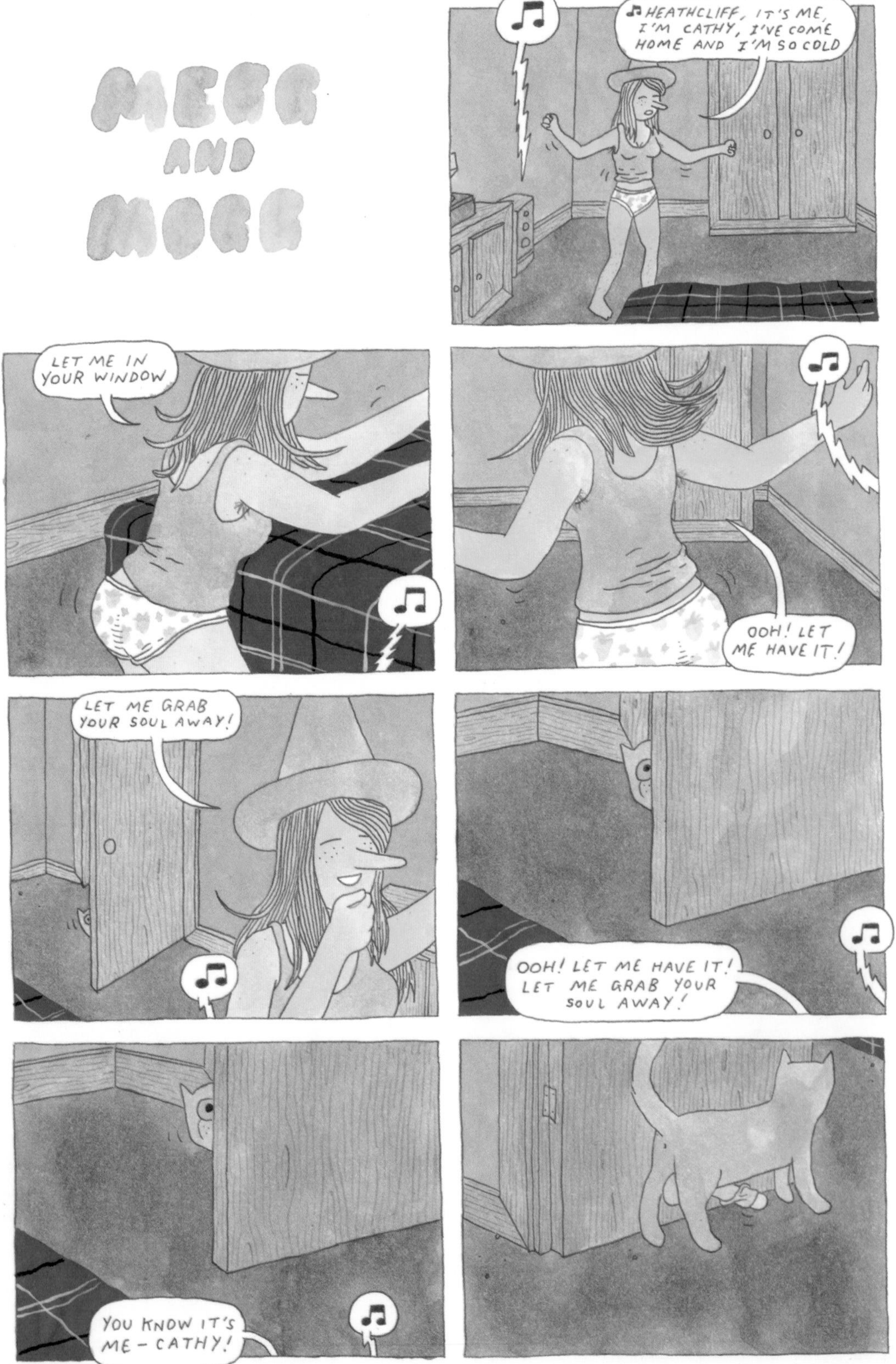
♫ HEATHCLIFF, IT'S ME, I'M CATHY, I'VE COME HOME AND I'M SO COLD
LET ME IN YOUR WINDOW
OOH! LET ME HAVE IT!
LET ME GRAB YOUR SOUL AWAY!
OOH! LET ME HAVE IT! LET ME GRAB YOUR SOUL AWAY!
YOU KNOW IT'S ME - CATHY!

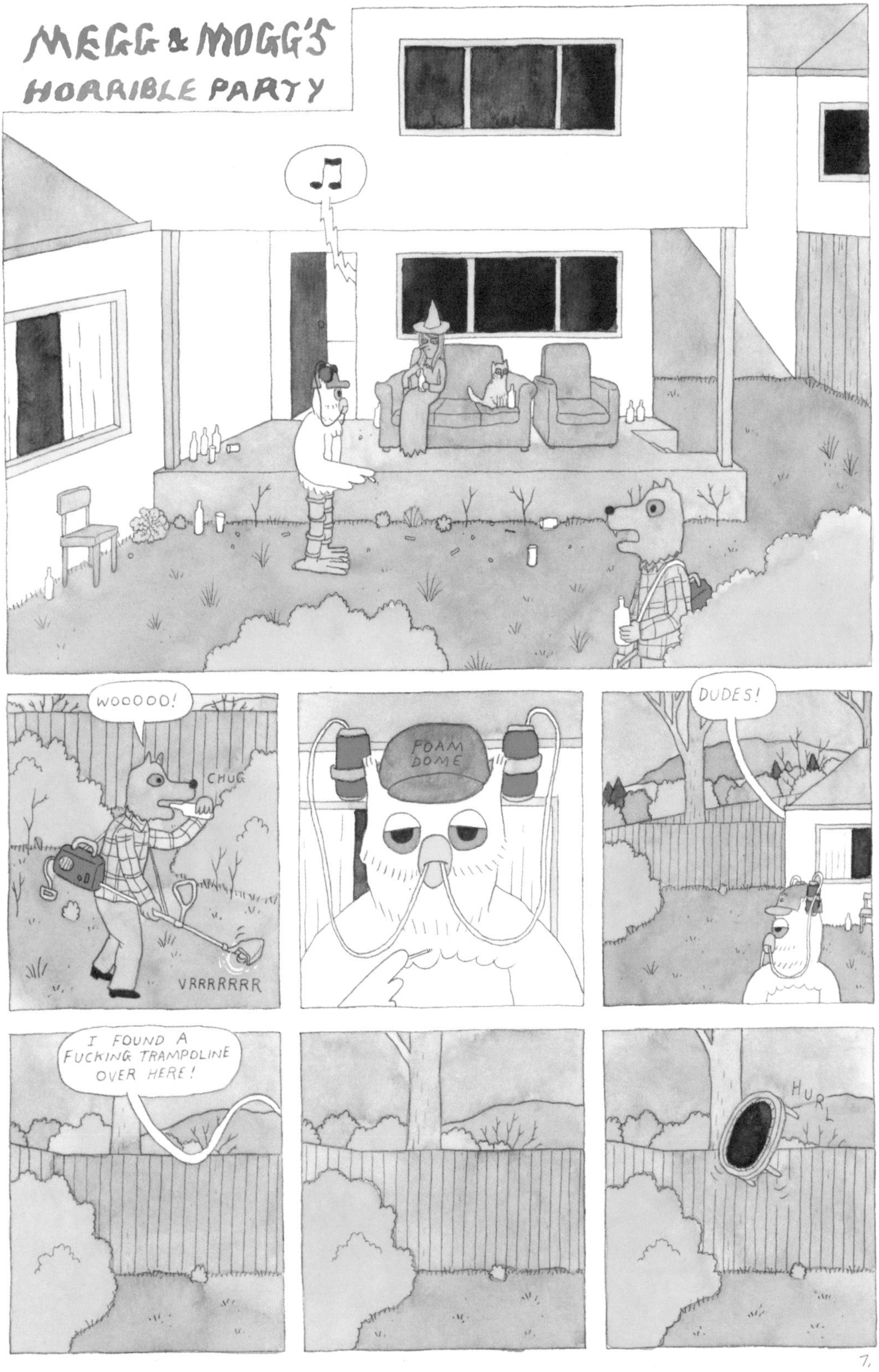
MEGG & MOGG'S
HORRIBLE PARTY
WOOOOO!
CHUG
VRRRRRRR
FOAM DOME
DUDES!
I FOUND A FUCKING TRAMPOLINE OVER HERE!
HURL

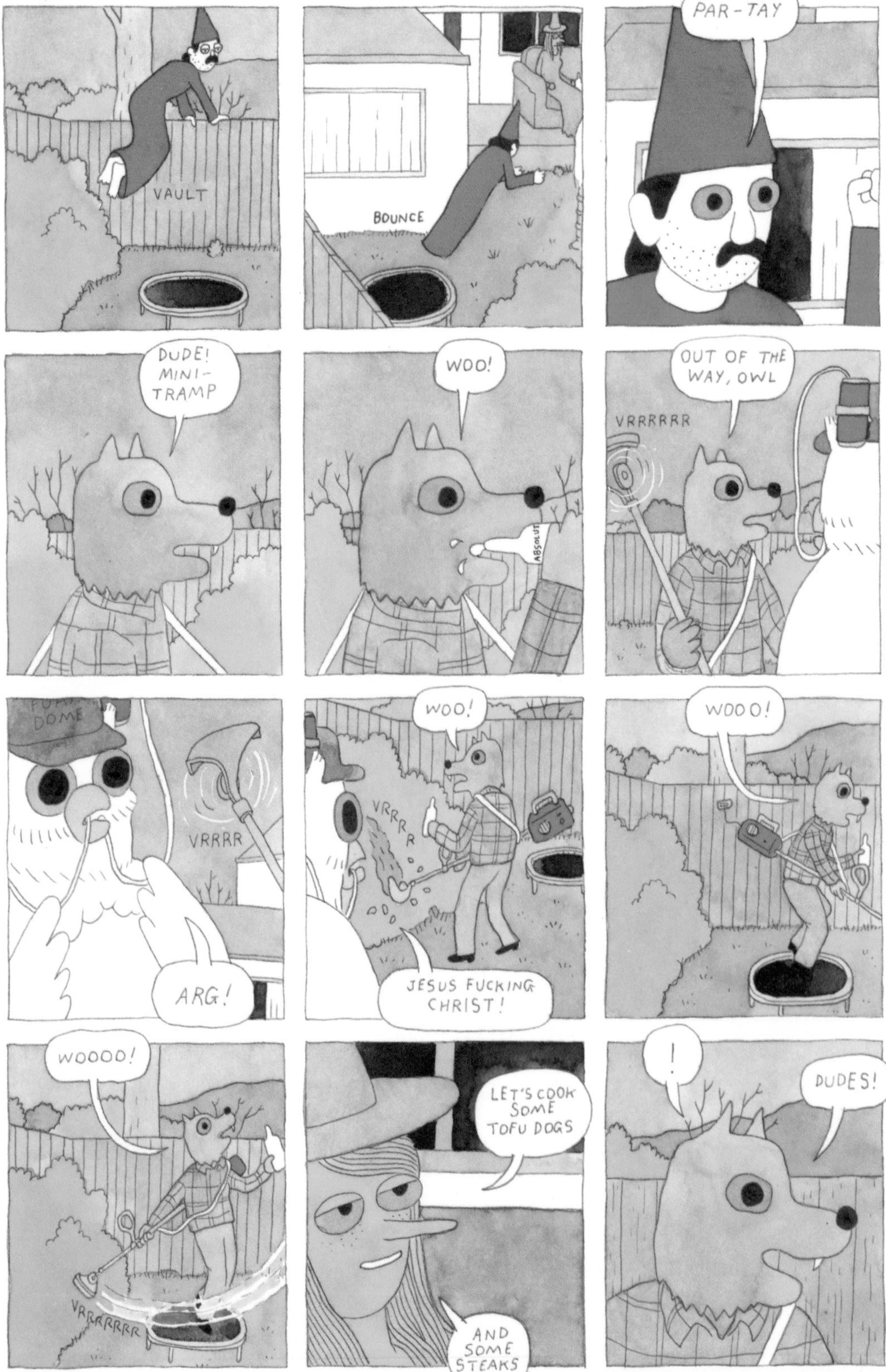

VAULT
BOUNCE
PAR-TAY
DUDE! MINI-TRAMP
WOO!
ABSOLUT
OUT OF THE WAY, OWL
VRRRRRR
VRRRR
ARG!
WOO!
VRRRR
JESUS FUCKING CHRIST!
WOOO!
WOOOO!
VRRRRRRR
LET'S COOK SOME TOFU DOGS
AND SOME STEAKS
!
DUDES!

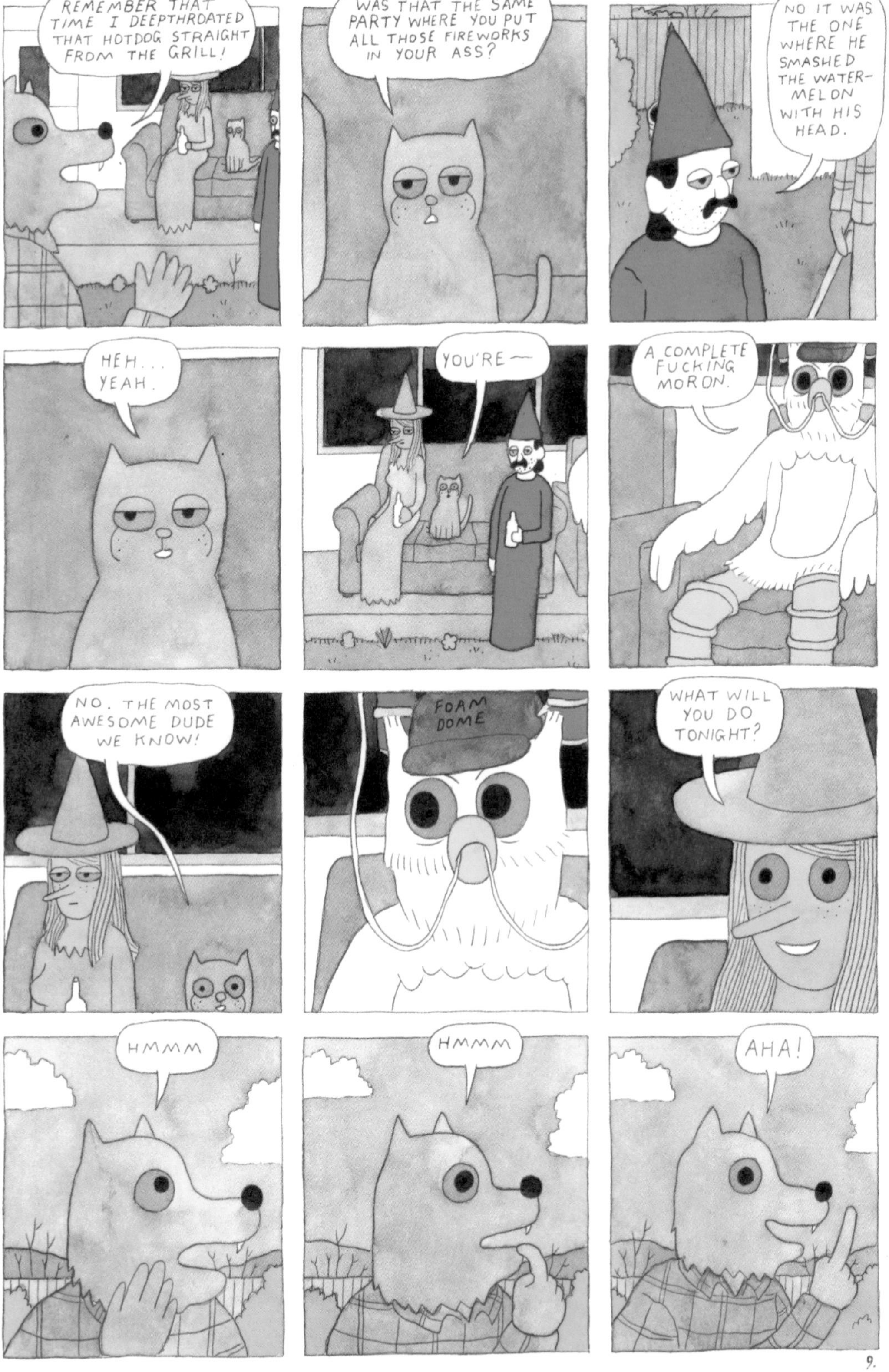
REMEMBER THAT TIME I DEEPTHROATED THAT HOTDOG STRAIGHT FROM THE GRILL!
WAS THAT THE SAME PARTY WHERE YOU PUT ALL THOSE FIREWORKS IN YOUR ASS?
NO IT WAS THE ONE WHERE HE SMASHED THE WATER-MELON WITH HIS HEAD.
HEH... YEAH.
YOU'RE—
A COMPLETE FUCKING MORON.
NO. THE MOST AWESOME DUDE WE KNOW!
FOAM DOME
WHAT WILL YOU DO TONIGHT?
HMMM
HMMM
AHA!

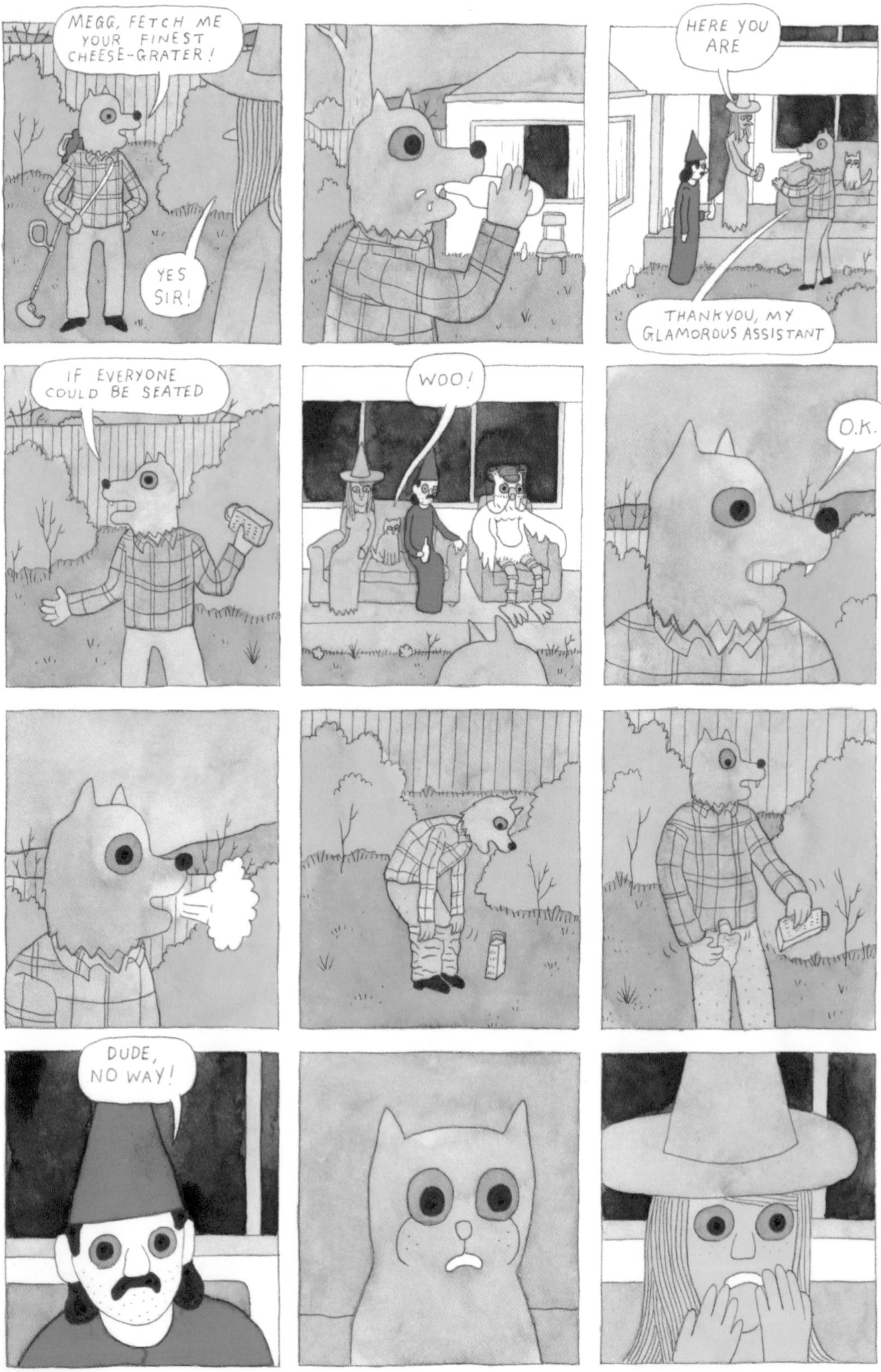
MEGG, FETCH ME YOUR FINEST CHEESE-GRATER!
YES SIR!
HERE YOU ARE
THANKYOU, MY GLAMOROUS ASSISTANT
IF EVERYONE COULD BE SEATED
WOO!
O.K.
DUDE, NO WAY!

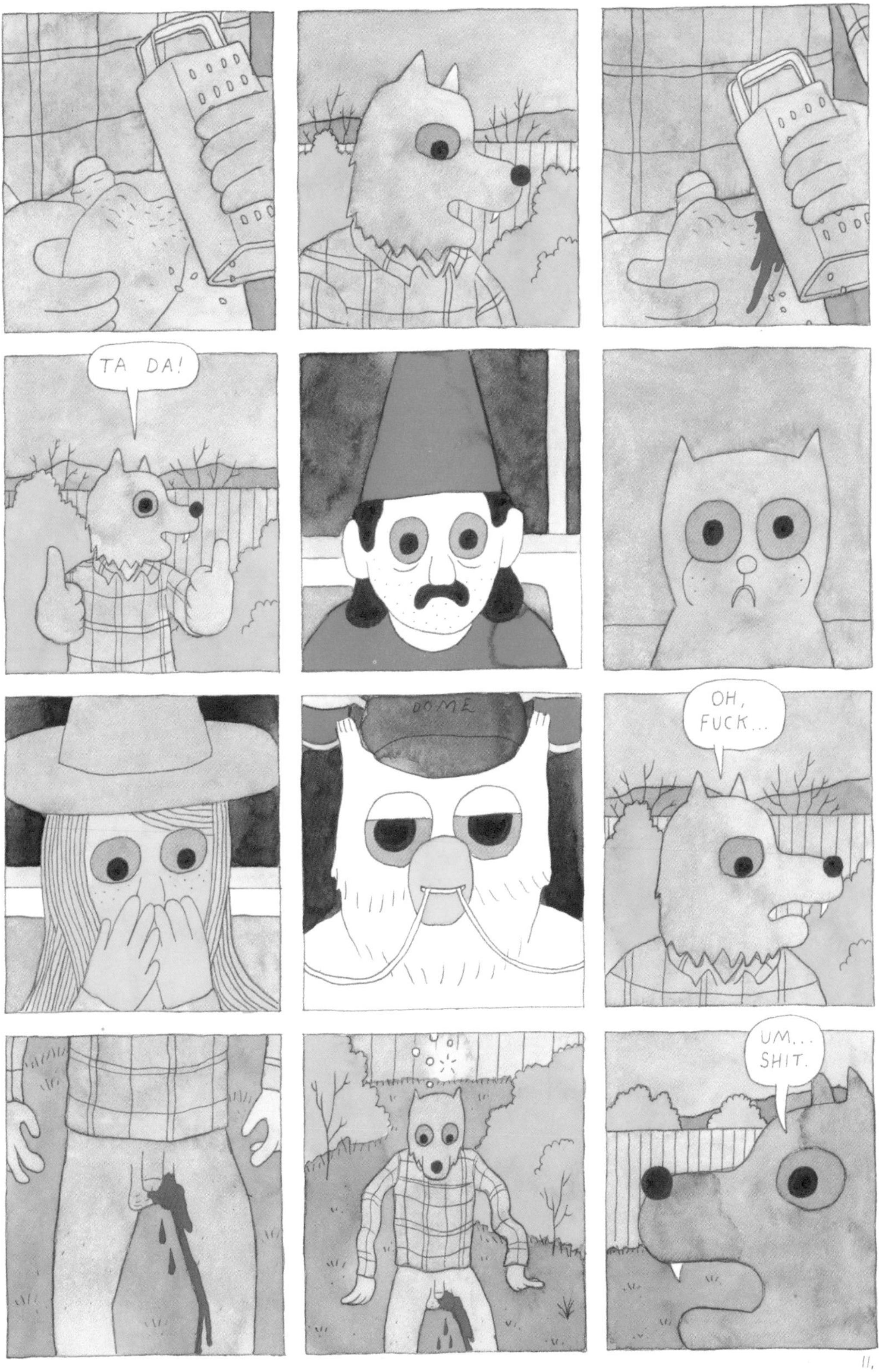
TA DA!
DOME
OH, FUCK...
UM... SHIT.

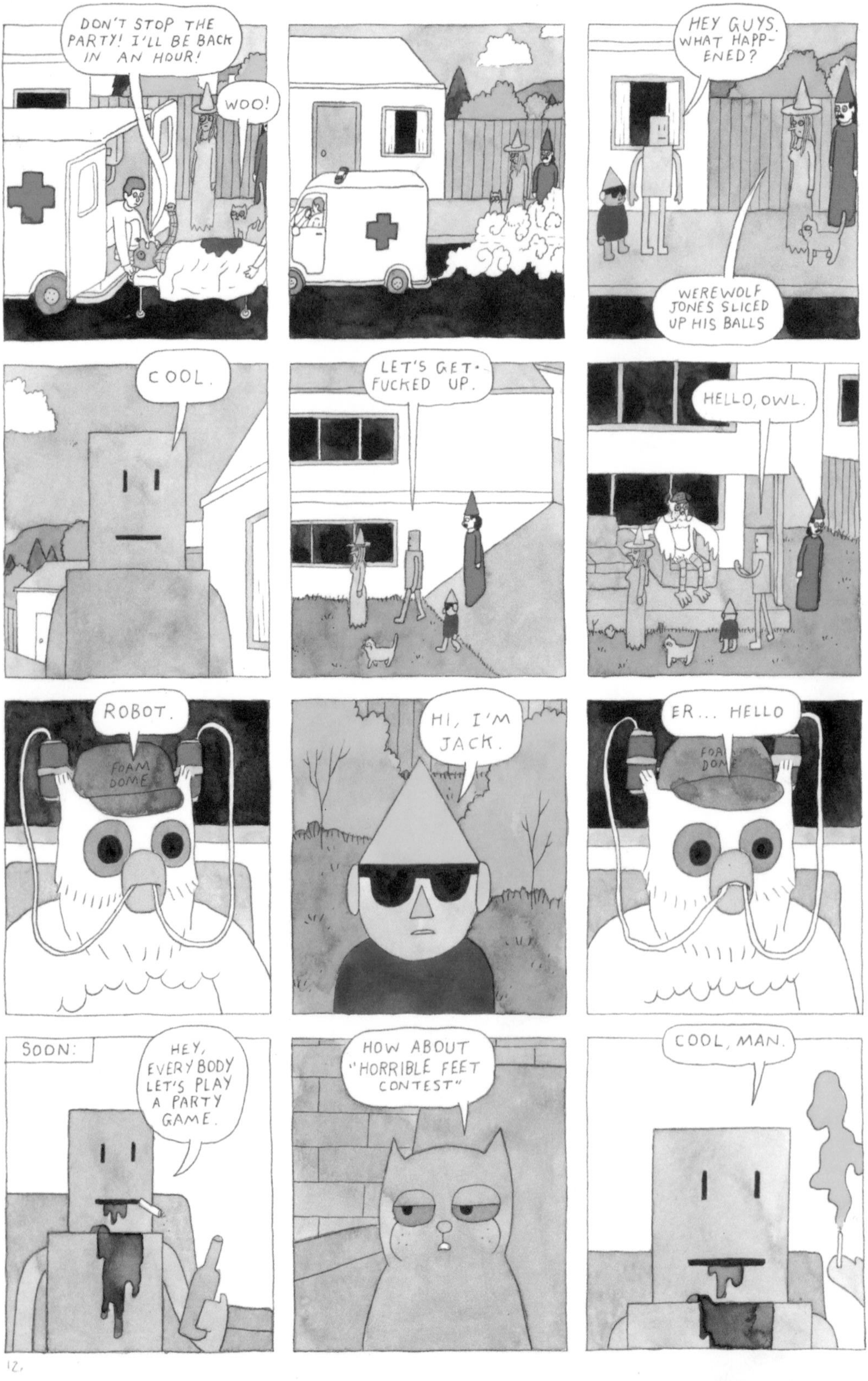
DON'T STOP THE PARTY! I'LL BE BACK IN AN HOUR!
WOO!
HEY GUYS. WHAT HAPP-ENED?
WEREWOLF JONES SLICED UP HIS BALLS
COOL.
LET'S GET FUCKED UP.
HELLO, OWL.
ROBOT.
FOAM DOME
HI, I'M JACK.
ER... HELLO
FOAM DOME
SOON:
HEY, EVERY BODY LET'S PLAY A PARTY GAME.
HOW ABOUT "HORRIBLE FEET CONTEST"
COOL, MAN.

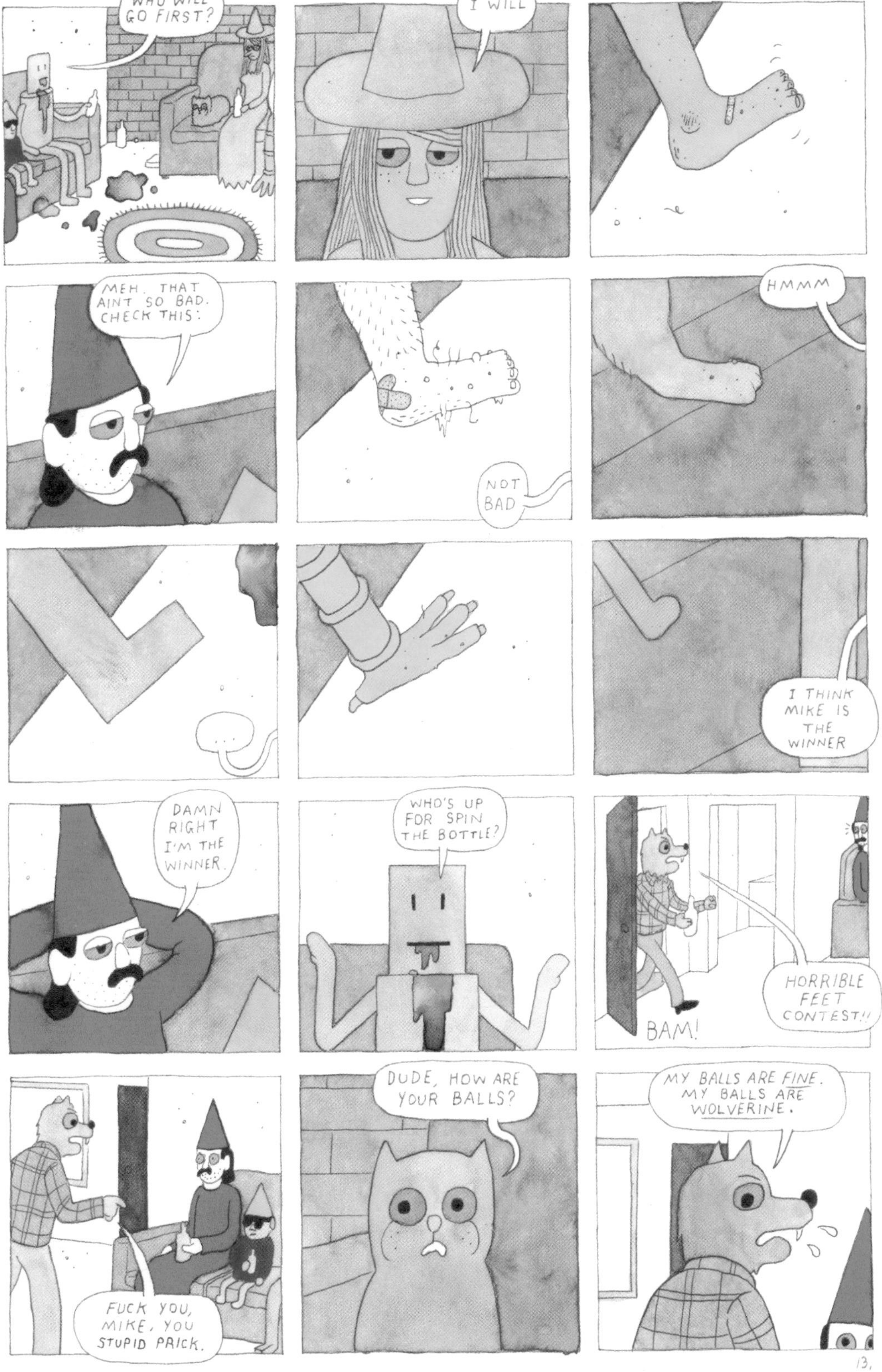
WHO WILL GO FIRST?
I WILL
MEH. THAT AINT SO BAD. CHECK THIS:
NOT BAD
HMMM
. . .
I THINK MIKE IS THE WINNER
DAMN RIGHT I'M THE WINNER.
WHO'S UP FOR SPIN THE BOTTLE?
BAM!
HORRIBLE FEET CONTEST!!
FUCK YOU, MIKE, YOU STUPID PRICK.
DUDE, HOW ARE YOUR BALLS?
MY BALLS ARE FINE. MY BALLS ARE WOLVERINE.

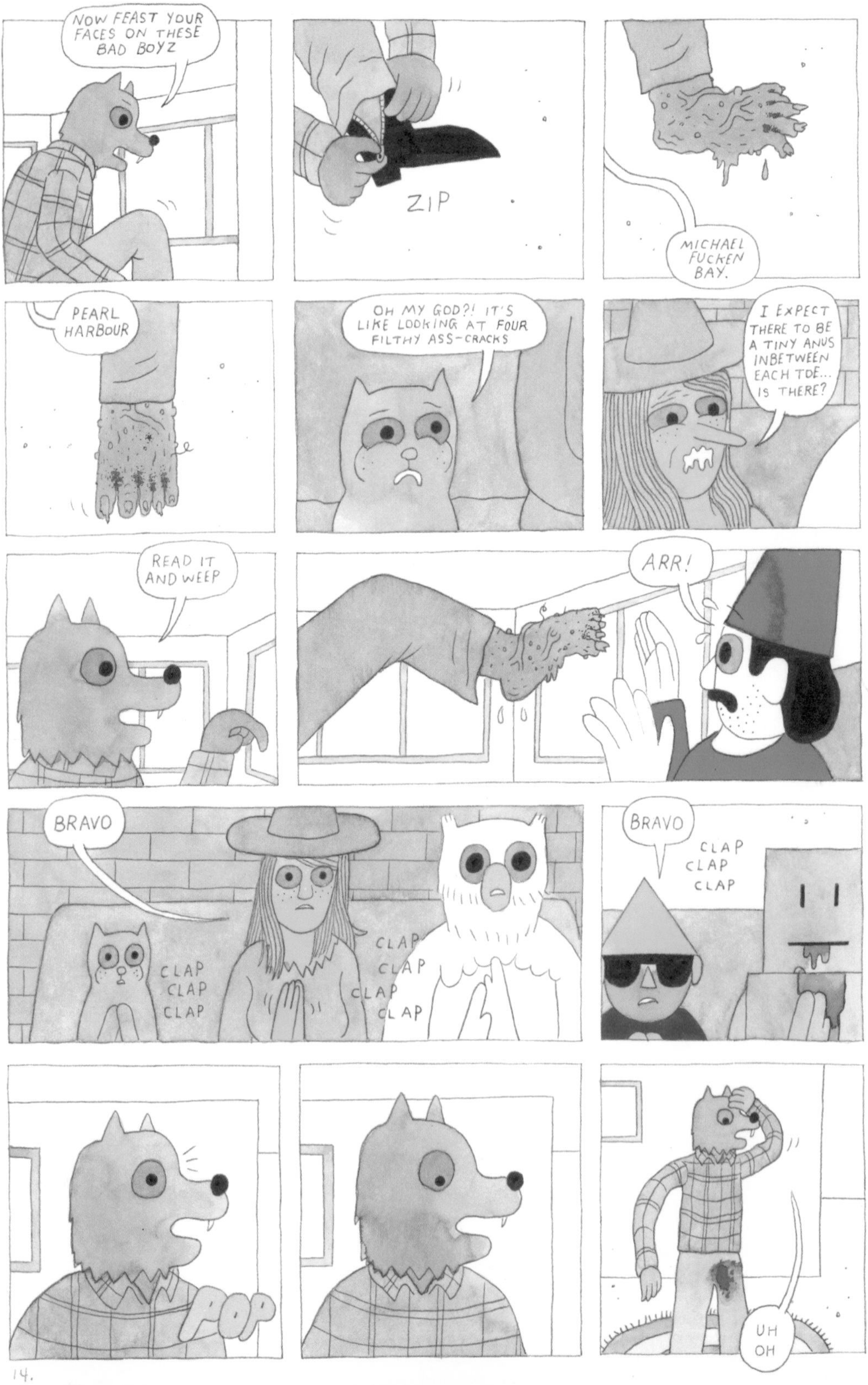
NOW FEAST YOUR FACES ON THESE BAD BOYZ
ZIP
MICHAEL FUCKEN BAY.
PEARL HARBOUR
OH MY GOD?! IT'S LIKE LOOKING AT FOUR FILTHY ASS-CRACKS
I EXPECT THERE TO BE A TINY ANUS INBETWEEN EACH TOE... IS THERE?
READ IT AND WEEP
ARR!
BRAVO
CLAP CLAP CLAP
CLAP CLAP CLAP CLAP
BRAVO
CLAP CLAP CLAP
POP
UH OH

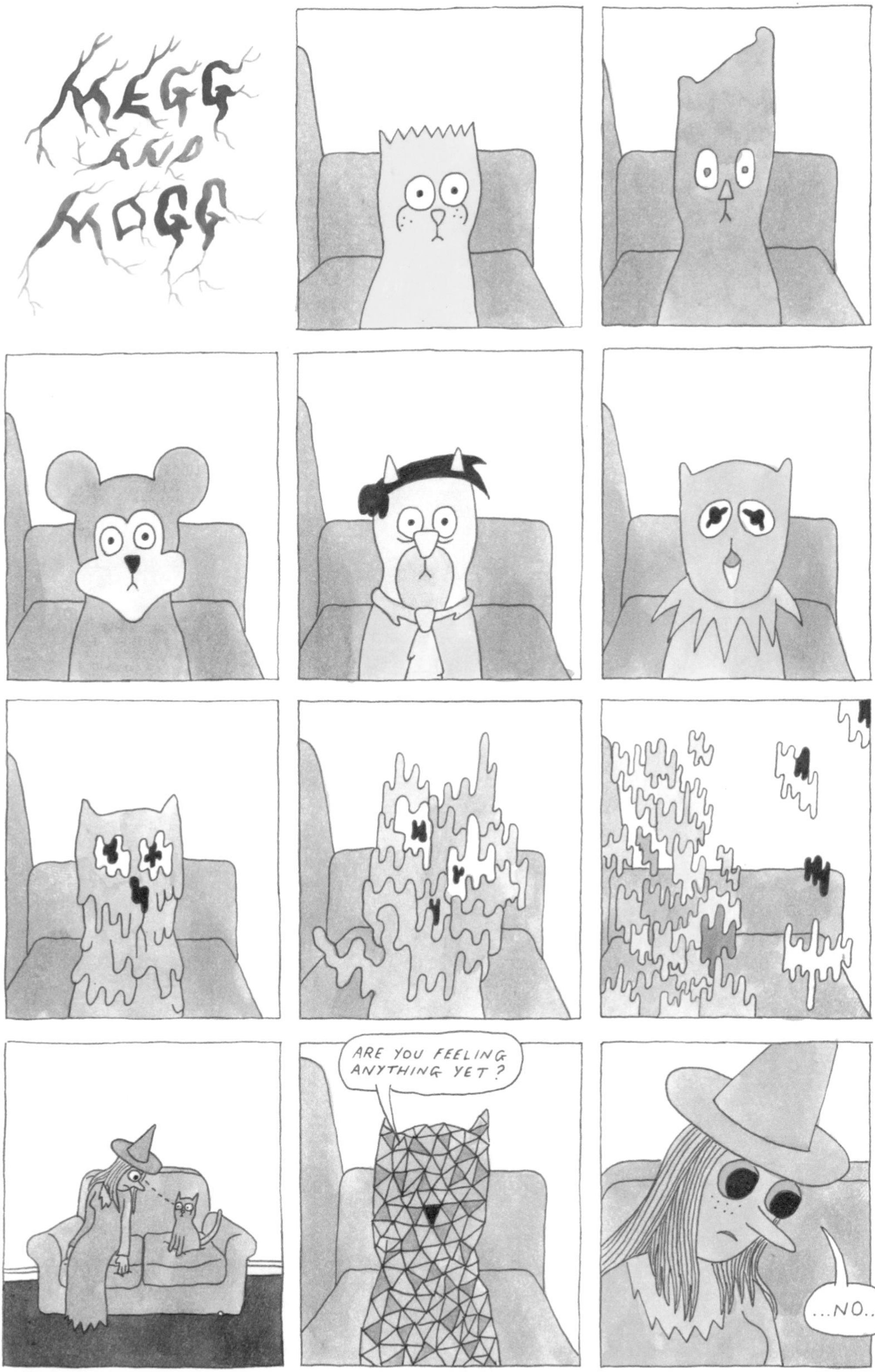
MEGG AND MOGG
ARE YOU FEELING ANYTHING YET?
...NO...

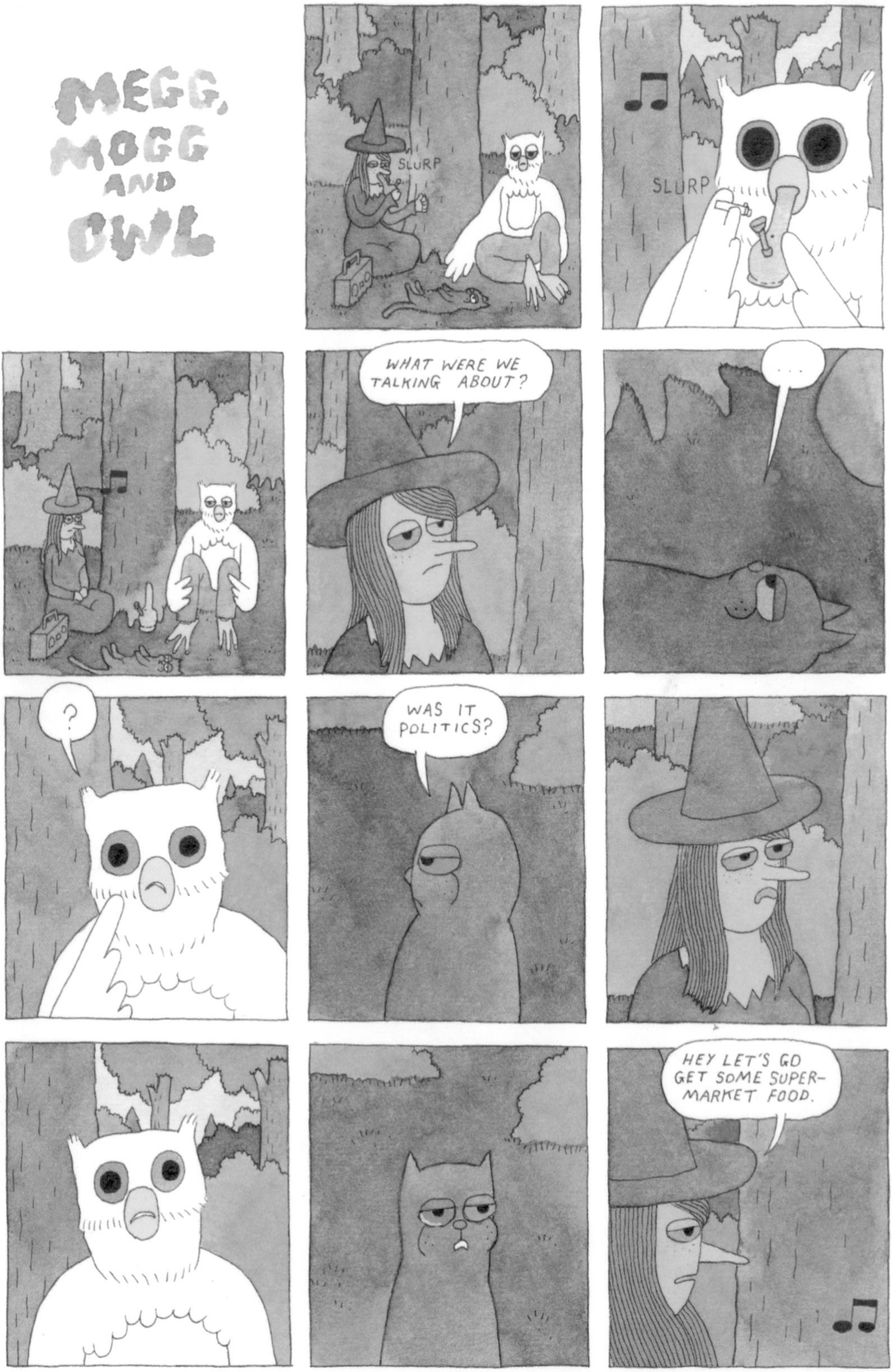
MEGG, MOGG AND OWL
SLURP
SLURP
WHAT WERE WE TALKING ABOUT?
. . .
?
WAS IT POLITICS?
HEY LET'S GO GET SOME SUPER-MARKET FOOD.

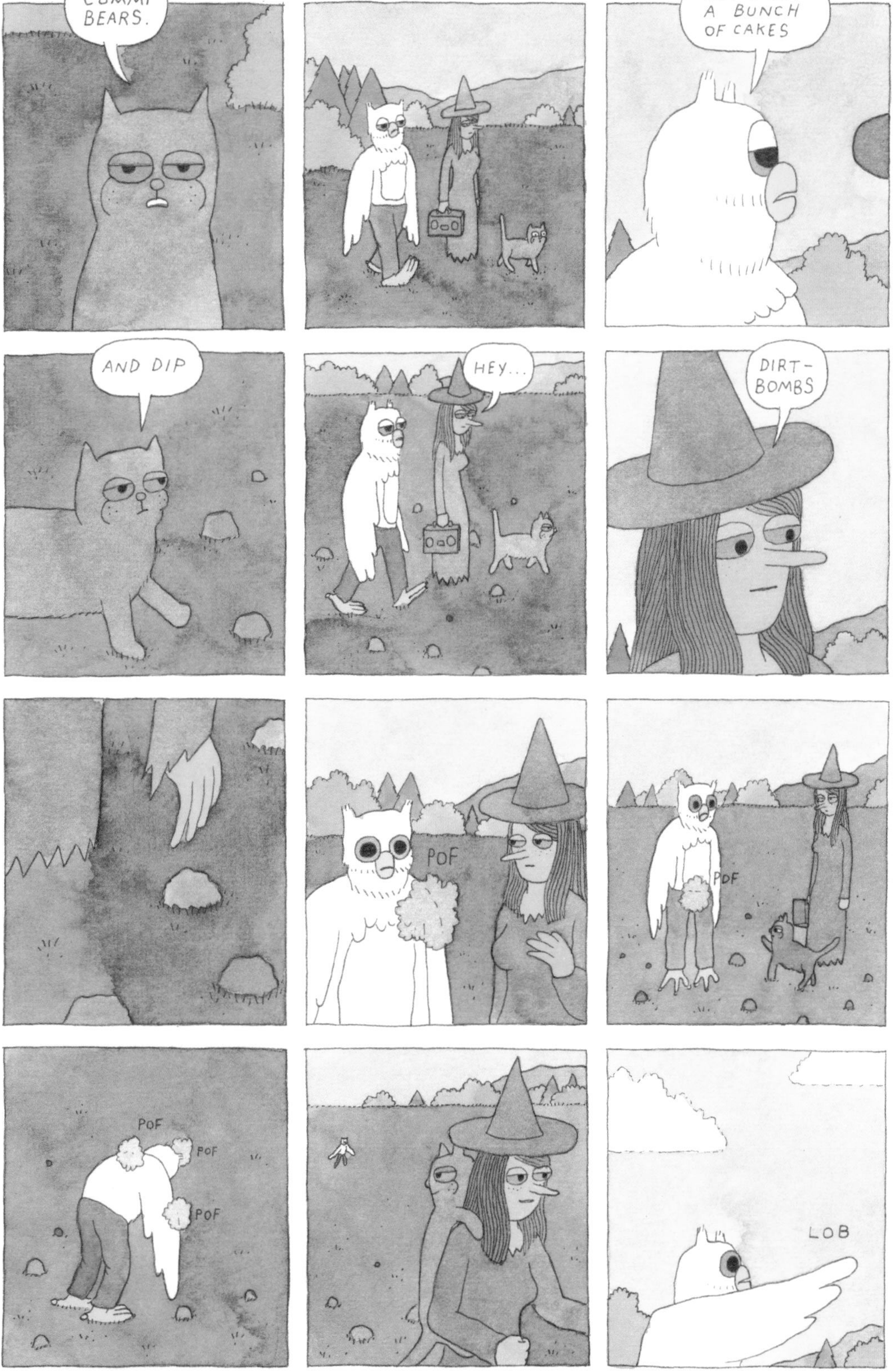
CUMMI BEARS.
LET'S GET A BUNCH OF CAKES
AND DIP
HEY...
DIRT-BOMBS
POF
POF
POF
POF
POF
LOB

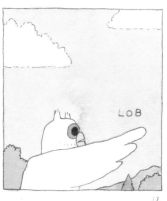

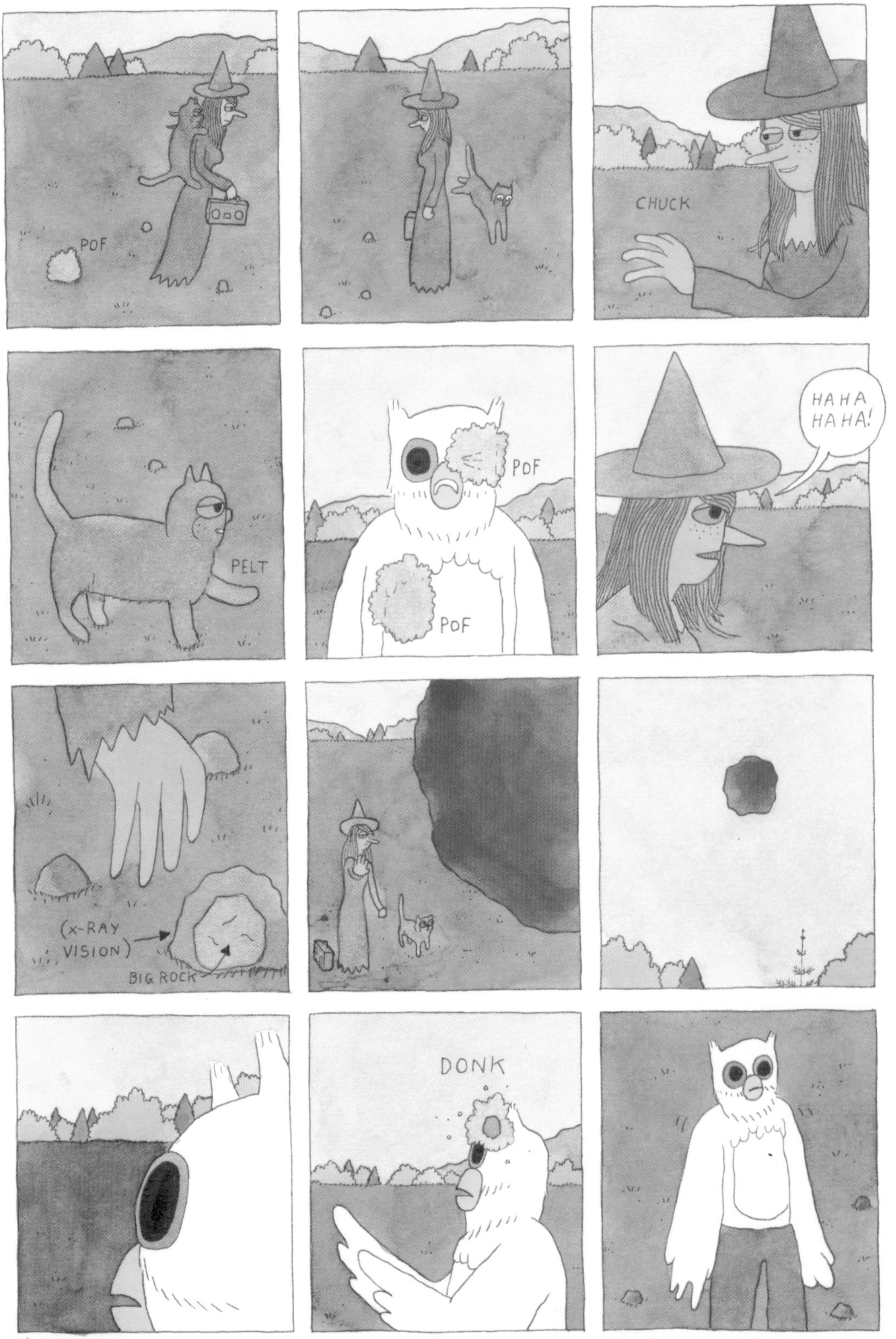
POF
CHUCK
PELT
POF
POF
HAHA HAHA!
(X-RAY VISION)
BIG ROCK
DONK

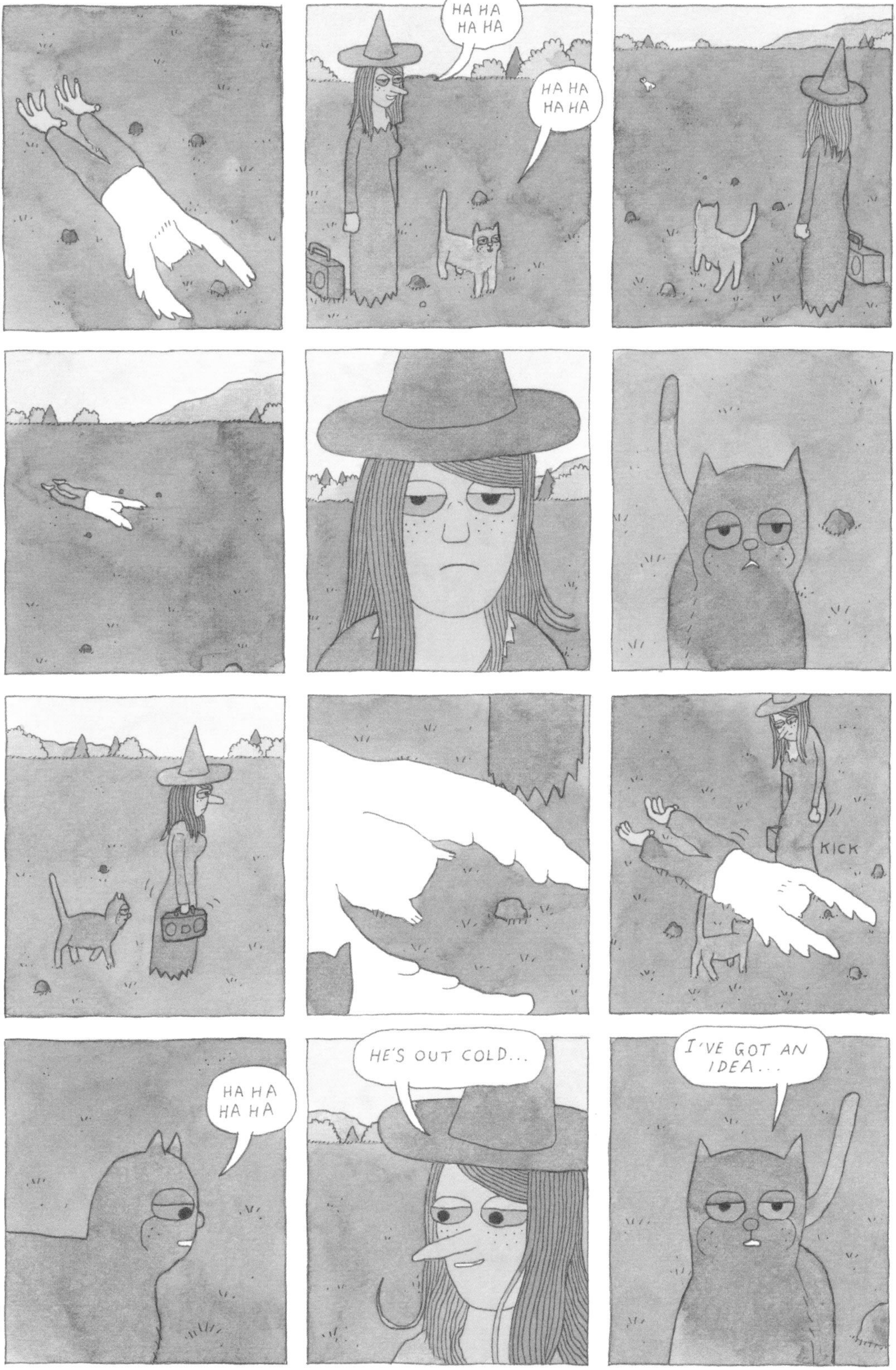
HA HA
HA HA
HA HA
HA HA
KICK
HA HA
HA HA
HE'S OUT COLD...
I'VE GOT AN IDEA...

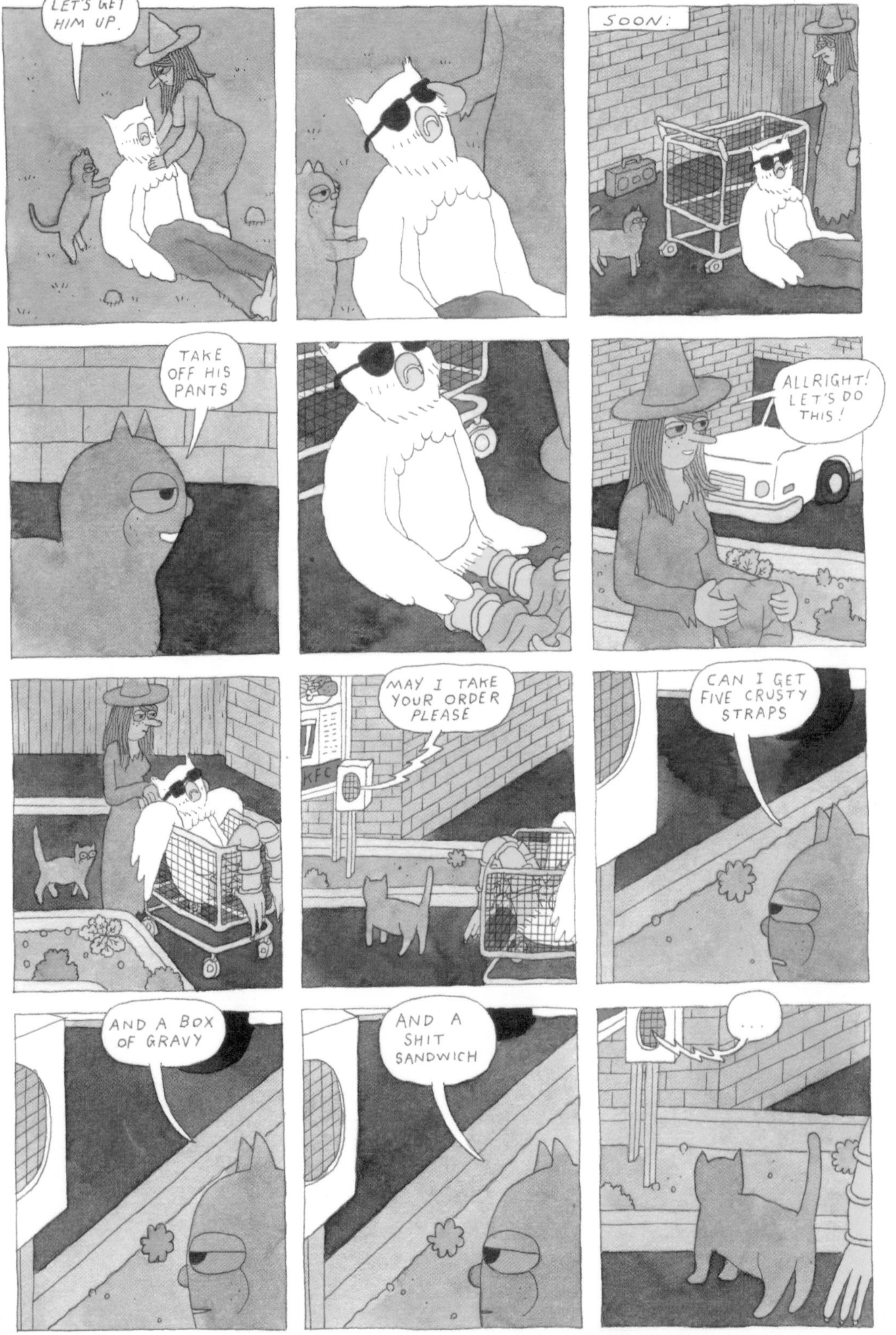

LET'S GET HIM UP.
SOON:
TAKE OFF HIS PANTS
ALLRIGHT! LET'S DO THIS!
MAY I TAKE YOUR ORDER PLEASE
KFC
CAN I GET FIVE CRUSTY STRAPS
AND A BOX OF GRAVY
AND A SHIT SANDWICH
...

DRIVE THROUGH PLEASE
SHOVE
KFC
SQUEAK
SQUEAK SQUEAK
KFC
GASP

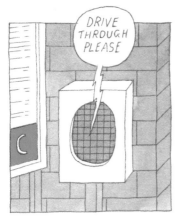

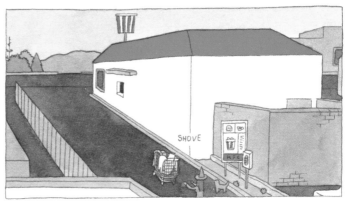

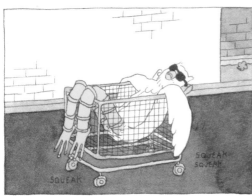

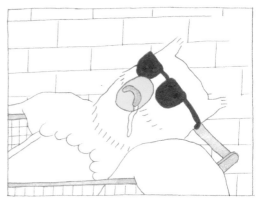

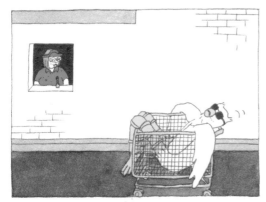

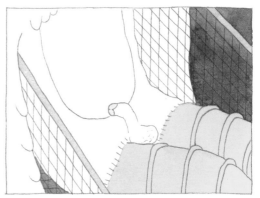

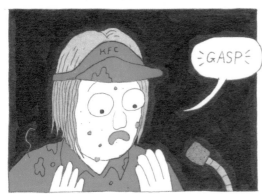

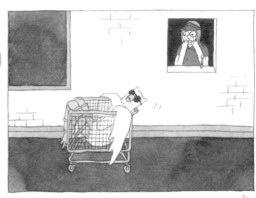

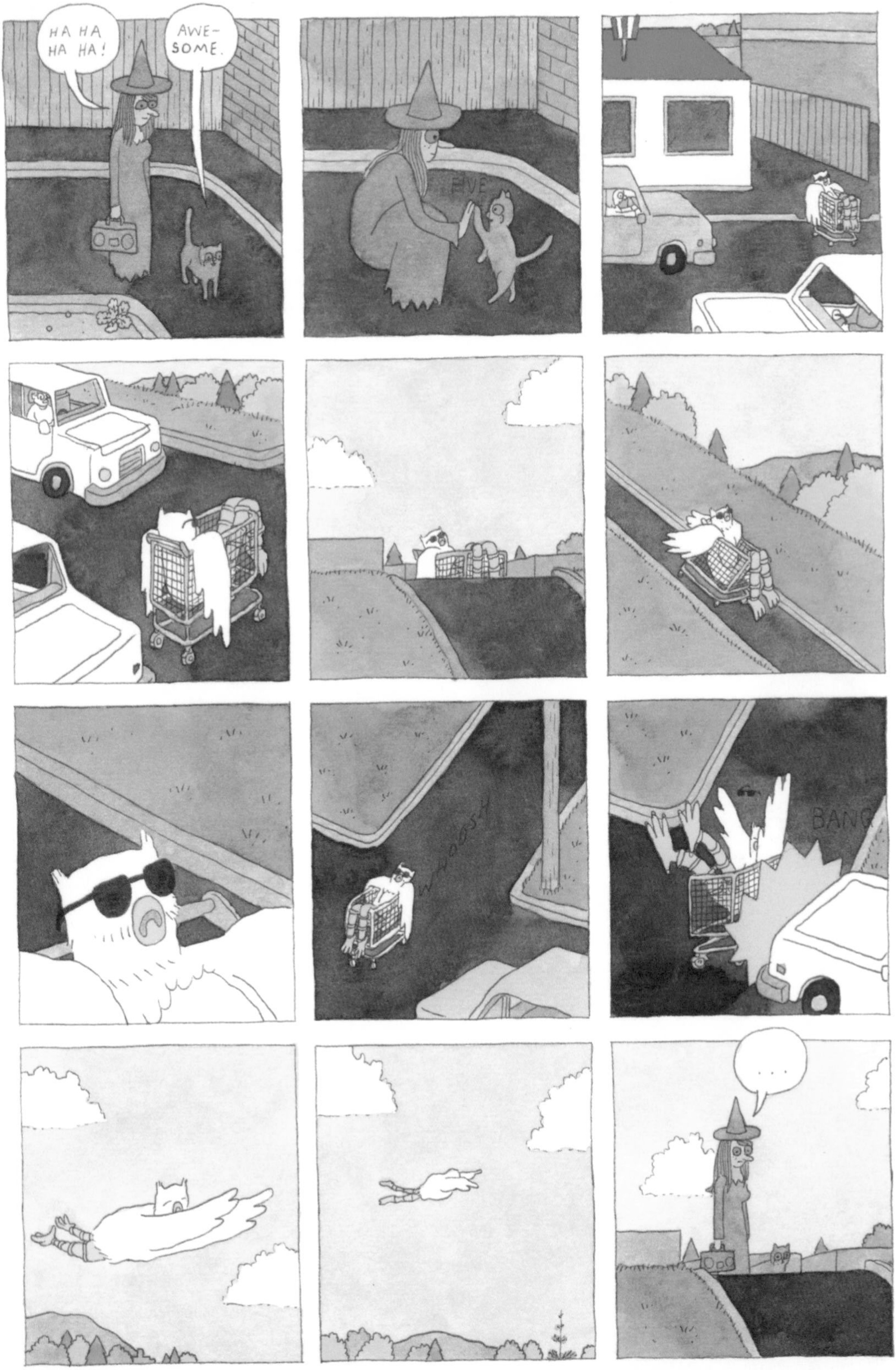
HA HA
HA HA!
AWE-
SOME.
FIVE
WHOOSH
BANG
. . .

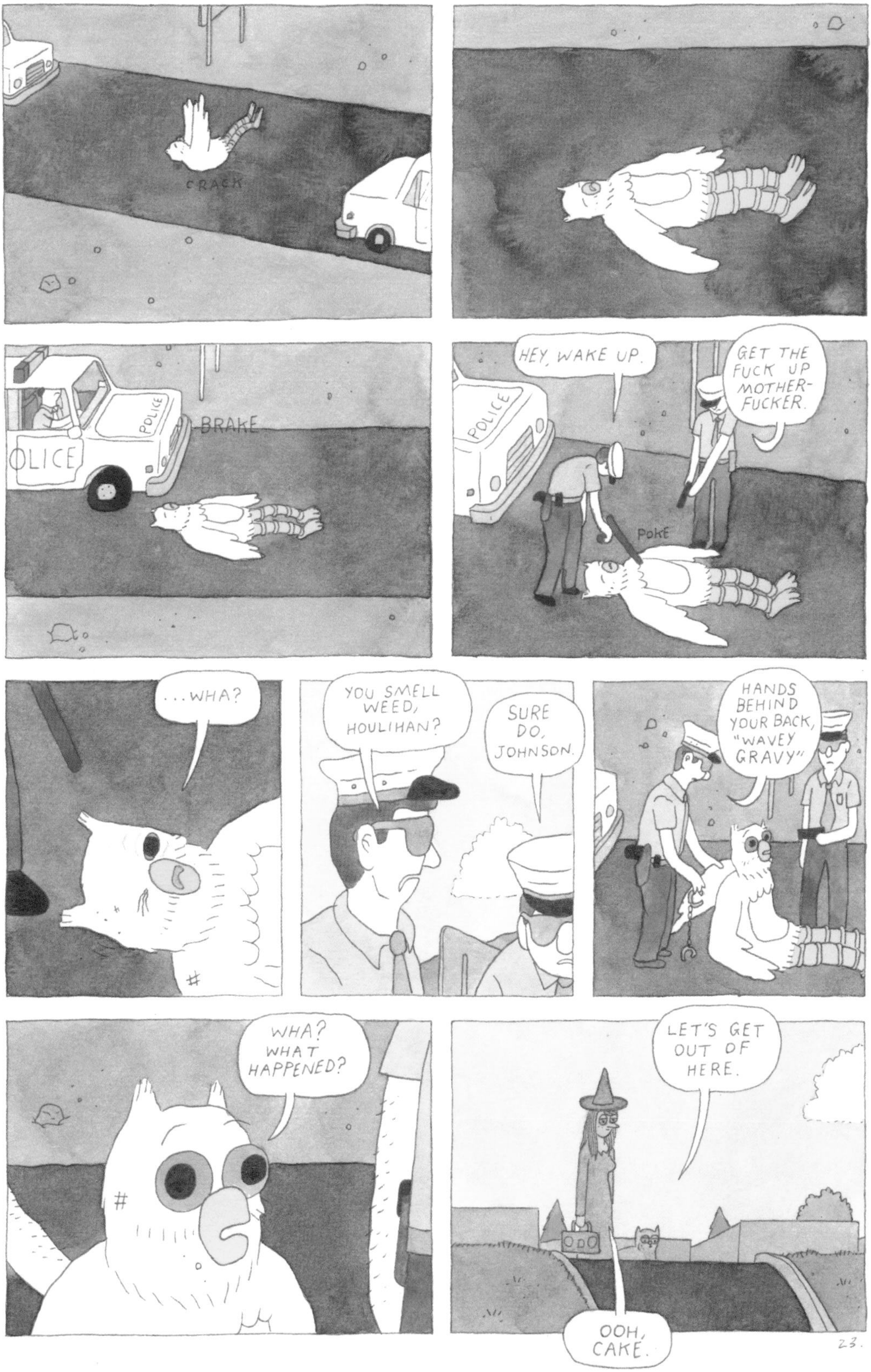
CRACK
POLICE
POLICE
BRAKE
HEY, WAKE UP.
GET THE FUCK UP MOTHER-FUCKER.
POLICE
POKE
...WHA?
YOU SMELL WEED, HOULIHAN?
SURE DO, JOHNSON.
HANDS BEHIND YOUR BACK, "WAVEY GRAVY"
WHA? WHAT HAPPENED?
LET'S GET OUT OF HERE.
OOH, CAKE.

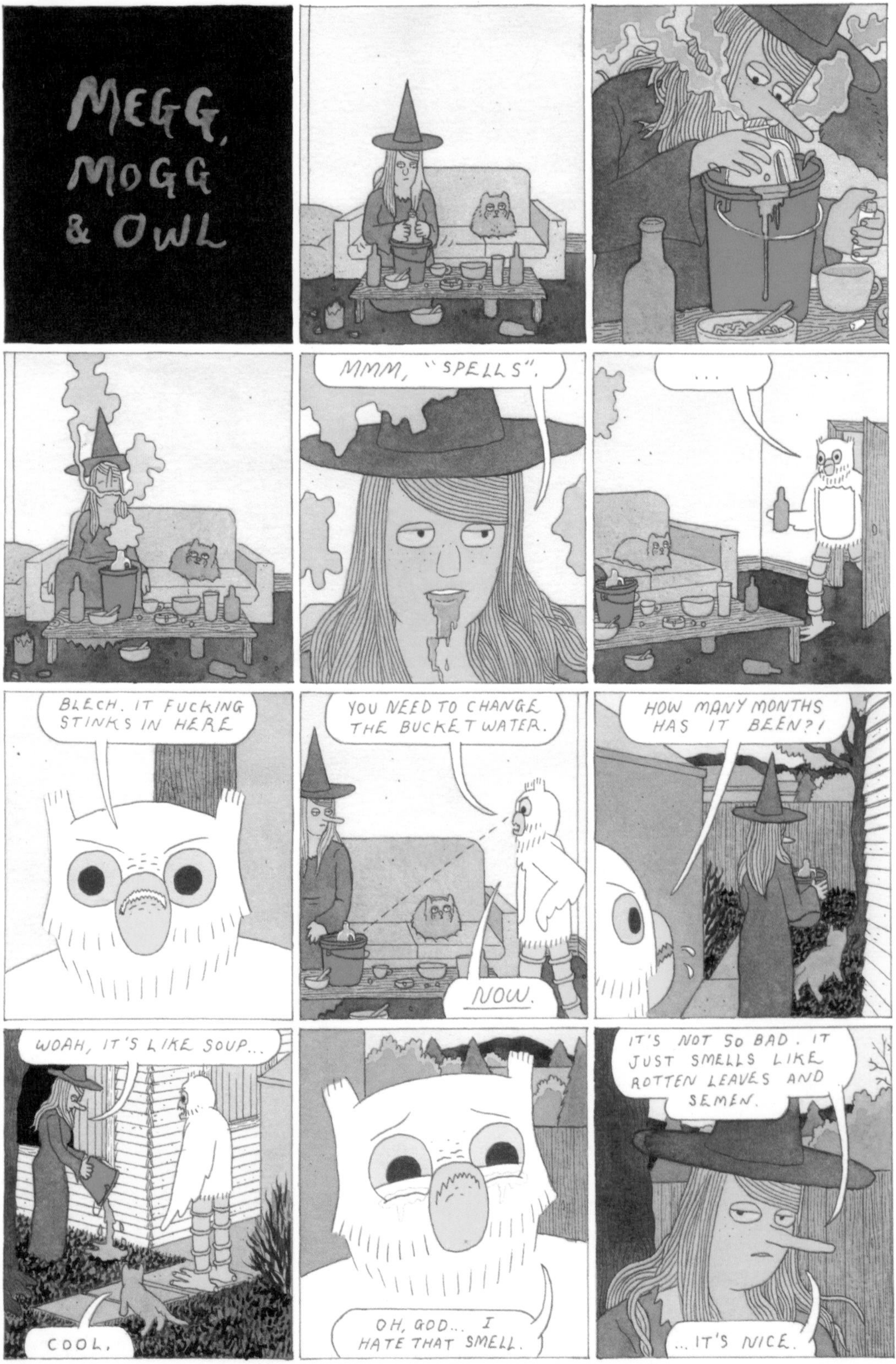
MEGG, MOGG & OWL
MMM, "SPELLS".
...
BLECH. IT FUCKING STINKS IN HERE
YOU NEED TO CHANGE THE BUCKET WATER.
NOW.
HOW MANY MONTHS HAS IT BEEN?!
WOAH, IT'S LIKE SOUP...
COOL.
OH, GOD... I HATE THAT SMELL.
IT'S NOT SO BAD. IT JUST SMELLS LIKE ROTTEN LEAVES AND SEMEN.
... IT'S NICE.

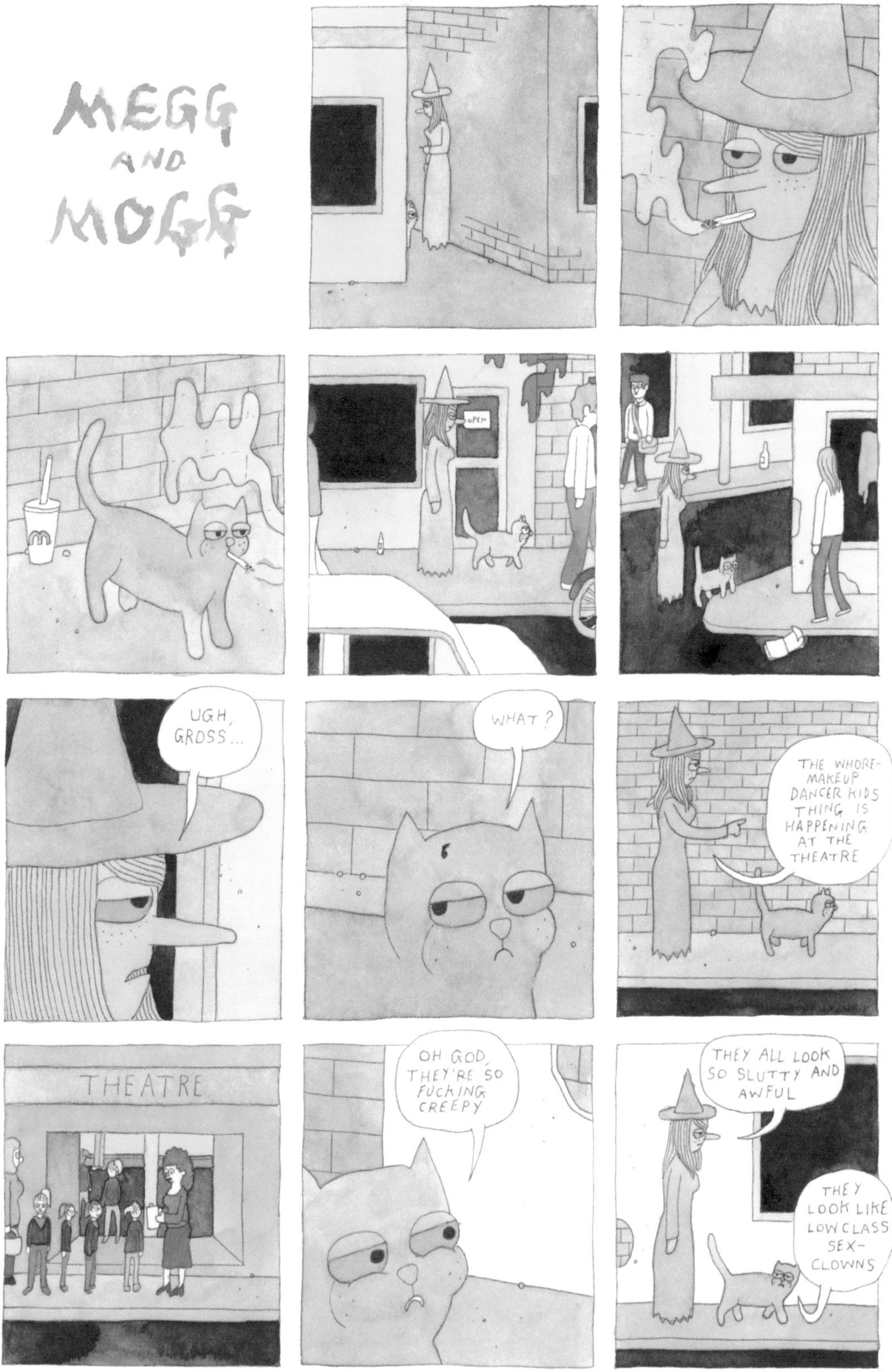
MEGG AND MOGG
OPEN
UGH, GROSS...
WHAT?
THE WHORE-MAKEUP DANCER KIDS THING IS HAPPENING AT THE THEATRE
THEATRE
OH GOD, THEY'RE SO FUCKING CREEPY
THEY ALL LOOK SO SLUTTY AND AWFUL
THEY LOOK LIKE LOWCLASS SEX-CLOWNS

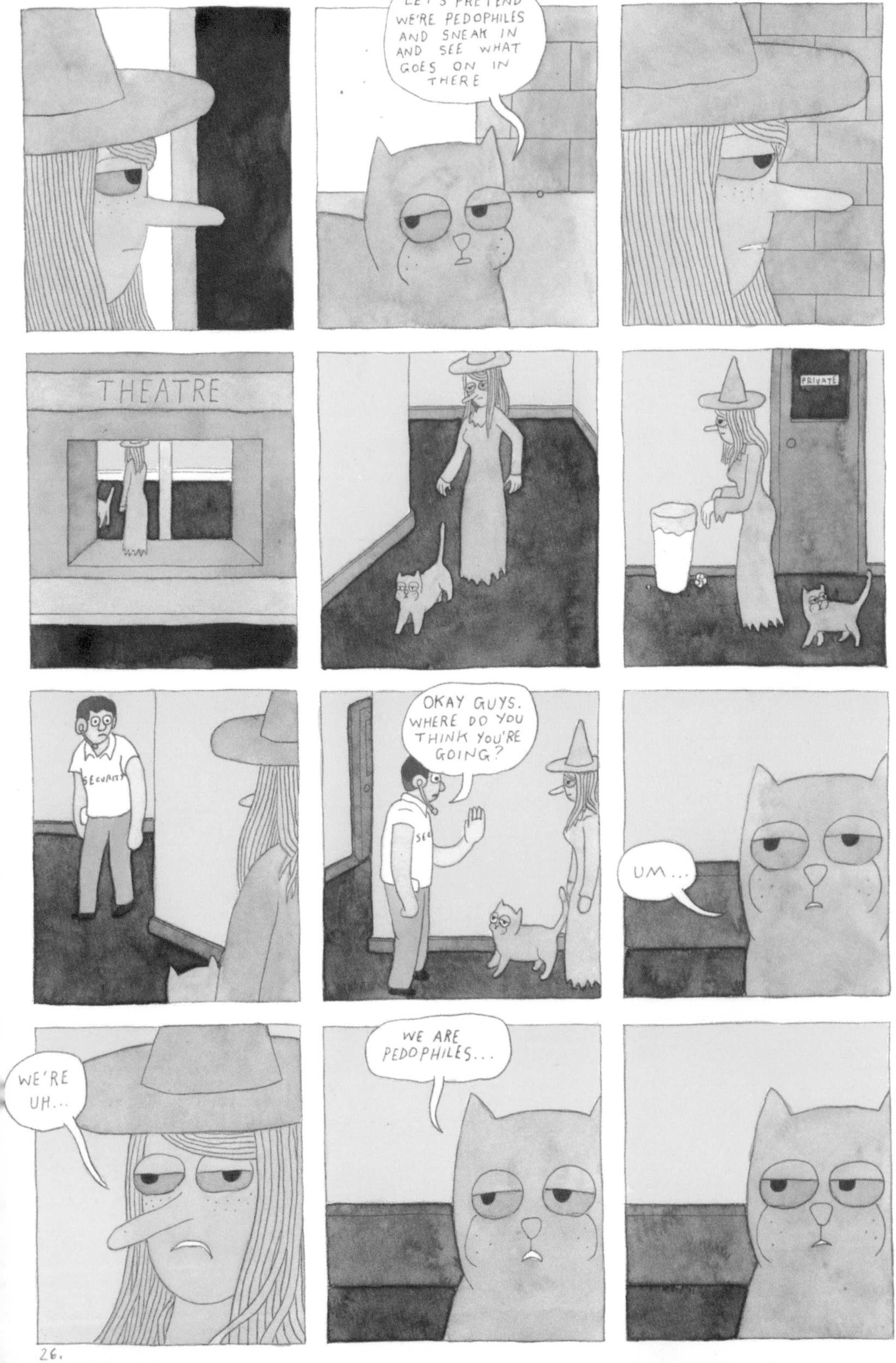
LET'S PRETEND WE'RE PEDOPHILES AND SNEAK IN AND SEE WHAT GOES ON IN THERE
THEATRE
PRIVATE
SECURITY
OKAY GUYS. WHERE DO YOU THINK YOU'RE GOING?
UM...
WE'RE UH...
WE ARE PEDOPHILES...

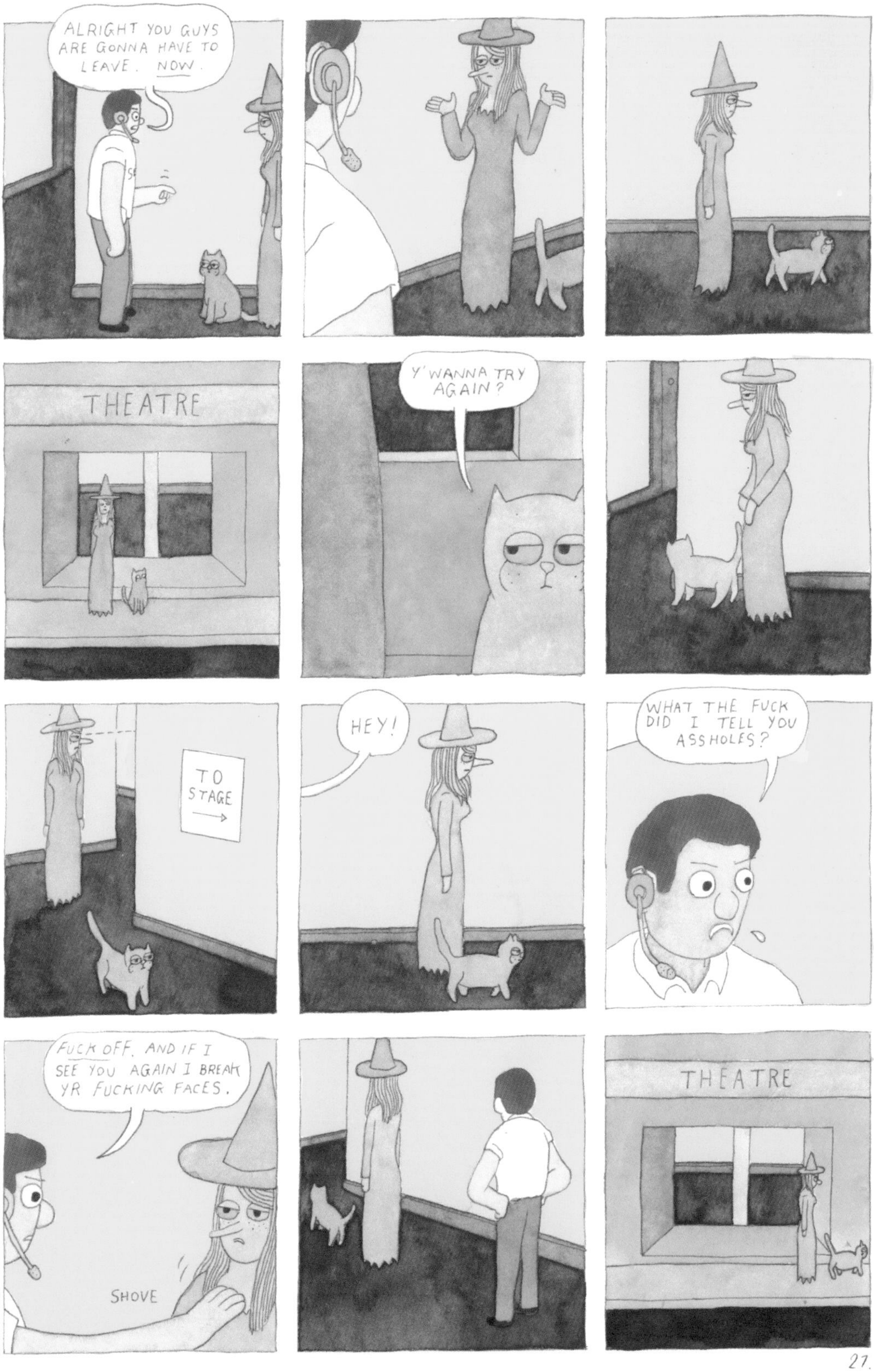
ALRIGHT YOU GUYS ARE GONNA HAVE TO LEAVE. NOW.
THEATRE
Y'WANNA TRY AGAIN?
TO STAGE →
HEY!
WHAT THE FUCK DID I TELL YOU ASSHOLES?
FUCK OFF. AND IF I SEE YOU AGAIN I BREAK YR FUCKING FACES.
SHOVE
THEATRE

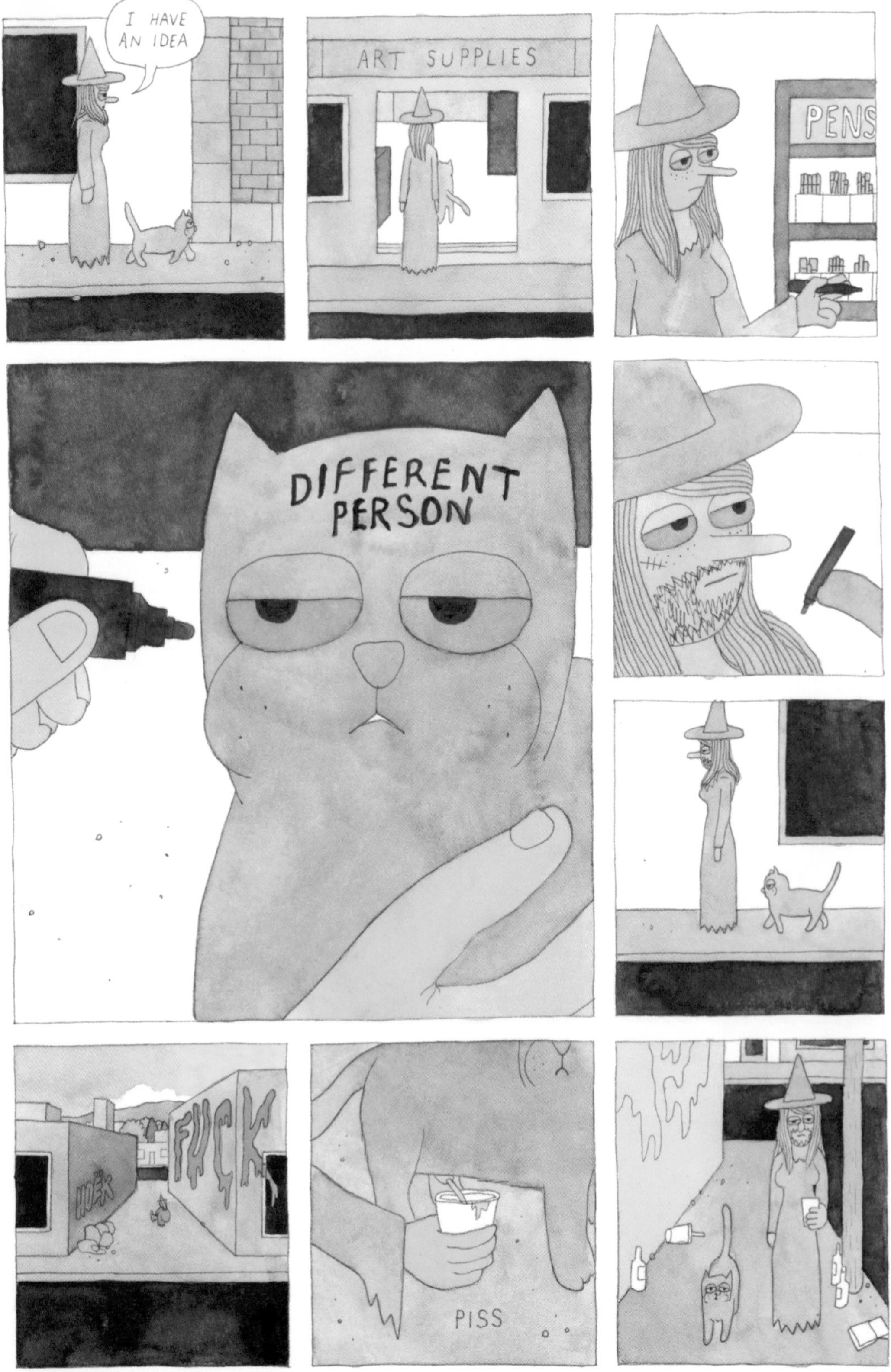
I HAVE AN IDEA
ART SUPPLIES
PENS
DIFFERENT PERSON
FUCK
PISS

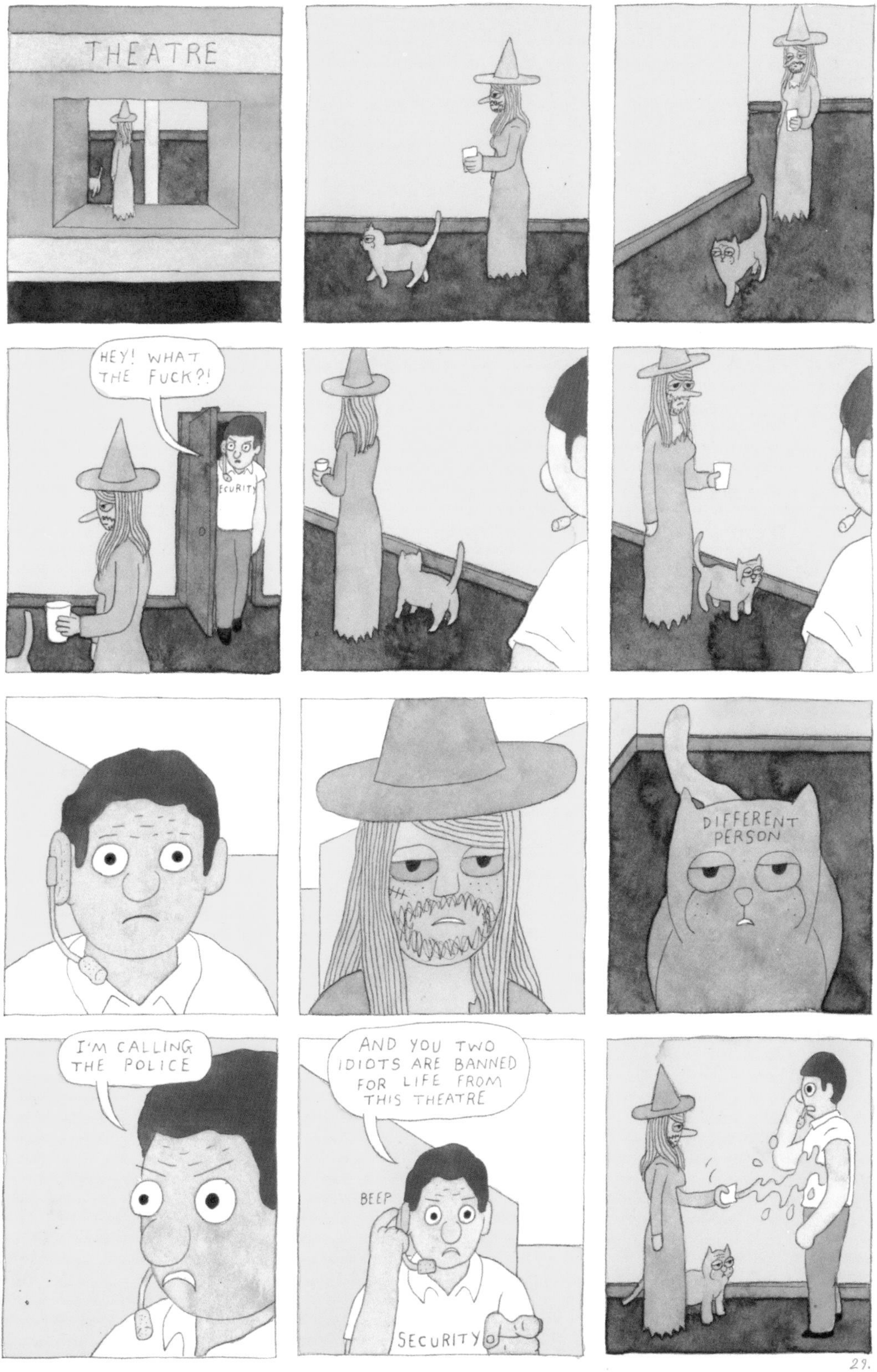
THEATRE
HEY! WHAT THE FUCK?!
SECURITY
DIFFERENT PERSON
I'M CALLING THE POLICE
AND YOU TWO IDIOTS ARE BANNED FOR LIFE FROM THIS THEATRE
BEEP
SECURITY

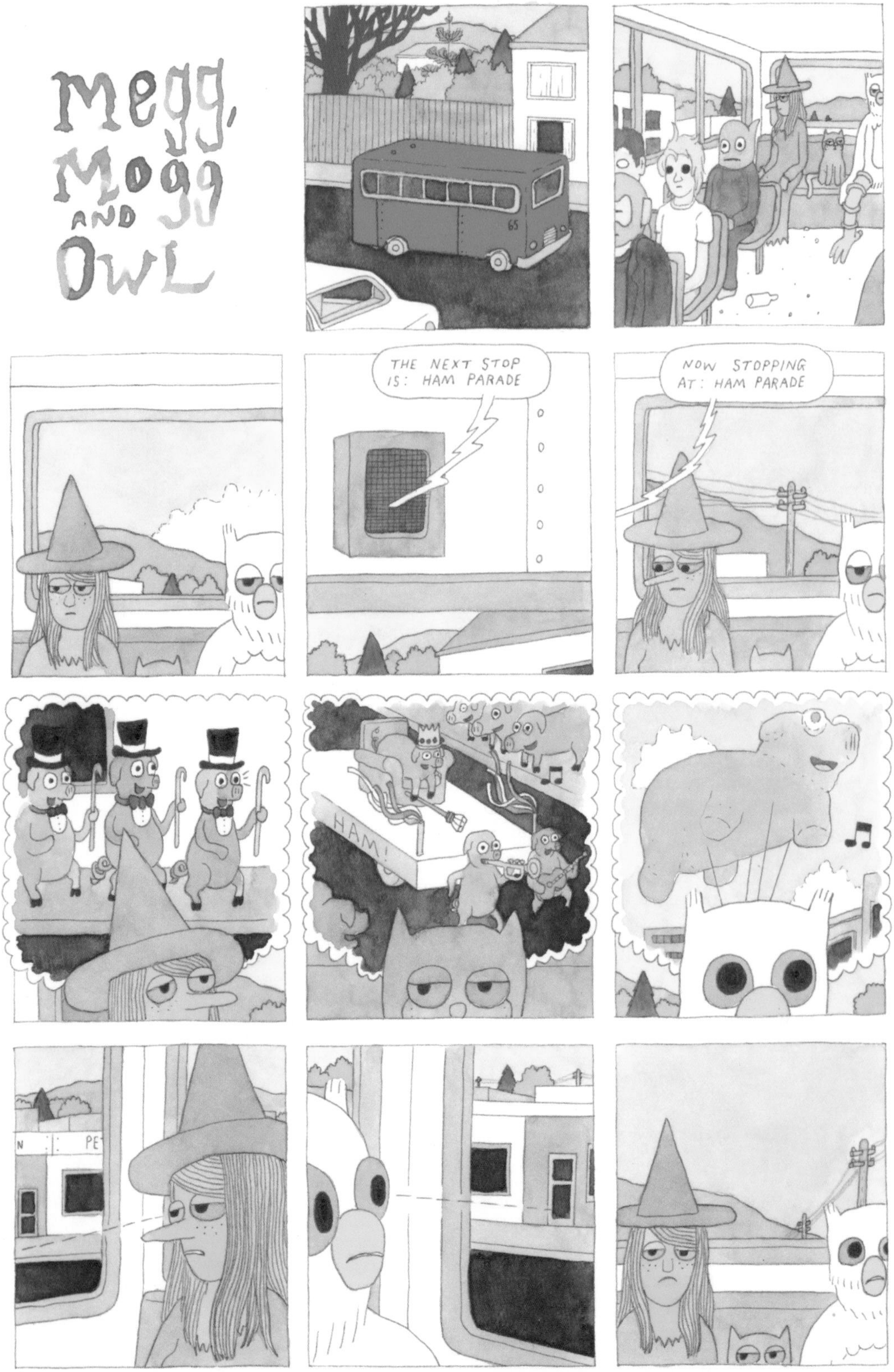
MEGG, MOGG AND OWL
65
THE NEXT STOP IS: HAM PARADE
NOW STOPPING AT: HAM PARADE
HAM!

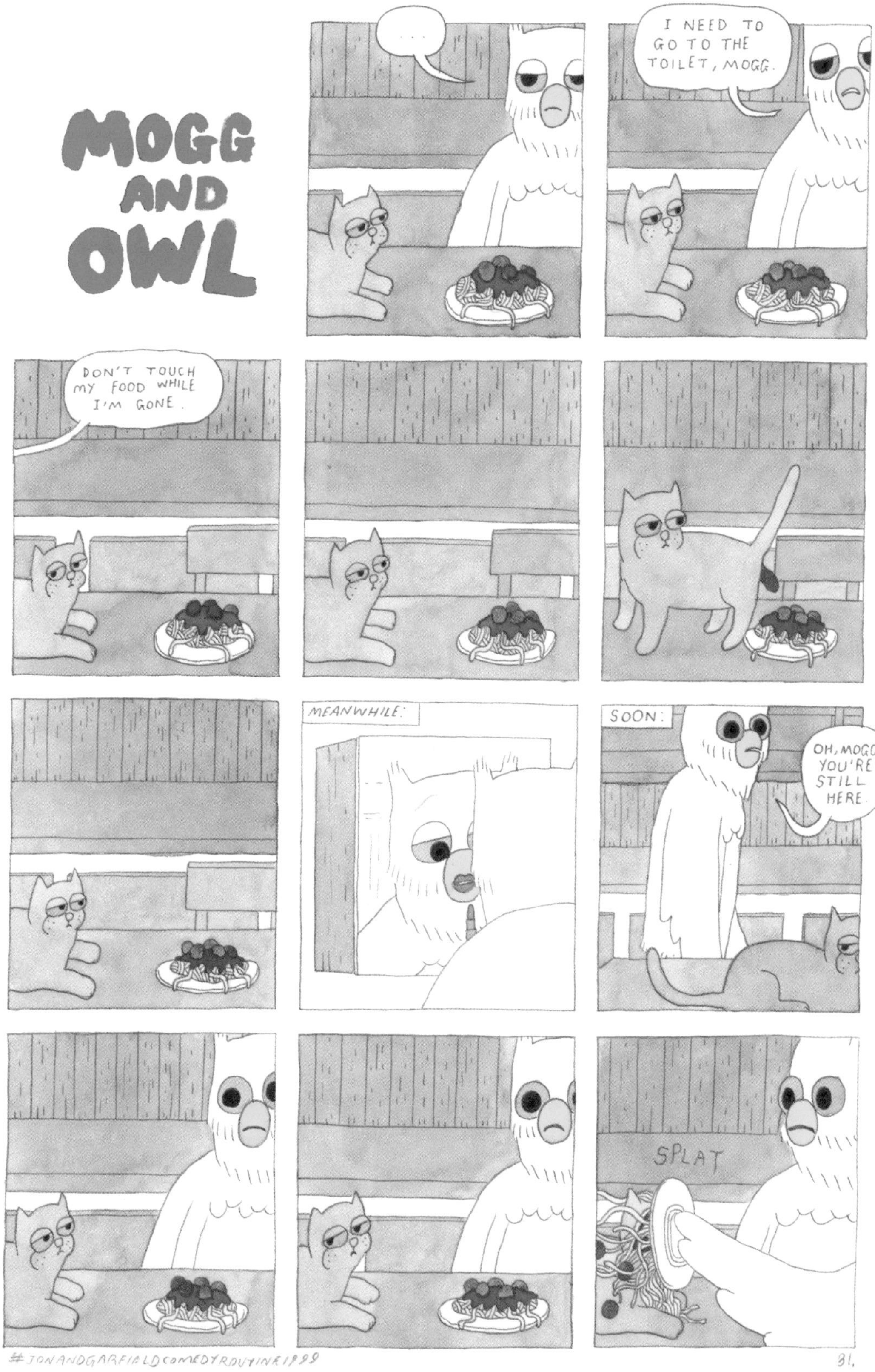
MOGG AND OWL
. . .
I NEED TO GO TO THE TOILET, MOGG.
DON'T TOUCH MY FOOD WHILE I'M GONE.
MEANWHILE:
SOON:
OH, MOGG, YOU'RE STILL HERE.
SPLAT

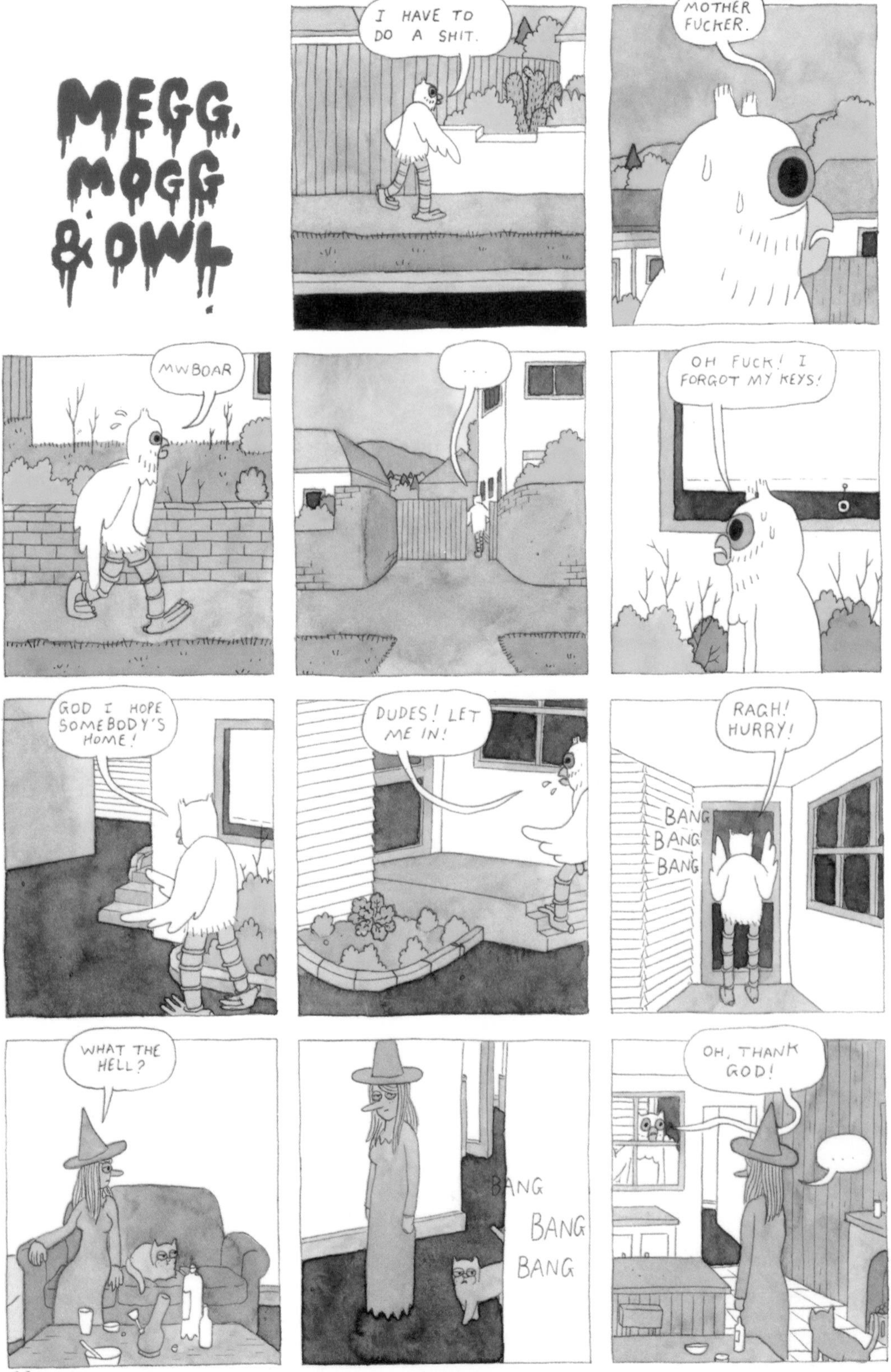
MEGG, MOGG & OWL
I HAVE TO DO A SHIT.
MOTHER FUCKER.
MWBOAR
...
OH FUCK! I FORGOT MY KEYS!
GOD I HOPE SOMEBODY'S HOME!
DUDES! LET ME IN!
RAGH! HURRY!
BANG
BANG
BANG
WHAT THE HELL?
BANG
BANG
BANG
OH, THANK GOD!
...

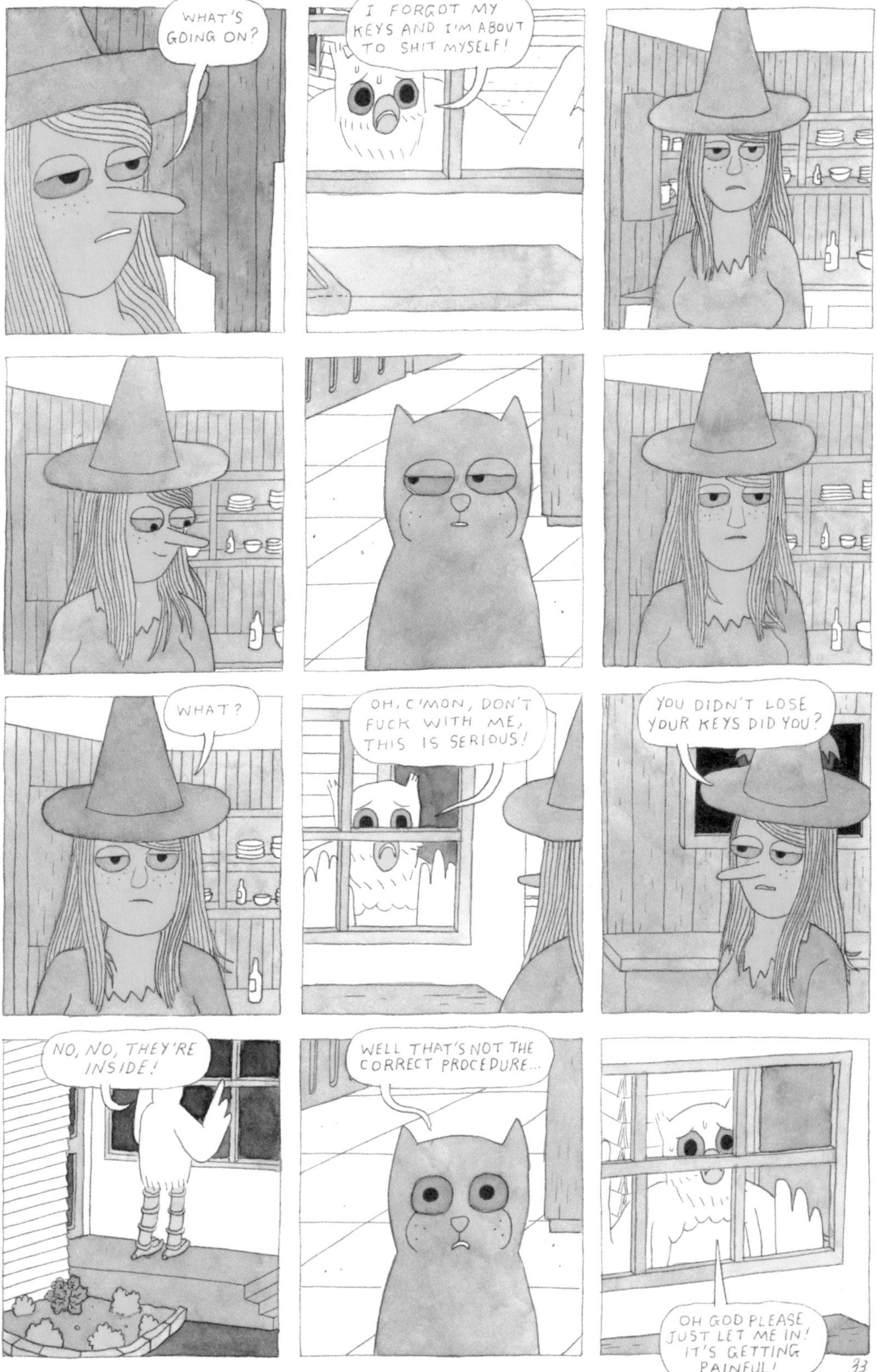
WHAT'S GOING ON?
I FORGOT MY KEYS AND I'M ABOUT TO SHIT MYSELF!
WHAT?
OH, C'MON, DON'T FUCK WITH ME, THIS IS SERIOUS!
YOU DIDN'T LOSE YOUR KEYS DID YOU?
NO, NO, THEY'RE INSIDE!
WELL THAT'S NOT THE CORRECT PROCEDURE...
OH GOD PLEASE JUST LET ME IN! IT'S GETTING PAINFUL!

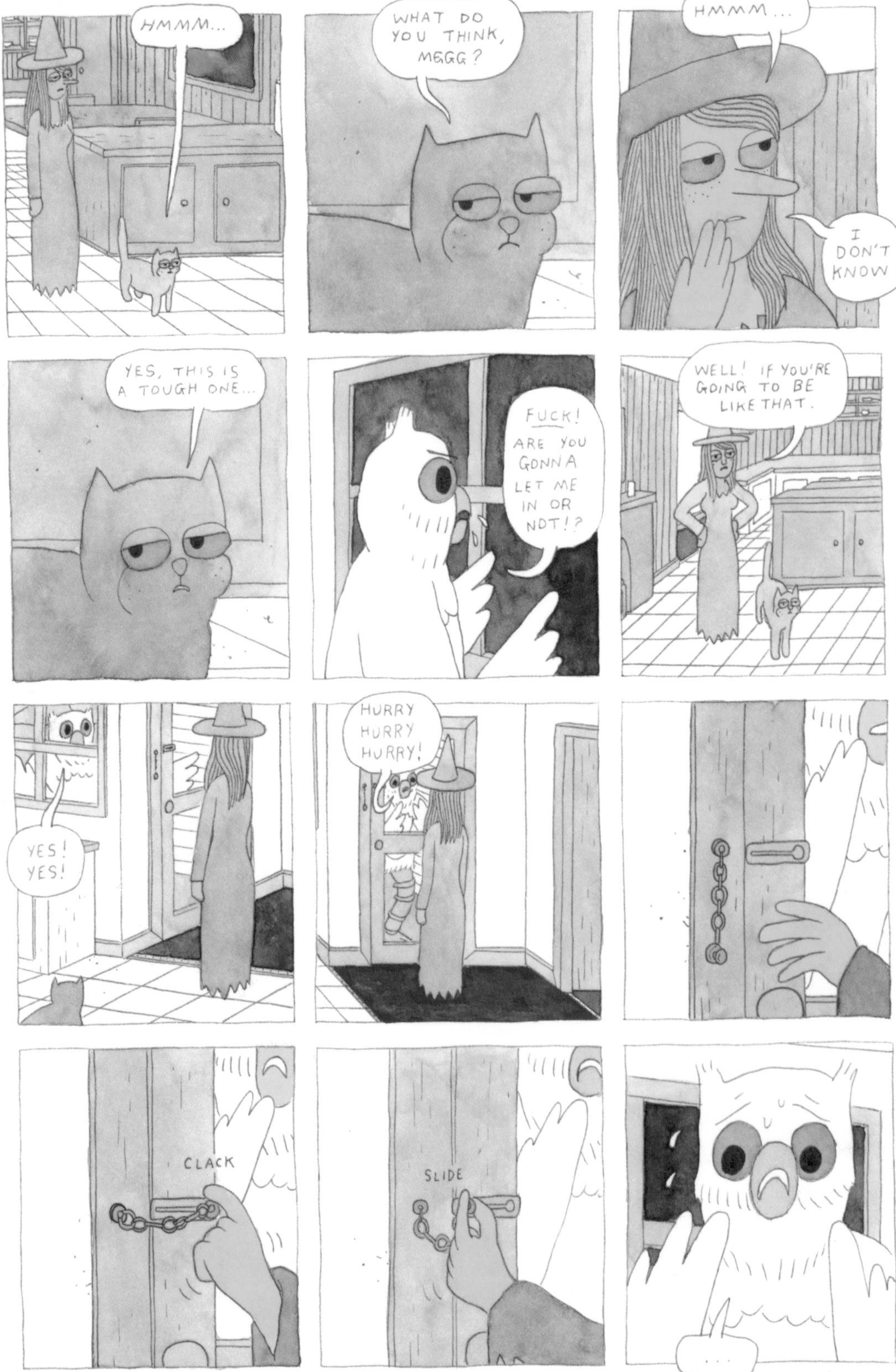
HMMM...
WHAT DO YOU THINK, MEGG?
HMMM...
I DON'T KNOW
YES, THIS IS A TOUGH ONE...
FUCK! ARE YOU GONNA LET ME IN OR NOT!?
WELL! IF YOU'RE GOING TO BE LIKE THAT.
YES! YES!
HURRY HURRY HURRY!
CLACK
SLIDE
...

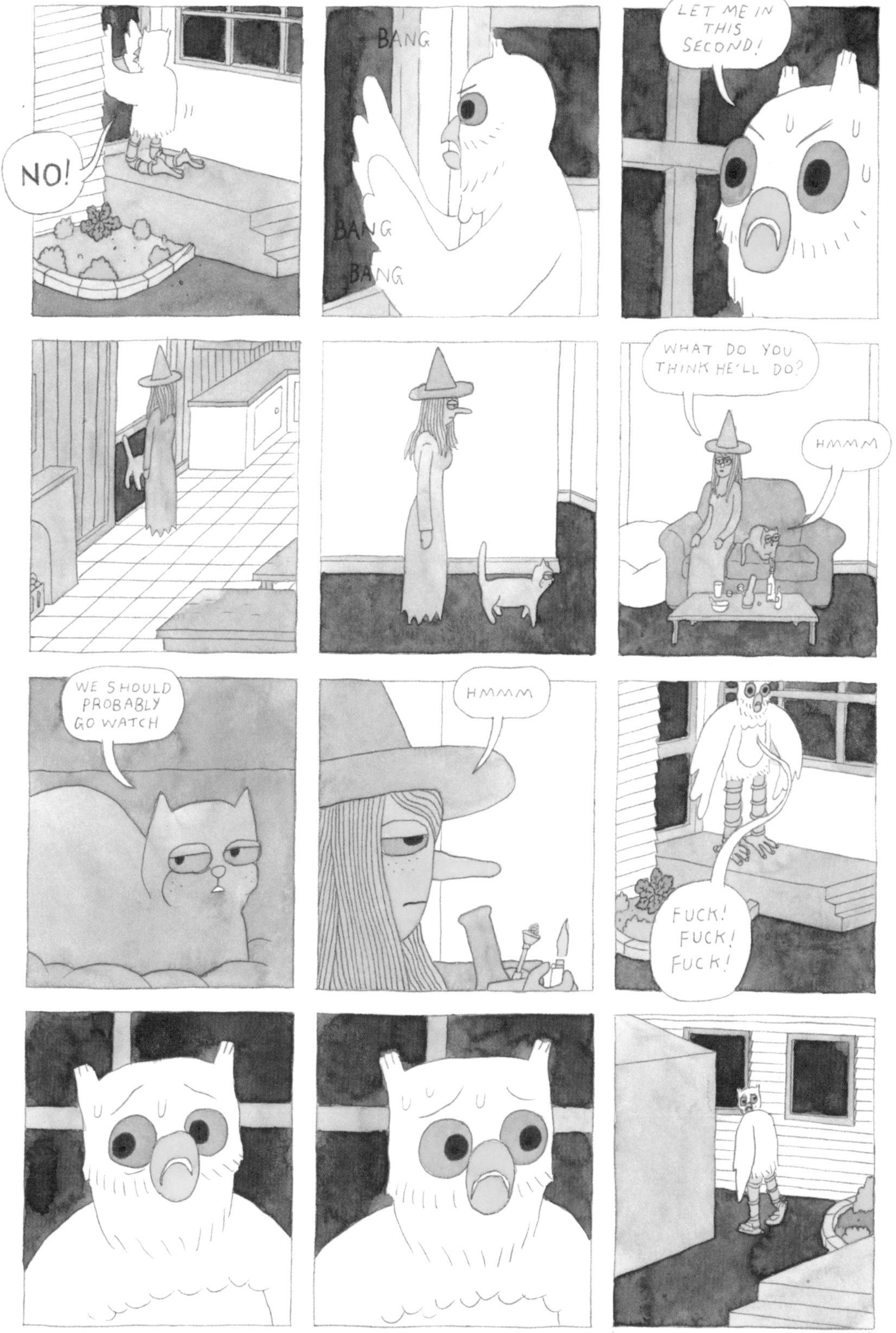
NO!
BANG
BANG
BANG
LET ME IN THIS SECOND!
WHAT DO YOU THINK HE'LL DO?
HMMM
WE SHOULD PROBABLY GO WATCH
HMMM
FUCK! FUCK! FUCK!

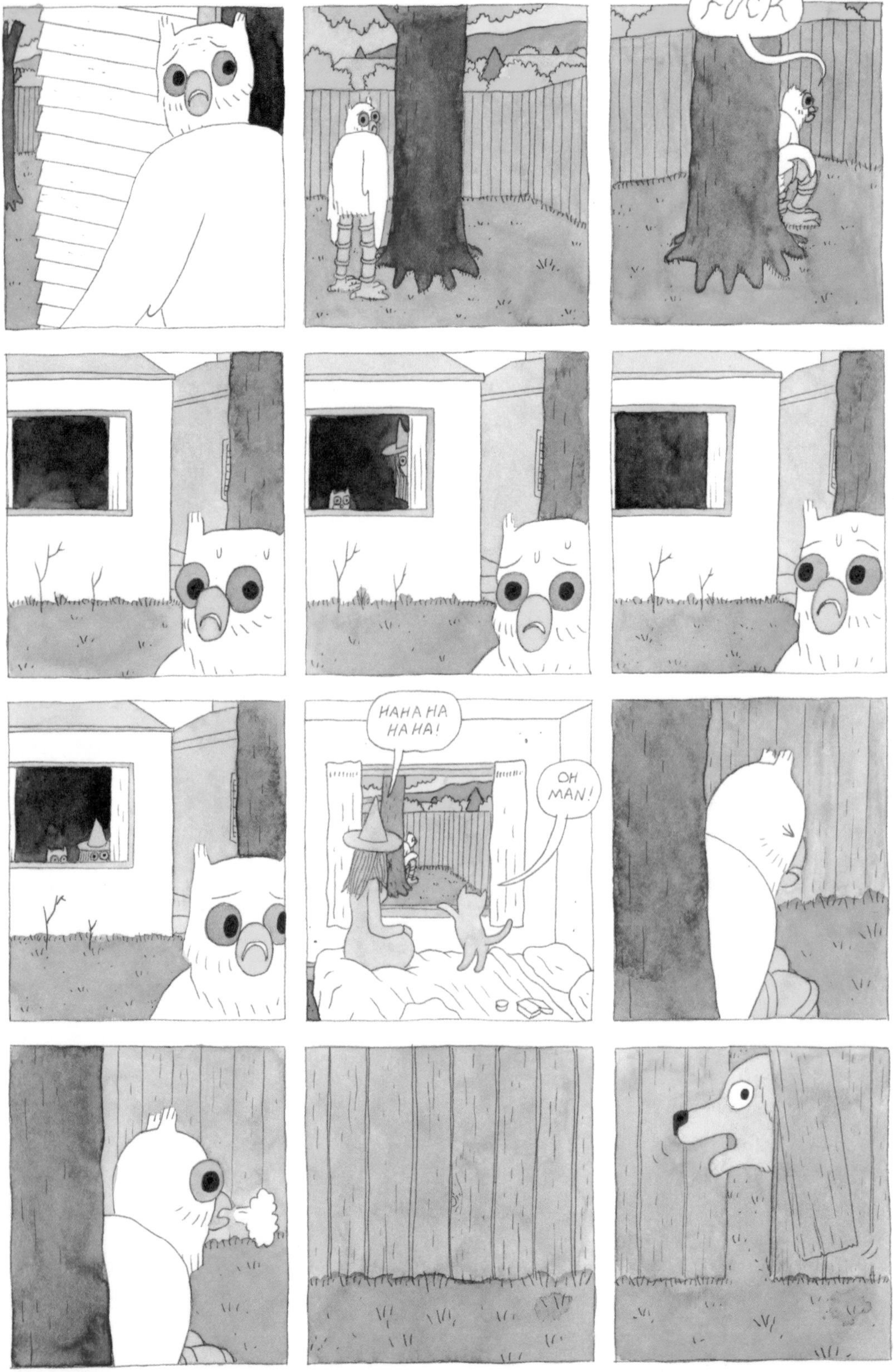
FUCK
HAHAHA HAHA!
OH MAN!

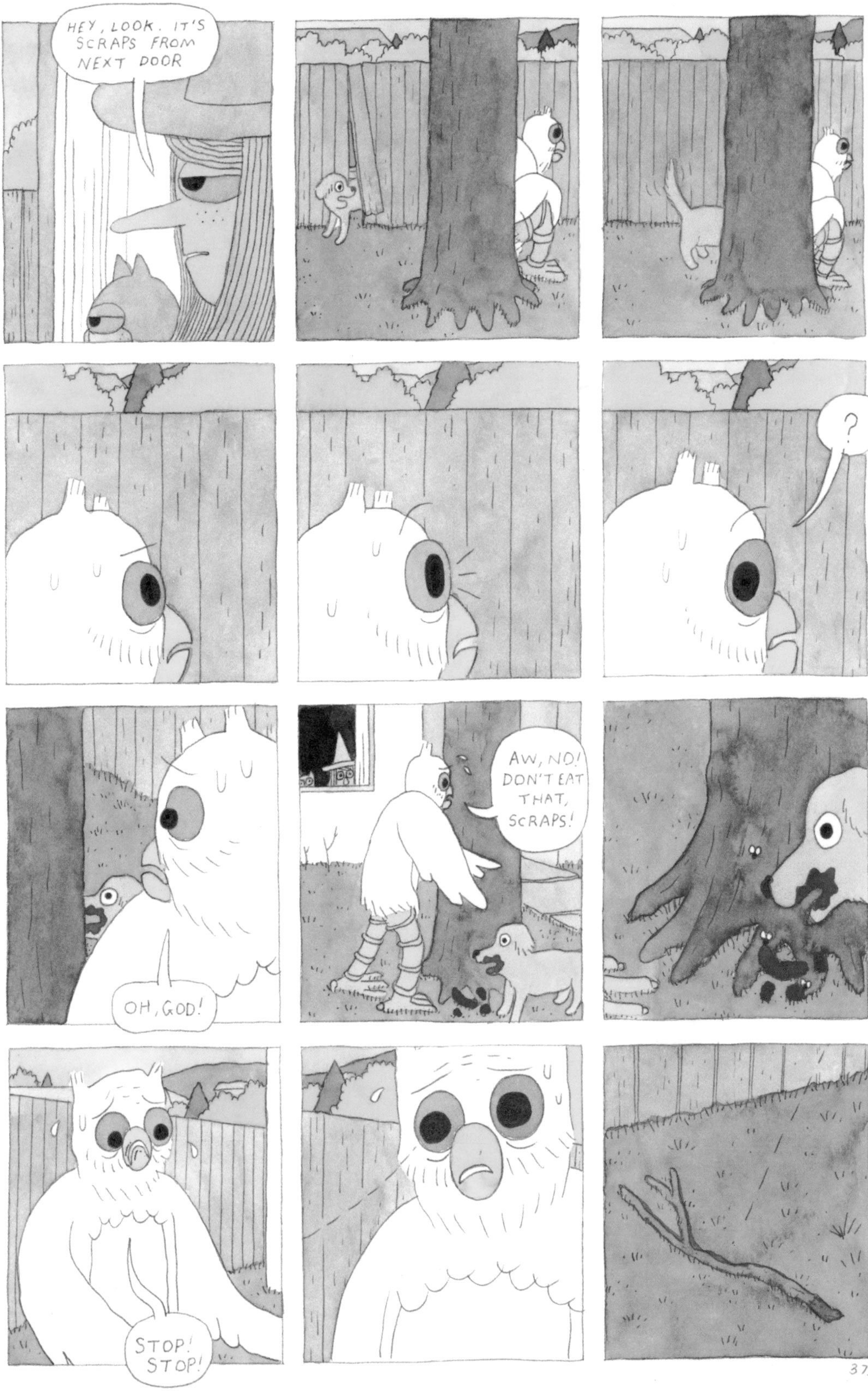
HEY, LOOK. IT'S SCRAPS FROM NEXT DOOR
?
OH, GOD!
AW, NO! DON'T EAT THAT, SCRAPS!
STOP! STOP!

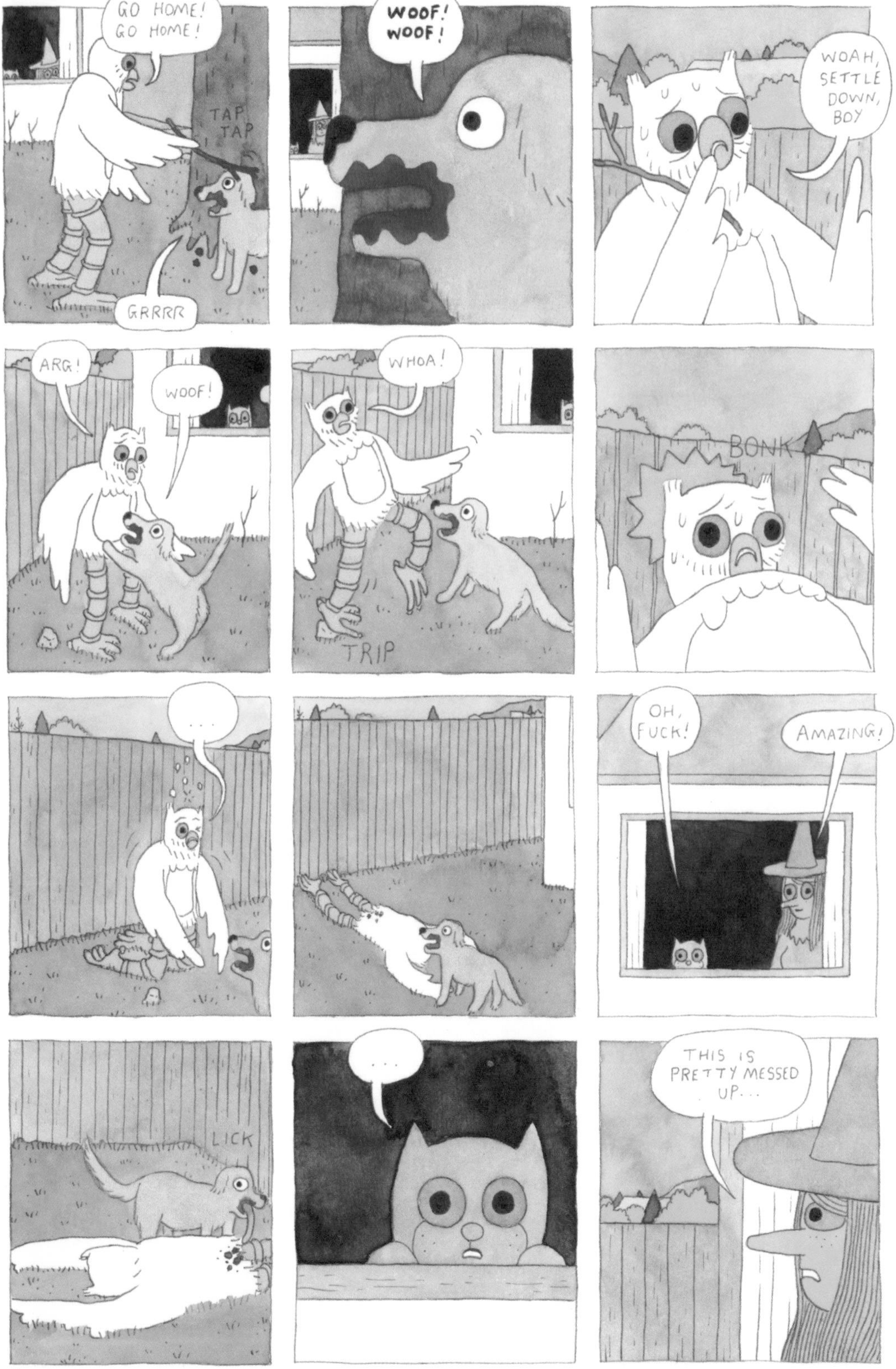
GO HOME! GO HOME!
TAP TAP
GRRRR
WOOF! WOOF!
WOAH, SETTLE DOWN, BOY
ARG!
WOOF!
WHOA!
TRIP
BONK
. . .
OH, FUCK!
AMAZING!
LICK
. . .
THIS IS PRETTY MESSED UP...

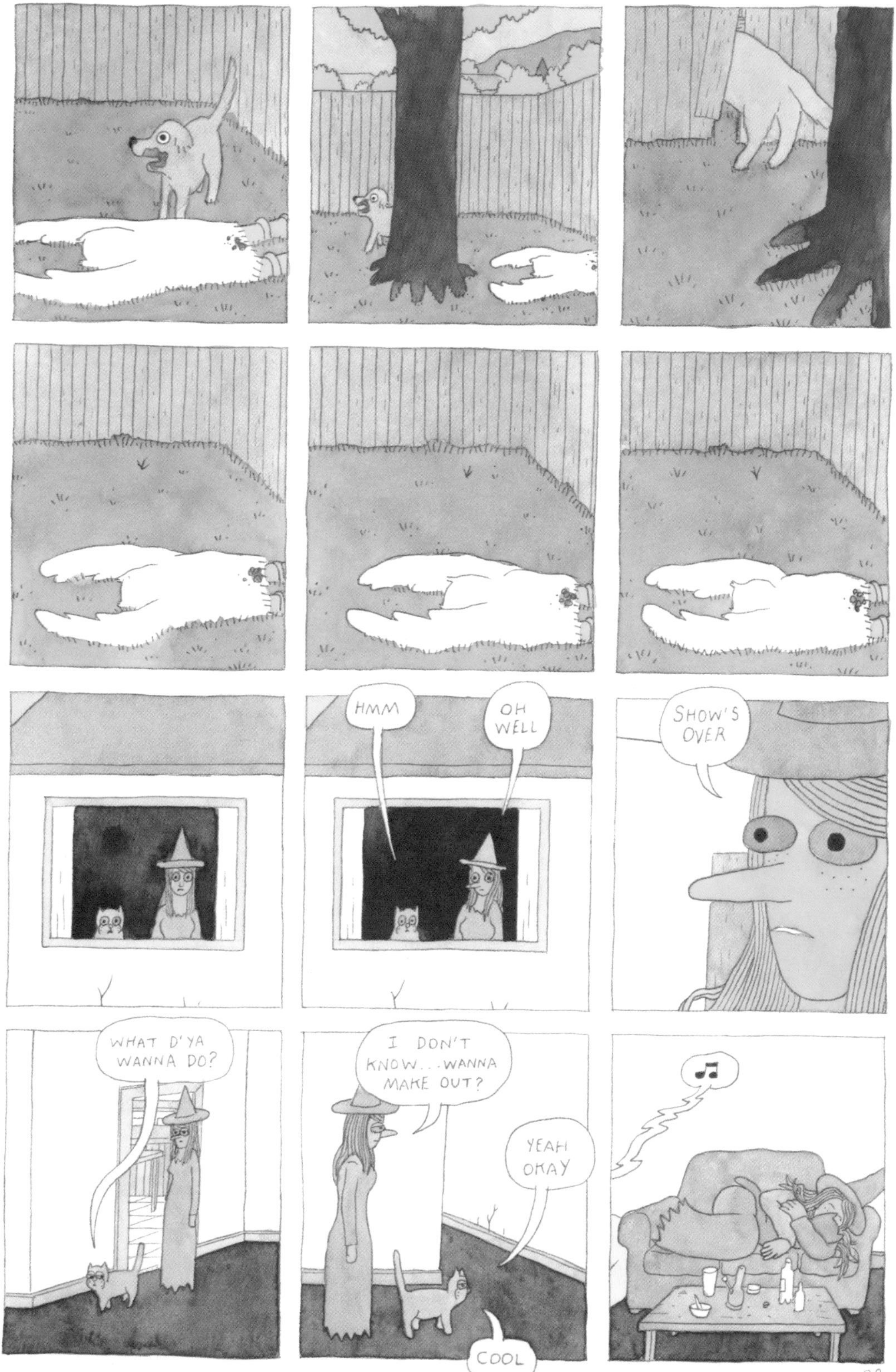
HMM
OH WELL
SHOW'S OVER
WHAT D'YA WANNA DO?
I DON'T KNOW... WANNA MAKE OUT?
YEAH OKAY
COOL

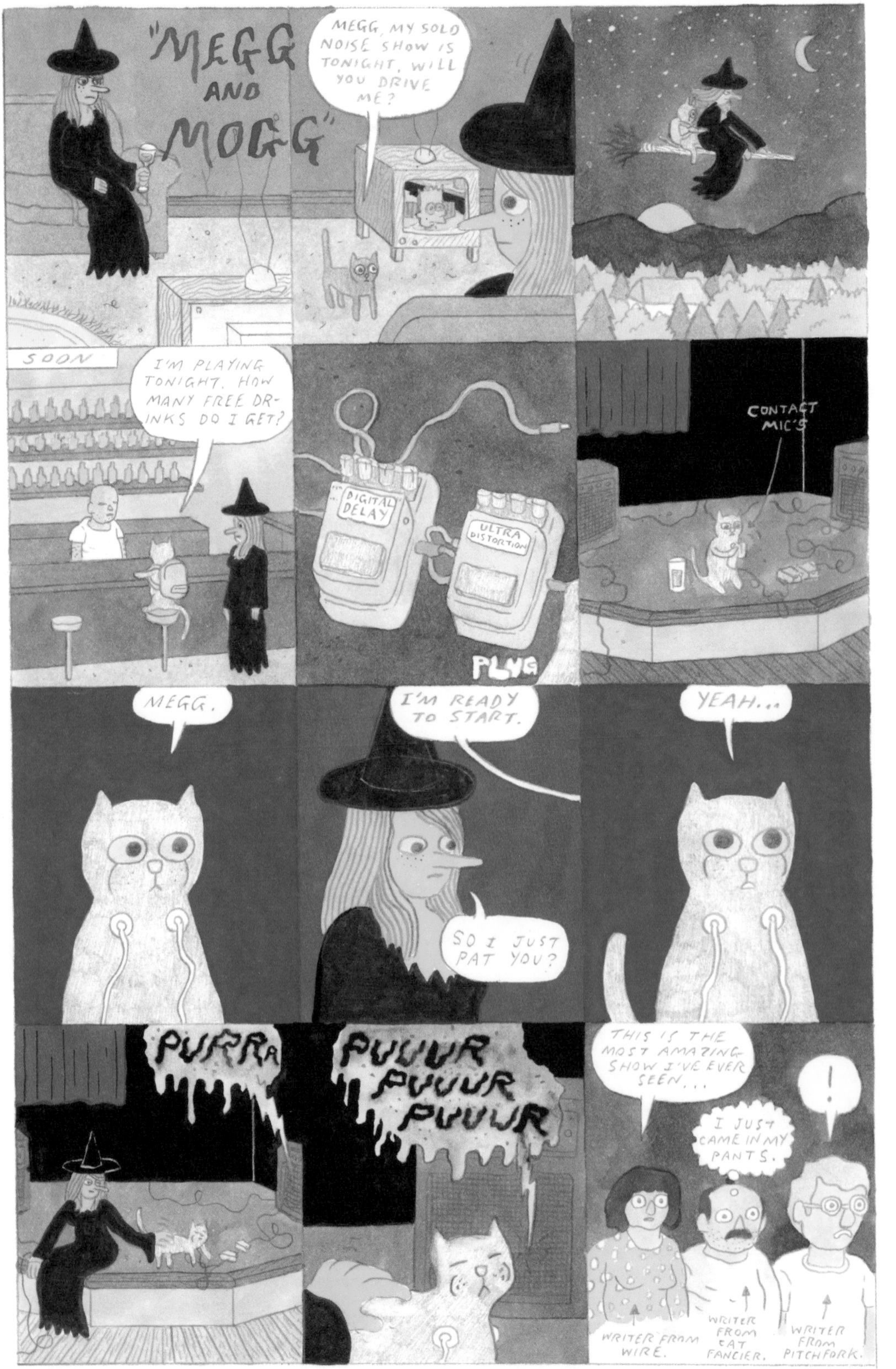
"MEGG AND MOGG"
MEGG, MY SOLO NOISE SHOW IS TONIGHT, WILL YOU DRIVE ME?
SOON
I'M PLAYING TONIGHT. HOW MANY FREE DRINKS DO I GET?
DIGITAL DELAY
ULTRA DISTORTION
PLUG
CONTACT MIC'S
MEGG.
I'M READY TO START.
SO I JUST PAT YOU?
YEAH...
PURRR
PUUUR PUUUR PUUUR
THIS IS THE MOST AMAZING SHOW I'VE EVER SEEN...
I JUST CAME IN MY PANTS.
!
WRITER FROM WIRE.
WRITER FROM CAT FANCIER.
WRITER FROM PITCHFORK.

TAUT
PSYCHOLOGICAL
THRILLER

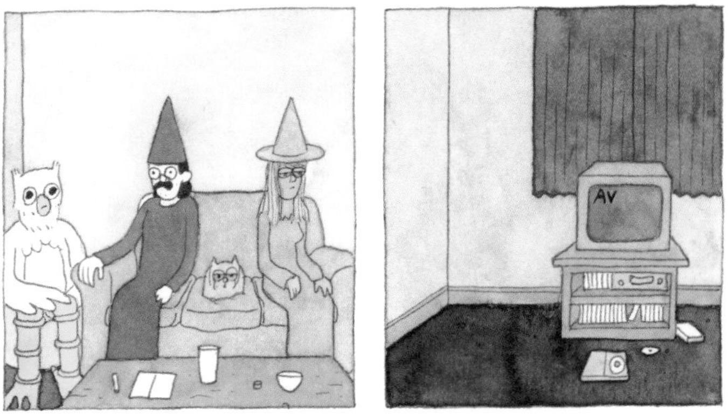
AV

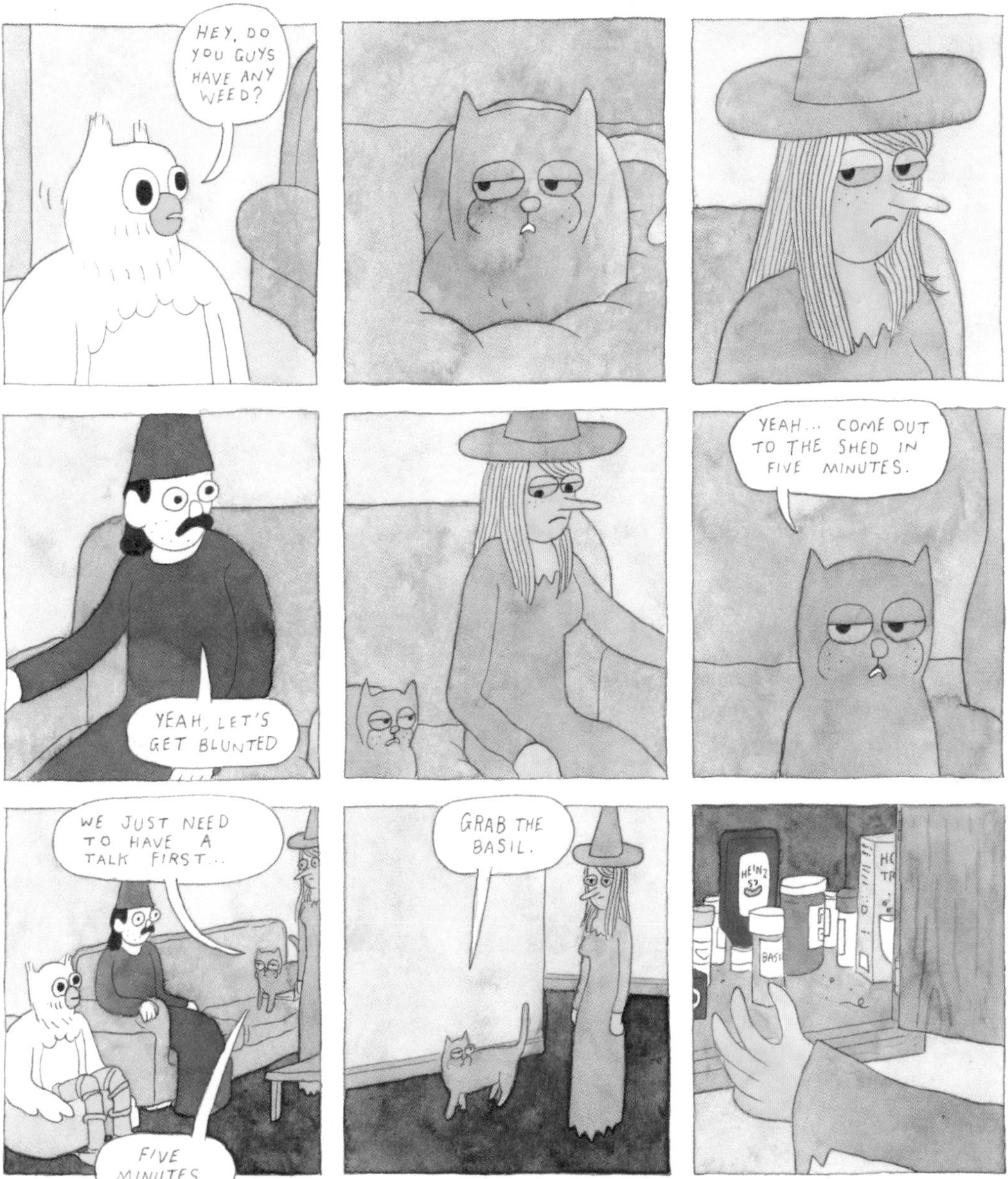
HEY, DO YOU GUYS HAVE ANY WEED?
YEAH, LET'S GET BLUNTED
YEAH... COME OUT TO THE SHED IN FIVE MINUTES.
WE JUST NEED TO HAVE A TALK FIRST...
FIVE MINUTES.
GRAB THE BASIL.
HEINZ 57
BASIL

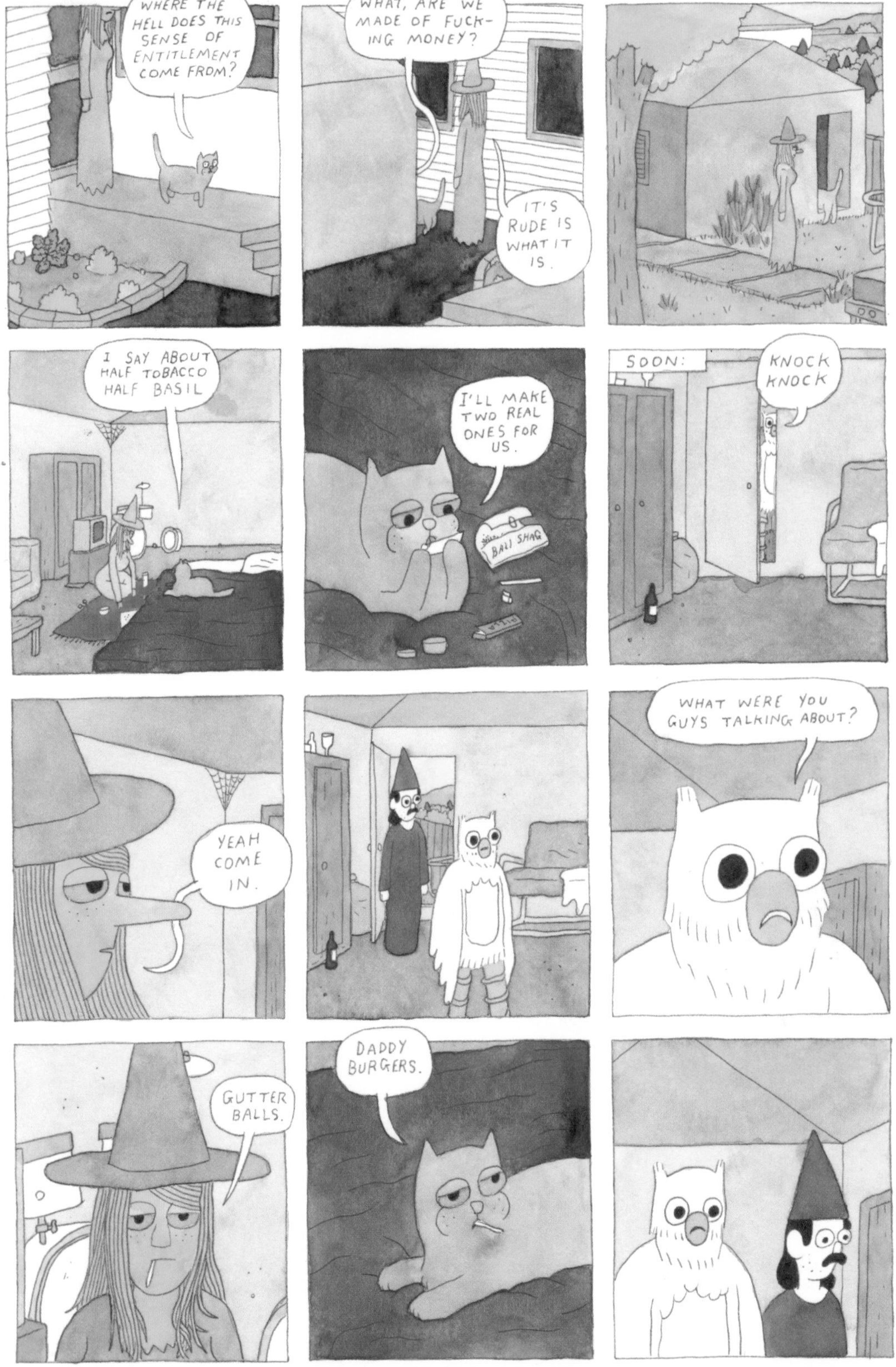
WHERE THE HELL DOES THIS SENSE OF ENTITLEMENT COME FROM?
WHAT, ARE WE MADE OF FUCK-ING MONEY?
IT'S RUDE IS WHAT IT IS.
I SAY ABOUT HALF TOBACCO HALF BASIL
I'LL MAKE TWO REAL ONES FOR US.
BALI SHAG
SOON:
KNOCK KNOCK
YEAH COME IN.
WHAT WERE YOU GUYS TALKING ABOUT?
GUTTER BALLS.
DADDY BURGERS.

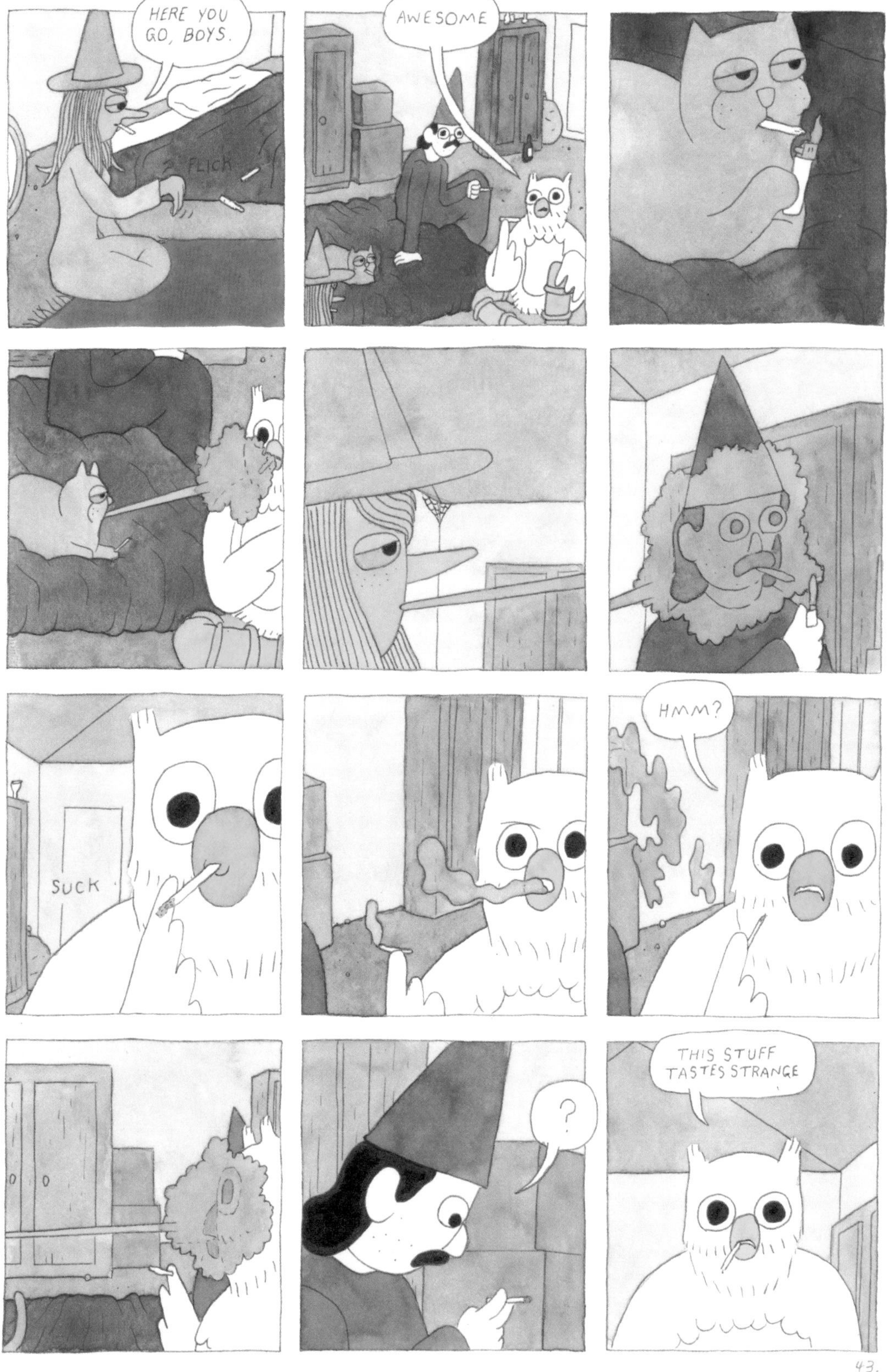
HERE YOU GO, BOYS.
FLICK
AWESOME
SUCK
HMM?
?
THIS STUFF TASTES STRANGE

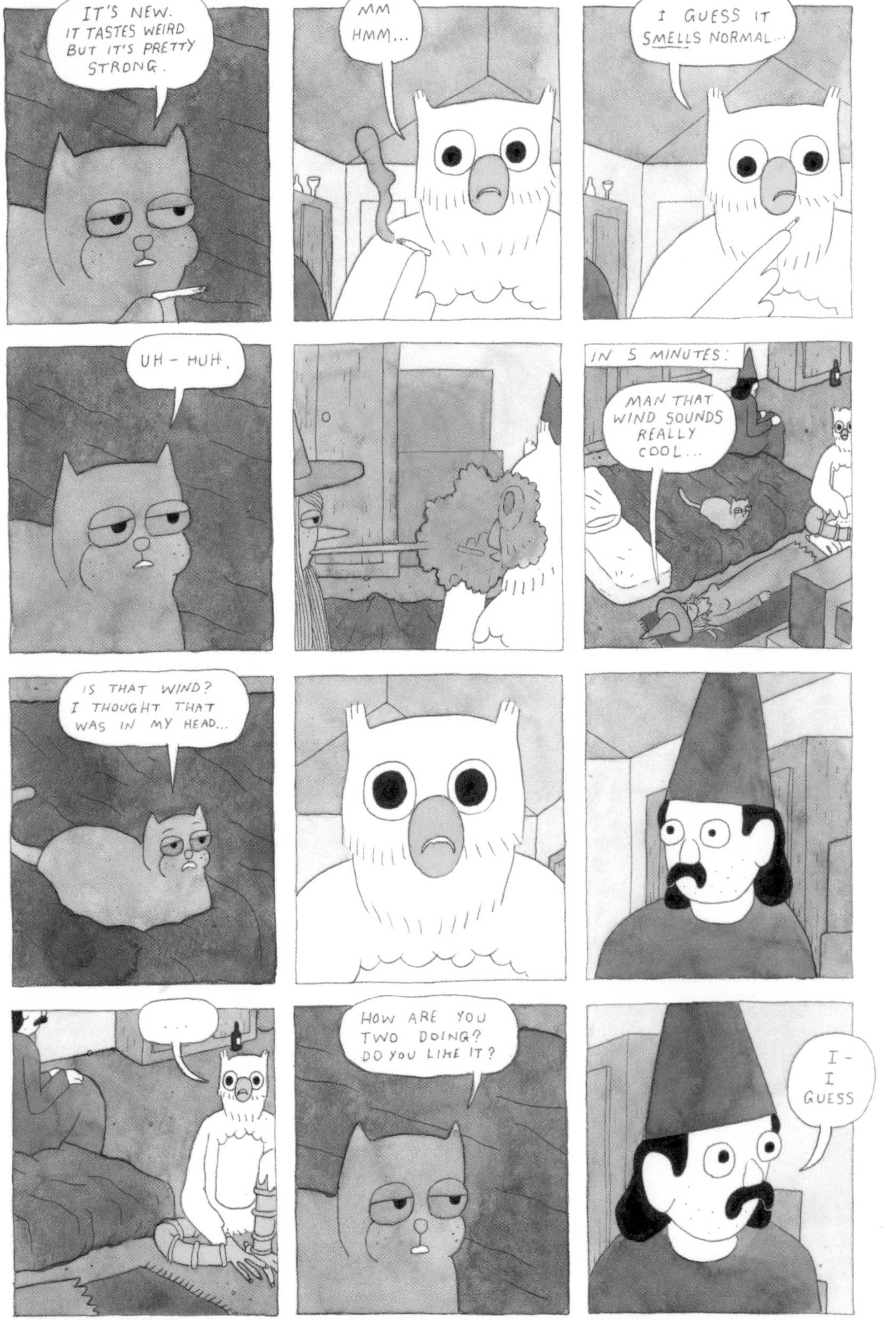
IT'S NEW. IT TASTES WEIRD BUT IT'S PRETTY STRONG.
MM HMM...
I GUESS IT SMELLS NORMAL...
UH-HUH.
IN 5 MINUTES:
MAN THAT WIND SOUNDS REALLY COOL...
IS THAT WIND? I THOUGHT THAT WAS IN MY HEAD...
...
HOW ARE YOU TWO DOING? DO YOU LIKE IT?
I- I GUESS

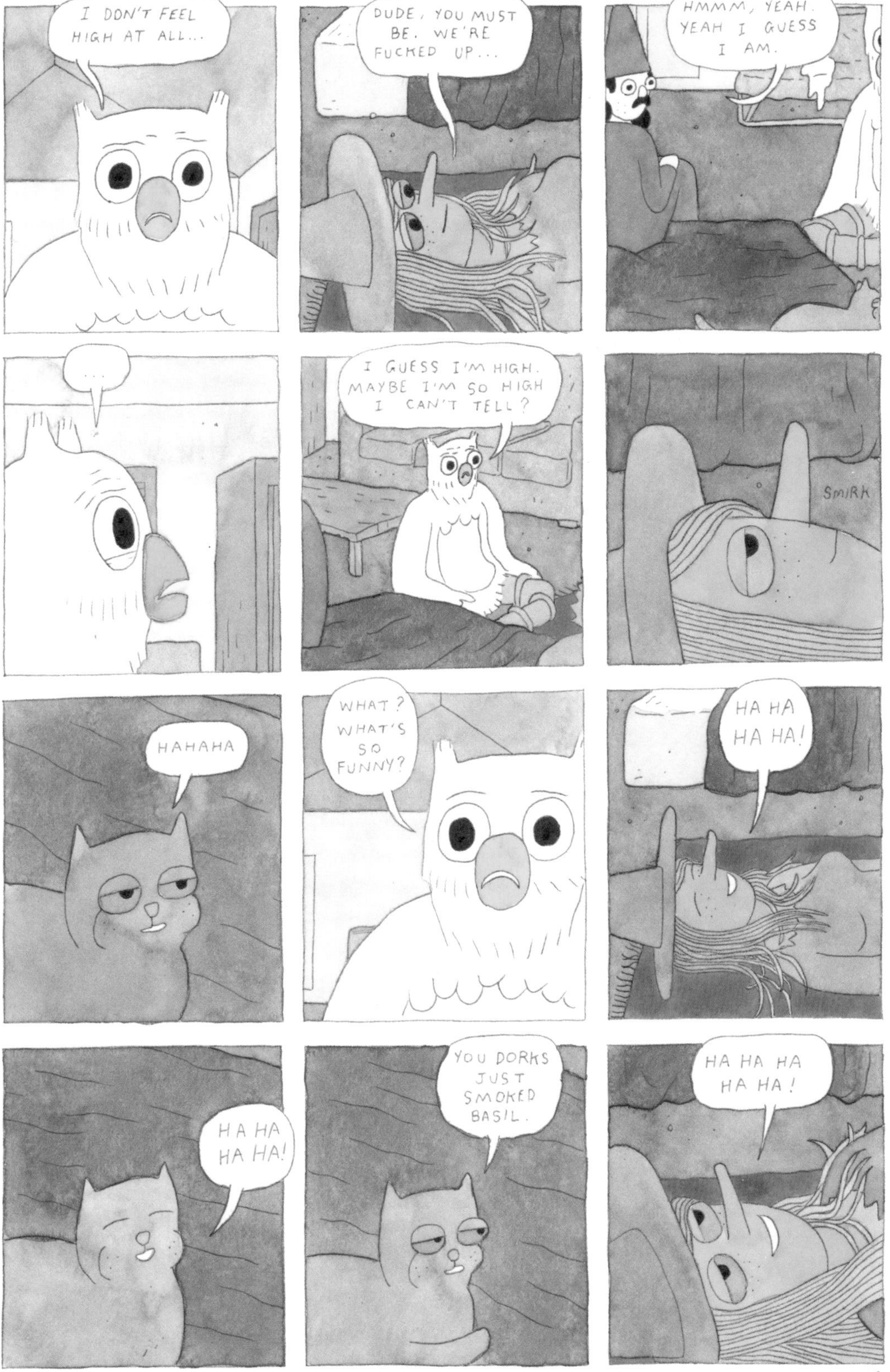
I DON'T FEEL HIGH AT ALL...
DUDE, YOU MUST BE. WE'RE FUCKED UP...
HMMM, YEAH. YEAH I GUESS I AM.
...
I GUESS I'M HIGH. MAYBE I'M SO HIGH I CAN'T TELL?
SMIRK
HAHAHA
WHAT? WHAT'S SO FUNNY?
HA HA HA HA!
HA HA HA HA!
YOU DORKS JUST SMOKED BASIL.
HA HA HA HA HA!

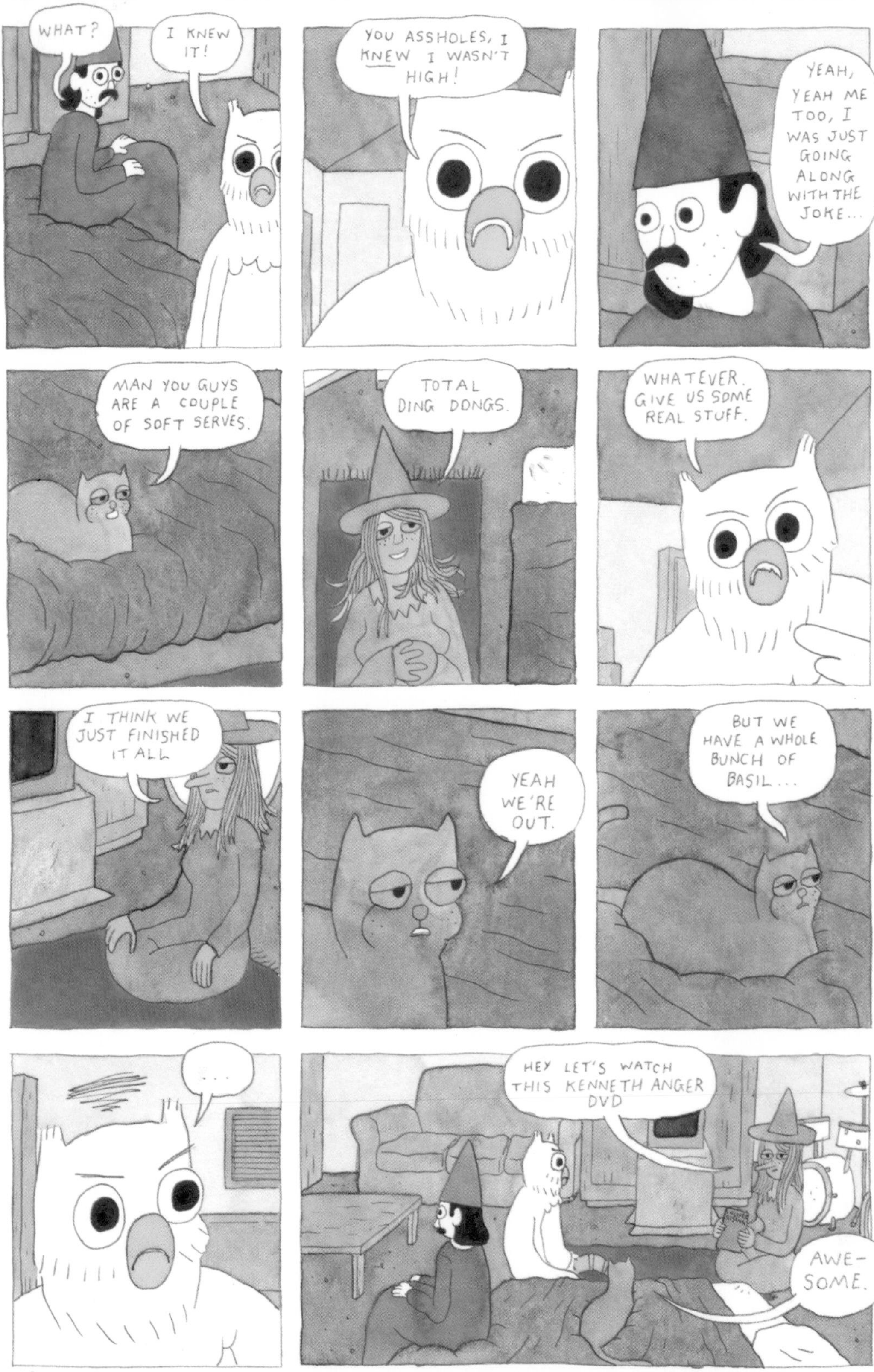
WHAT?
I KNEW IT!
YOU ASSHOLES, I KNEW I WASN'T HIGH!
YEAH, YEAH ME TOO, I WAS JUST GOING ALONG WITH THE JOKE...
MAN YOU GUYS ARE A COUPLE OF SOFT SERVES.
TOTAL DING DONGS.
WHATEVER. GIVE US SOME REAL STUFF.
I THINK WE JUST FINISHED IT ALL
YEAH WE'RE OUT.
BUT WE HAVE A WHOLE BUNCH OF BASIL...
...
HEY LET'S WATCH THIS KENNETH ANGER DVD
AWE-SOME.

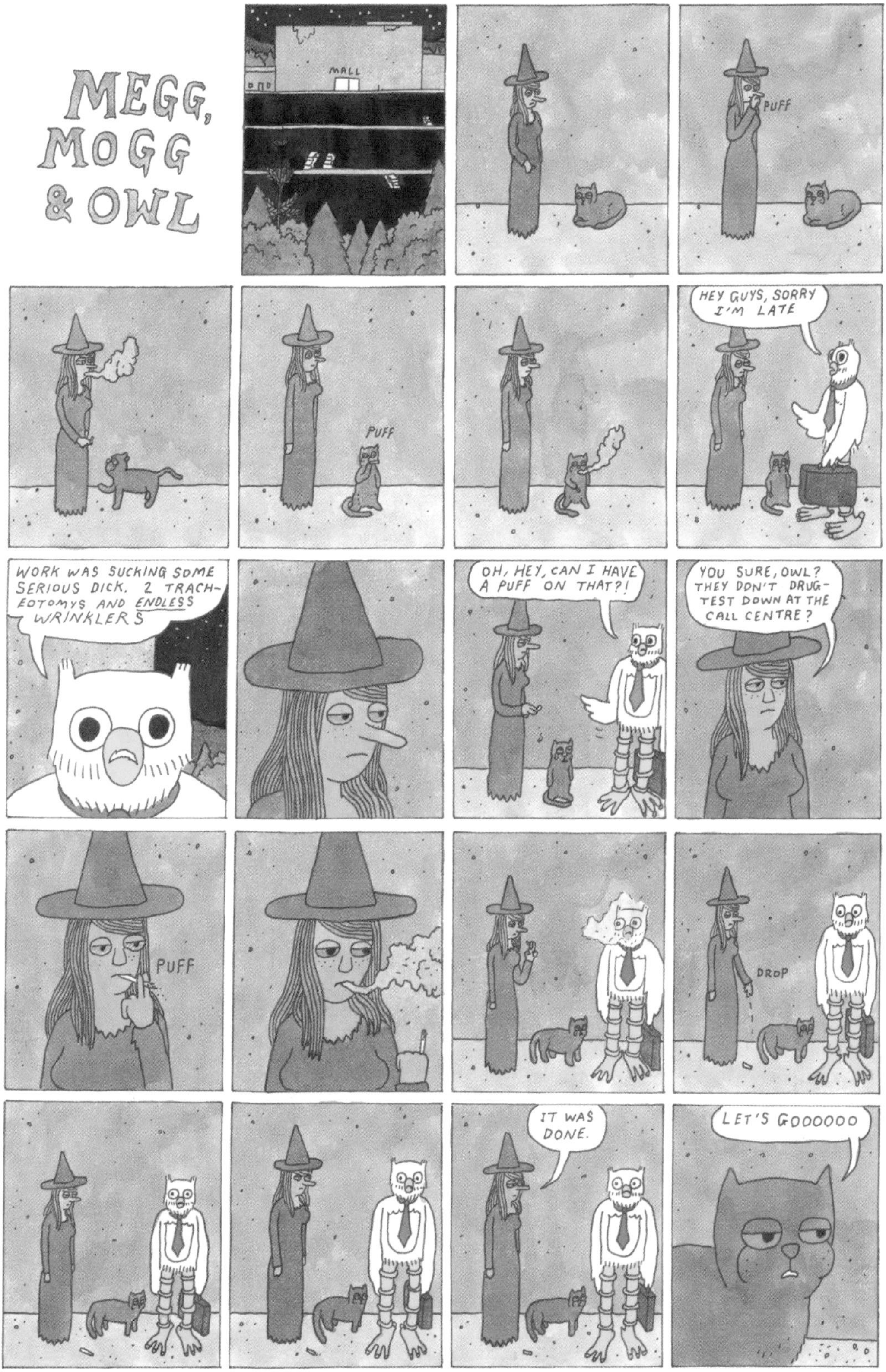
MEGG, MOGG & OWL
MALL
PUFF
PUFF
HEY GUYS, SORRY I'M LATE
WORK WAS SUCKING SOME SERIOUS DICK. 2 TRACHEOTOMYS AND ENDLESS WRINKLERS
OH, HEY, CAN I HAVE A PUFF ON THAT?!
YOU SURE, OWL? THEY DON'T DRUG-TEST DOWN AT THE CALL CENTRE?
PUFF
DROP
IT WAS DONE.
LET'S GOOOOOO

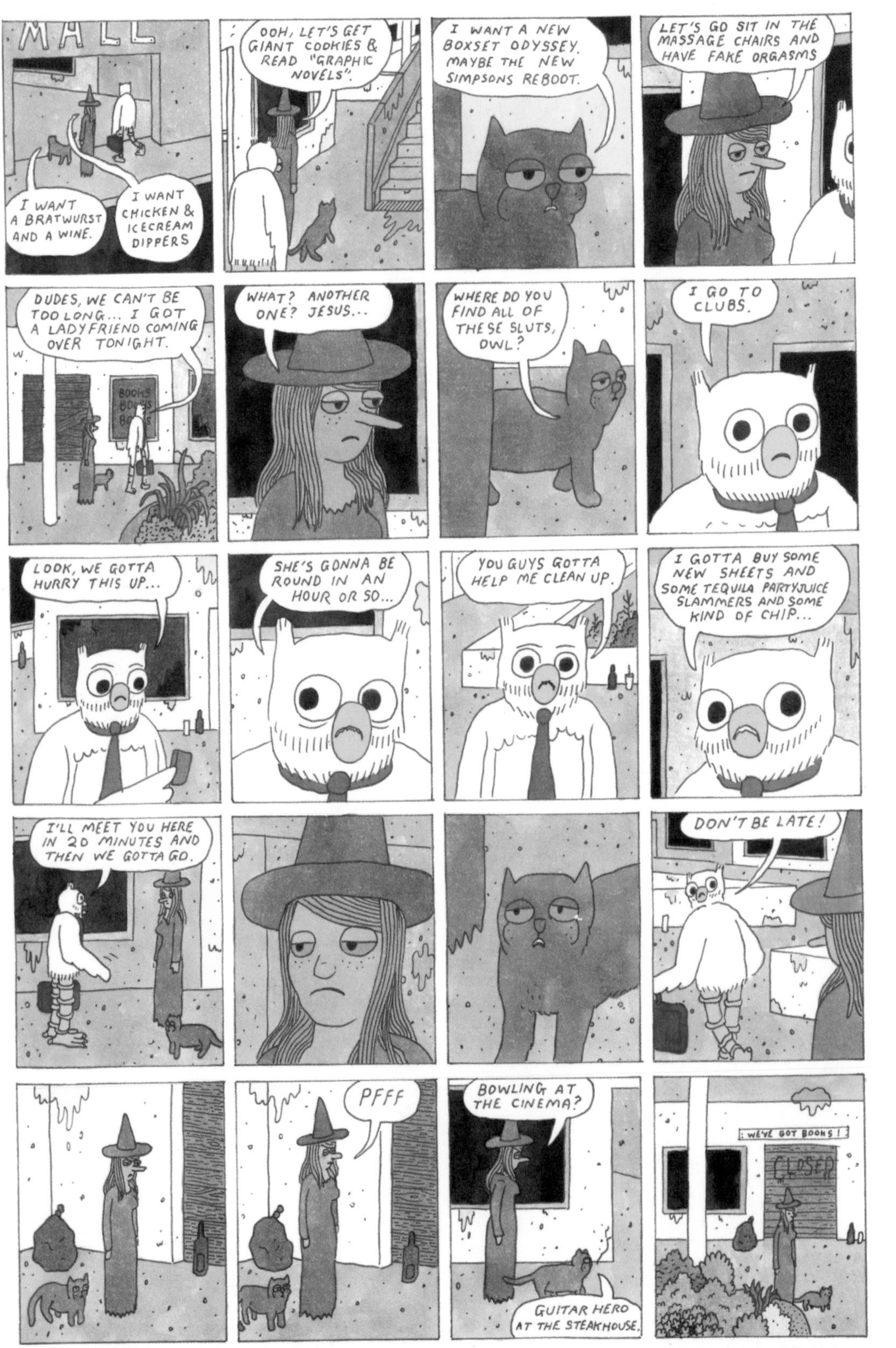
MALL
I WANT A BRATWURST AND A WINE.
I WANT CHICKEN & ICECREAM DIPPERS
OOH, LET'S GET GIANT COOKIES & READ "GRAPHIC NOVELS".
I WANT A NEW BOXSET ODYSSEY. MAYBE THE NEW SIMPSONS REBOOT.
LET'S GO SIT IN THE MASSAGE CHAIRS AND HAVE FAKE ORGASMS
DUDES, WE CAN'T BE TOO LONG... I GOT A LADYFRIEND COMING OVER TONIGHT.
BOOKS BOOKS BOOKS
WHAT? ANOTHER ONE? JESUS...
WHERE DO YOU FIND ALL OF THESE SLUTS, OWL?
I GO TO CLUBS.
LOOK, WE GOTTA HURRY THIS UP...
SHE'S GONNA BE ROUND IN AN HOUR OR SO...
YOU GUYS GOTTA HELP ME CLEAN UP.
I GOTTA BUY SOME NEW SHEETS AND SOME TEQUILA PARTYJUICE SLAMMERS AND SOME KIND OF CHIP...
I'LL MEET YOU HERE IN 20 MINUTES AND THEN WE GOTTA GO.
DON'T BE LATE!
PFFF
BOWLING AT THE CINEMA?
GUITAR HERO AT THE STEAKHOUSE.
WE'VE GOT BOOKS!
CLOSED

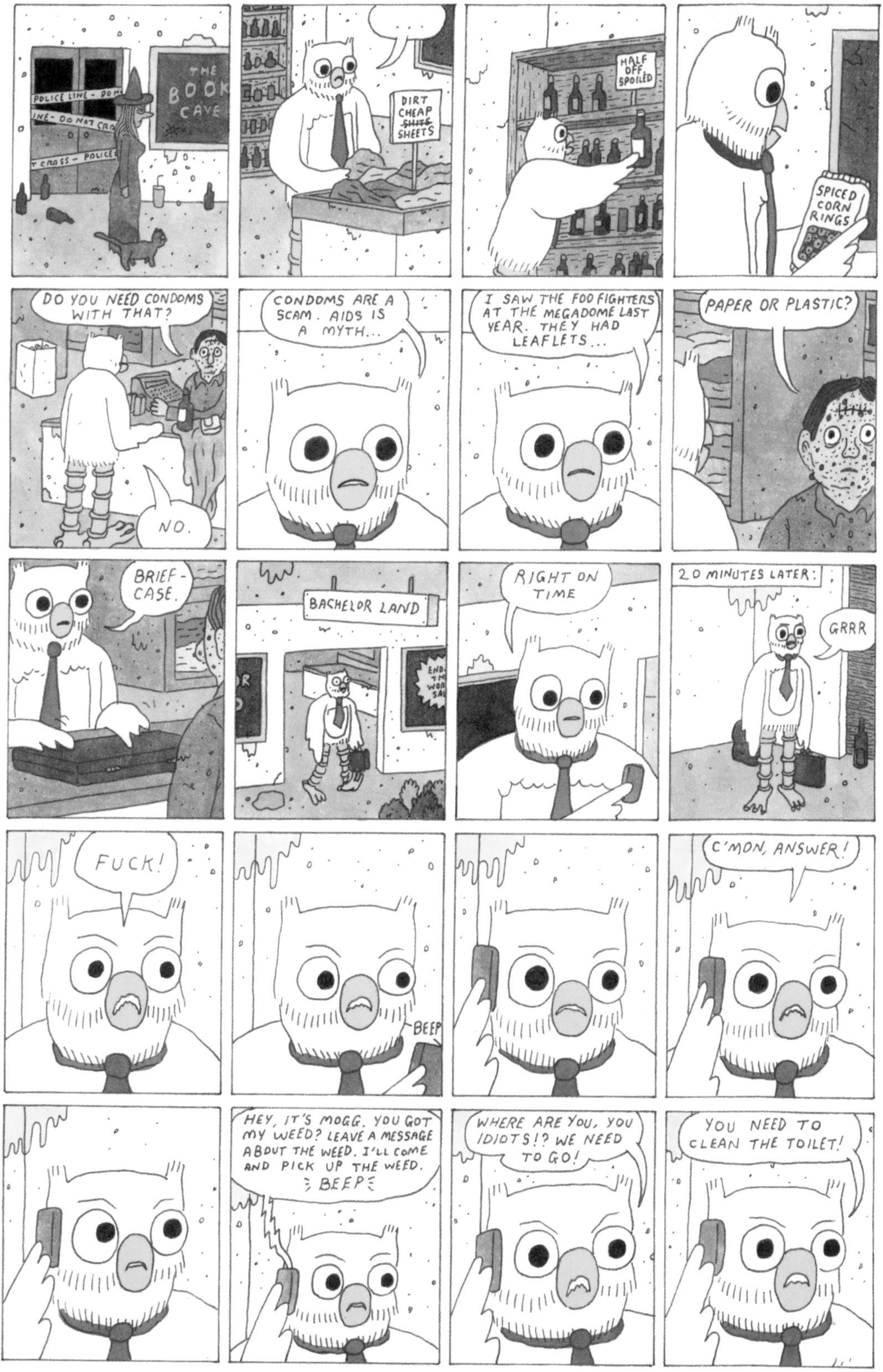
POLICE LINE - DO NOT CROSS
THE BOOK CAVE
DIRT CHEAP ~~SHITS~~ SHEETS
HALF OFF SPOILED
SPICED CORN RINGS
DO YOU NEED CONDOMS WITH THAT?
NO.
CONDOMS ARE A SCAM. AIDS IS A MYTH...
I SAW THE FOO FIGHTERS AT THE MEGADOME LAST YEAR. THEY HAD LEAFLETS...
PAPER OR PLASTIC?
BRIEF-CASE.
BACHELOR LAND
RIGHT ON TIME
20 MINUTES LATER:
GRRR
FUCK!
BEEP
C'MON, ANSWER!
HEY, IT'S MOGG. YOU GOT MY WEED? LEAVE A MESSAGE ABOUT THE WEED. I'LL COME AND PICK UP THE WEED. BEEP
WHERE ARE YOU, YOU IDIOTS!? WE NEED TO GO!
YOU NEED TO CLEAN THE TOILET!

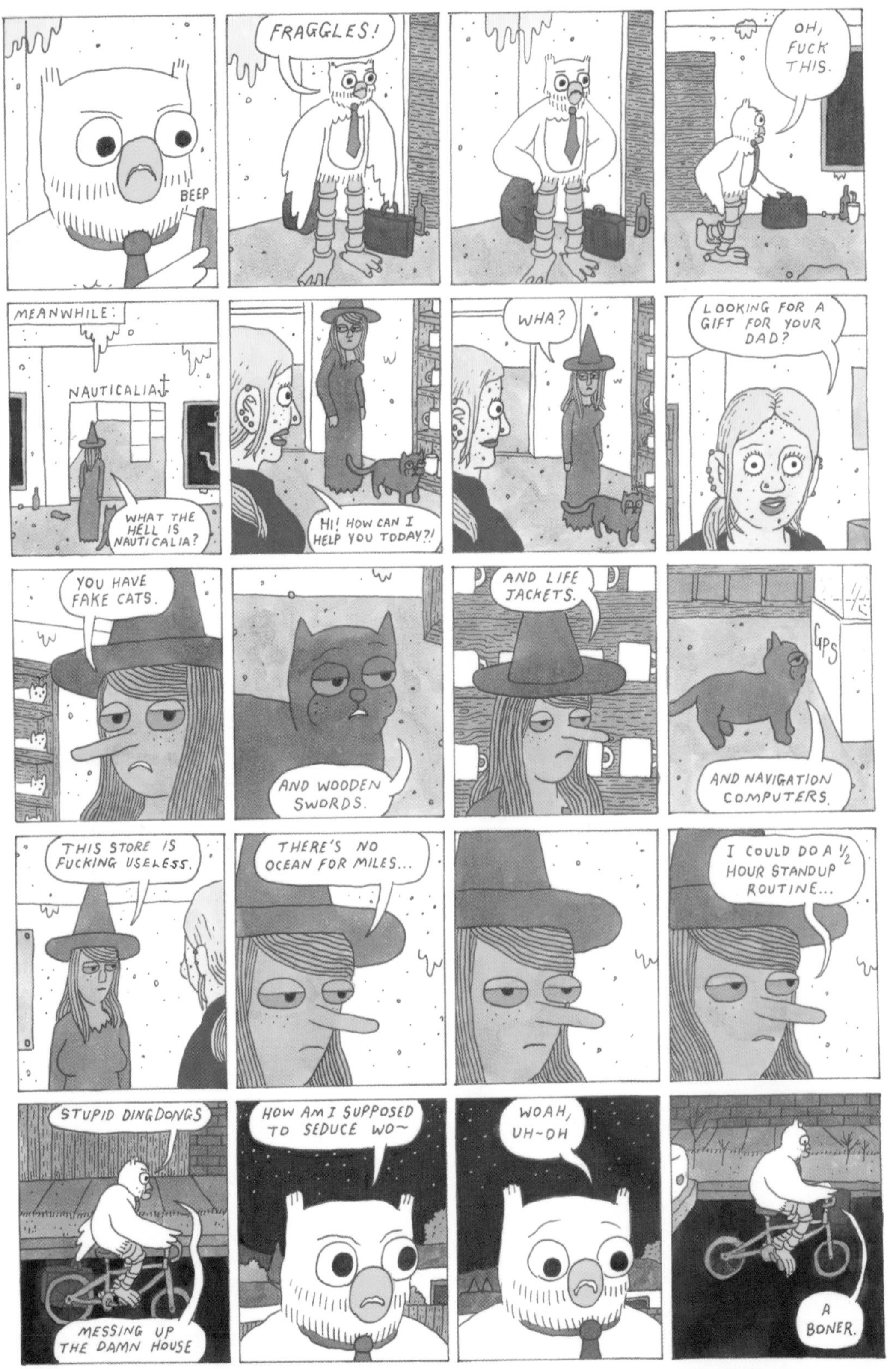
BEEP
FRAGGLES!
OH, FUCK THIS.
MEANWHILE:
NAUTICALIA
WHAT THE HELL IS NAUTICALIA?
HI! HOW CAN I HELP YOU TODAY?!
WHA?
LOOKING FOR A GIFT FOR YOUR DAD?
YOU HAVE FAKE CATS.
AND WOODEN SWORDS.
AND LIFE JACKETS.
GPS
AND NAVIGATION COMPUTERS.
THIS STORE IS FUCKING USELESS.
THERE'S NO OCEAN FOR MILES...
I COULD DO A 1/2 HOUR STANDUP ROUTINE...
STUPID DINGDONGS
MESSING UP THE DAMN HOUSE
HOW AM I SUPPOSED TO SEDUCE WO~
WOAH, UH-OH
A BONER.

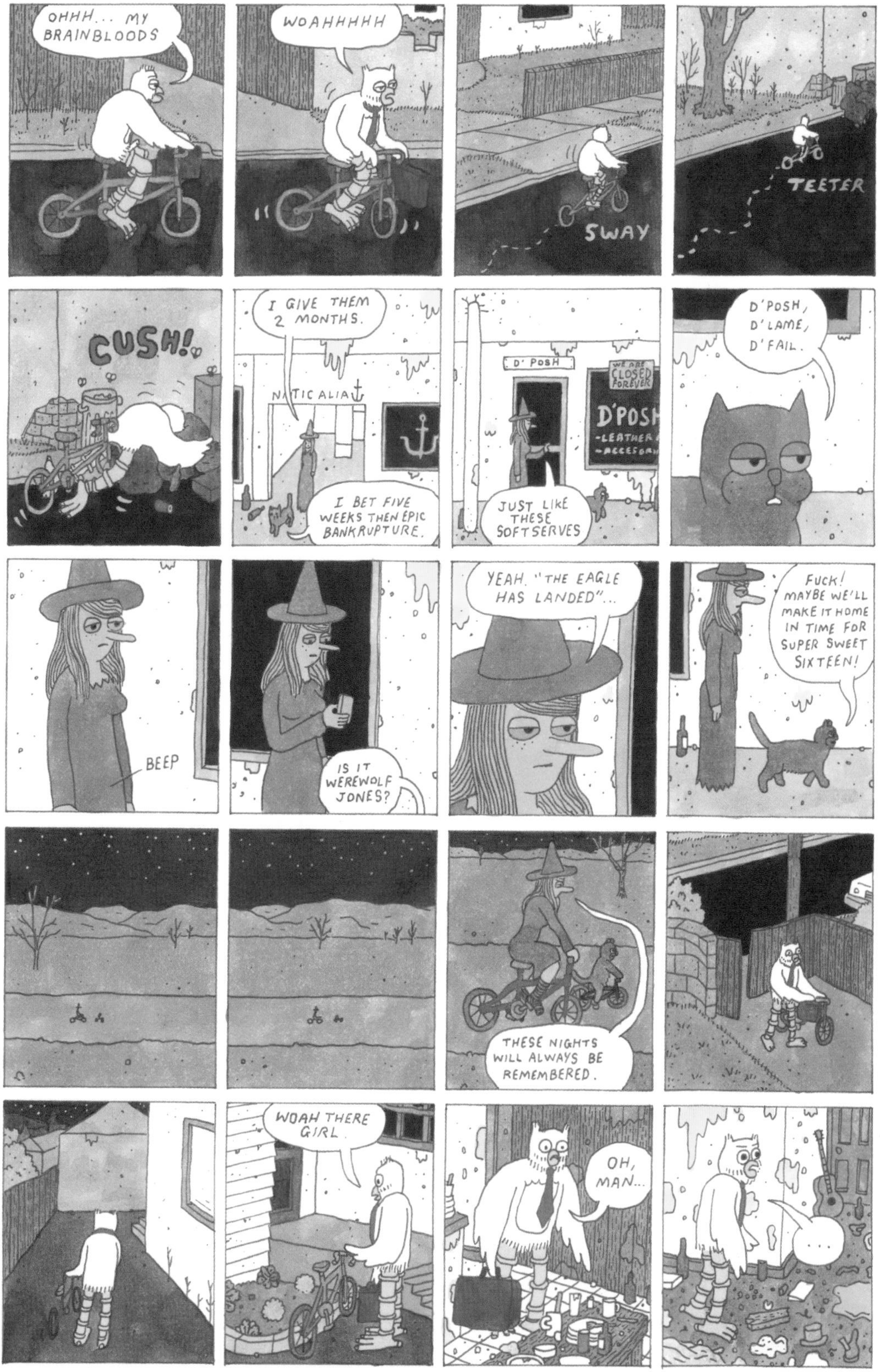
OHHH... MY BRAINBLOODS
WOAHHHHH
SWAY
TEETER
CUSH!
I GIVE THEM 2 MONTHS.
I BET FIVE WEEKS THEN EPIC BANKRUPTURE.
D' POSH
WE ARE CLOSED FOREVER
D'POSH
-LEATHER
JUST LIKE THESE SOFTSERVES
D'POSH, D'LAME, D'FAIL.
BEEP
IS IT WEREWOLF JONES?
YEAH. "THE EAGLE HAS LANDED"...
FUCK! MAYBE WE'LL MAKE IT HOME IN TIME FOR SUPER SWEET SIXTEEN!
THESE NIGHTS WILL ALWAYS BE REMEMBERED.
WOAH THERE GIRL
OH, MAN...
...

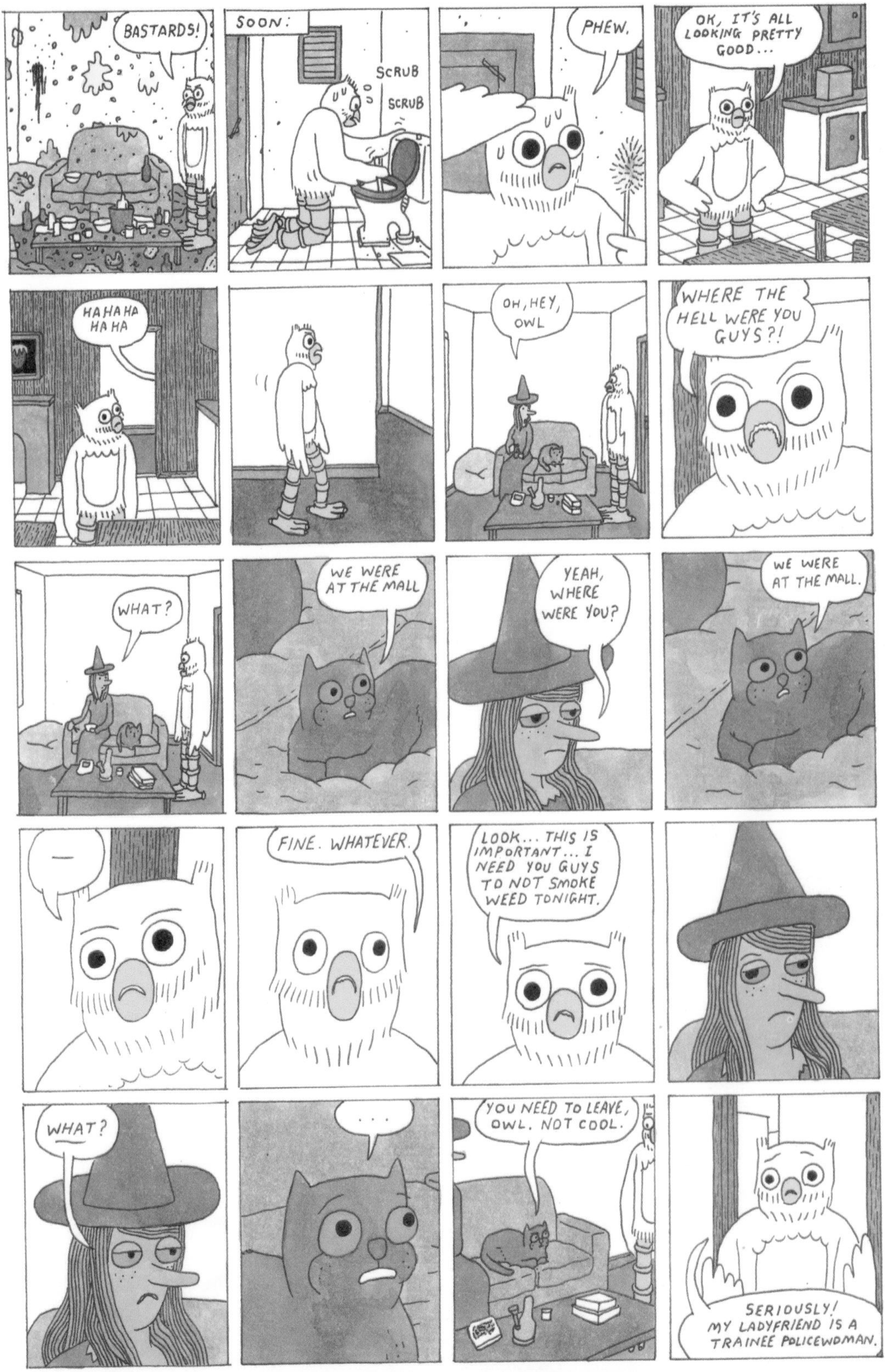
BASTARDS!
SOON:
SCRUB
SCRUB
PHEW.
OK, IT'S ALL LOOKING PRETTY GOOD...
HA HA HA HA HA
OH, HEY, OWL
WHERE THE HELL WERE YOU GUYS?!
WHAT?
WE WERE AT THE MALL
YEAH, WHERE WERE YOU?
WE WERE AT THE MALL.
FINE. WHATEVER.
LOOK... THIS IS IMPORTANT... I NEED YOU GUYS TO NOT SMOKE WEED TONIGHT.
WHAT?
. . .
YOU NEED TO LEAVE, OWL. NOT COOL.
SERIOUSLY! MY LADYFRIEND IS A TRAINEE POLICEWOMAN.

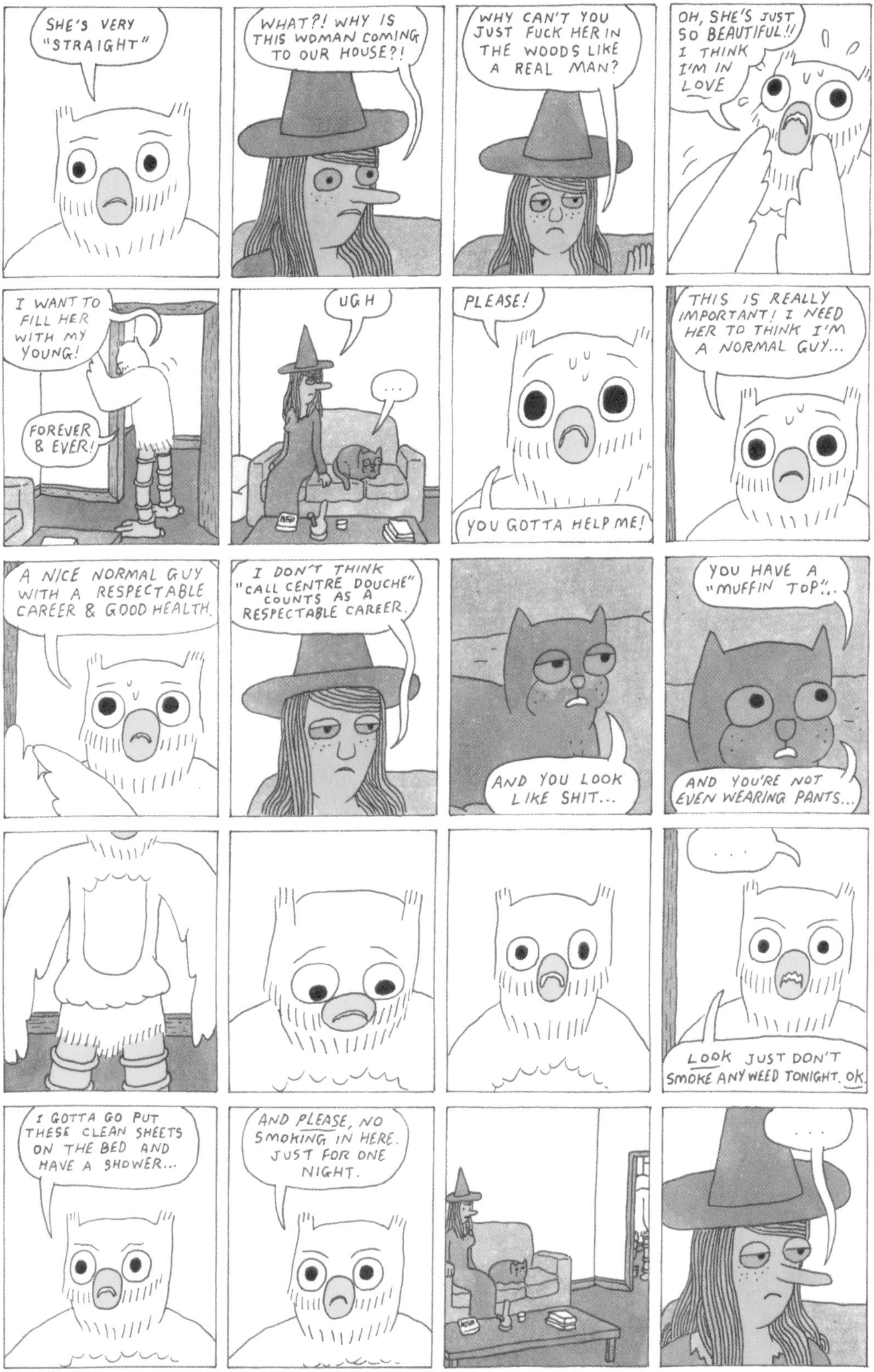
SHE'S VERY "STRAIGHT"
WHAT?! WHY IS THIS WOMAN COMING TO OUR HOUSE?!
WHY CAN'T YOU JUST FUCK HER IN THE WOODS LIKE A REAL MAN?
OH, SHE'S JUST SO BEAUTIFUL!! I THINK I'M IN LOVE
I WANT TO FILL HER WITH MY YOUNG!
FOREVER & EVER!
UGH
...
PLEASE!
YOU GOTTA HELP ME!
THIS IS REALLY IMPORTANT! I NEED HER TO THINK I'M A NORMAL GUY...
A NICE NORMAL GUY WITH A RESPECTABLE CAREER & GOOD HEALTH.
I DON'T THINK "CALL CENTRE DOUCHE" COUNTS AS A RESPECTABLE CAREER.
AND YOU LOOK LIKE SHIT...
YOU HAVE A "MUFFIN TOP"...
AND YOU'RE NOT EVEN WEARING PANTS...
...
LOOK JUST DON'T SMOKE ANY WEED TONIGHT. OK.
I GOTTA GO PUT THESE CLEAN SHEETS ON THE BED AND HAVE A SHOWER...
AND PLEASE, NO SMOKING IN HERE. JUST FOR ONE NIGHT.
...

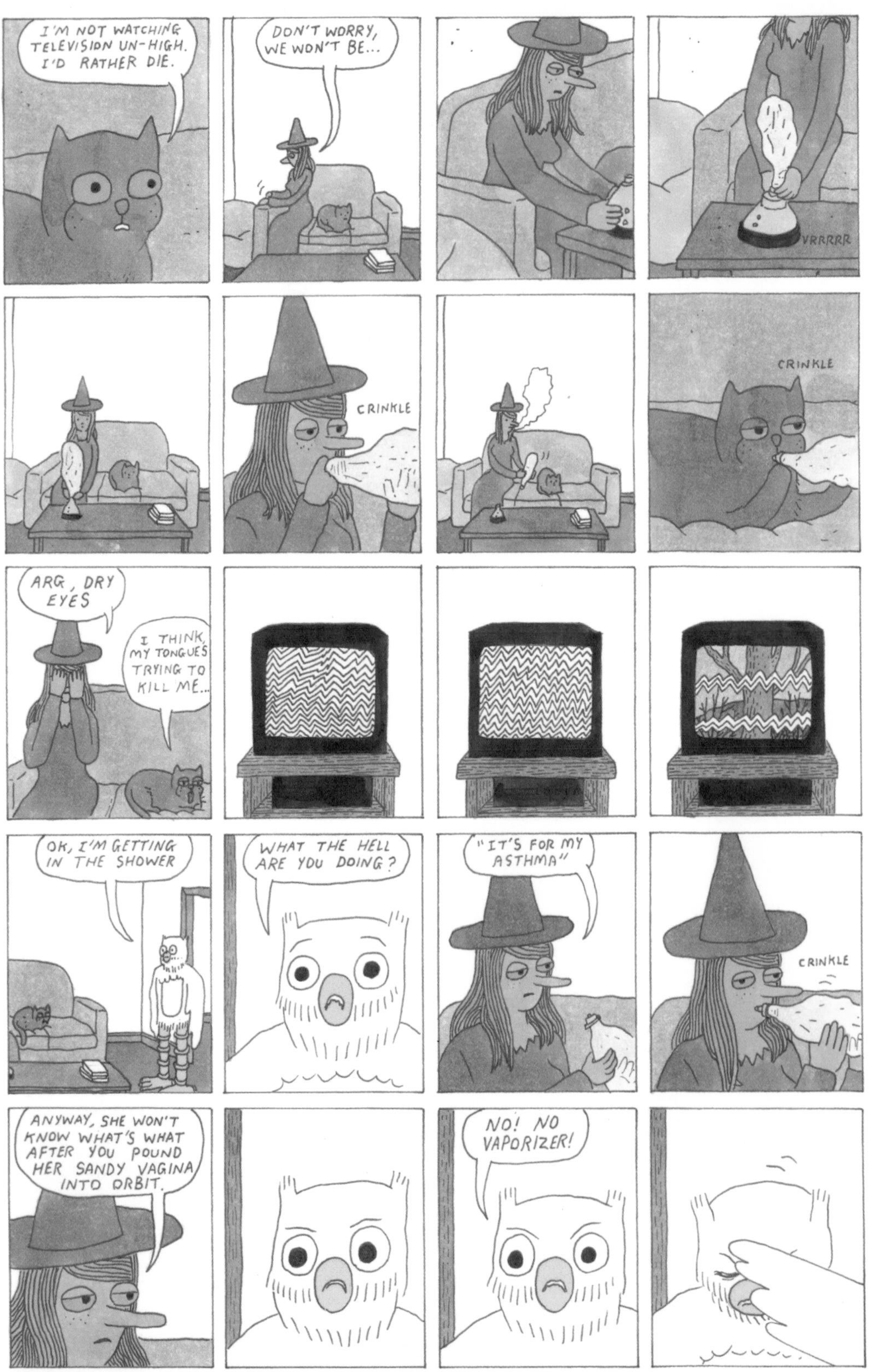
I'M NOT WATCHING TELEVISION UN-HIGH. I'D RATHER DIE.
DON'T WORRY, WE WON'T BE...
VRRRRR
CRINKLE
CRINKLE
ARG, DRY EYES
I THINK, MY TONGUE'S TRYING TO KILL ME...
OK, I'M GETTING IN THE SHOWER
WHAT THE HELL ARE YOU DOING?
"IT'S FOR MY ASTHMA"
CRINKLE
ANYWAY, SHE WON'T KNOW WHAT'S WHAT AFTER YOU POUND HER SANDY VAGINA INTO ORBIT.
NO! NO VAPORIZER!

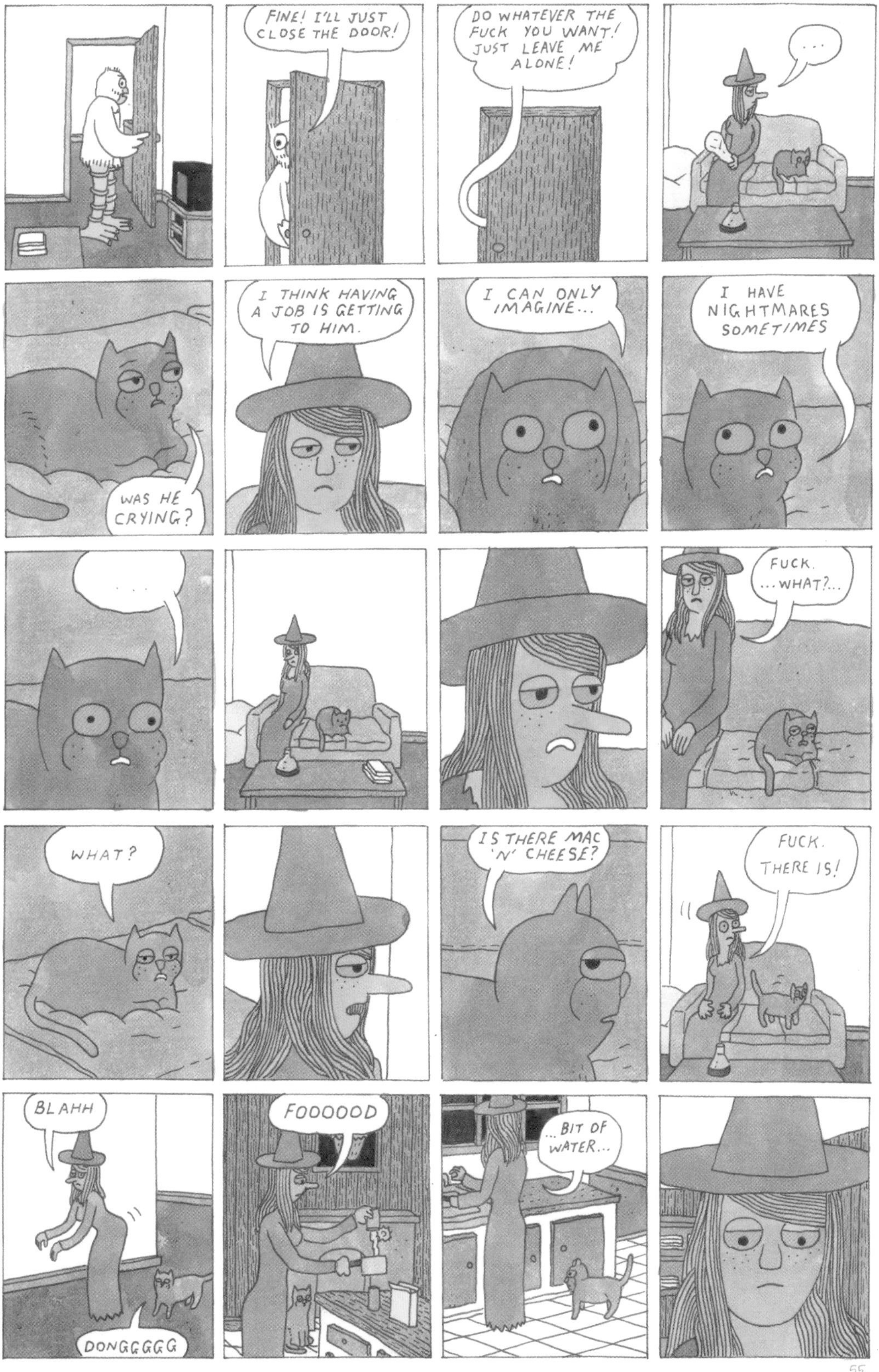
FINE! I'LL JUST CLOSE THE DOOR!
DO WHATEVER THE FUCK YOU WANT! JUST LEAVE ME ALONE!
...
WAS HE CRYING?
I THINK HAVING A JOB IS GETTING TO HIM.
I CAN ONLY IMAGINE...
I HAVE NIGHTMARES SOMETIMES
...
FUCK. ...WHAT?...
WHAT?
IS THERE MAC 'N' CHEESE?
FUCK. THERE IS!
BLAHH
DONGGGGG
FOOOOOD
...BIT OF WATER...

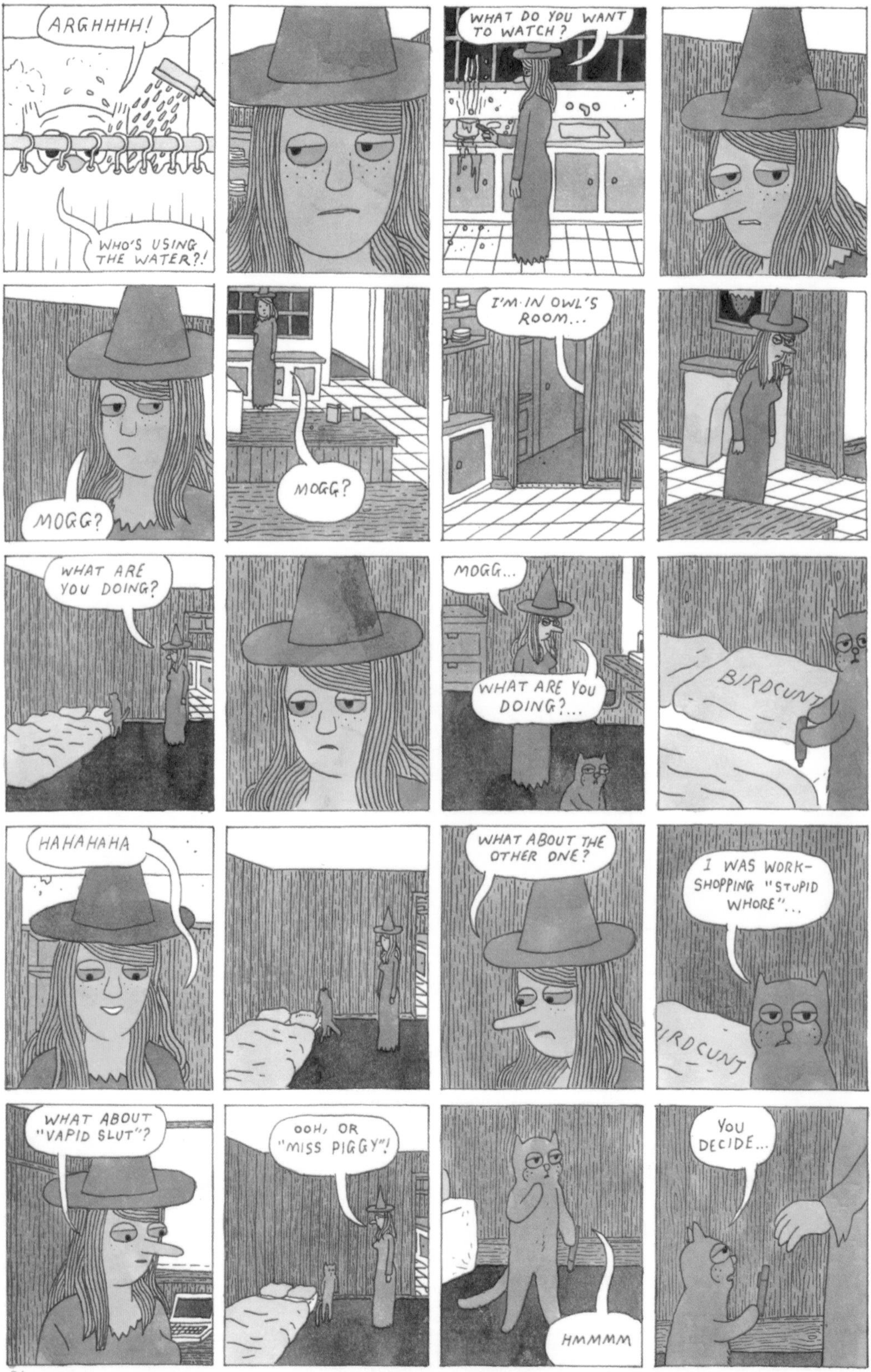
ARGHHHH!
WHO'S USING THE WATER?!
WHAT DO YOU WANT TO WATCH?
MOGG?
MOGG?
I'M IN OWL'S ROOM...
WHAT ARE YOU DOING?
MOGG...
WHAT ARE YOU DOING?...
BIRDCUNT
HAHAHAHA
WHAT ABOUT THE OTHER ONE?
I WAS WORK-SHOPPING "STUPID WHORE"...
WHAT ABOUT "VAPID SLUT"?
OOH, OR "MISS PIGGY"!
HMMMM
YOU DECIDE...

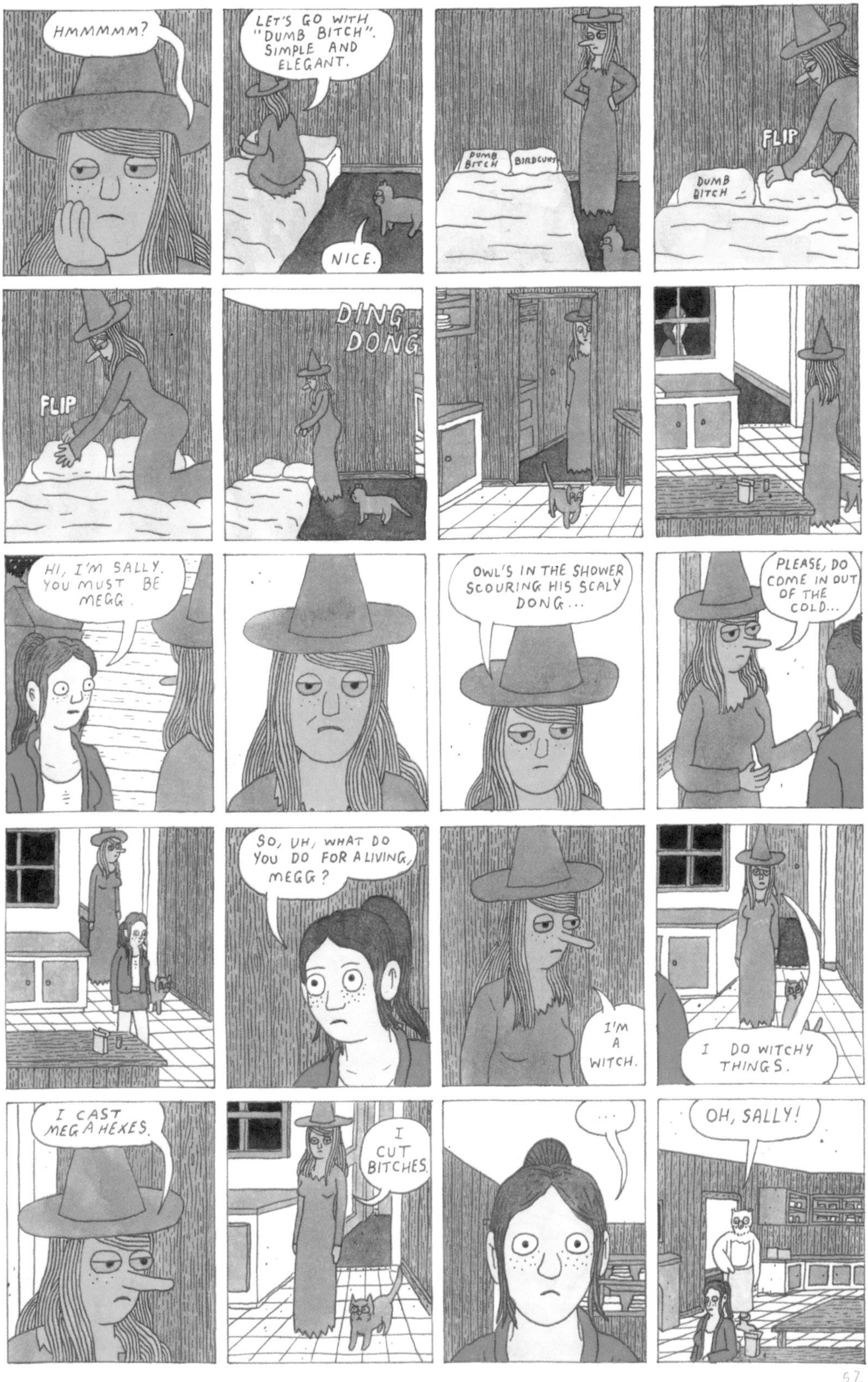
HMMMMM?
LET'S GO WITH "DUMB BITCH". SIMPLE AND ELEGANT.
NICE.
DUMB BITCH
BIRDCUNT
DUMB BITCH
FLIP
FLIP
DING DONG
HI, I'M SALLY. YOU MUST BE MEGG.
OWL'S IN THE SHOWER SCOURING HIS SCALY DONG...
PLEASE, DO COME IN OUT OF THE COLD...
SO, UH, WHAT DO YOU DO FOR A LIVING, MEGG?
I'M A WITCH.
I DO WITCHY THINGS.
I CAST MEGA HEXES.
I CUT BITCHES.
...
OH, SALLY!

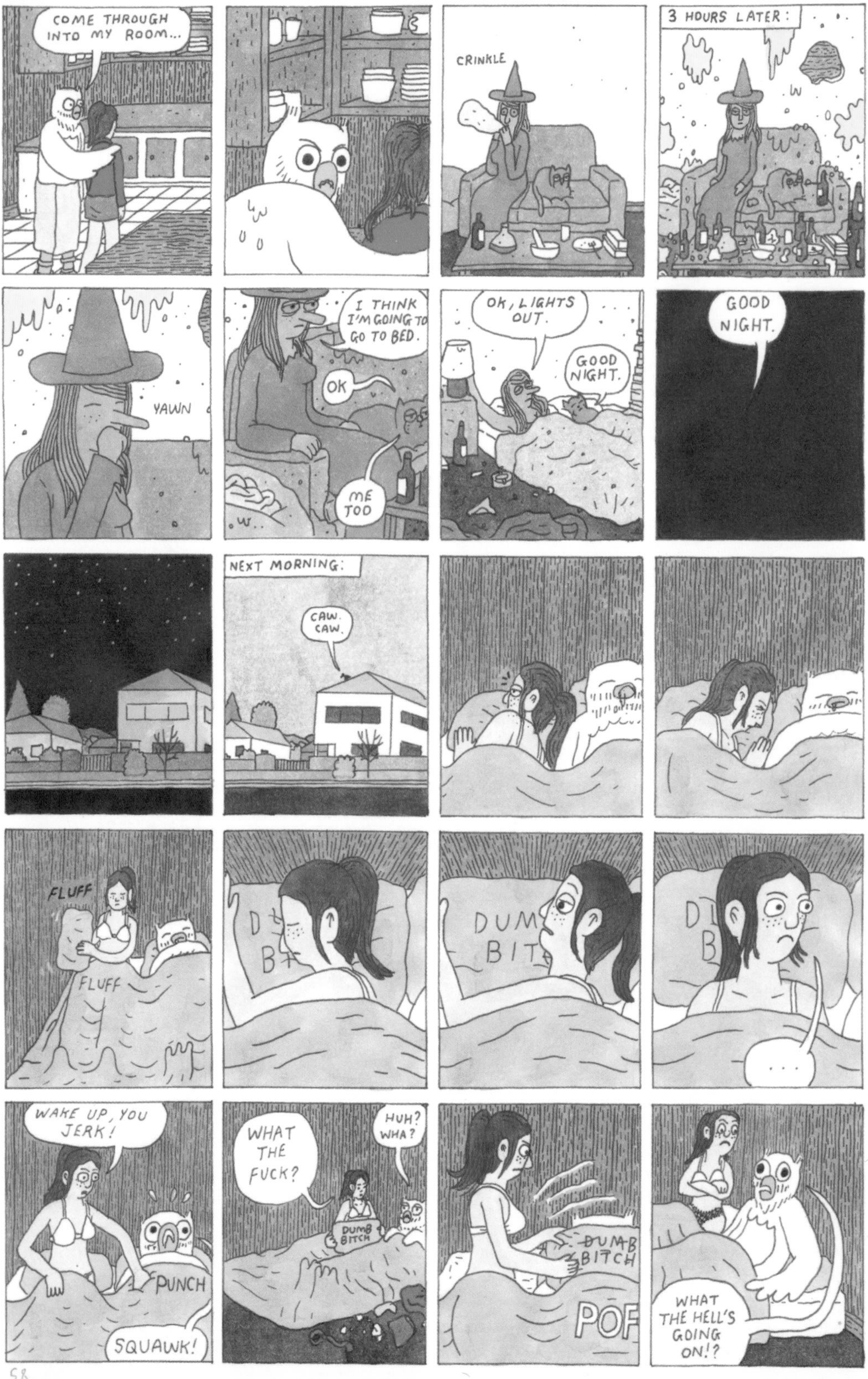
COME THROUGH INTO MY ROOM...
CRINKLE
3 HOURS LATER:
YAWN
I THINK I'M GOING TO GO TO BED.
OK
ME TOO
OK, LIGHTS OUT.
GOOD NIGHT.
GOOD NIGHT.
NEXT MORNING:
CAW. CAW.
FLUFF
FLUFF
DUMB BITCH
...
WAKE UP, YOU JERK!
PUNCH
SQUAWK!
WHAT THE FUCK?
HUH? WHA?
DUMB BITCH
DUMB BITCH
POF
WHAT THE HELL'S GOING ON!?

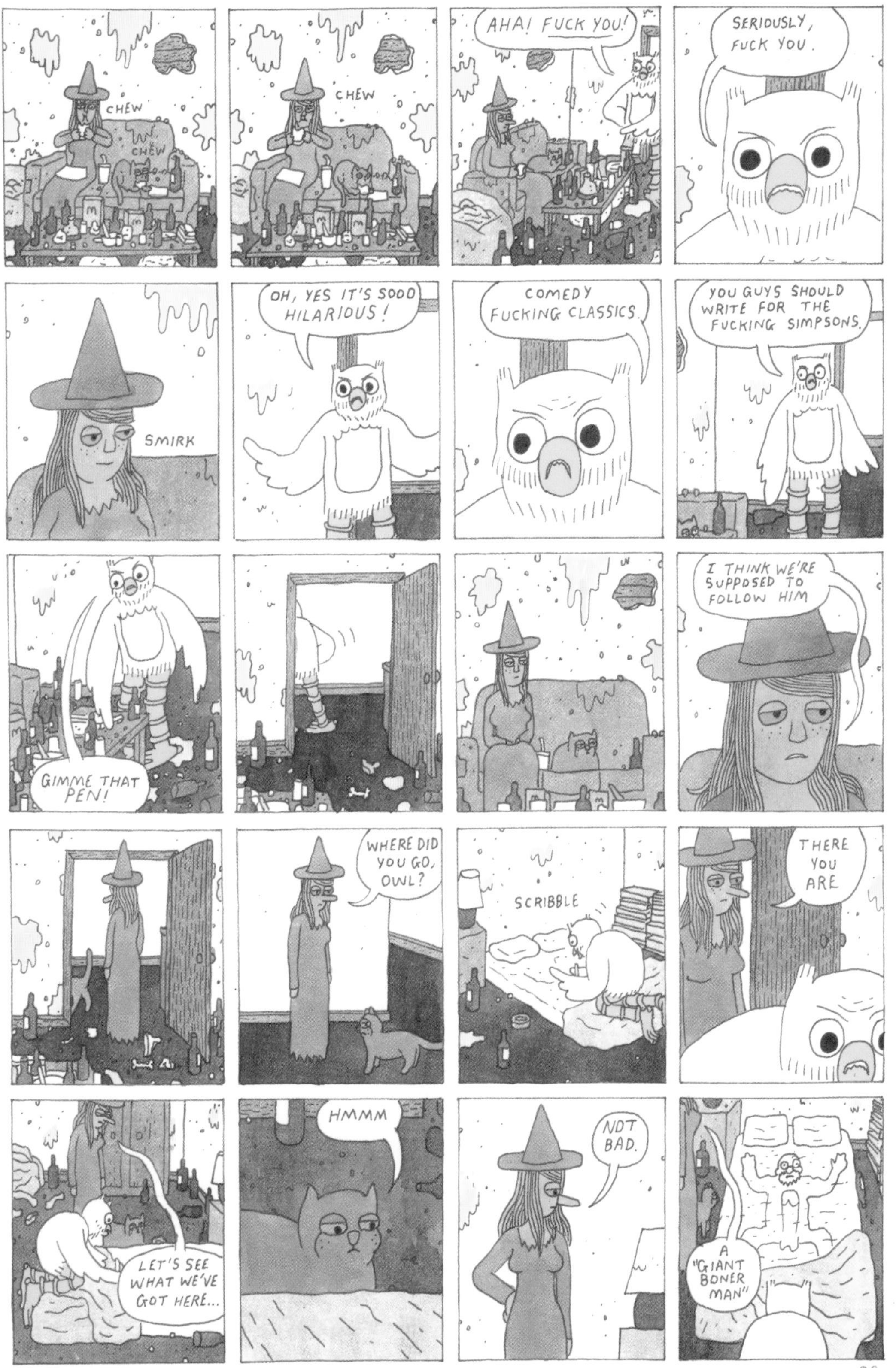

CHEW
CHEW
CHEW
AHA! FUCK YOU!
SERIOUSLY, FUCK YOU.
SMIRK
OH, YES IT'S SOOO HILARIOUS!
COMEDY FUCKING CLASSICS.
YOU GUYS SHOULD WRITE FOR THE FUCKING SIMPSONS.
GIMME THAT PEN!
I THINK WE'RE SUPPOSED TO FOLLOW HIM
WHERE DID YOU GO, OWL?
SCRIBBLE
THERE YOU ARE
LET'S SEE WHAT WE'VE GOT HERE...
HMMM
NOT BAD.
A "GIANT BONER MAN"

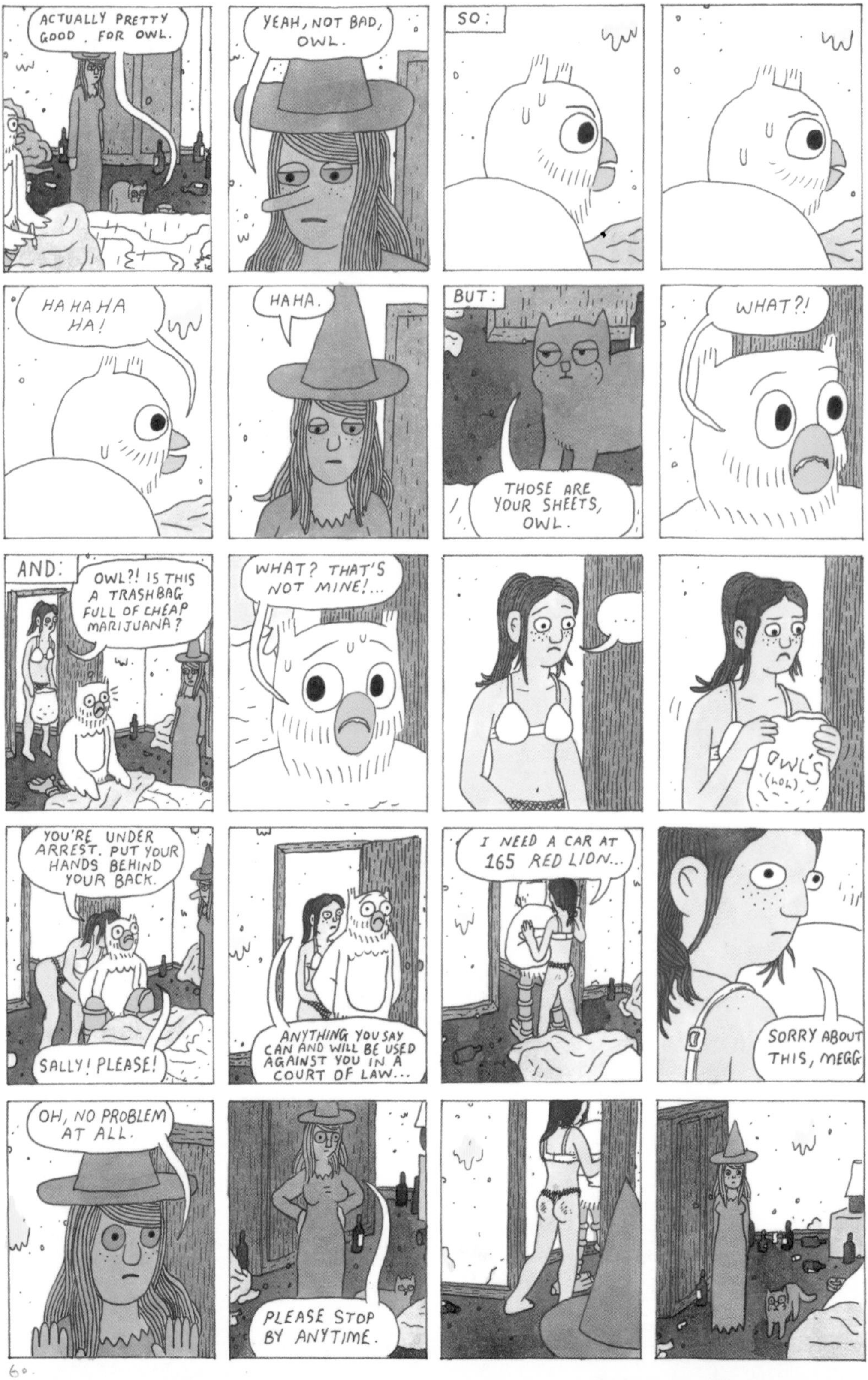
ACTUALLY PRETTY GOOD. FOR OWL.
YEAH, NOT BAD, OWL.
SO:
HA HA HA HA!
HAHA.
BUT:
THOSE ARE YOUR SHEETS, OWL.
WHAT?!
AND:
OWL?! IS THIS A TRASHBAG FULL OF CHEAP MARIJUANA?
WHAT? THAT'S NOT MINE!...
...
OWL'S (LOL)
YOU'RE UNDER ARREST. PUT YOUR HANDS BEHIND YOUR BACK.
SALLY! PLEASE!
ANYTHING YOU SAY CAN AND WILL BE USED AGAINST YOU IN A COURT OF LAW...
I NEED A CAR AT 165 RED LION...
SORRY ABOUT THIS, MEGG
OH, NO PROBLEM AT ALL.
PLEASE STOP BY ANYTIME.

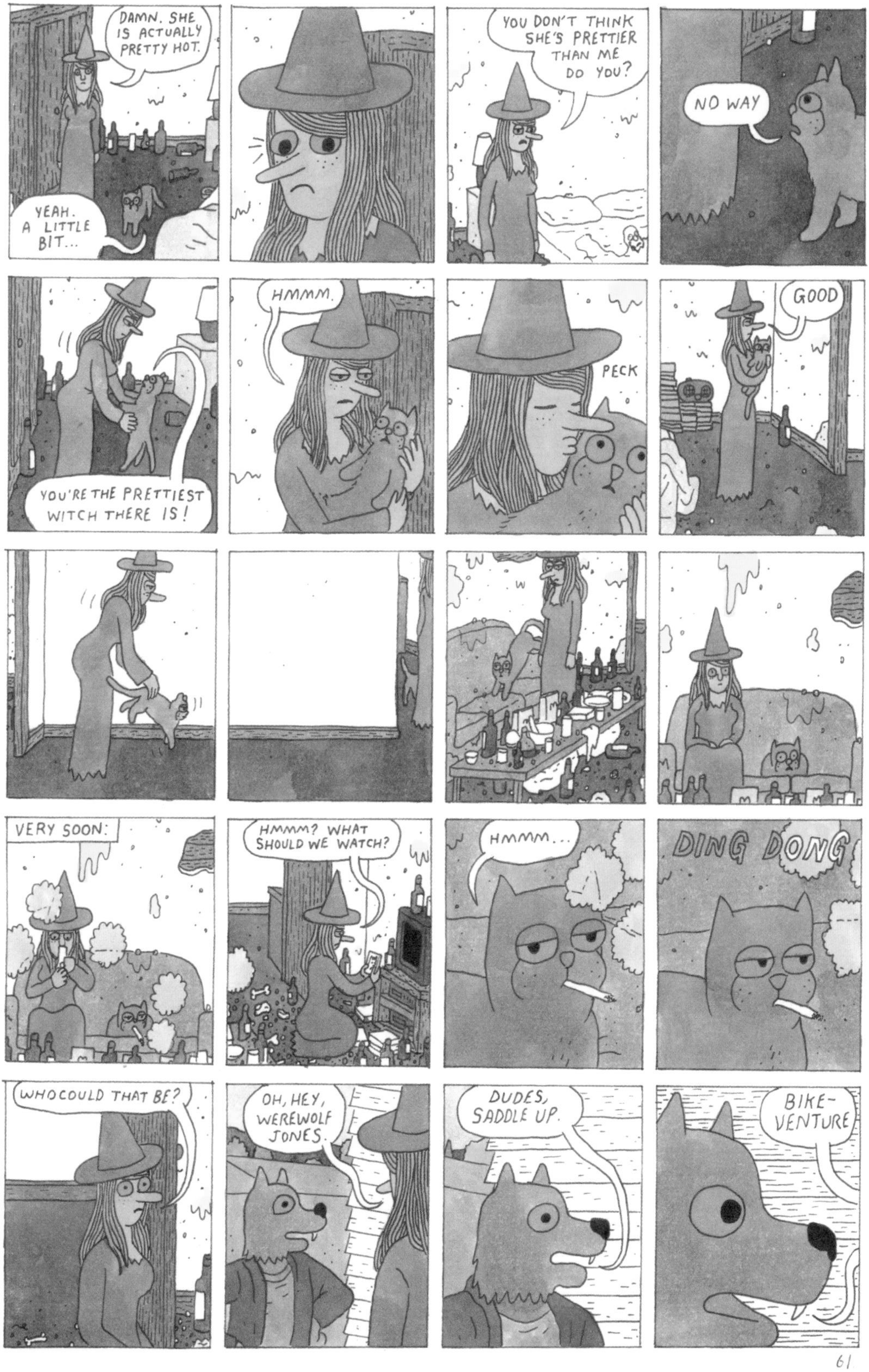
DAMN. SHE IS ACTUALLY PRETTY HOT.
YEAH. A LITTLE BIT...
YOU DON'T THINK SHE'S PRETTIER THAN ME DO YOU?
NO WAY
YOU'RE THE PRETTIEST WITCH THERE IS!
HMMM.
PECK
GOOD
VERY SOON:
HMMM? WHAT SHOULD WE WATCH?
HMMM...
DING DONG
WHO COULD THAT BE?
OH, HEY, WEREWOLF JONES.
DUDES, SADDLE UP.
BIKE-VENTURE

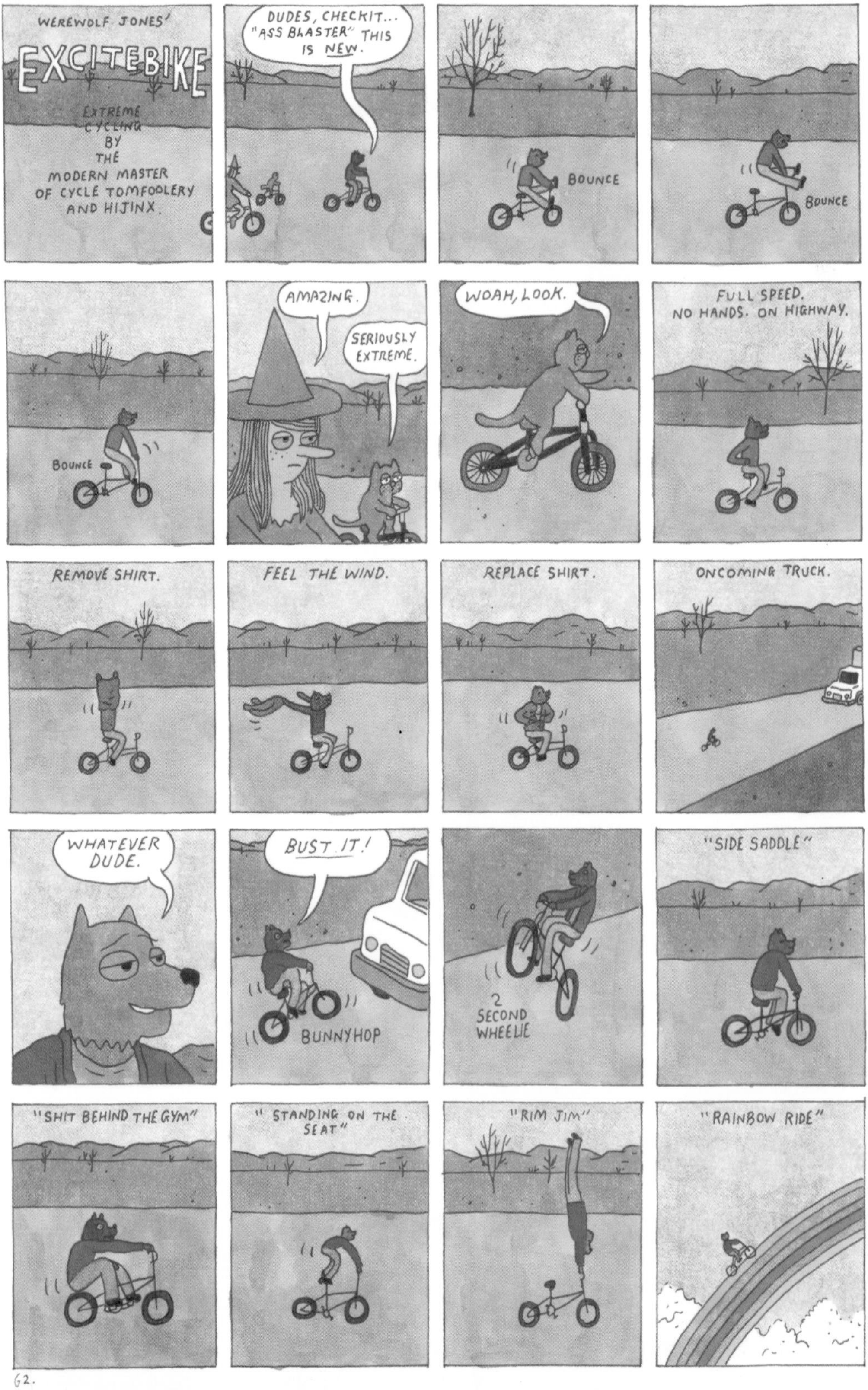
WEREWOLF JONES'
EXCITEBIKE
EXTREME CYCLING BY THE MODERN MASTER OF CYCLE TOMFOOLERY AND HIJINX.
DUDES, CHECKIT... "ASS BLASTER" THIS IS NEW.
BOUNCE
BOUNCE
BOUNCE
AMAZING.
SERIOUSLY EXTREME.
WOAH, LOOK.
FULL SPEED. NO HANDS. ON HIGHWAY.
REMOVE SHIRT.
FEEL THE WIND.
REPLACE SHIRT.
ONCOMING TRUCK.
WHATEVER DUDE.
BUST IT!
BUNNYHOP
2 SECOND WHEELIE
"SIDE SADDLE"
"SHIT BEHIND THE GYM"
"STANDING ON THE SEAT"
"RIM JIM"
"RAINBOW RIDE"

OWL'S BIRTHDAY

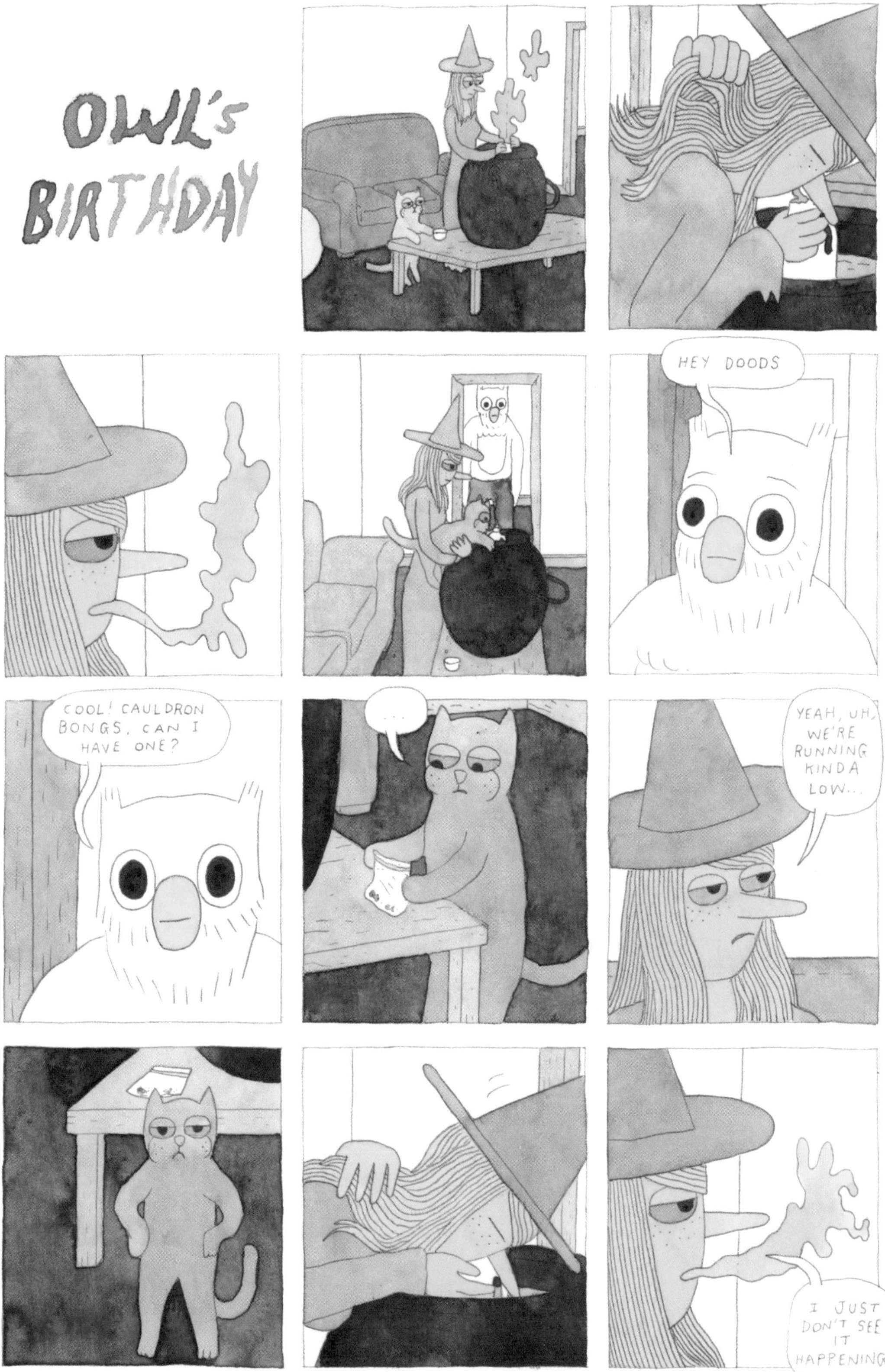

HEY DOODS
COOL! CAULDRON BONGS, CAN I HAVE ONE?
...
YEAH, UH, WE'RE RUNNING KINDA LOW...
I JUST DON'T SEE IT HAPPENING

YOU GUYS DO KNOW IT'S MY BIRTHDAY TODAY DON'T YOU?

IS THAT WHY YOU'RE WEARING THOSE STUPID PANTS?

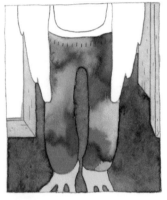

MY DAD GAVE ME THESE... THEY'RE "HAPPY PANTS"

OWL & HIS TECHNICOLOUR D'REAM PANTS

TECHNICOLOUR EROTIC D'REAMS ABOUT SUCKING NEON DICKSS

YOU GUYS SUCK! YOU'RE THE WORST FRIENDS EVER!

DUMB JERKS!

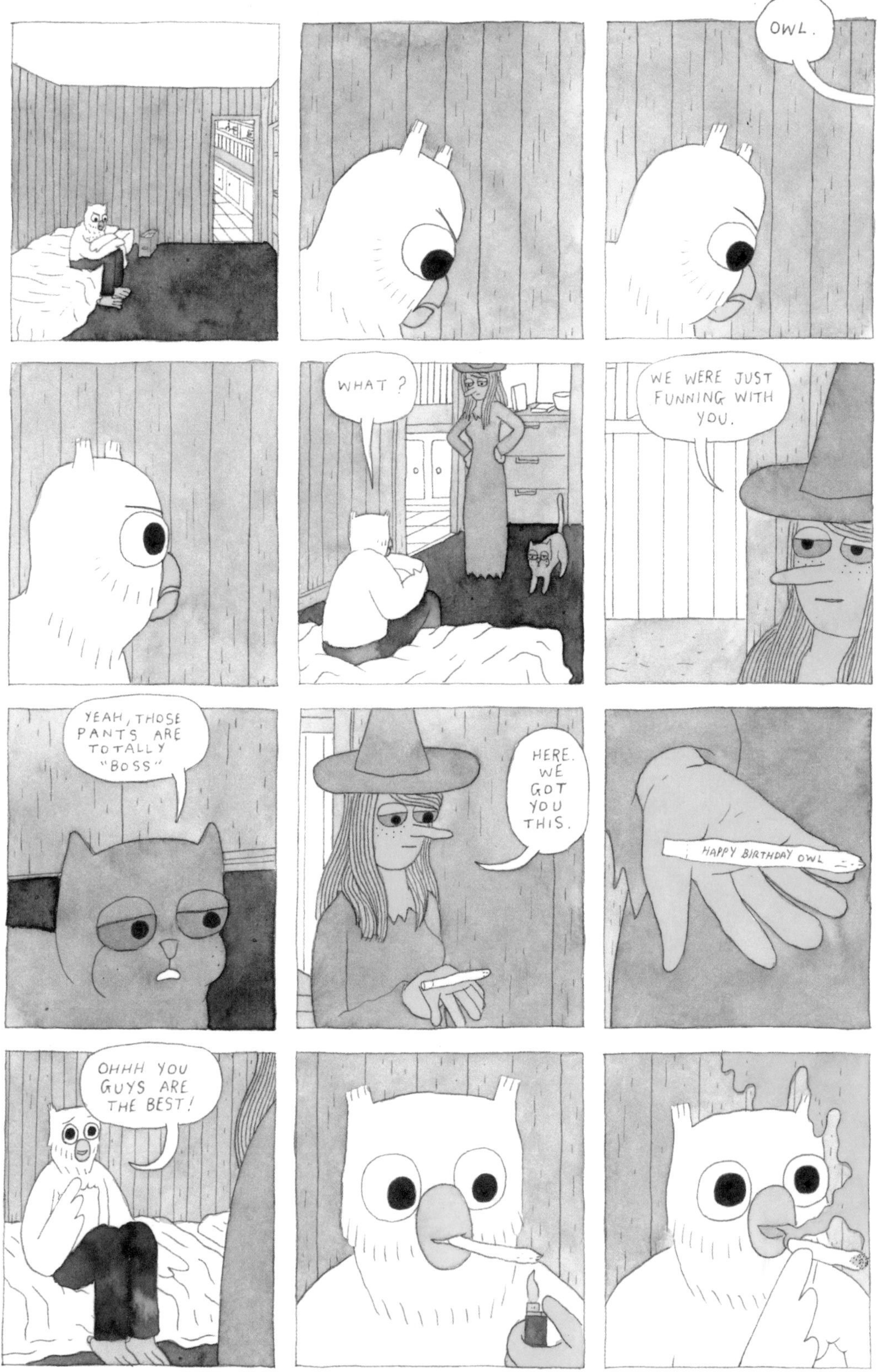
OWL.
WHAT ?
WE WERE JUST FUNNING WITH YOU.
YEAH, THOSE PANTS ARE TOTALLY "BOSS"
HERE. WE GOT YOU THIS.
HAPPY BIRTHDAY OWL
OHHH YOU GUYS ARE THE BEST!

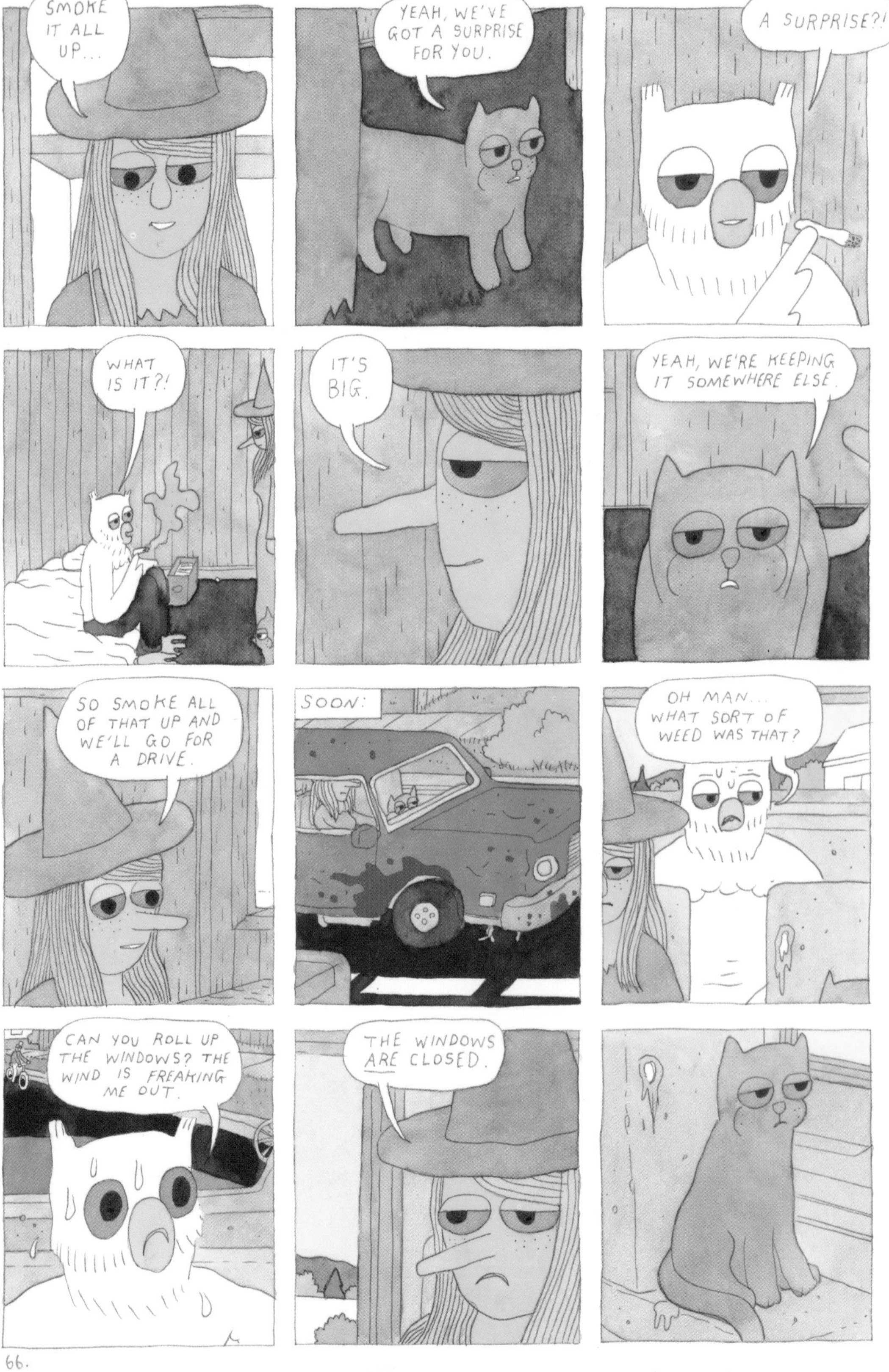
SMOKE IT ALL UP...
YEAH, WE'VE GOT A SURPRISE FOR YOU.
A SURPRISE?!
WHAT IS IT?!
IT'S BIG.
YEAH, WE'RE KEEPING IT SOMEWHERE ELSE.
SO SMOKE ALL OF THAT UP AND WE'LL GO FOR A DRIVE.
SOON:
OH MAN... WHAT SORT OF WEED WAS THAT?
CAN YOU ROLL UP THE WINDOWS? THE WIND IS FREAKING ME OUT.
THE WINDOWS ARE CLOSED.

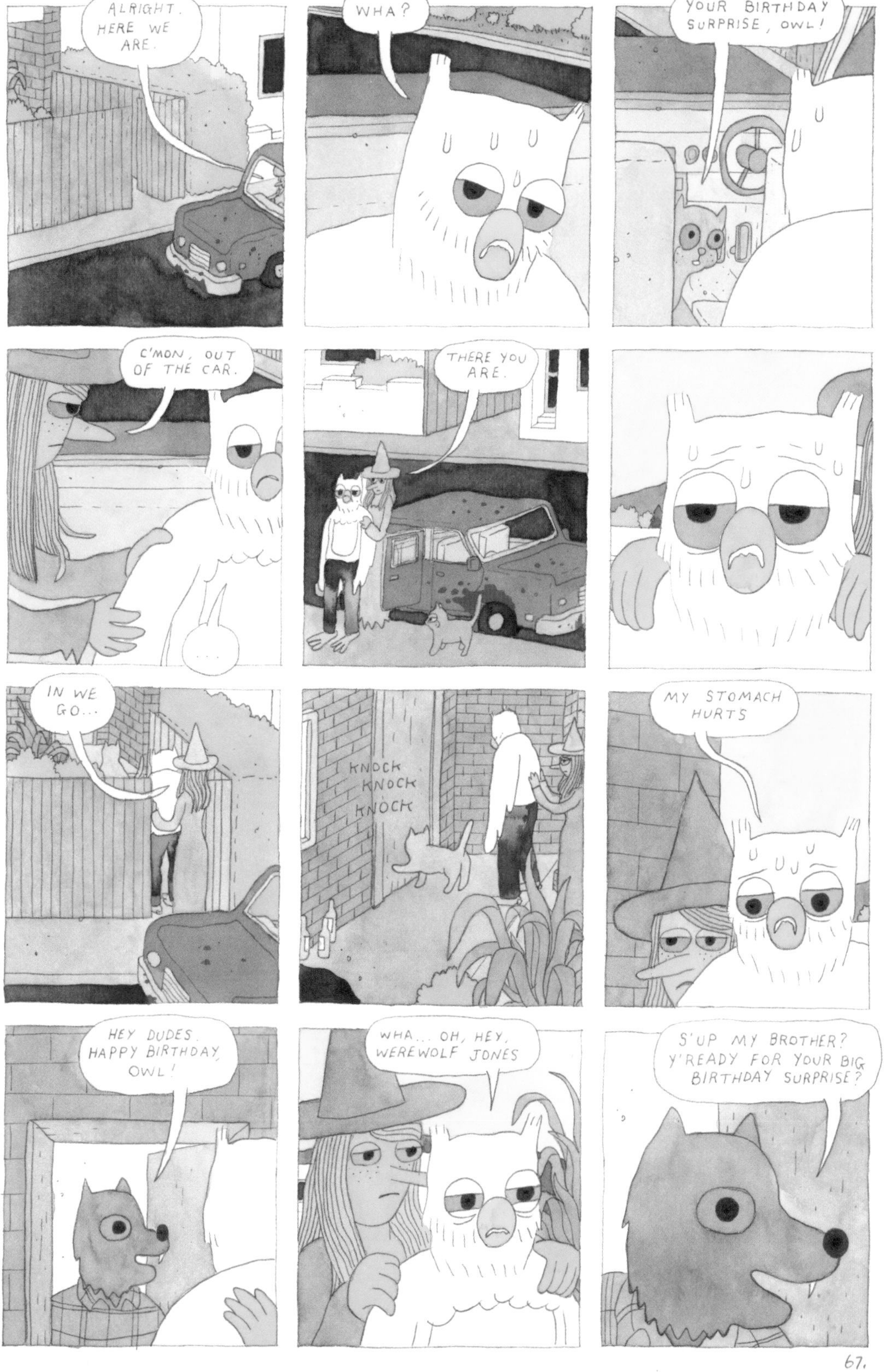
ALRIGHT. HERE WE ARE.
WHA?
YOUR BIRTHDAY SURPRISE, OWL!
C'MON, OUT OF THE CAR.
...
THERE YOU ARE.
IN WE GO...
KNOCK KNOCK KNOCK
MY STOMACH HURTS
HEY DUDES. HAPPY BIRTHDAY, OWL!
WHA... OH, HEY, WEREWOLF JONES
S'UP MY BROTHER? Y'READY FOR YOUR BIG BIRTHDAY SURPRISE?

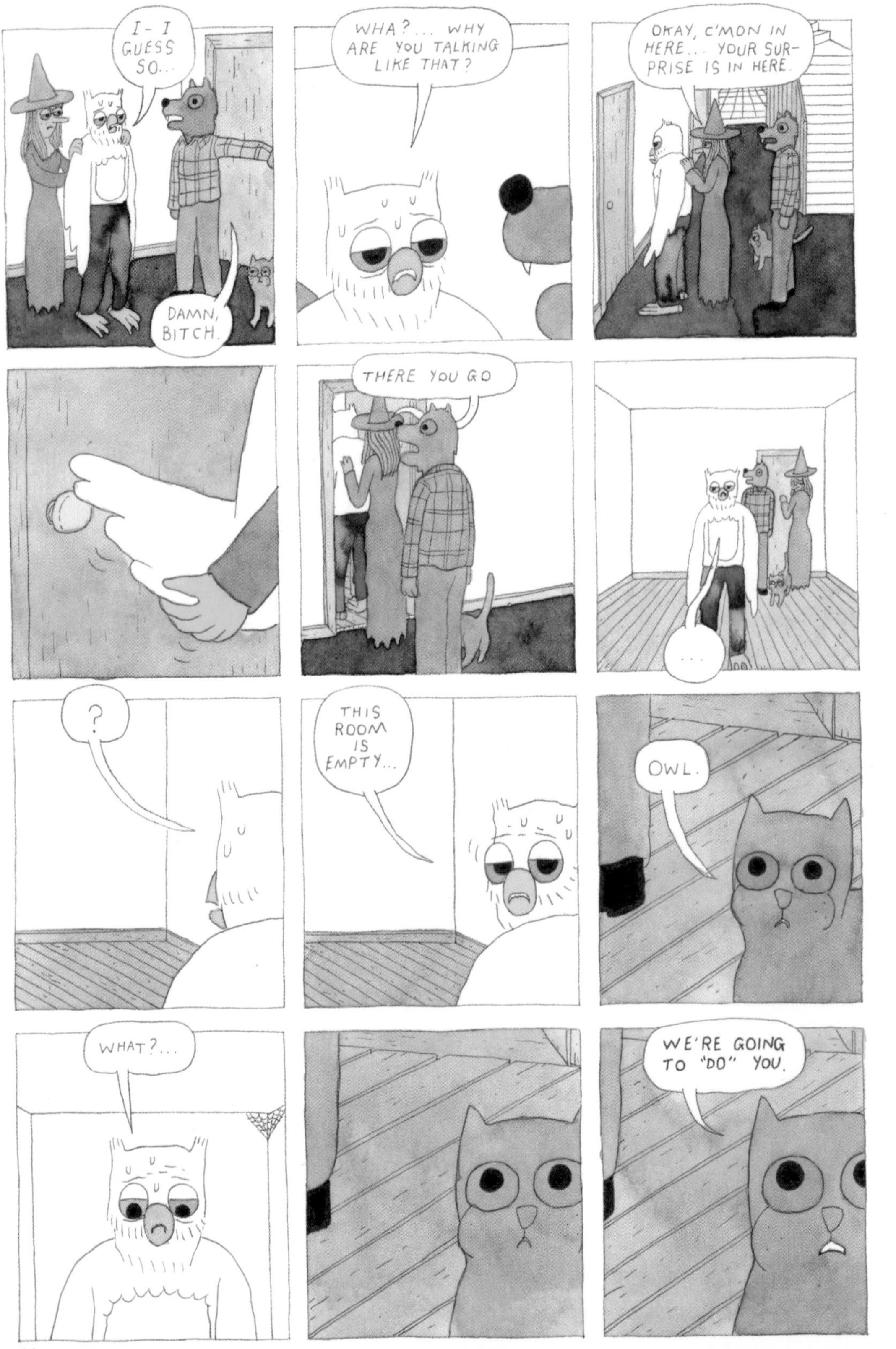
I- I GUESS SO...
DAMN, BITCH.
WHA?... WHY ARE YOU TALKING LIKE THAT?
OKAY, C'MON IN HERE... YOUR SURPRISE IS IN HERE.
THERE YOU GO
...
?
THIS ROOM IS EMPTY...
OWL.
WHAT?...
WE'RE GOING TO "DO" YOU.

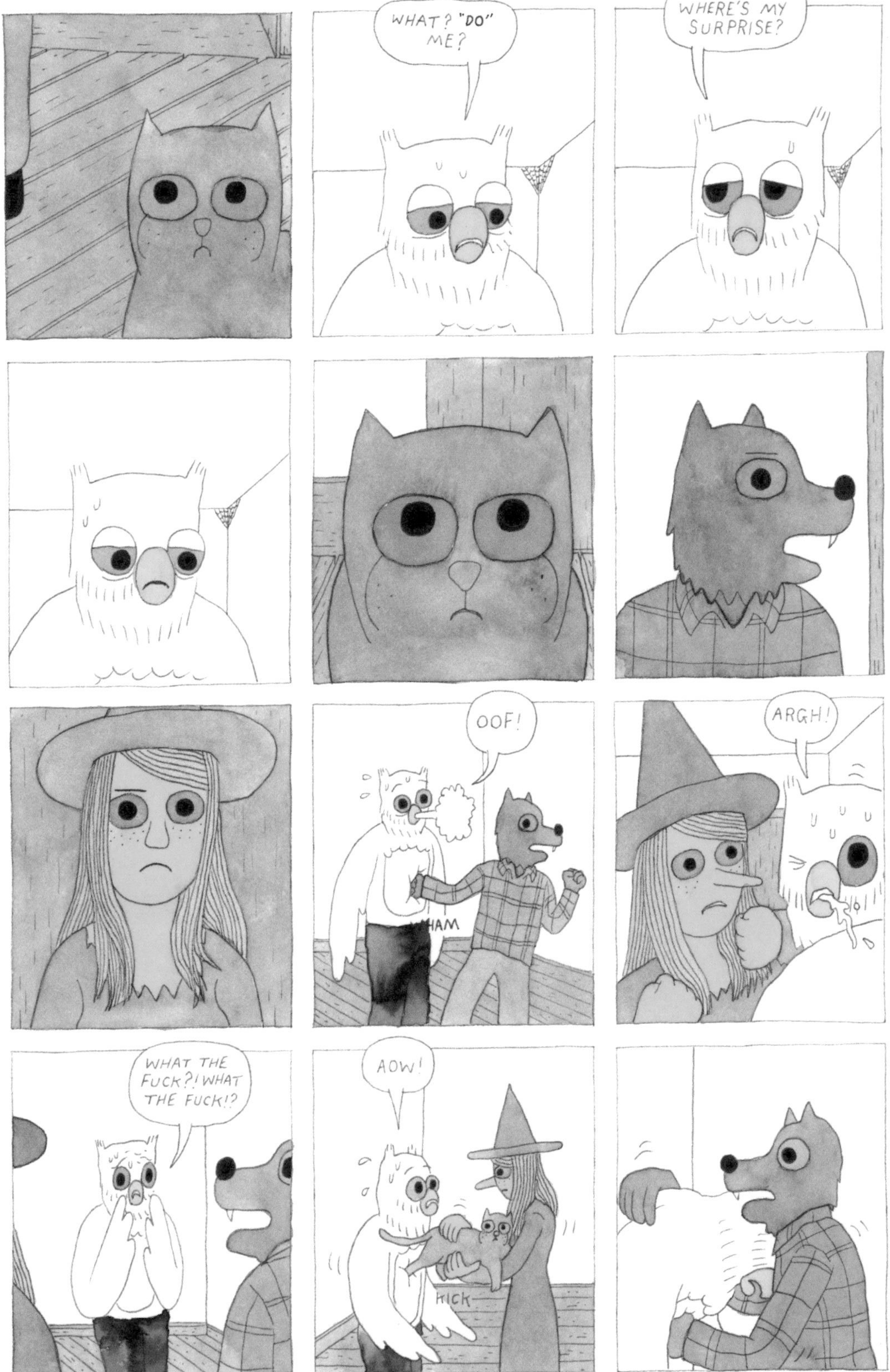
WHAT? "DO" ME?
WHERE'S MY SURPRISE?
OOF!
WHAM
ARGH!
WHAT THE FUCK?! WHAT THE FUCK!?
AOW!
KICK

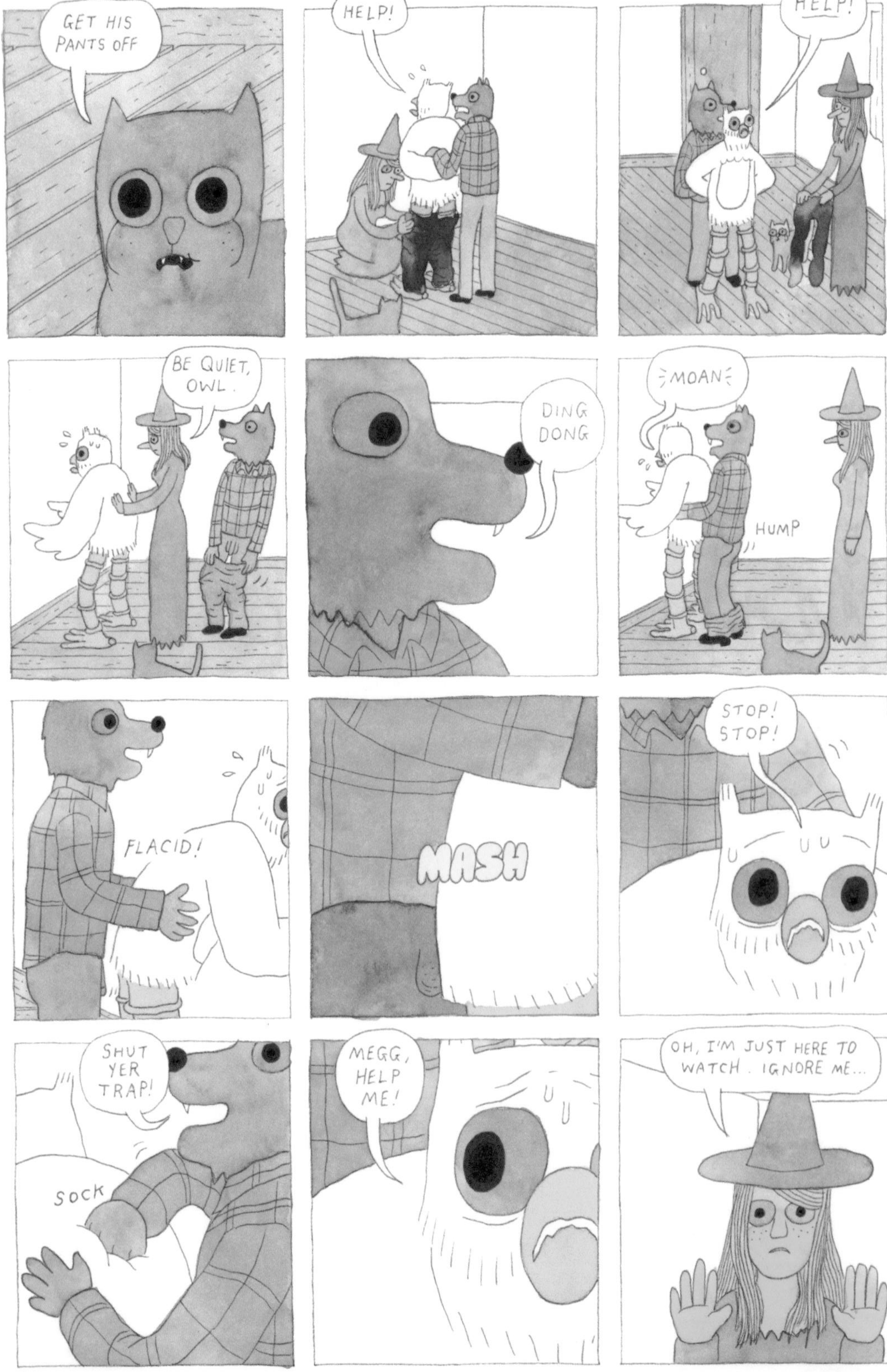
GET HIS PANTS OFF
HELP!
HELP!
BE QUIET, OWL.
DING DONG
MOAN
HUMP
FLACID!
MASH
STOP! STOP!
SHUT YER TRAP!
SOCK
MEGG, HELP ME!
OH, I'M JUST HERE TO WATCH. IGNORE ME...

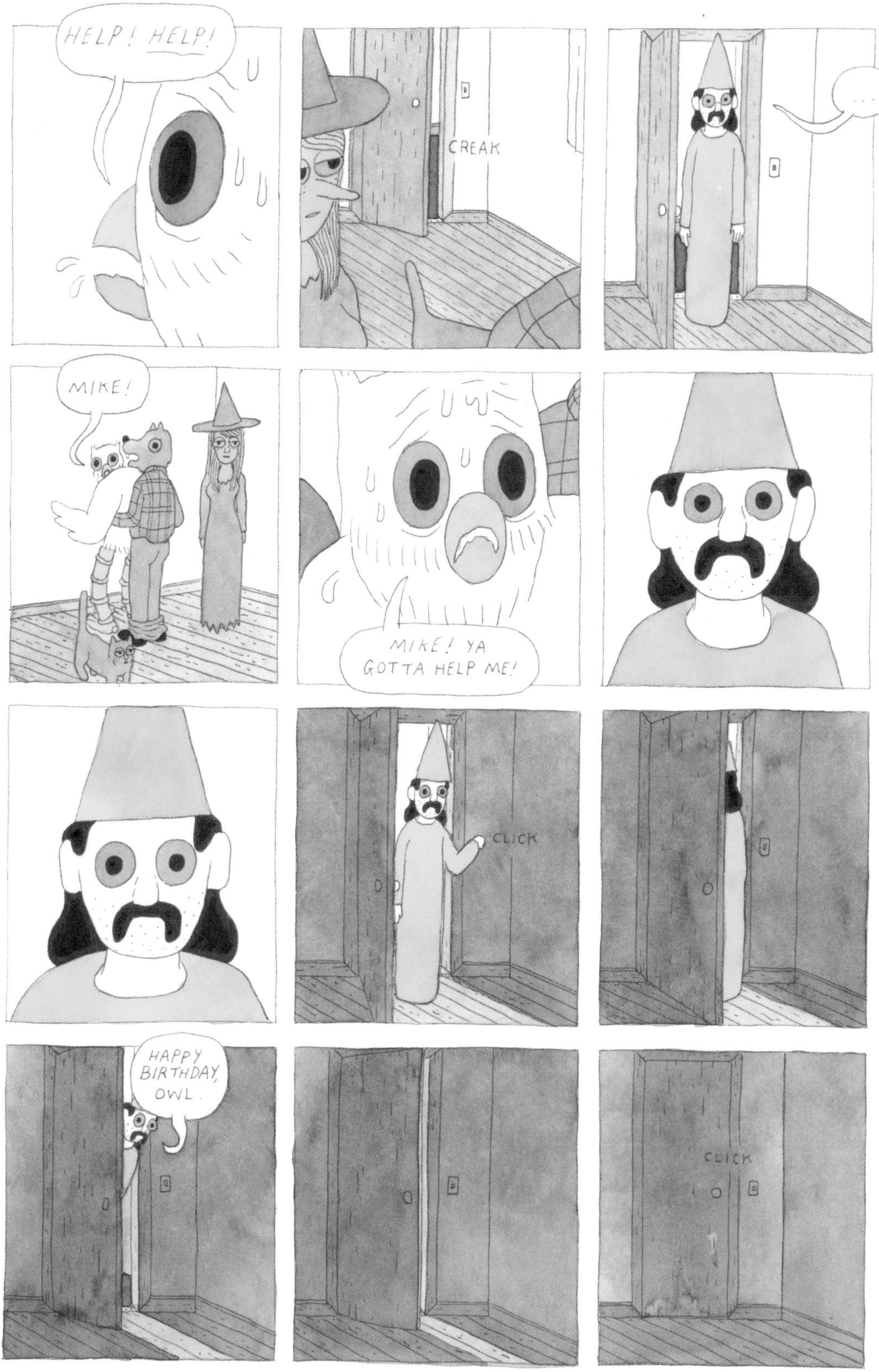
HELP! HELP!
CREAK
MIKE!
MIKE! YA GOTTA HELP ME!
CLICK
HAPPY BIRTHDAY, OWL.
CLICK

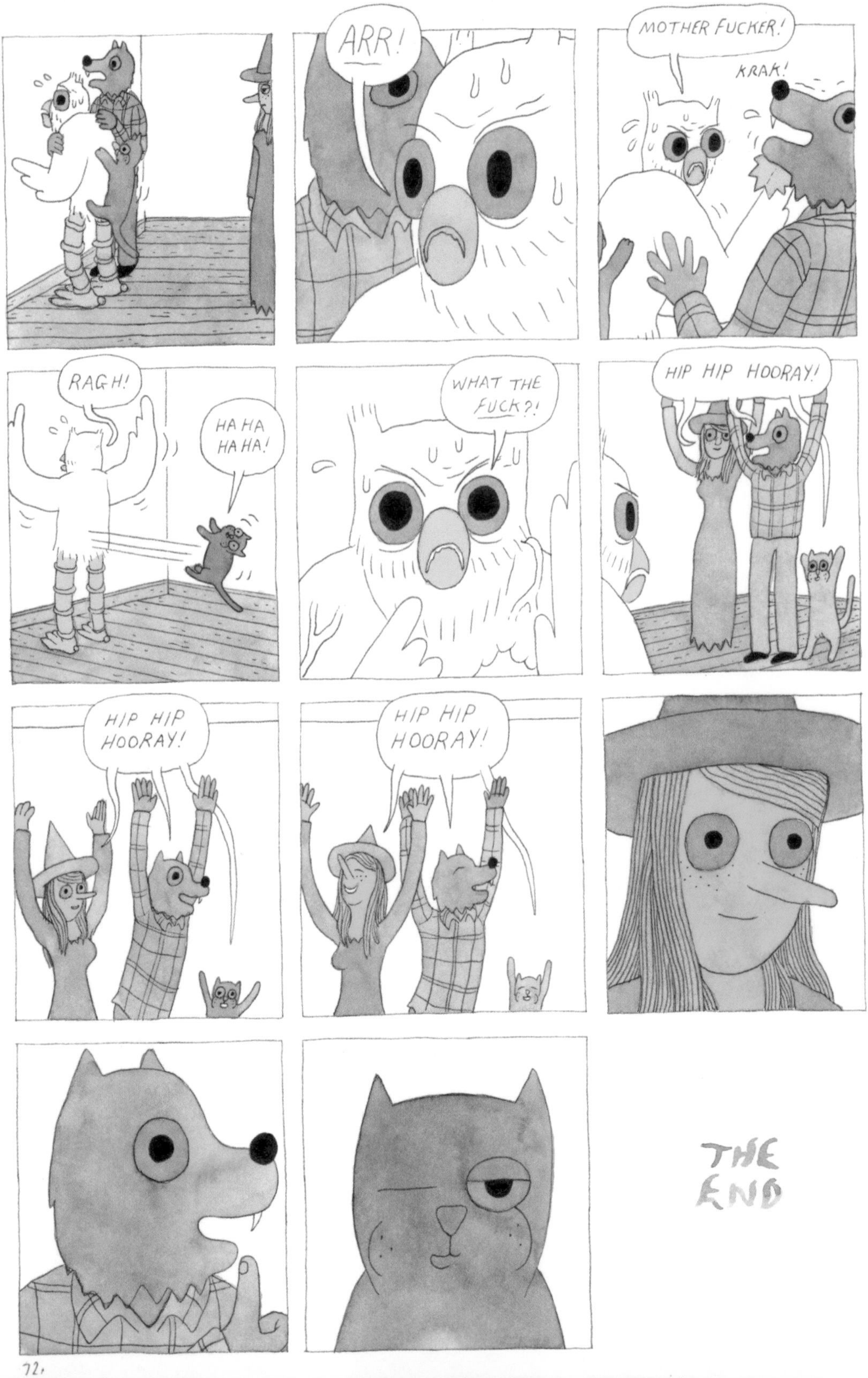
ARR!
MOTHER FUCKER!
KRAK!
RAGH!
HA HA HA HA!
WHAT THE FUCK?!
HIP HIP HOORAY!
HIP HIP HOORAY!
HIP HIP HOORAY!
THE END

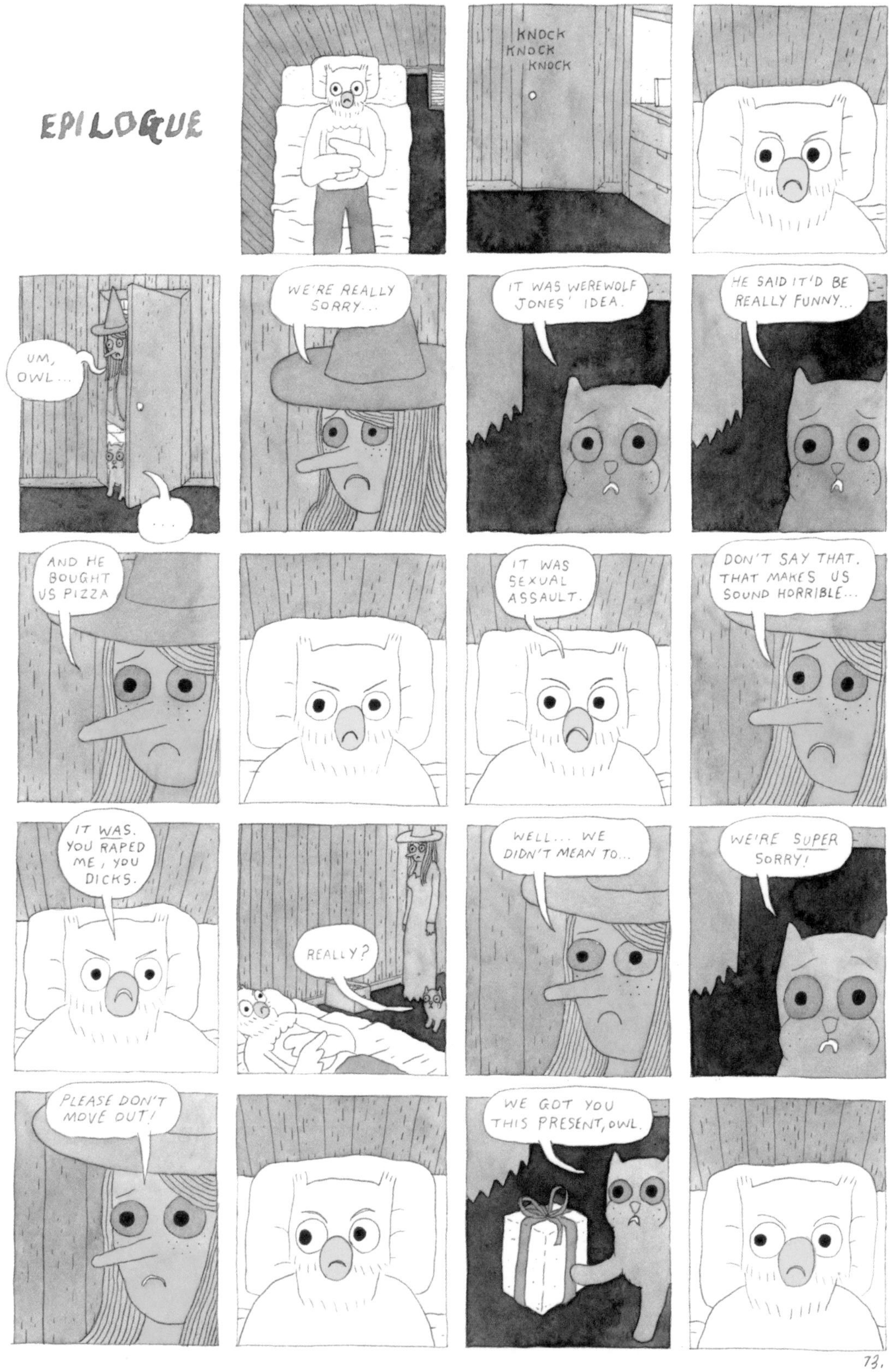
EPILOGUE
KNOCK KNOCK KNOCK
UM, OWL...
...
WE'RE REALLY SORRY...
IT WAS WEREWOLF JONES' IDEA.
HE SAID IT'D BE REALLY FUNNY...
AND HE BOUGHT US PIZZA
IT WAS SEXUAL ASSAULT.
DON'T SAY THAT. THAT MAKES US SOUND HORRIBLE...
IT WAS. YOU RAPED ME, YOU DICKS.
REALLY?
WELL... WE DIDN'T MEAN TO...
WE'RE SUPER SORRY!
PLEASE DON'T MOVE OUT!
WE GOT YOU THIS PRESENT, OWL.

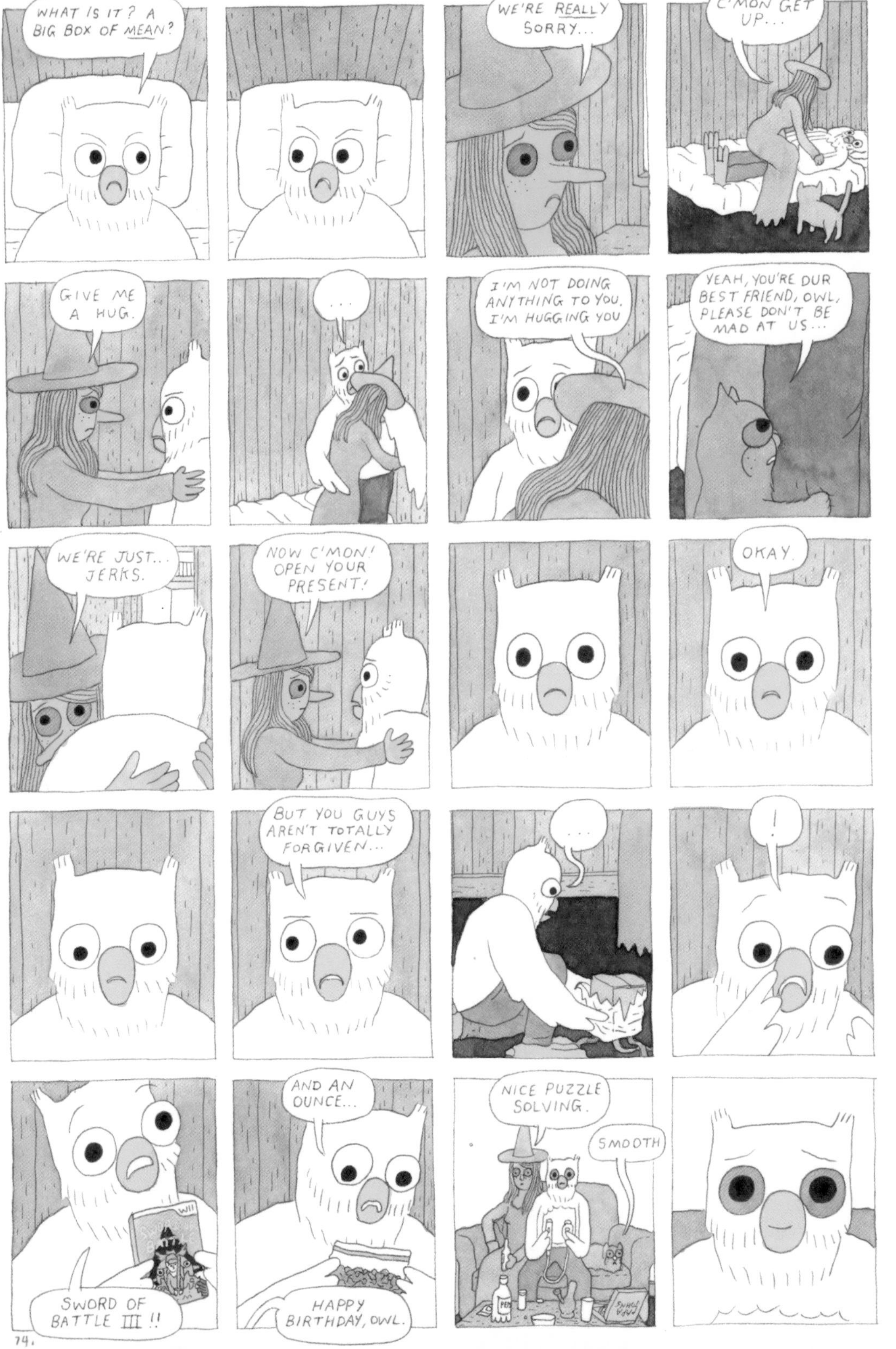
WHAT IS IT? A BIG BOX OF MEAN?
WE'RE REALLY SORRY...
C'MON GET UP...
GIVE ME A HUG.
...
I'M NOT DOING ANYTHING TO YOU. I'M HUGGING YOU
YEAH, YOU'RE OUR BEST FRIEND, OWL, PLEASE DON'T BE MAD AT US...
WE'RE JUST... JERKS.
NOW C'MON! OPEN YOUR PRESENT!
OKAY.
BUT YOU GUYS AREN'T TOTALLY FORGIVEN...
...
!
SWORD OF BATTLE III !!
AND AN OUNCE...
HAPPY BIRTHDAY, OWL.
NICE PUZZLE SOLVING.
SMOOTH

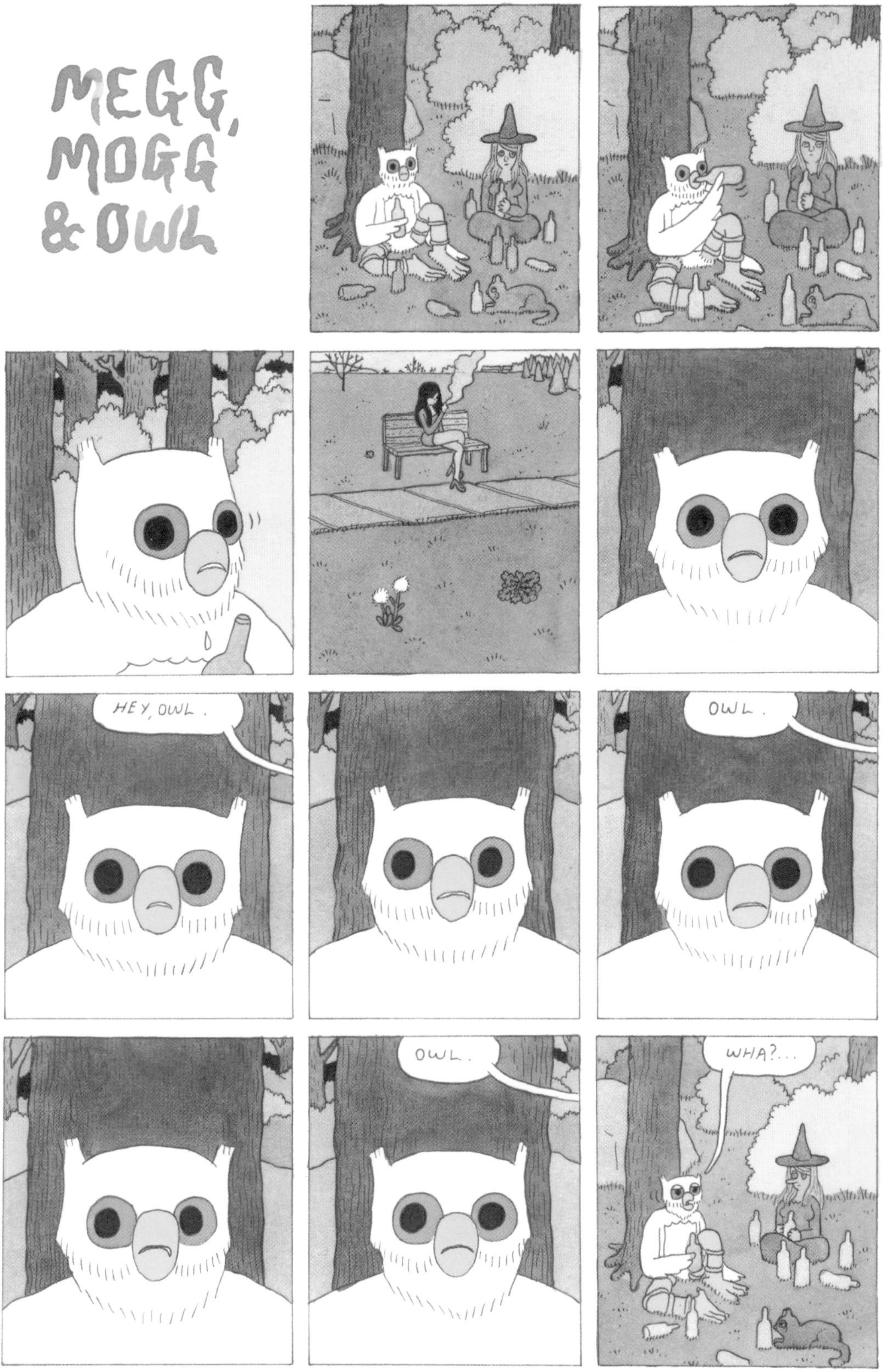
MEGG, MOGG & OWL
HEY, OWL.
OWL.
OWL.
WHA?...

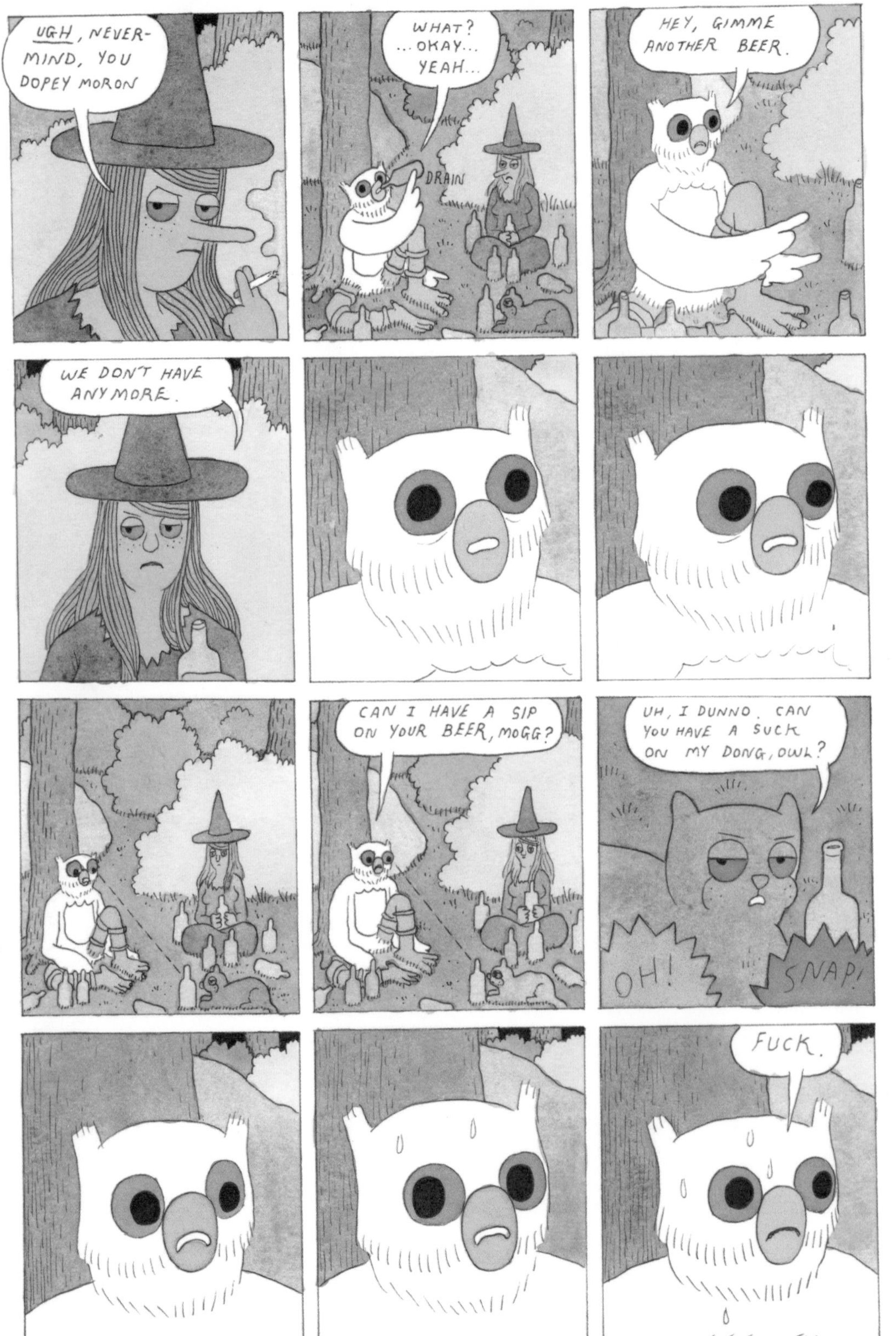
UGH, NEVER-MIND, YOU DOPEY MORON
WHAT? ...OKAY... YEAH...
DRAIN
HEY, GIMME ANOTHER BEER.
WE DON'T HAVE ANYMORE.
CAN I HAVE A SIP ON YOUR BEER, MOGG?
UH, I DUNNO. CAN YOU HAVE A SUCK ON MY DONG, OWL?
OH!
SNAP!
FUCK.

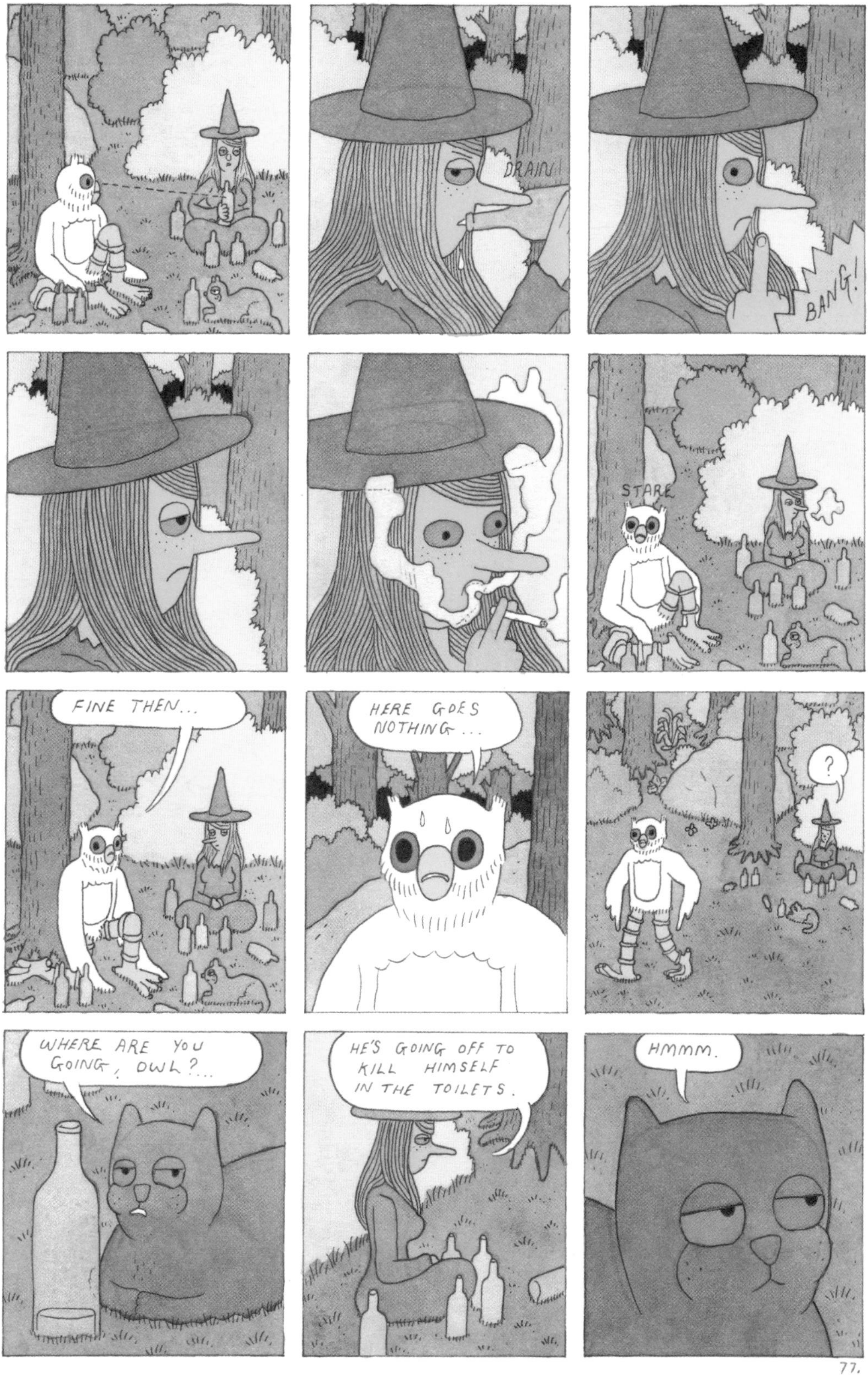
DRAIN
BANG!
STARE
FINE THEN...
HERE GOES NOTHING...
?
WHERE ARE YOU GOING, OWL?...
HE'S GOING OFF TO KILL HIMSELF IN THE TOILETS.
HMMM.

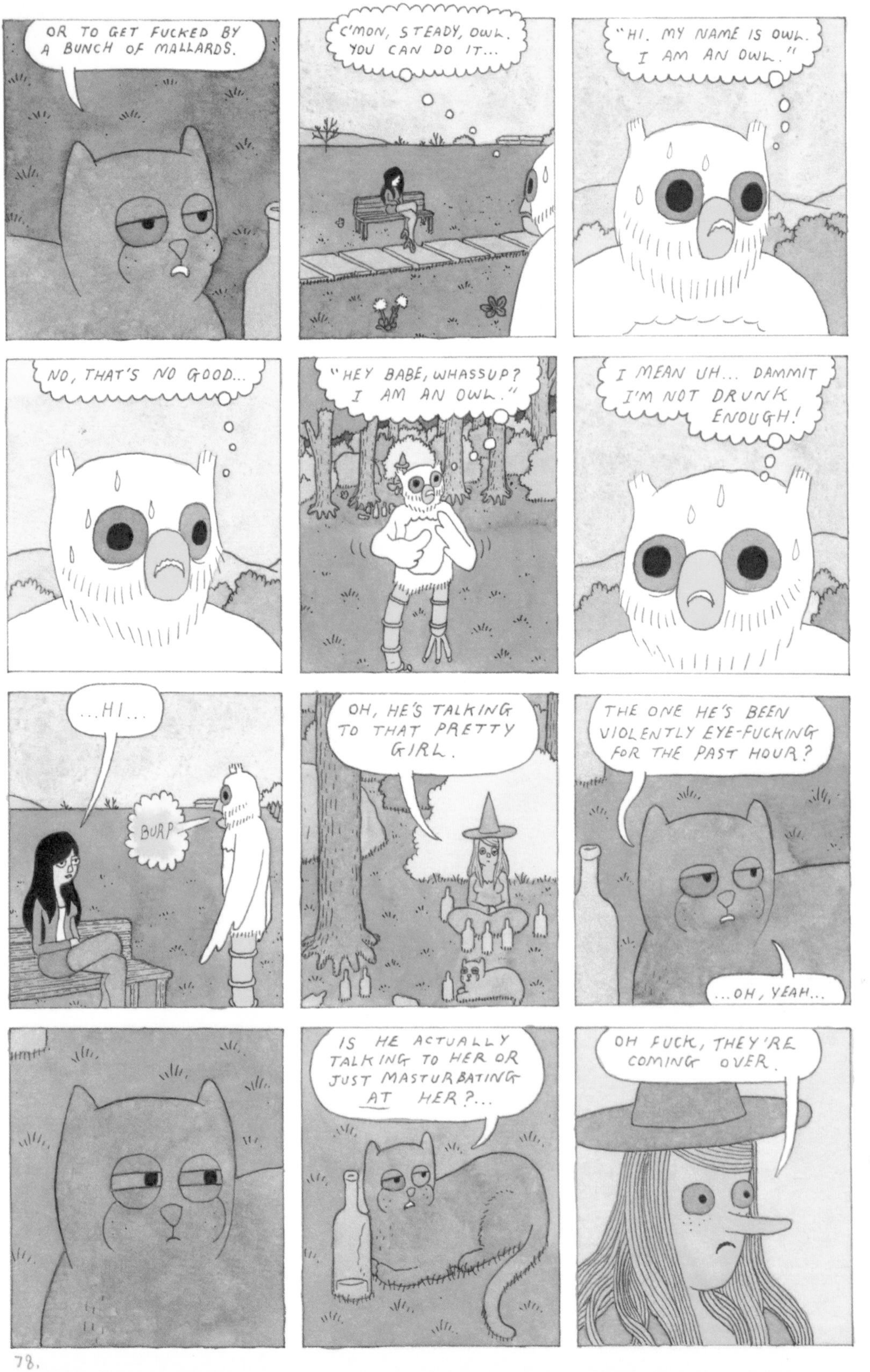
OR TO GET FUCKED BY A BUNCH OF MALLARDS.
C'MON, STEADY, OWL. YOU CAN DO IT...
"HI. MY NAME IS OWL. I AM AN OWL."
NO, THAT'S NO GOOD...
"HEY BABE, WHASSUP? I AM AN OWL."
I MEAN UH... DAMMIT I'M NOT DRUNK ENOUGH!
...HI...
BURP
OH, HE'S TALKING TO THAT PRETTY GIRL.
THE ONE HE'S BEEN VIOLENTLY EYE-FUCKING FOR THE PAST HOUR?
...OH, YEAH...
IS HE ACTUALLY TALKING TO HER OR JUST MASTURBATING AT HER?...
OH FUCK, THEY'RE COMING OVER.

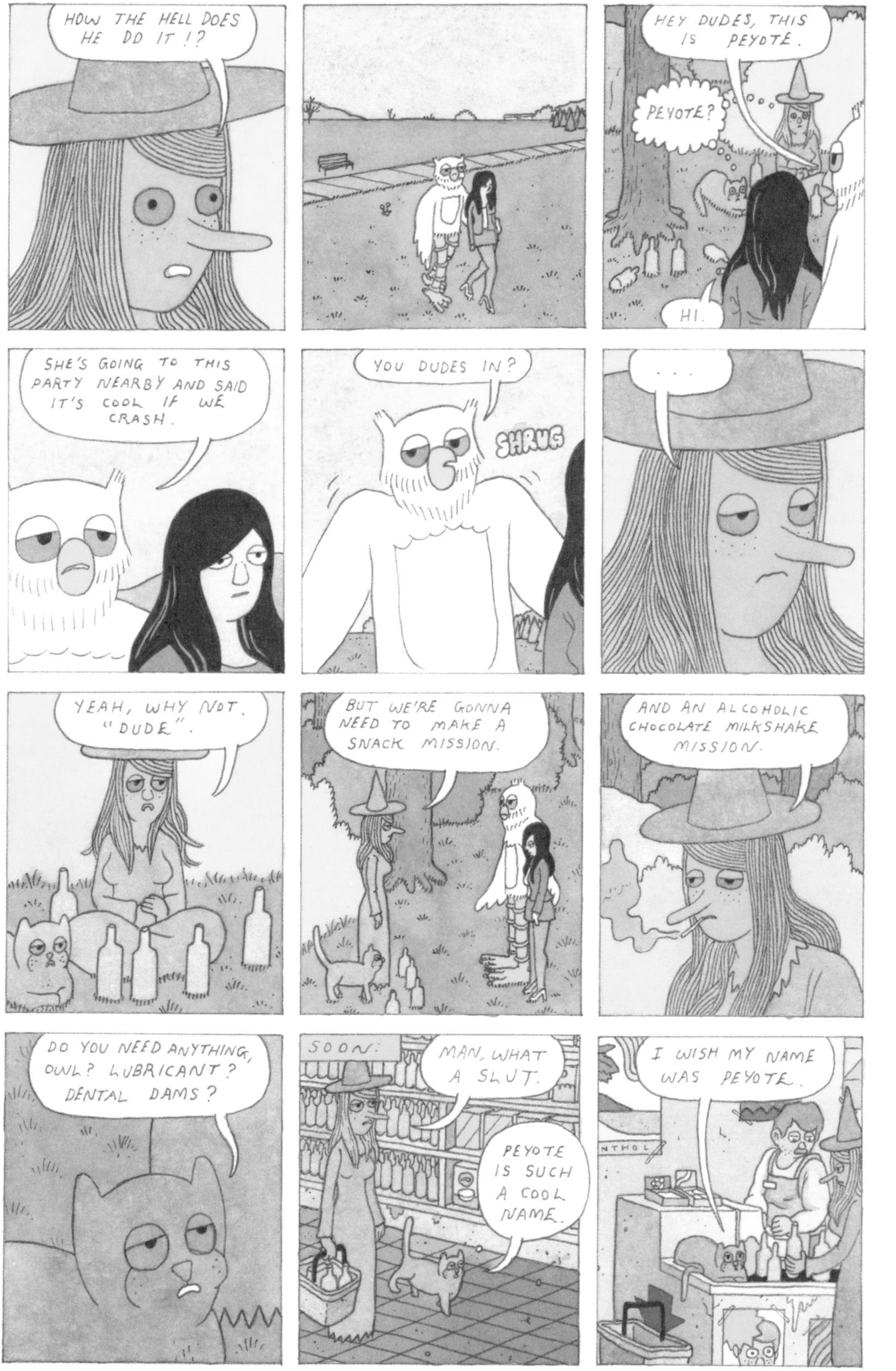
HOW THE HELL DOES HE DO IT !?
HEY DUDES, THIS IS PEYOTE.
PEYOTE?
HI.
SHE'S GOING TO THIS PARTY NEARBY AND SAID IT'S COOL IF WE CRASH.
YOU DUDES IN?
SHRUG
. . .
YEAH, WHY NOT. "DUDE".
BUT WE'RE GONNA NEED TO MAKE A SNACK MISSION.
AND AN ALCOHOLIC CHOCOLATE MILKSHAKE MISSION.
DO YOU NEED ANYTHING, OWL? LUBRICANT? DENTAL DAMS?
SOON:
MAN, WHAT A SLUT.
PEYOTE IS SUCH A COOL NAME.
I WISH MY NAME WAS PEYOTE.
NTHOL

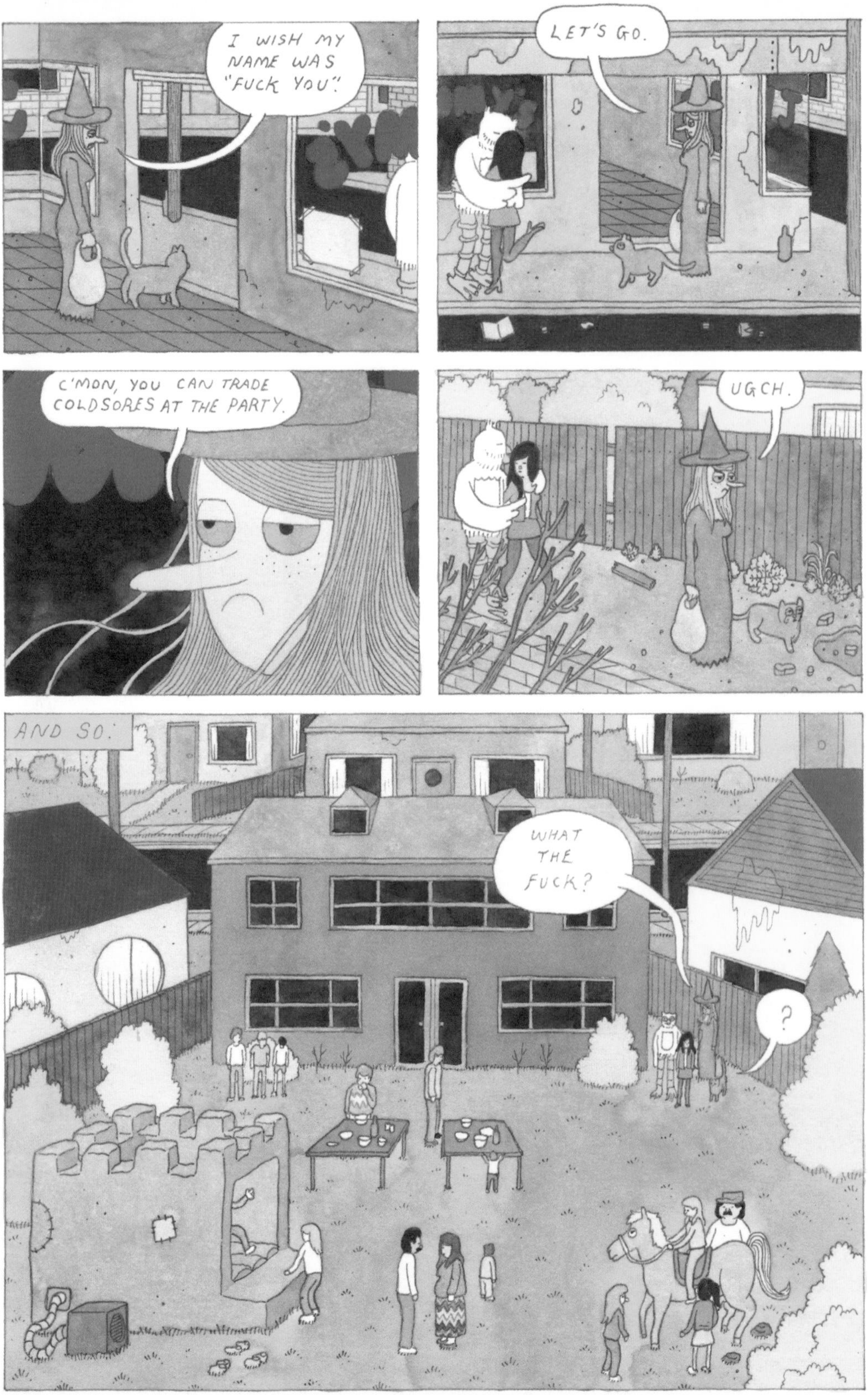
I WISH MY NAME WAS "FUCK YOU".
LET'S GO.
C'MON, YOU CAN TRADE COLDSORES AT THE PARTY.
UGCH.
AND SO.
WHAT THE FUCK?
?

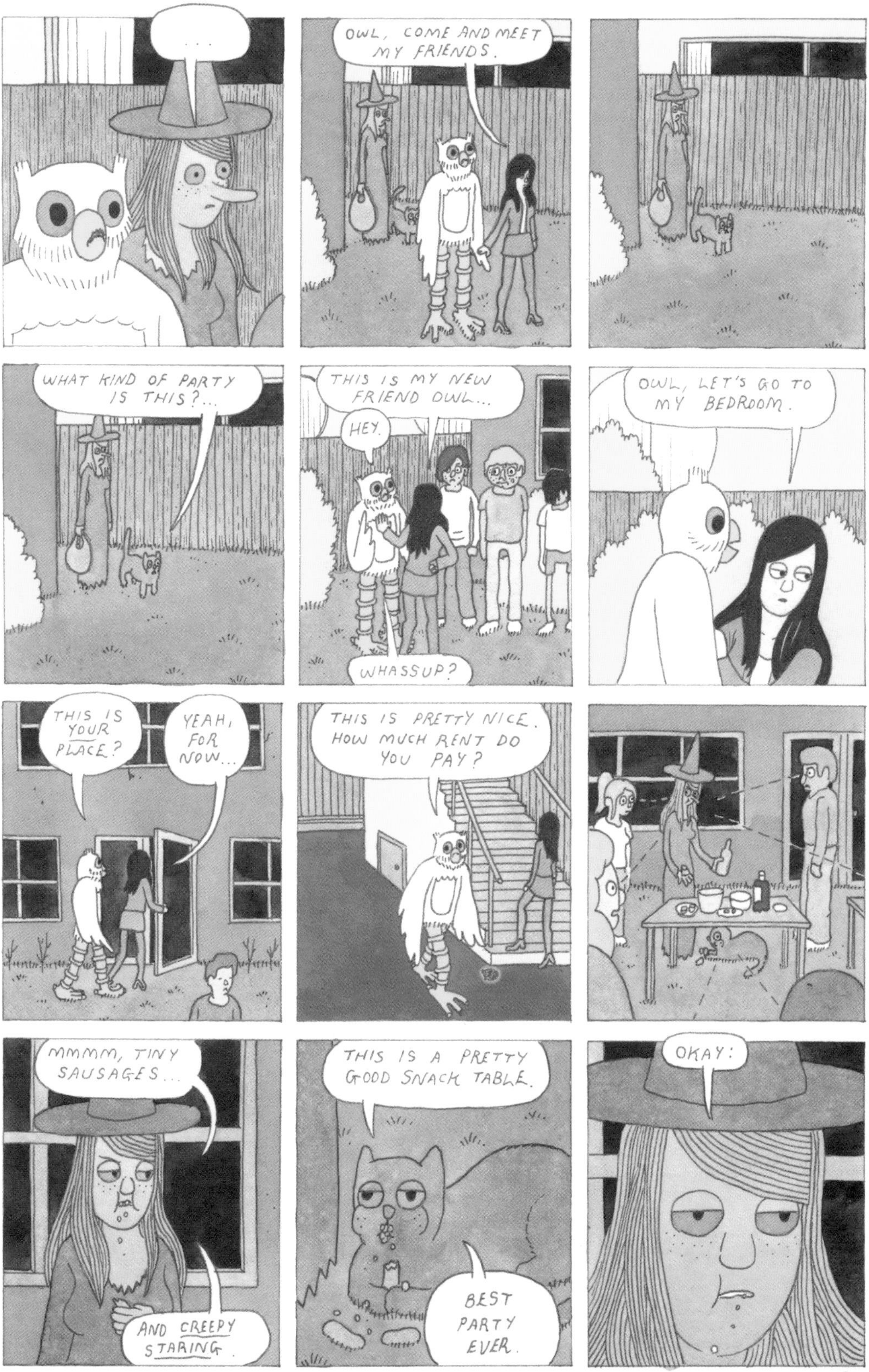
...
OWL, COME AND MEET MY FRIENDS.
WHAT KIND OF PARTY IS THIS?...
THIS IS MY NEW FRIEND OWL...
HEY.
WHASSUP?
OWL, LET'S GO TO MY BEDROOM.
THIS IS YOUR PLACE?
YEAH, FOR NOW...
THIS IS PRETTY NICE. HOW MUCH RENT DO YOU PAY?
MMMM, TINY SAUSAGES...
AND CREEPY STARING.
THIS IS A PRETTY GOOD SNACK TABLE.
BEST PARTY EVER.
OKAY:

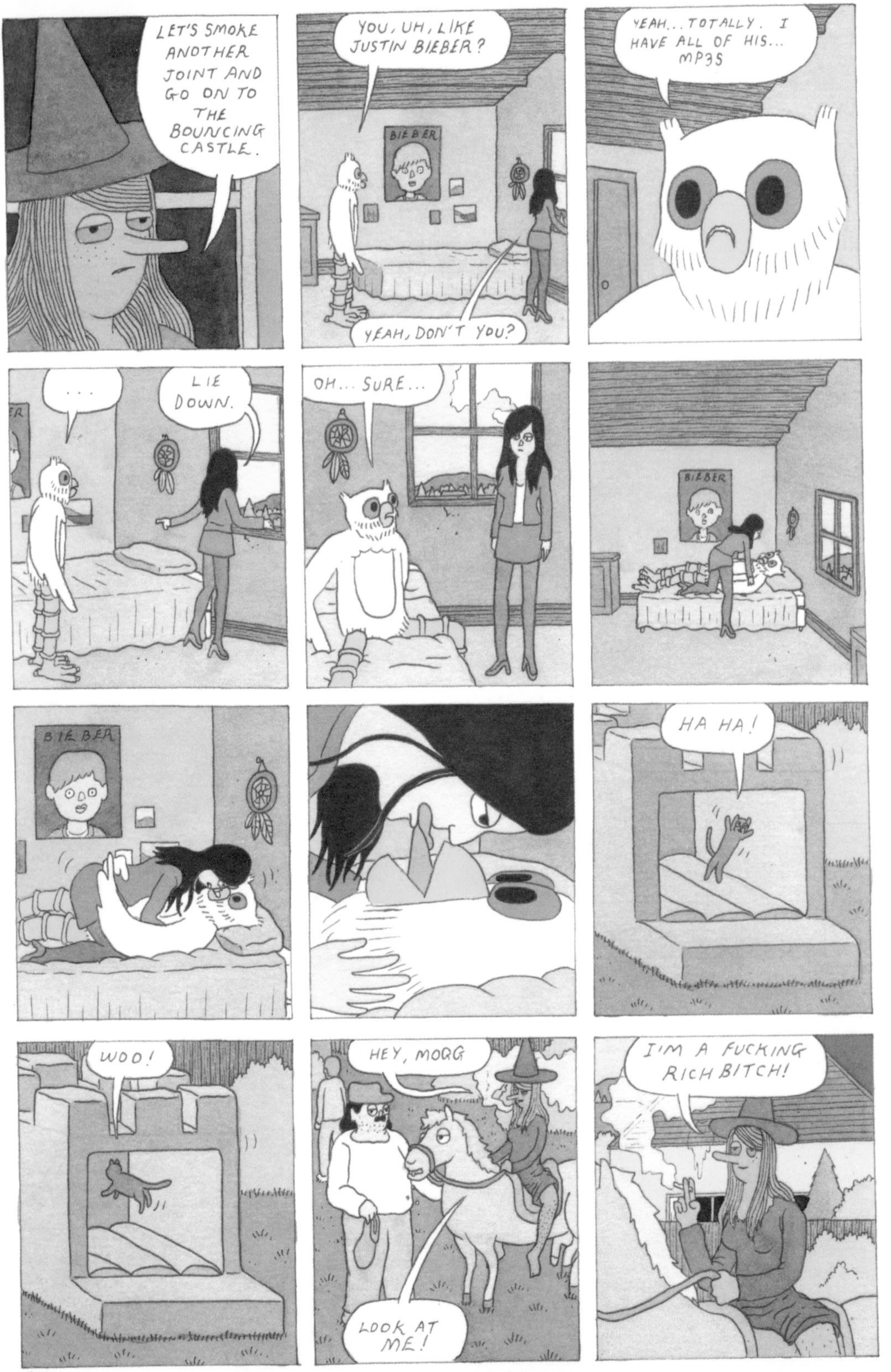
LET'S SMOKE ANOTHER JOINT AND GO ON TO THE BOUNCING CASTLE.
YOU, UH, LIKE JUSTIN BIEBER?
BIEBER
YEAH, DON'T YOU?
YEAH... TOTALLY. I HAVE ALL OF HIS... MP3S
...
LIE DOWN.
OH... SURE...
BIEBER
BIEBER
HA HA!
WOO!
HEY, MORG
LOOK AT ME!
I'M A FUCKING RICH BITCH!

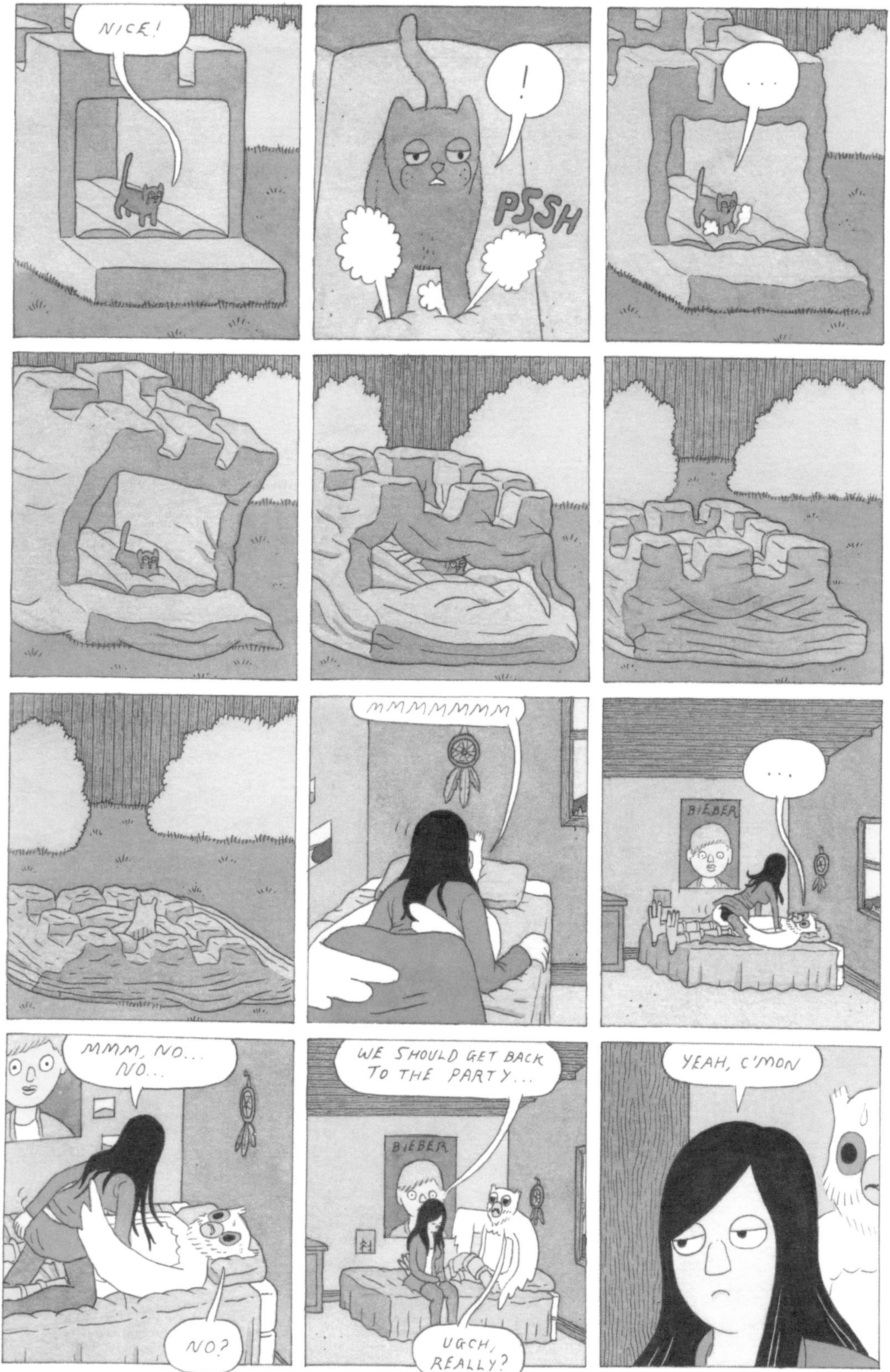
NICE!
!
PSSH
. . .
MMMMMMMM
. . .
BIEBER
MMM, NO...
NO...
NO?
WE SHOULD GET BACK
TO THE PARTY...
BIEBER
UGCH,
REALLY?
YEAH, C'MON

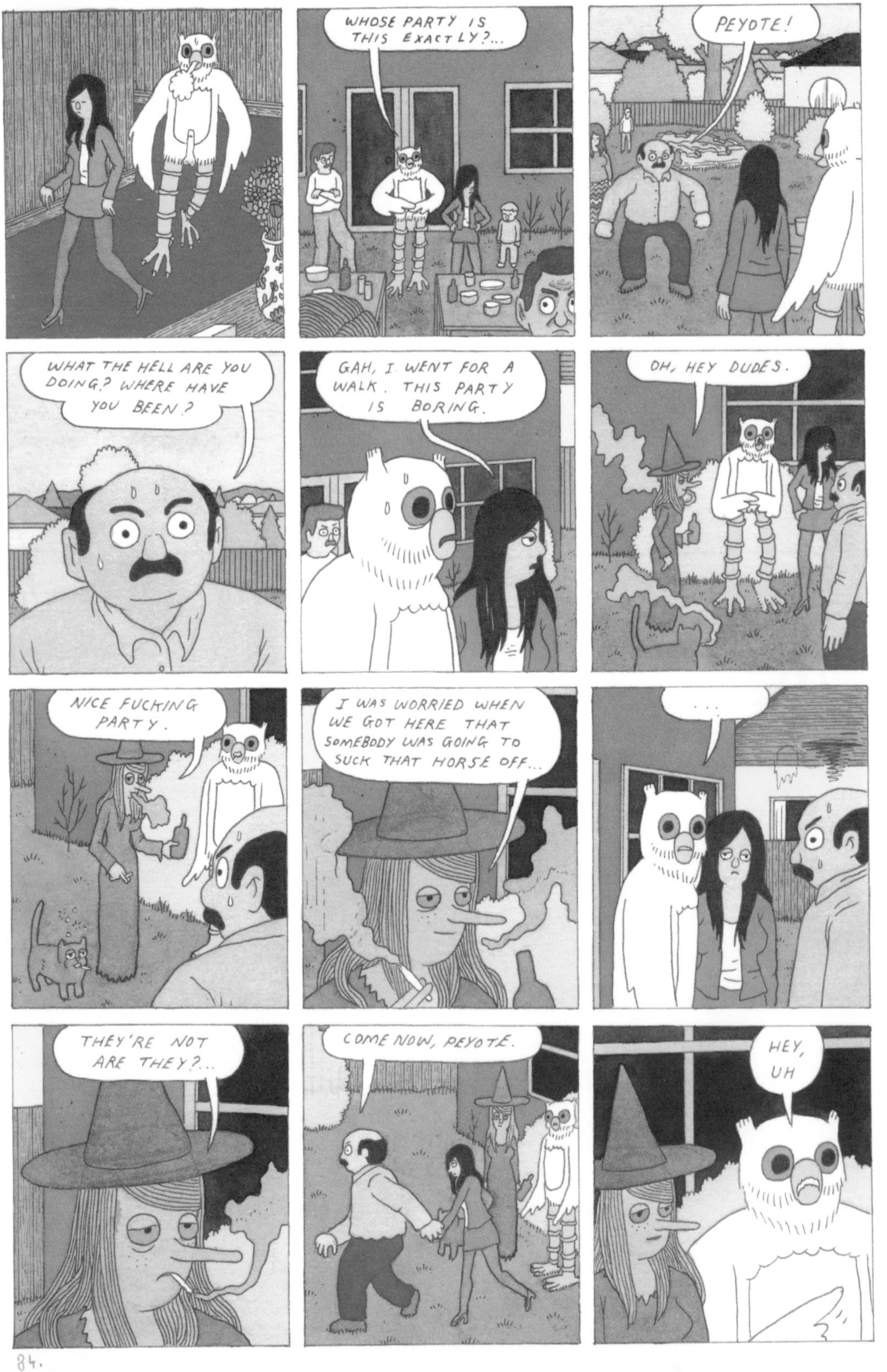
WHOSE PARTY IS THIS EXACTLY?...
PEYOTE!
WHAT THE HELL ARE YOU DOING? WHERE HAVE YOU BEEN?
GAH, I WENT FOR A WALK. THIS PARTY IS BORING.
OH, HEY DUDES.
NICE FUCKING PARTY.
I WAS WORRIED WHEN WE GOT HERE THAT SOMEBODY WAS GOING TO SUCK THAT HORSE OFF...
...
THEY'RE NOT ARE THEY?...
COME NOW, PEYOTE.
HEY, UH

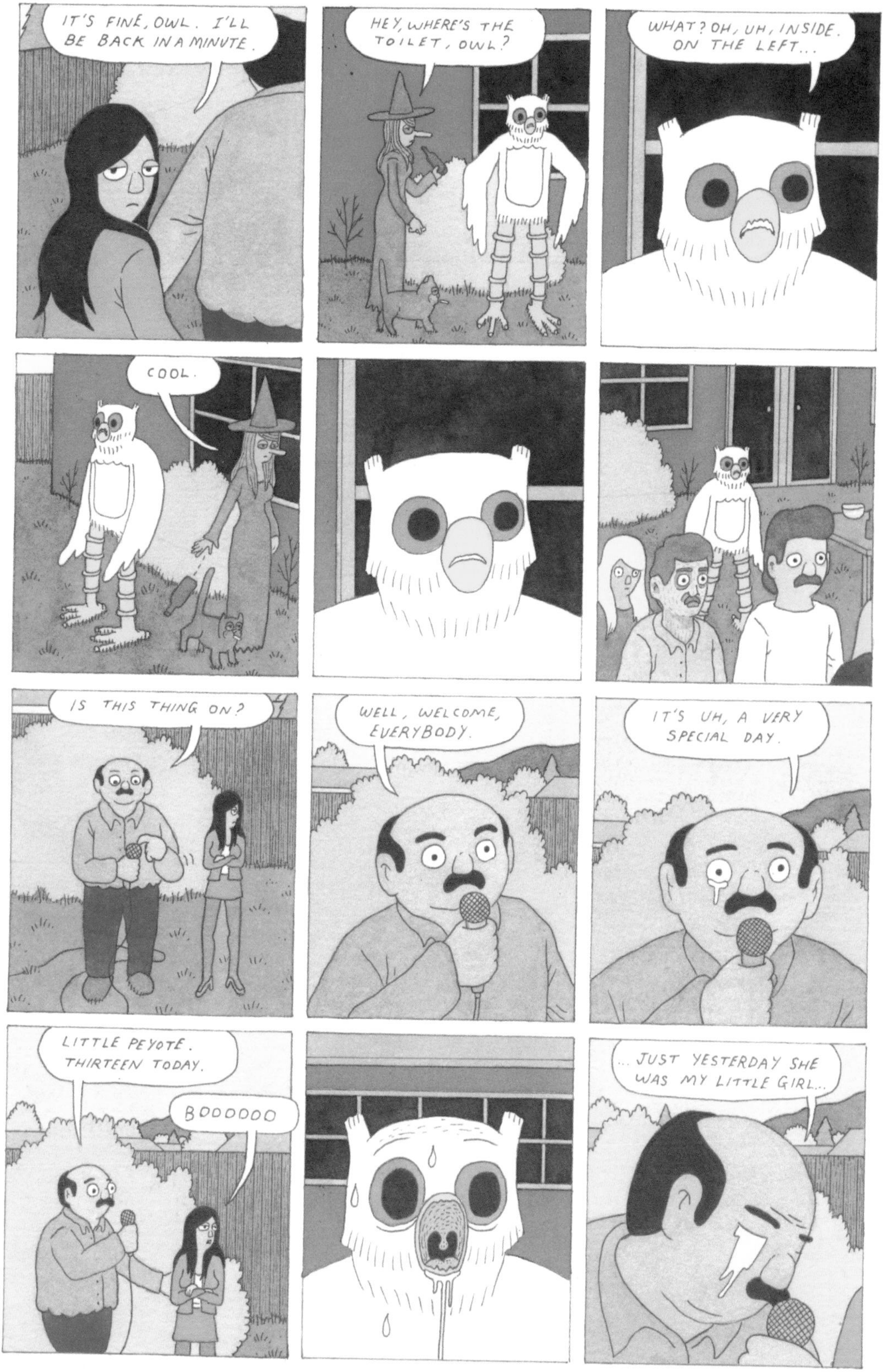
IT'S FINE, OWL. I'LL BE BACK IN A MINUTE.
HEY, WHERE'S THE TOILET, OWL?
WHAT? OH, UH, INSIDE. ON THE LEFT...
COOL.
IS THIS THING ON?
WELL, WELCOME, EVERYBODY.
IT'S UH, A VERY SPECIAL DAY.
LITTLE PEYOTE. THIRTEEN TODAY.
BOOOOOO
... JUST YESTERDAY SHE WAS MY LITTLE GIRL...

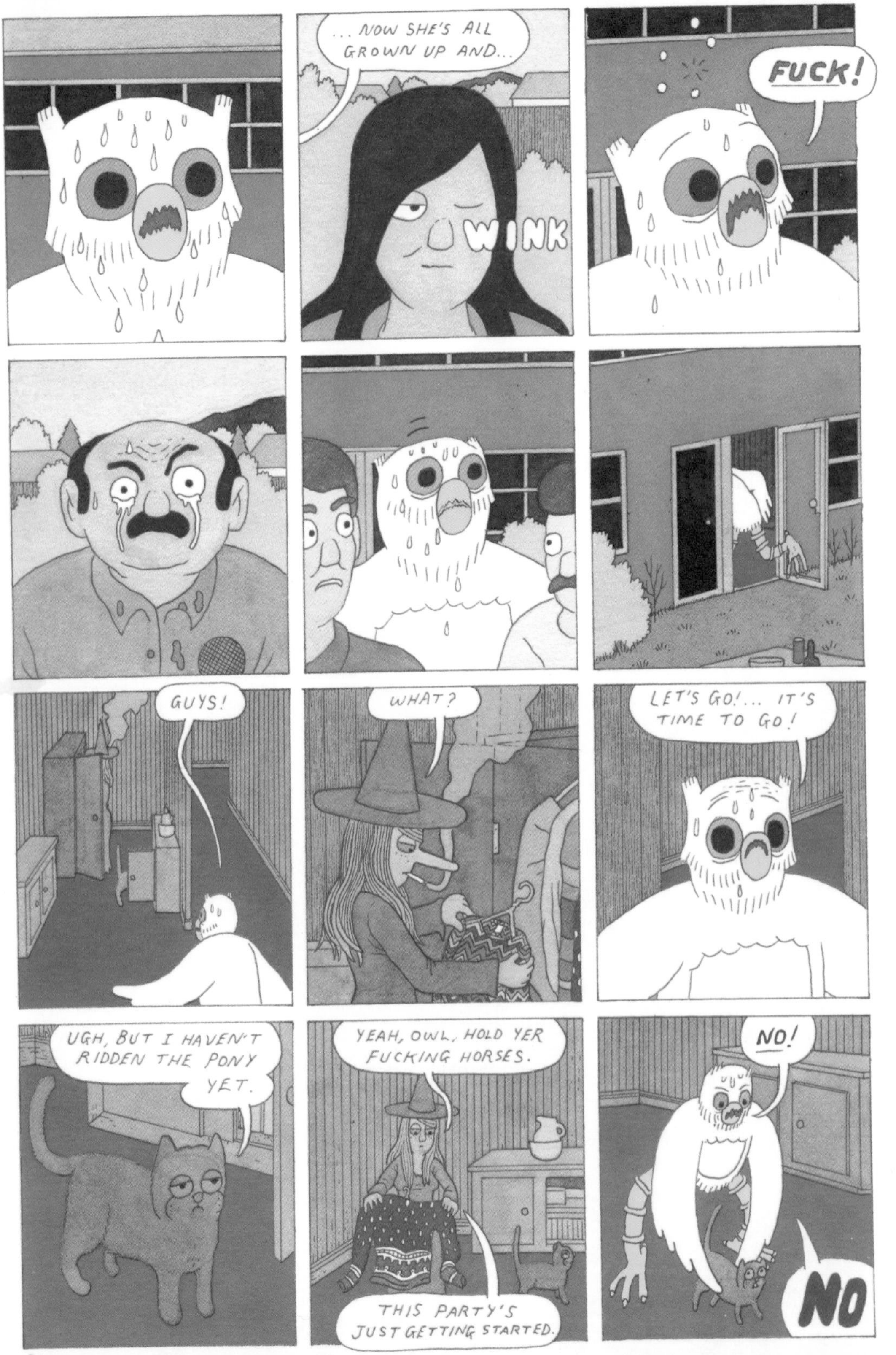

... NOW SHE'S ALL GROWN UP AND...
WINK
FUCK!
GUYS!
WHAT?
LET'S GO!... IT'S TIME TO GO!
UGH, BUT I HAVEN'T RIDDEN THE PONY YET.
YEAH, OWL, HOLD YER FUCKING HORSES.
THIS PARTY'S JUST GETTING STARTED.
NO!
NO

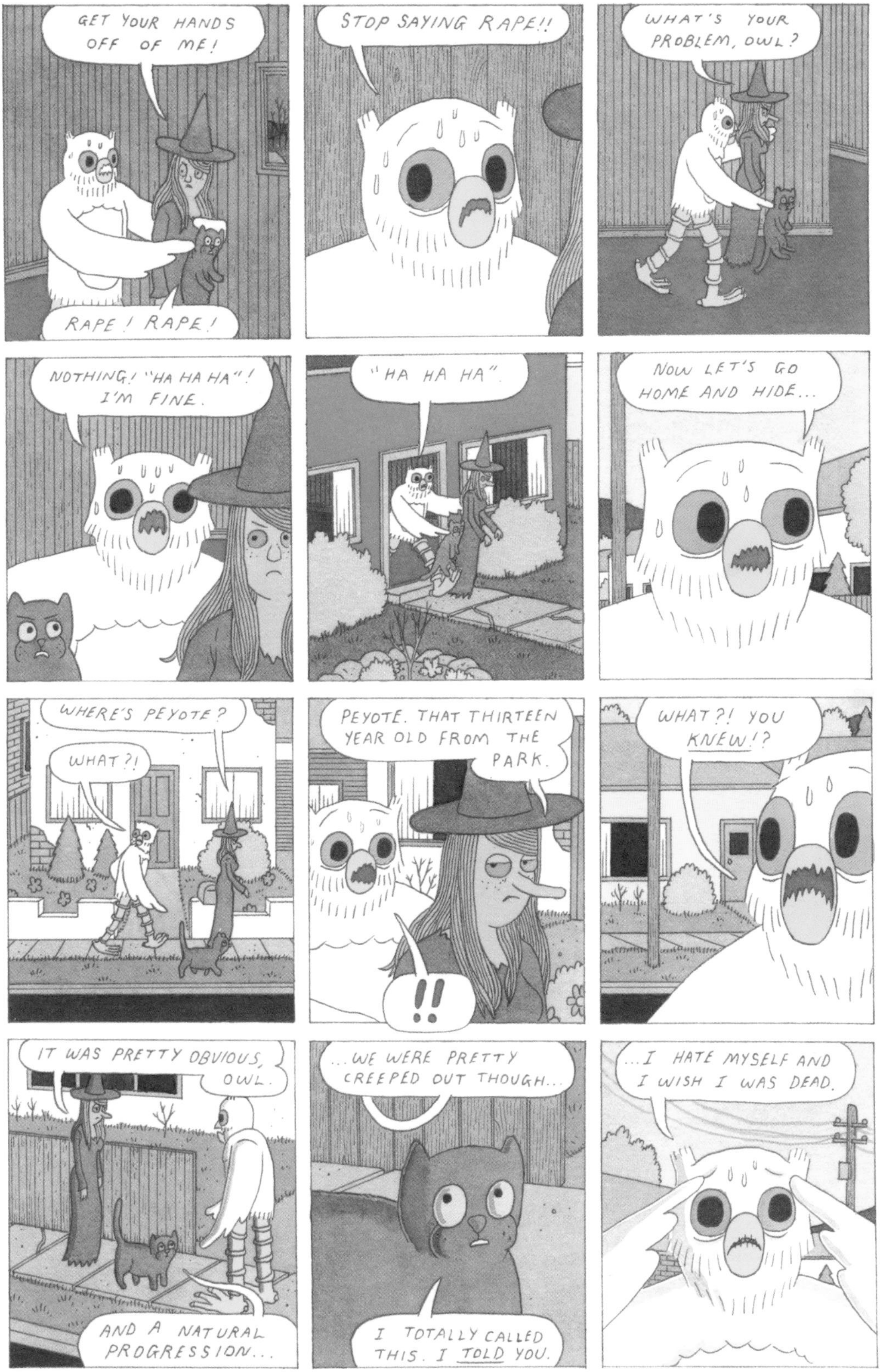
GET YOUR HANDS OFF OF ME!
RAPE! RAPE!
STOP SAYING RAPE!!
WHAT'S YOUR PROBLEM, OWL?
NOTHING! "HA HA HA"! I'M FINE.
"HA HA HA".
NOW LET'S GO HOME AND HIDE...
WHERE'S PEYOTE?
WHAT?!
PEYOTE. THAT THIRTEEN YEAR OLD FROM THE PARK.
!!
WHAT?! YOU KNEW!?
IT WAS PRETTY OBVIOUS, OWL.
AND A NATURAL PROGRESSION...
...WE WERE PRETTY CREEPED OUT THOUGH...
I TOTALLY CALLED THIS. I TOLD YOU.
...I HATE MYSELF AND I WISH I WAS DEAD.

MEGG, MOGG & OWL

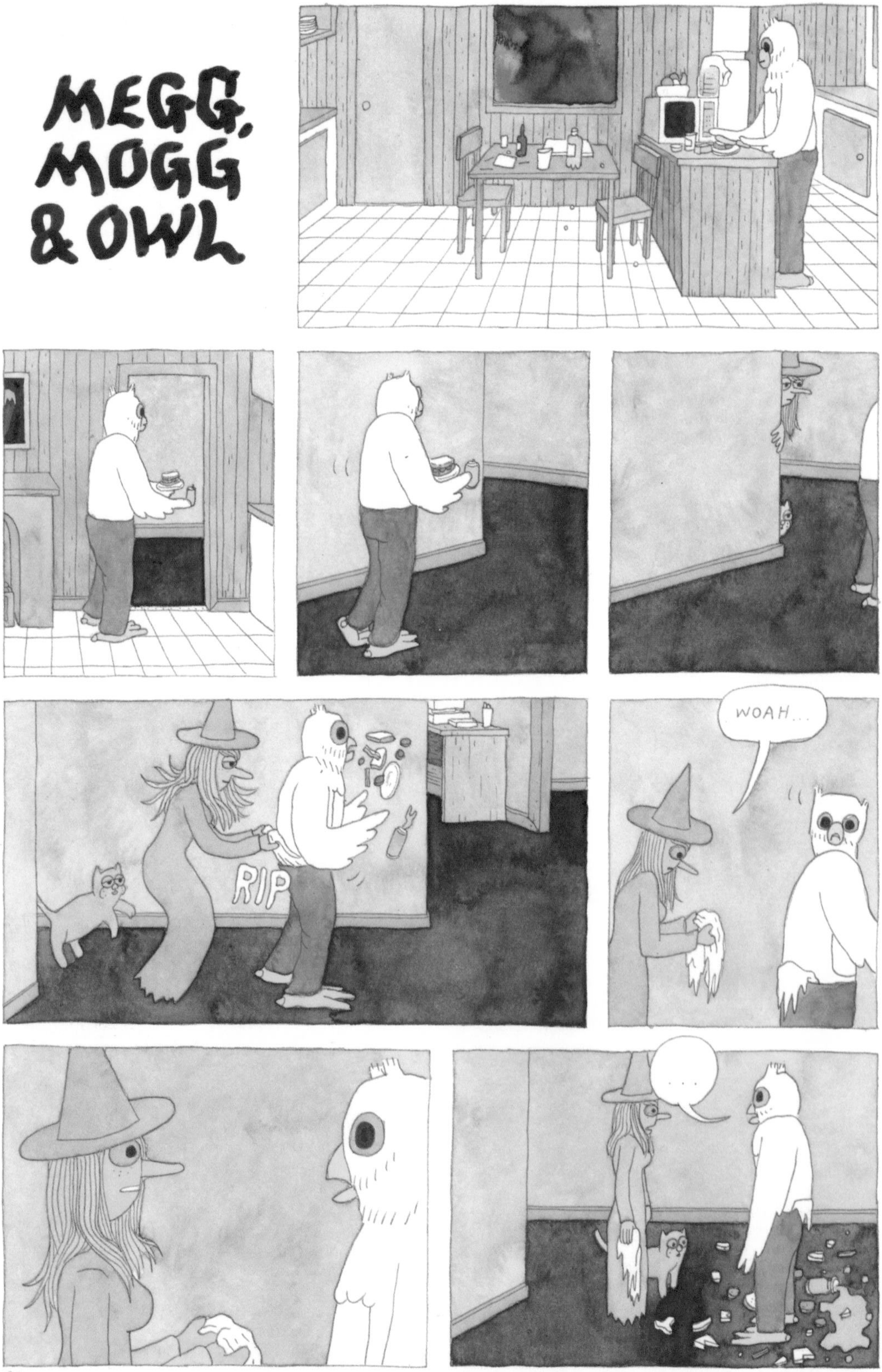
RIP
WOAH...
...

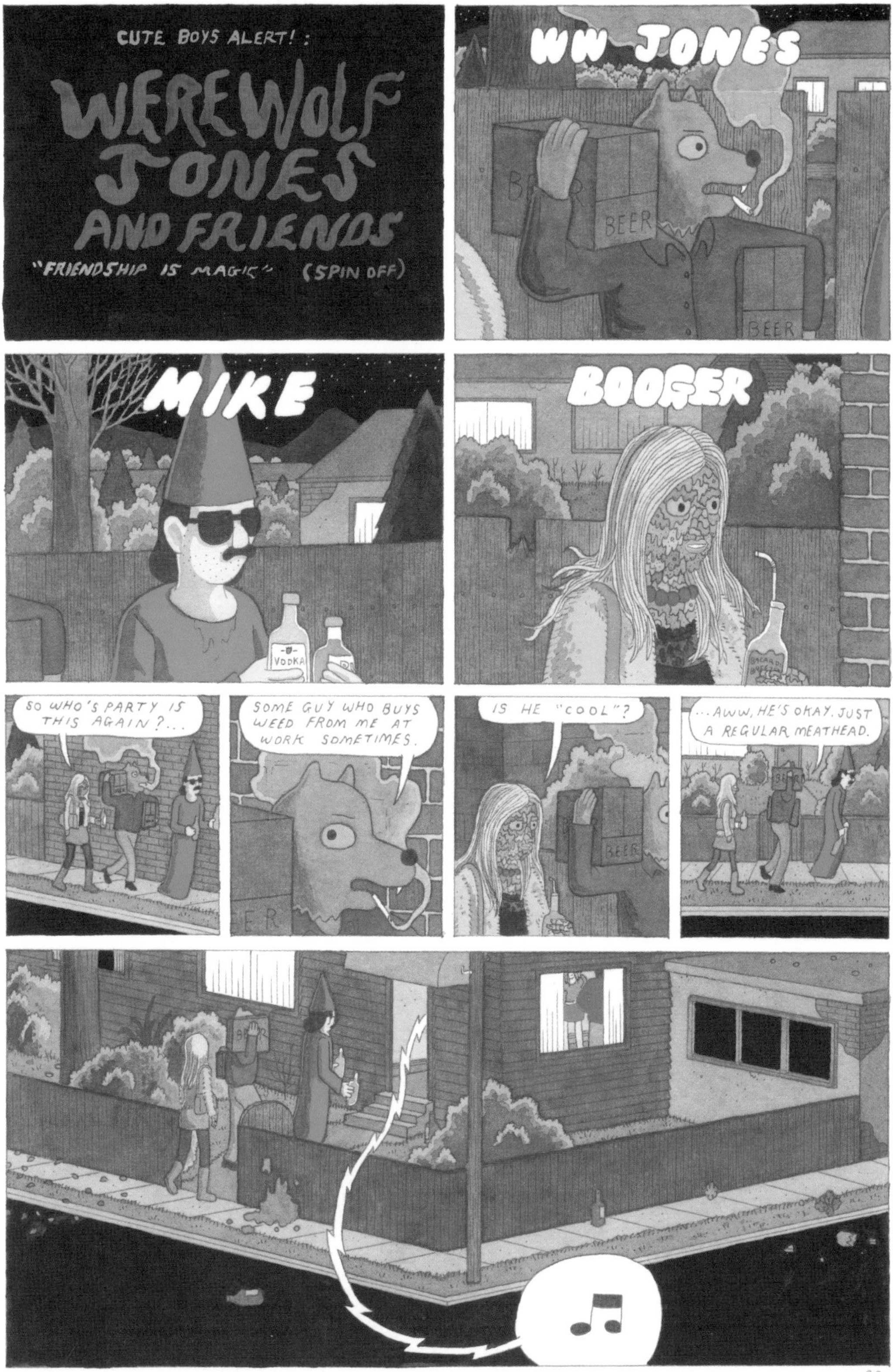
CUTE BOYS ALERT! :
WEREWOLF JONES AND FRIENDS
"FRIENDSHIP IS MAGIC" (SPIN OFF)
WW JONES
BEER
BEER
BEER
BEER
MIKE
VODKA
BOOGER
SO WHO'S PARTY IS THIS AGAIN?...
SOME GUY WHO BUYS WEED FROM ME AT WORK SOMETIMES.
IS HE "COOL"?
BEER
...AWW, HE'S OKAY. JUST A REGULAR MEATHEAD.

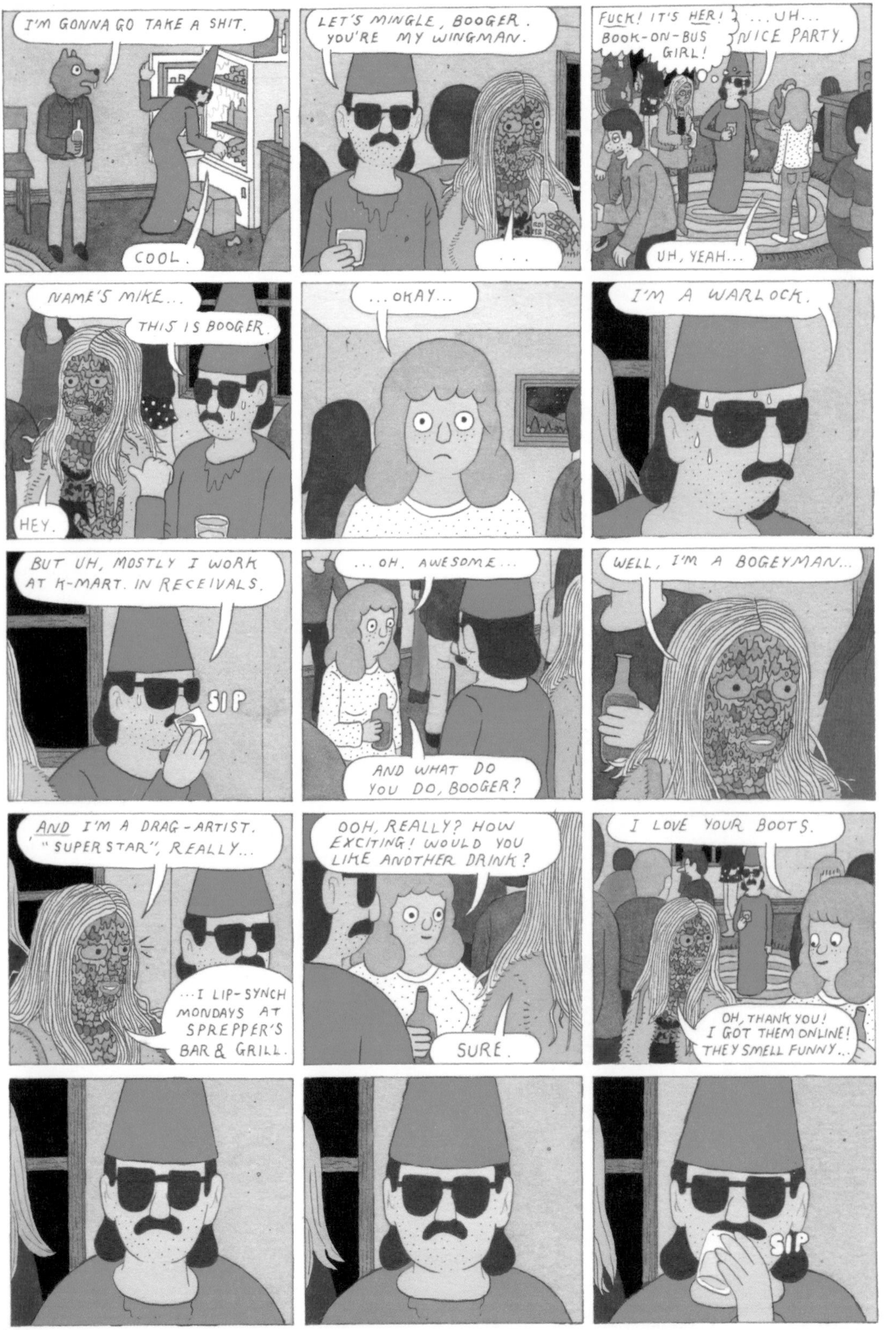

I'M GONNA GO TAKE A SHIT.
COOL.
LET'S MINGLE, BOOGER. YOU'RE MY WINGMAN.
...
FUCK! IT'S HER! BOOK-ON-BUS GIRL!
...UH... NICE PARTY.
UH, YEAH...
NAME'S MIKE...
THIS IS BOOGER.
HEY.
...OKAY...
I'M A WARLOCK.
BUT UH, MOSTLY I WORK AT K-MART. IN RECEIVALS.
SIP
...OH. AWESOME...
AND WHAT DO YOU DO, BOOGER?
WELL, I'M A BOGEYMAN...
AND I'M A DRAG-ARTIST. "SUPER STAR", REALLY...
...I LIP-SYNCH MONDAYS AT SPREPPER'S BAR & GRILL.
OOH, REALLY? HOW EXCITING! WOULD YOU LIKE ANOTHER DRINK?
SURE.
I LOVE YOUR BOOTS.
OH, THANK YOU! I GOT THEM ONLINE! THEY SMELL FUNNY...
SIP

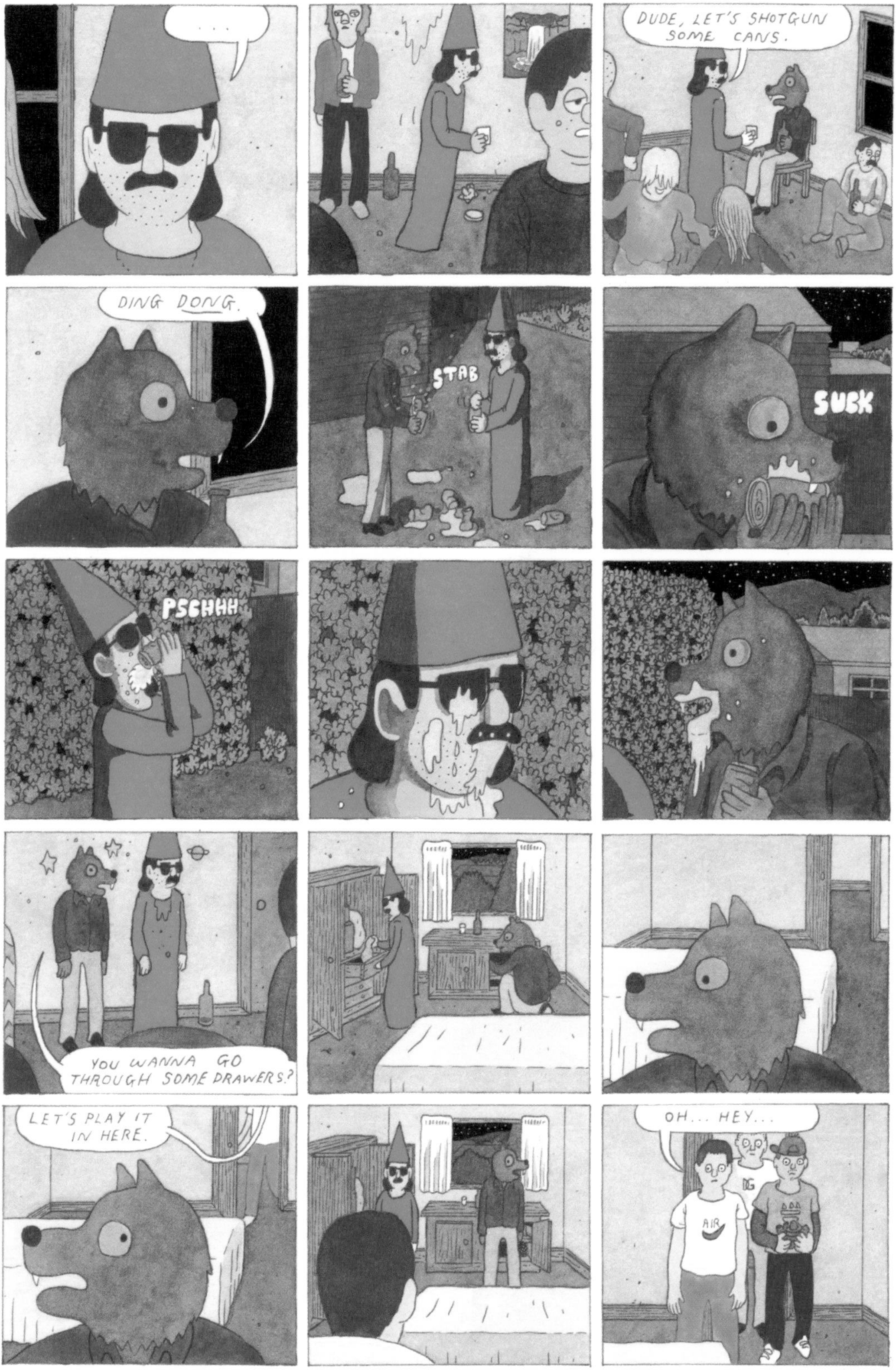

. . .
DUDE, LET'S SHOTGUN SOME CANS.
DING DONG.
STAB
SUCK
PSCHHH
YOU WANNA GO THROUGH SOME DRAWERS?
LET'S PLAY IT IN HERE.
OH... HEY...
AIR
DG

...WE'RE ABOUT TO PLAY THIS AWESOME GAME WE FOUND.

YOU IN?

YOU BETCHA.

YES.

...OKAY.

BOOP!

LAST ONE TO HIT THE BUTTON AFTER THE BEEP GETS ZAPPED. HAW!

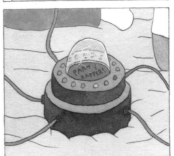

PARTY ZAPPER!

!BEEEEEEEP!

TAP TAP TAP BZZZ TAP TAP

ARRGHHH! CRAP!

OH, FUDGE THAT HURTS!

HAHAH! AGHH!

HAW! HA HA HA

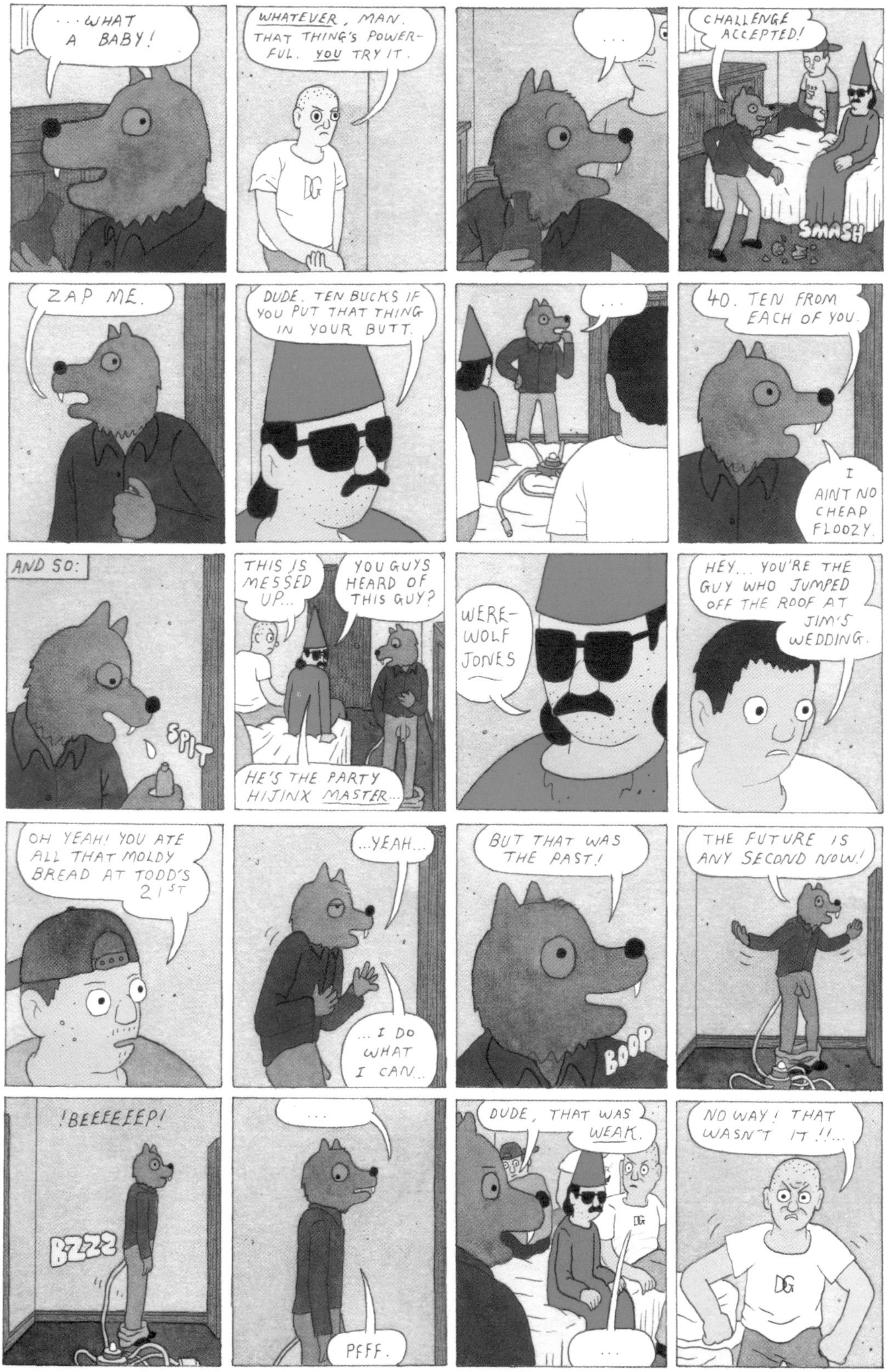
...WHAT A BABY!
WHATEVER, MAN. THAT THING'S POWERFUL. YOU TRY IT.
...
CHALLENGE ACCEPTED!
SMASH
ZAP ME.
DUDE. TEN BUCKS IF YOU PUT THAT THING IN YOUR BUTT.
...
40. TEN FROM EACH OF YOU.
I AINT NO CHEAP FLOOZY.
AND SO:
SPIT
THIS IS MESSED UP...
YOU GUYS HEARD OF THIS GUY?
HE'S THE PARTY HIJINX MASTER...
WERE-WOLF JONES
HEY... YOU'RE THE GUY WHO JUMPED OFF THE ROOF AT JIM'S WEDDING.
OH YEAH! YOU ATE ALL THAT MOLDY BREAD AT TODD'S 21ST
...YEAH...
...I DO WHAT I CAN...
BUT THAT WAS THE PAST!
BOOP
THE FUTURE IS ANY SECOND NOW!
!BEEEEEEP!
BZZZ
...
PFFF.
DUDE, THAT WAS WEAK.
...
NO WAY! THAT WASN'T IT!!...

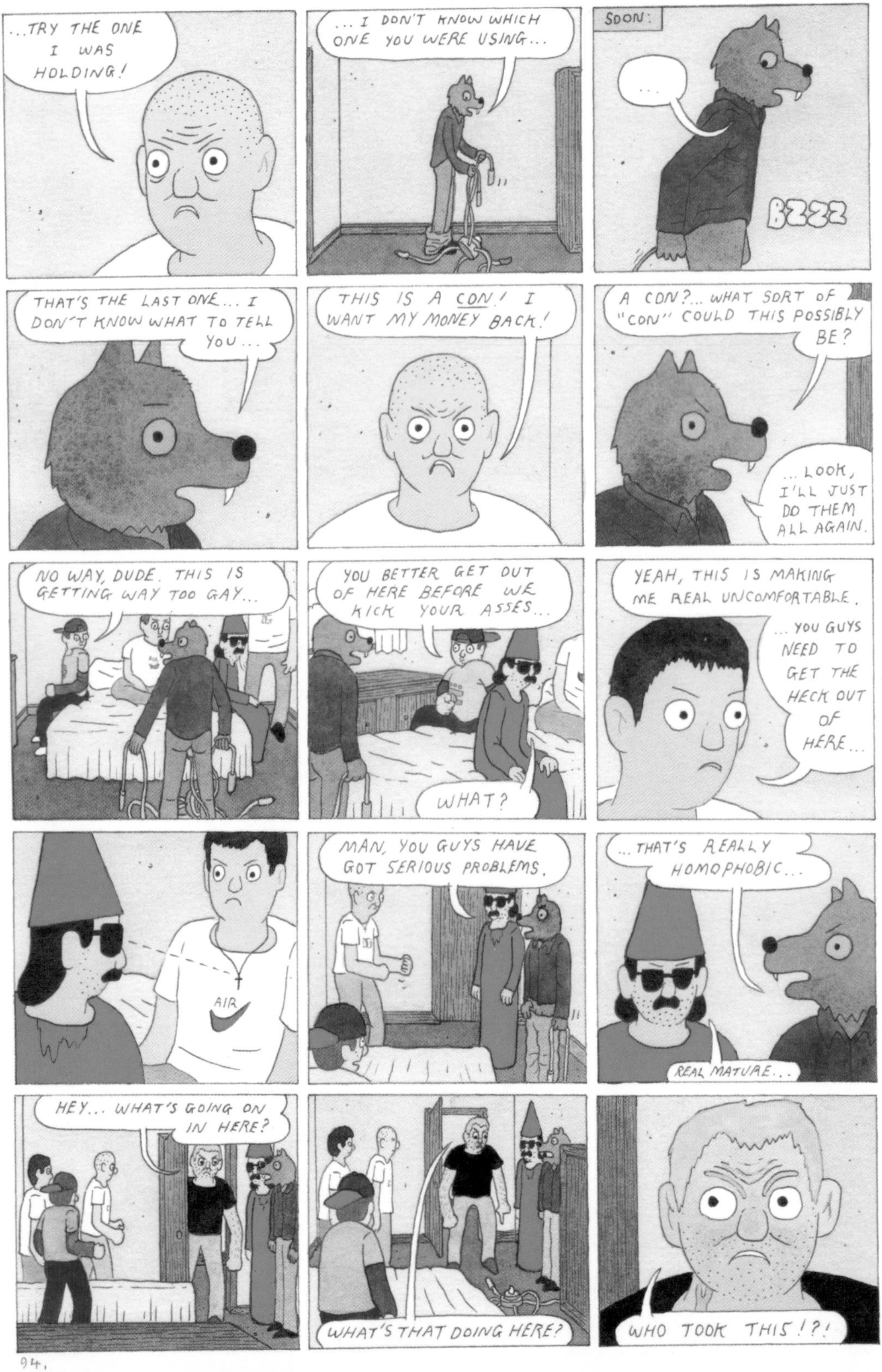
...TRY THE ONE I WAS HOLDING!
... I DON'T KNOW WHICH ONE YOU WERE USING...
SOON:
...
BZZZ
THAT'S THE LAST ONE... I DON'T KNOW WHAT TO TELL YOU...
THIS IS A CON! I WANT MY MONEY BACK!
A CON?... WHAT SORT OF "CON" COULD THIS POSSIBLY BE?
...LOOK, I'LL JUST DO THEM ALL AGAIN.
NO WAY, DUDE. THIS IS GETTING WAY TOO GAY...
YOU BETTER GET OUT OF HERE BEFORE WE KICK YOUR ASSES...
WHAT?
YEAH, THIS IS MAKING ME REAL UNCOMFORTABLE.
...YOU GUYS NEED TO GET THE HECK OUT OF HERE...
AIR
MAN, YOU GUYS HAVE GOT SERIOUS PROBLEMS.
...THAT'S REALLY HOMOPHOBIC...
REAL MATURE...
HEY... WHAT'S GOING ON IN HERE?
WHAT'S THAT DOING HERE?
WHO TOOK THIS!?!

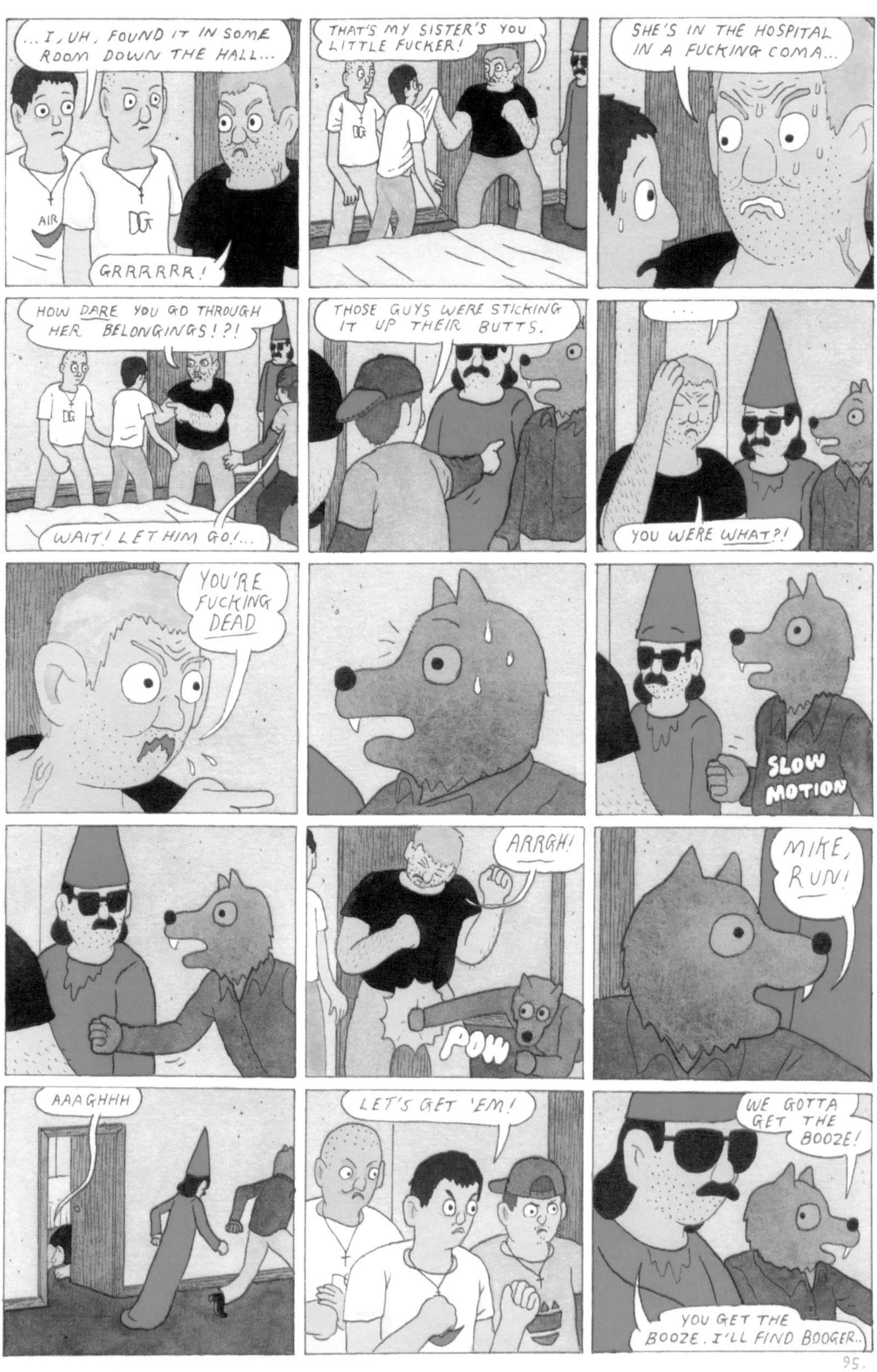
...I, UH, FOUND IT IN SOME ROOM DOWN THE HALL...
GRRRRRR!
AIR
DG
THAT'S MY SISTER'S YOU LITTLE FUCKER!
SHE'S IN THE HOSPITAL IN A FUCKING COMA...
HOW DARE YOU GO THROUGH HER BELONGINGS!?!
WAIT! LET HIM GO!...
THOSE GUYS WERE STICKING IT UP THEIR BUTTS.
...
YOU WERE WHAT?!
YOU'RE FUCKING DEAD
SLOW MOTION
ARRGH!
POW
MIKE, RUN!
AAAGHHH
LET'S GET 'EM!
WE GOTTA GET THE BOOZE!
YOU GET THE BOOZE. I'LL FIND BOOGER..

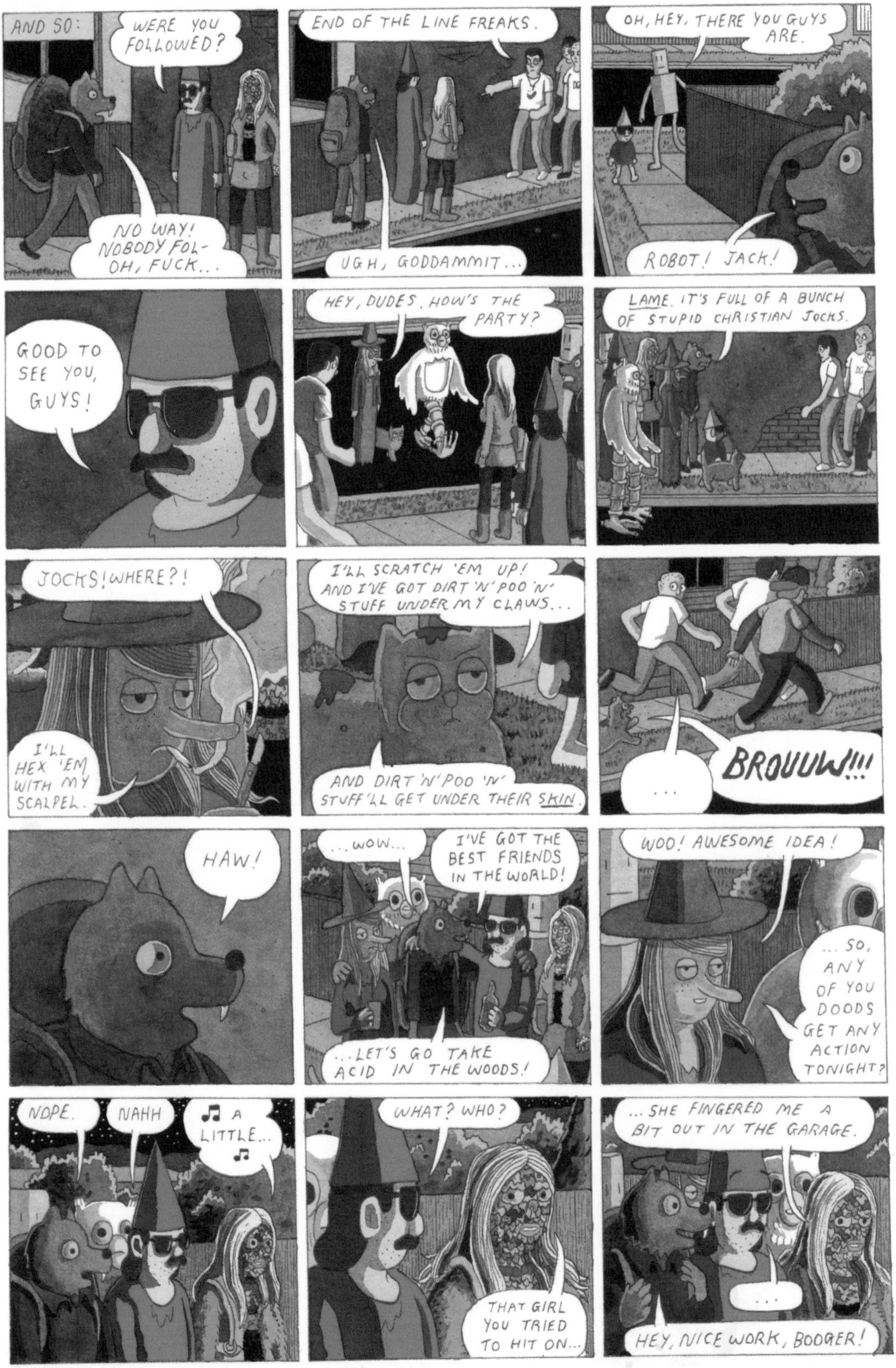
AND SO:
WERE YOU FOLLOWED?
NO WAY! NOBODY FOL- OH, FUCK...
END OF THE LINE FREAKS.
UGH, GODDAMMIT...
OH, HEY. THERE YOU GUYS ARE.
ROBOT! JACK!
GOOD TO SEE YOU, GUYS!
HEY, DUDES. HOW'S THE PARTY?
LAME. IT'S FULL OF A BUNCH OF STUPID CHRISTIAN JOCKS.
JOCKS! WHERE?!
I'LL HEX 'EM WITH MY SCALPEL.
I'LL SCRATCH 'EM UP! AND I'VE GOT DIRT 'N' POO 'N' STUFF UNDER MY CLAWS...
AND DIRT 'N' POO 'N' STUFF'LL GET UNDER THEIR SKIN.
...
BROUUW!!!!
HAW!
...WOW...
I'VE GOT THE BEST FRIENDS IN THE WORLD!
...LET'S GO TAKE ACID IN THE WOODS!
WOO! AWESOME IDEA!
...SO, ANY OF YOU DOODS GET ANY ACTION TONIGHT?
NOPE.
NAHH
♫ A LITTLE... ♫
WHAT? WHO?
THAT GIRL YOU TRIED TO HIT ON...
...SHE FINGERED ME A BIT OUT IN THE GARAGE.
...
HEY, NICE WORK, BOOGER!

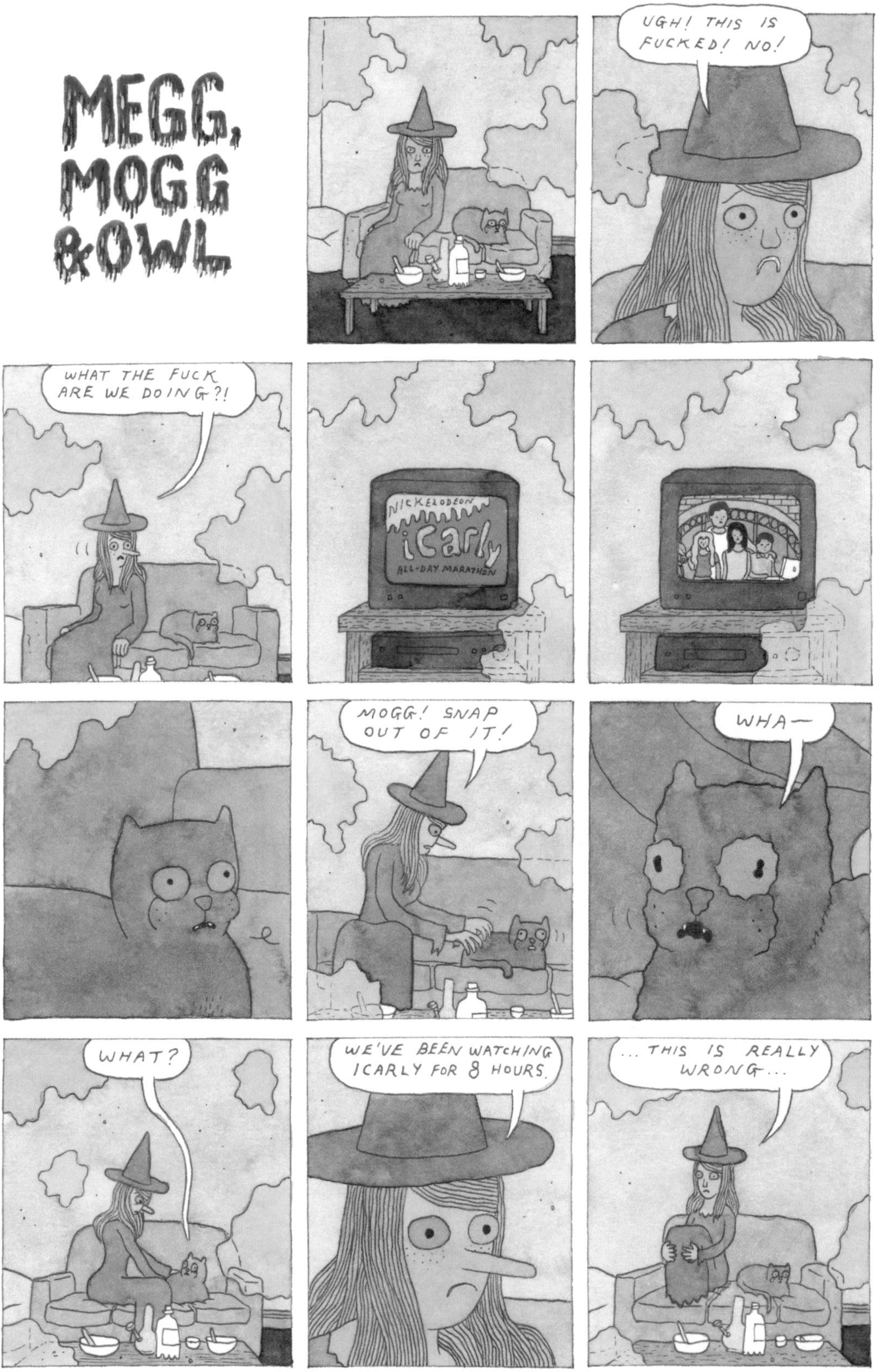
MEGG, MOGG & OWL
UGH! THIS IS FUCKED! NO!
WHAT THE FUCK ARE WE DOING?!
NICKELODEON
iCarly
ALL-DAY MARATHON
MOGG! SNAP OUT OF IT!
WHA—
WHAT?
WE'VE BEEN WATCHING ICARLY FOR 8 HOURS.
... THIS IS REALLY WRONG...

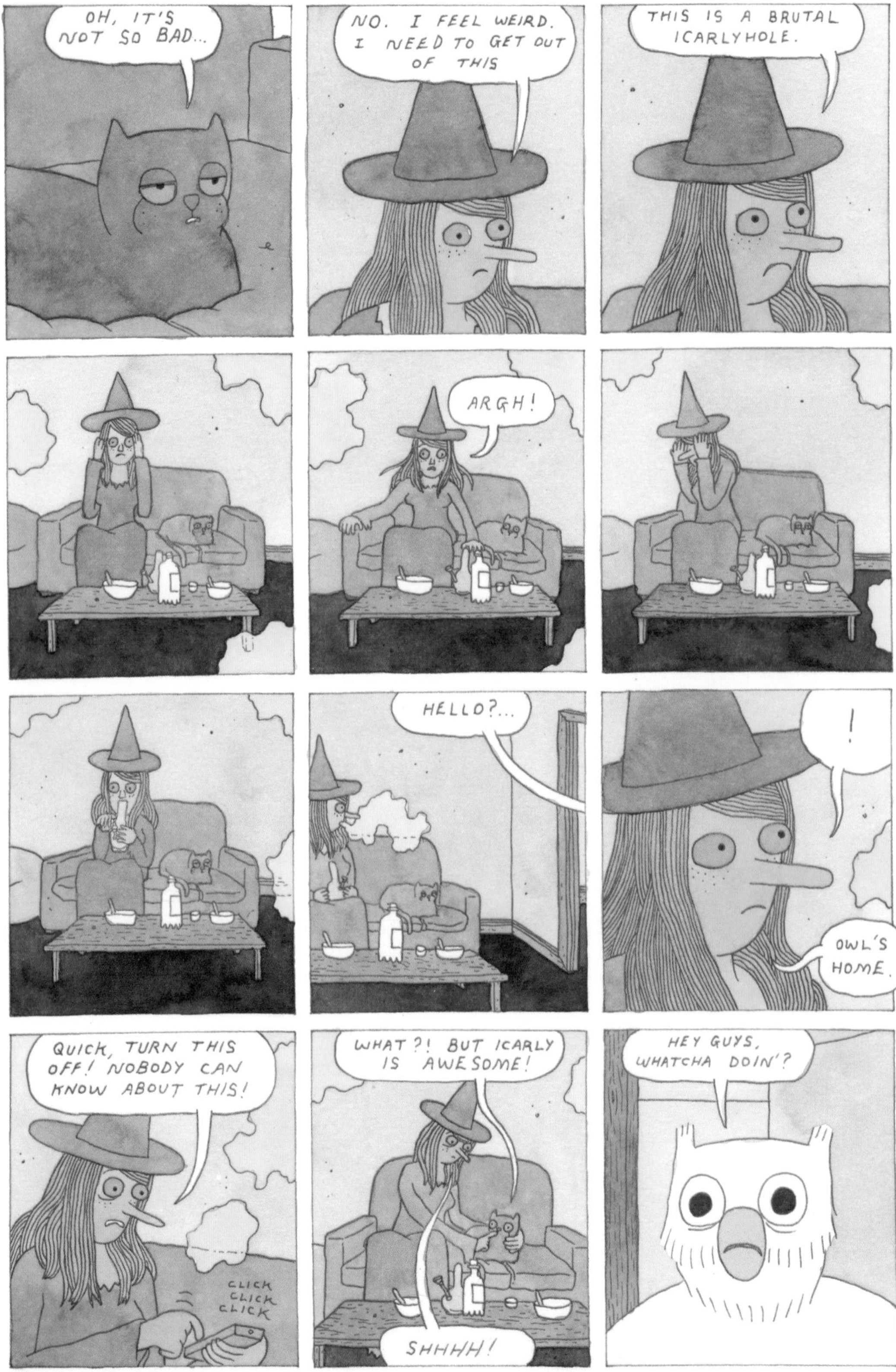

OH, IT'S NOT SO BAD...
NO. I FEEL WEIRD. I NEED TO GET OUT OF THIS
THIS IS A BRUTAL ICARLYHOLE.
ARGH!
HELLO?...
!
OWL'S HOME.
QUICK, TURN THIS OFF! NOBODY CAN KNOW ABOUT THIS!
CLICK CLICK CLICK
WHAT?! BUT ICARLY IS AWESOME!
SHHHH!
HEY GUYS, WHATCHA DOIN'?

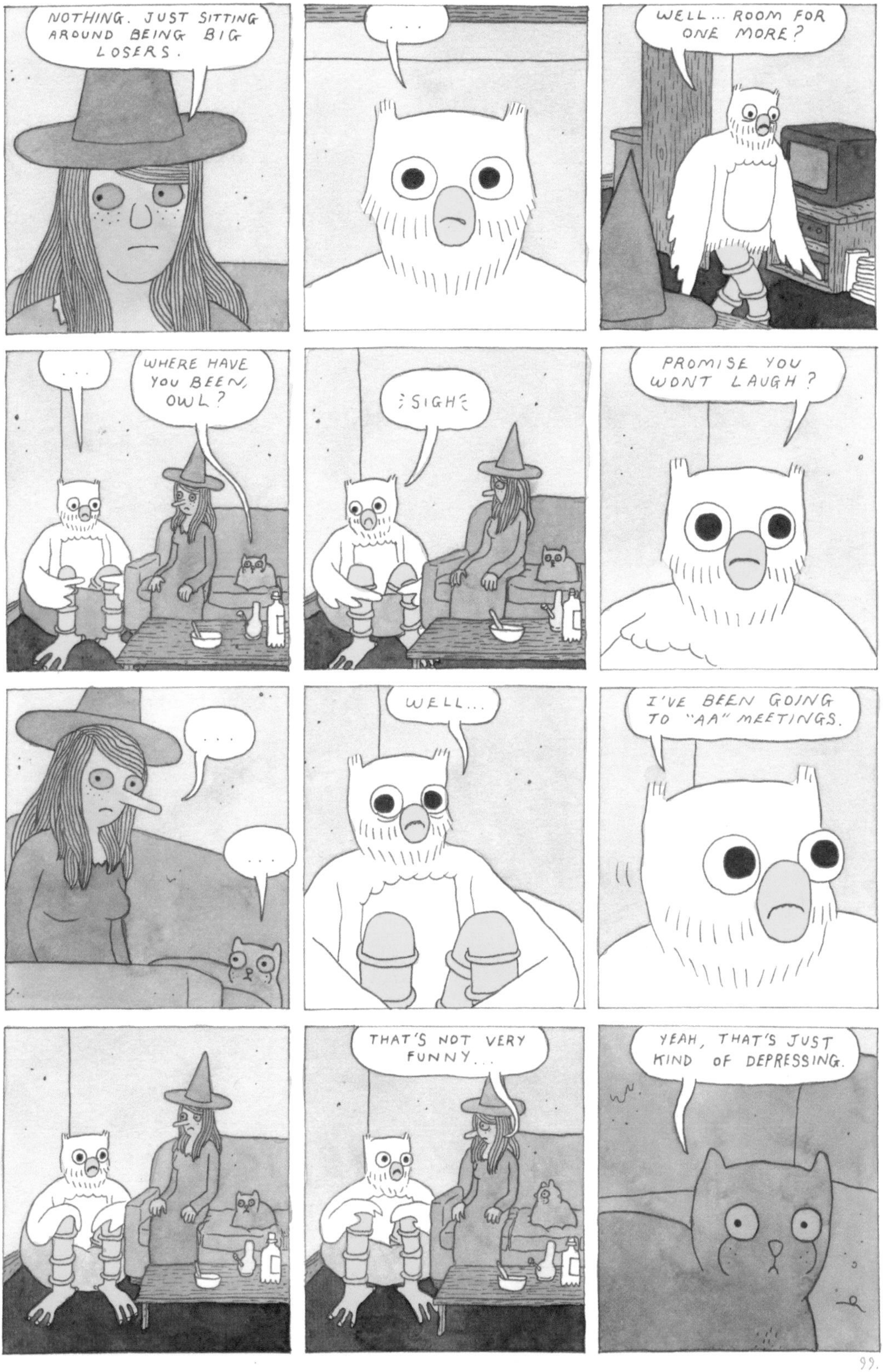
NOTHING. JUST SITTING AROUND BEING BIG LOSERS.
. . .
WELL... ROOM FOR ONE MORE?
. . .
WHERE HAVE YOU BEEN, OWL?
SIGH
PROMISE YOU WONT LAUGH?
. . .
. . .
WELL...
I'VE BEEN GOING TO "AA" MEETINGS.
THAT'S NOT VERY FUNNY...
YEAH, THAT'S JUST KIND OF DEPRESSING.

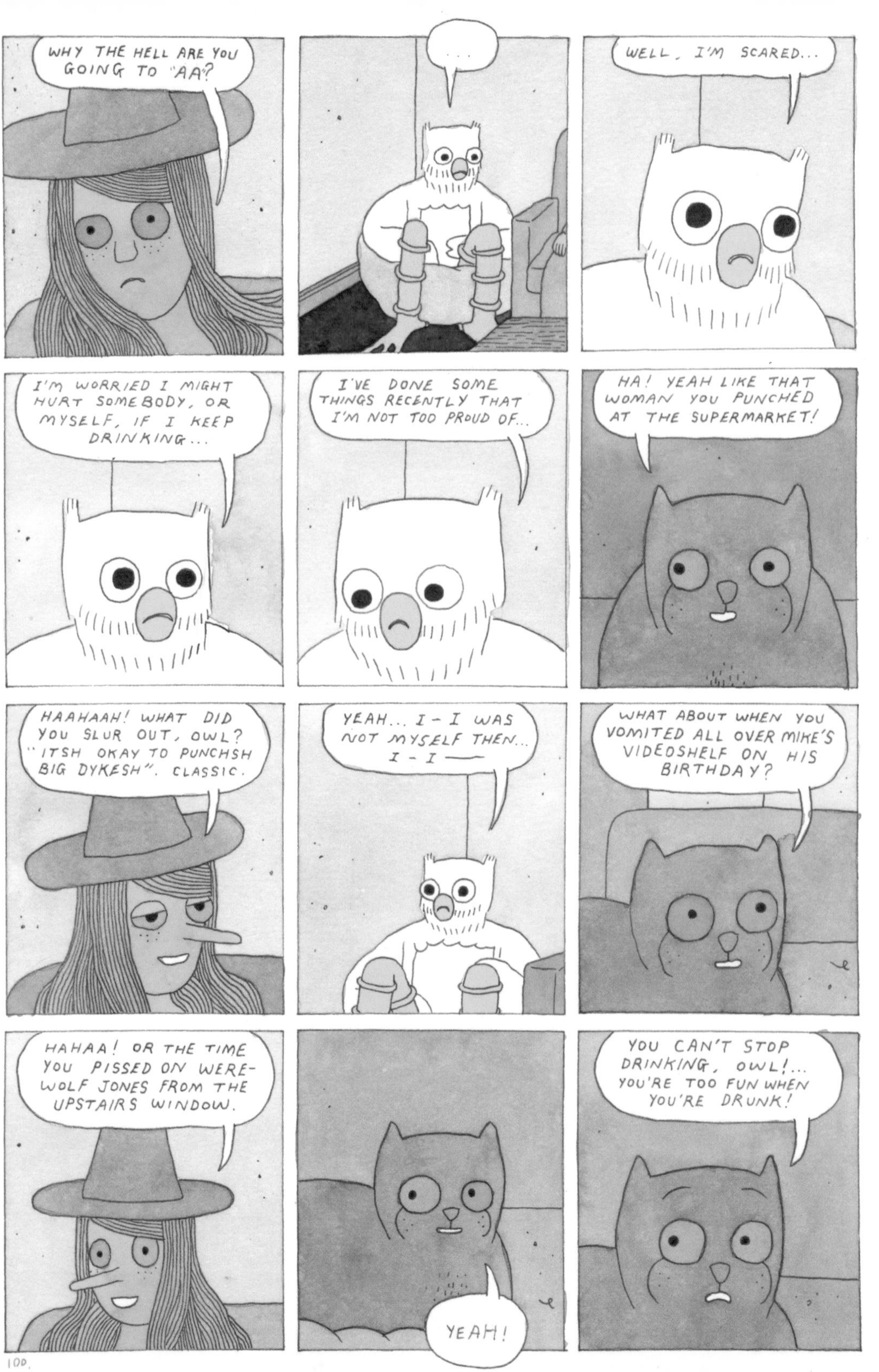
WHY THE HELL ARE YOU GOING TO "AA"?
. . .
WELL, I'M SCARED...
I'M WORRIED I MIGHT HURT SOMEBODY, OR MYSELF, IF I KEEP DRINKING...
I'VE DONE SOME THINGS RECENTLY THAT I'M NOT TOO PROUD OF...
HA! YEAH LIKE THAT WOMAN YOU PUNCHED AT THE SUPERMARKET!
HAAHAAH! WHAT DID YOU SLUR OUT, OWL? "ITSH OKAY TO PUNCHSH BIG DYKESH". CLASSIC.
YEAH... I - I WAS NOT MYSELF THEN... I - I —
WHAT ABOUT WHEN YOU VOMITED ALL OVER MIKE'S VIDEOSHELF ON HIS BIRTHDAY?
HAHAA! OR THE TIME YOU PISSED ON WERE-WOLF JONES FROM THE UPSTAIRS WINDOW.
YEAH!
YOU CAN'T STOP DRINKING, OWL!... YOU'RE TOO FUN WHEN YOU'RE DRUNK!

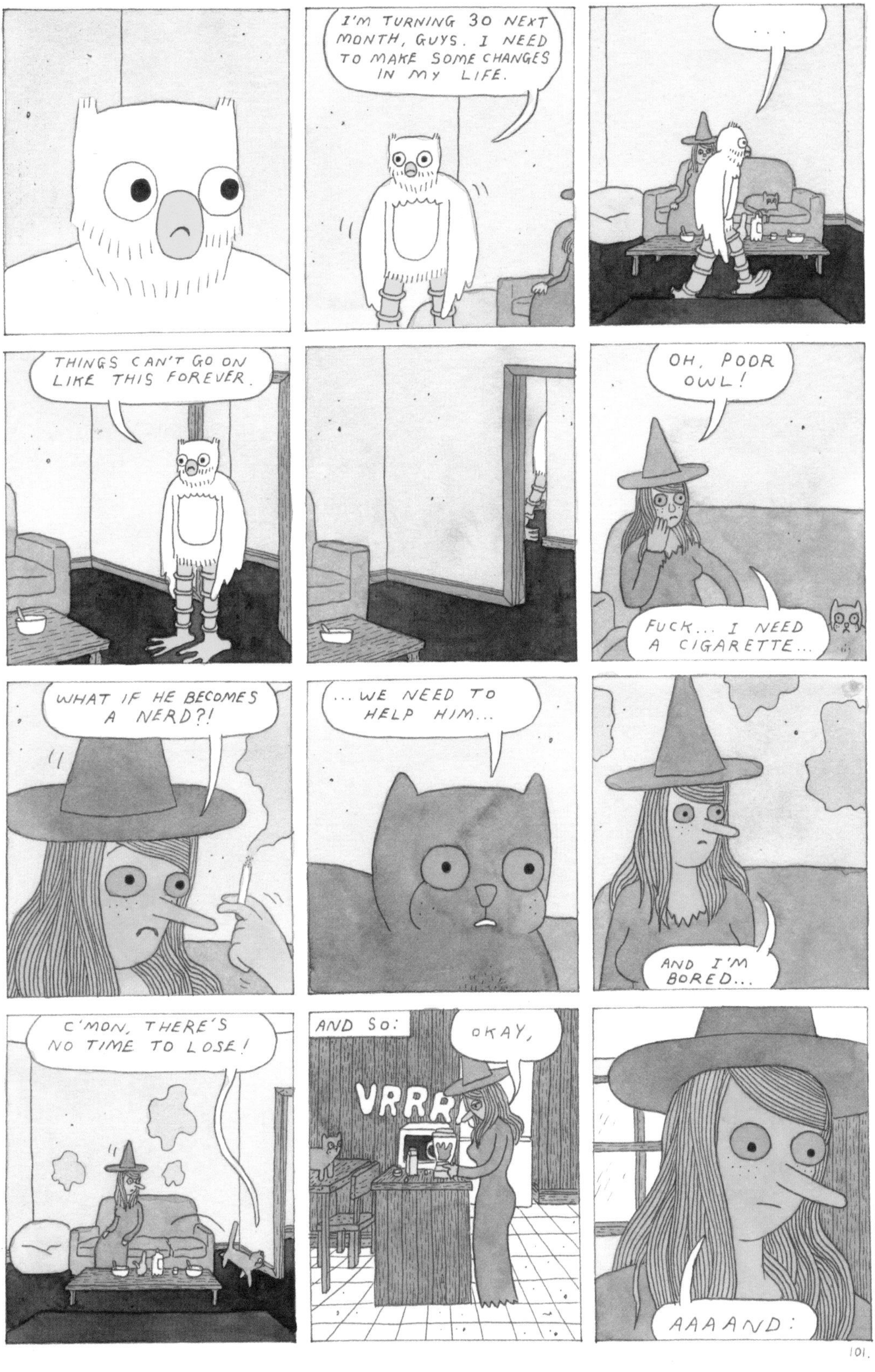
I'M TURNING 30 NEXT MONTH, GUYS. I NEED TO MAKE SOME CHANGES IN MY LIFE.
. . .
THINGS CAN'T GO ON LIKE THIS FOREVER.
OH, POOR OWL!
FUCK... I NEED A CIGARETTE...
WHAT IF HE BECOMES A NERD?!
...WE NEED TO HELP HIM...
AND I'M BORED...
C'MON, THERE'S NO TIME TO LOSE!
AND SO:
OKAY,
VRRR
AAAAND:

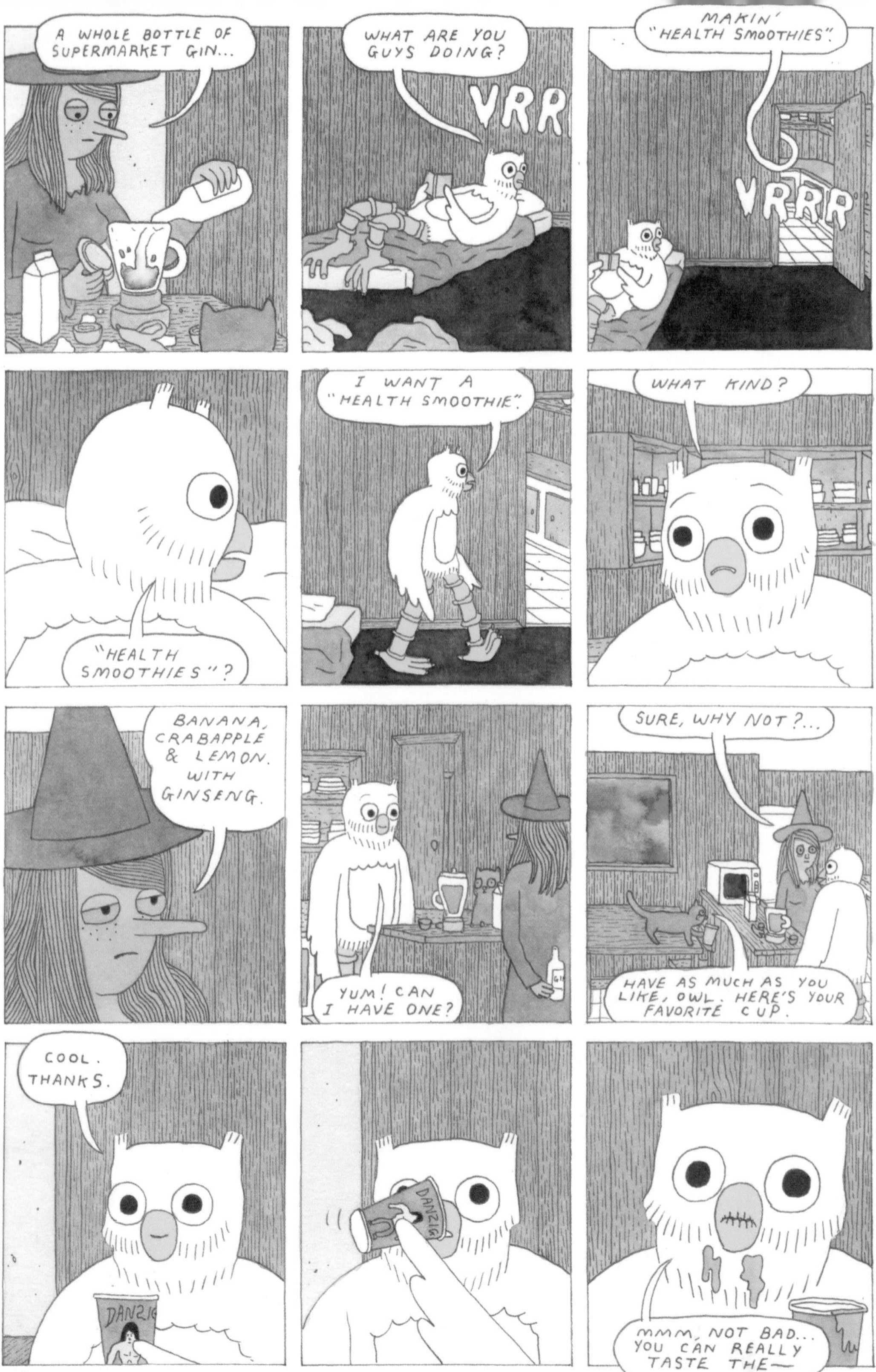
A WHOLE BOTTLE OF SUPERMARKET GIN...
WHAT ARE YOU GUYS DOING?
VRR
MAKIN' "HEALTH SMOOTHIES".
VRRR
"HEALTH SMOOTHIES"?
I WANT A "HEALTH SMOOTHIE".
WHAT KIND?
BANANA, CRABAPPLE & LEMON. WITH GINSENG.
YUM! CAN I HAVE ONE?
SURE, WHY NOT?...
HAVE AS MUCH AS YOU LIKE, OWL. HERE'S YOUR FAVORITE CUP.
COOL. THANKS.
DANZIG
DANZIG
MMM, NOT BAD... YOU CAN REALLY TASTE THE—

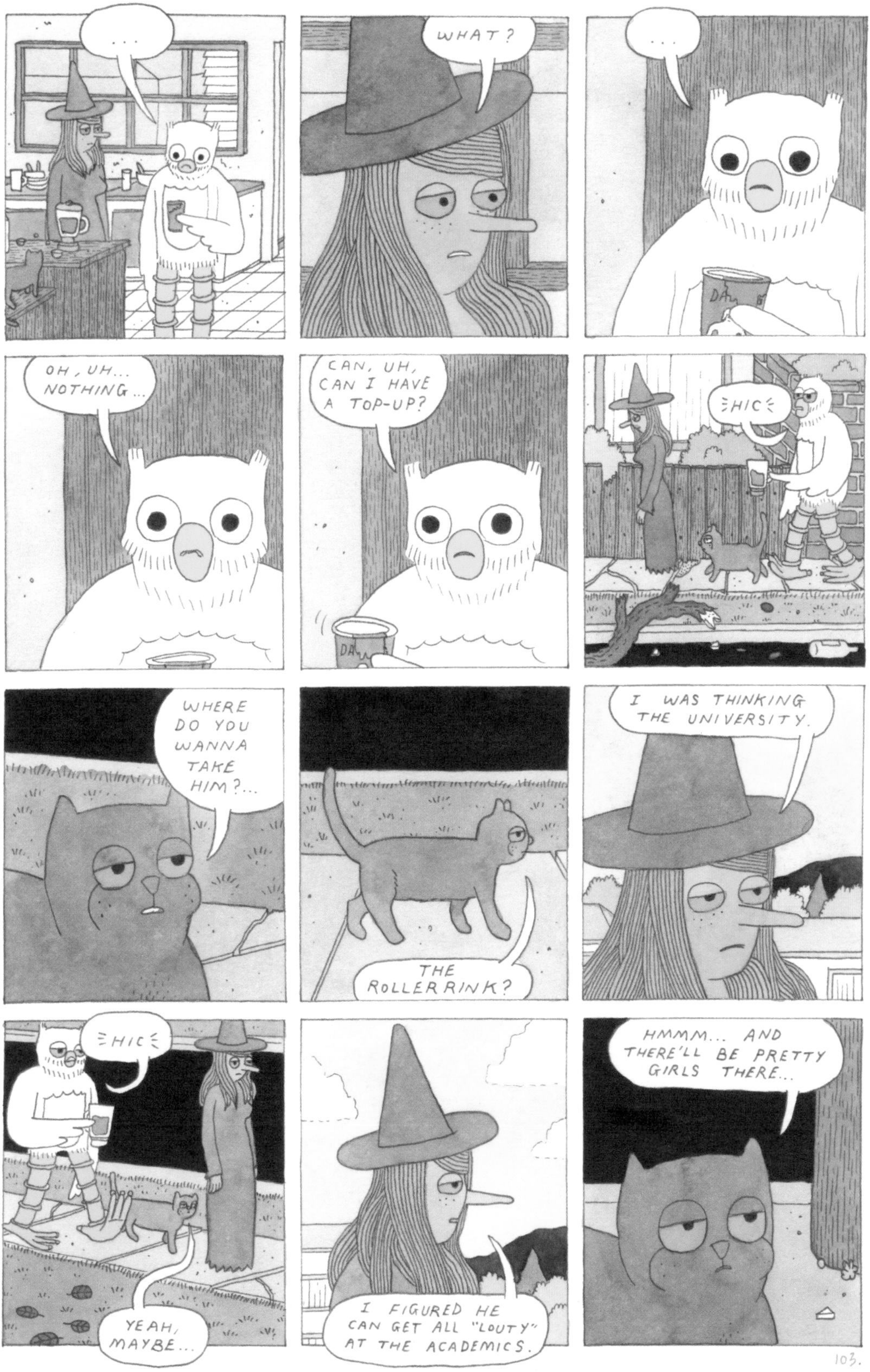
. . .
WHAT?
. . .
OH, UH... NOTHING...
CAN, UH, CAN I HAVE A TOP-UP?
HIC
WHERE DO YOU WANNA TAKE HIM?...
THE ROLLERRINK?
I WAS THINKING THE UNIVERSITY.
HIC
YEAH, MAYBE...
I FIGURED HE CAN GET ALL "LOUTY" AT THE ACADEMICS.
HMMM... AND THERE'LL BE PRETTY GIRLS THERE...

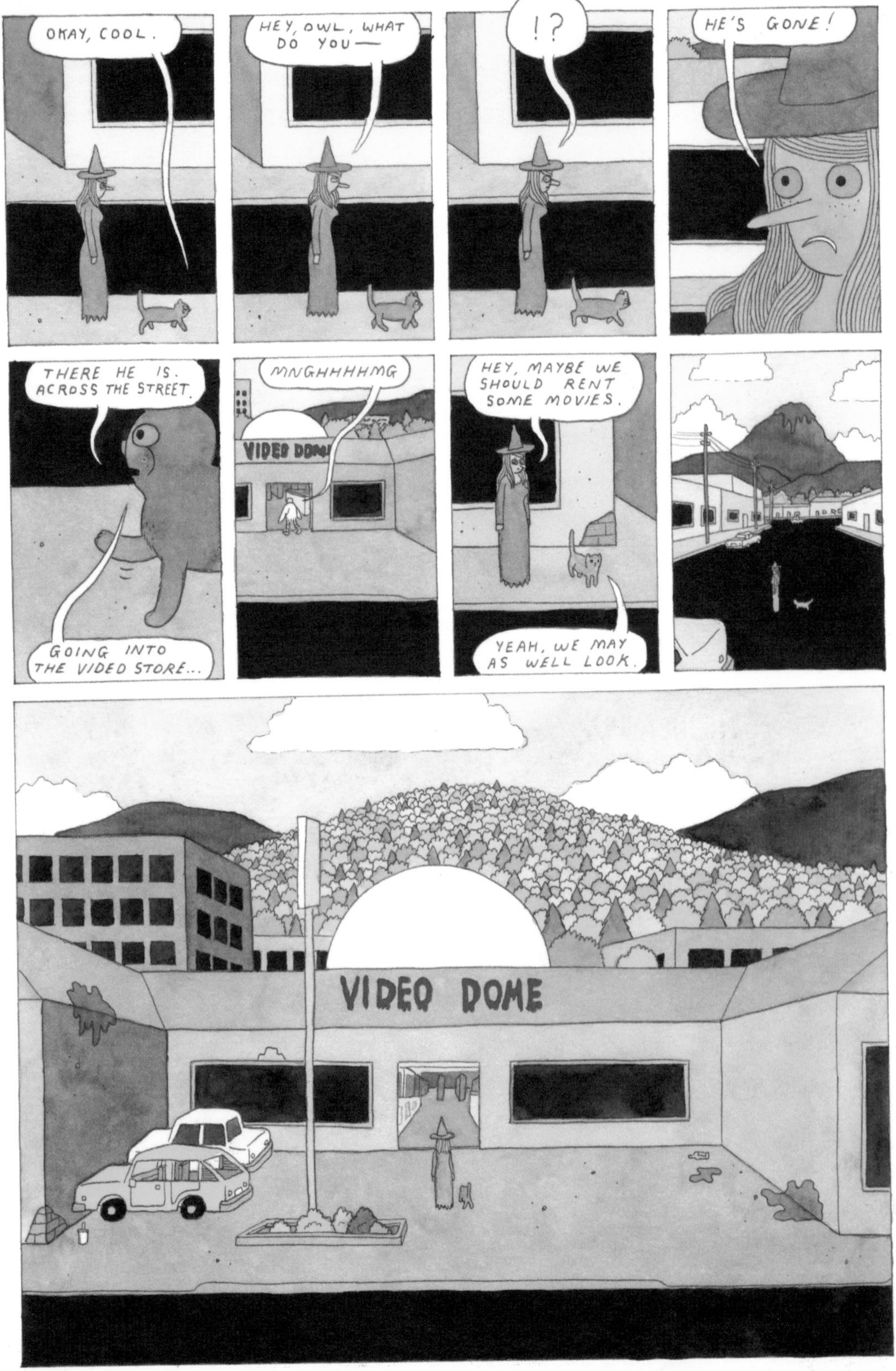
OKAY, COOL.
HEY, OWL, WHAT DO YOU—
!?
HE'S GONE!
THERE HE IS. ACROSS THE STREET.
GOING INTO THE VIDEO STORE...
MNGHHHHMG
HEY, MAYBE WE SHOULD RENT SOME MOVIES.
YEAH, WE MAY AS WELL LOOK.
VIDEO DOME

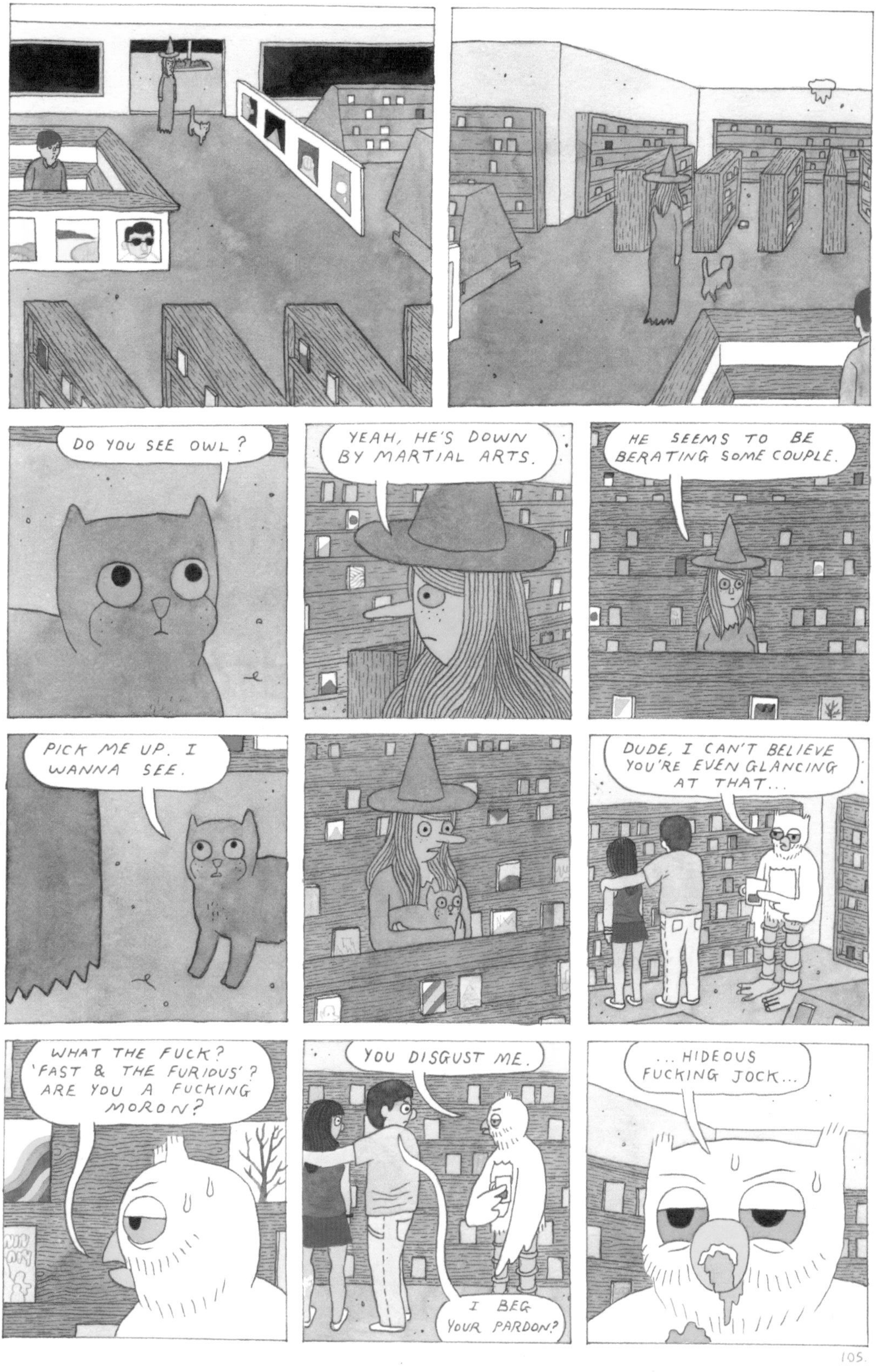
DO YOU SEE OWL?
YEAH, HE'S DOWN BY MARTIAL ARTS.
HE SEEMS TO BE BERATING SOME COUPLE.
PICK ME UP. I WANNA SEE.
DUDE, I CAN'T BELIEVE YOU'RE EVEN GLANCING AT THAT...
WHAT THE FUCK? 'FAST & THE FURIOUS'? ARE YOU A FUCKING MORON?
YOU DISGUST ME.
I BEG YOUR PARDON?
...HIDEOUS FUCKING JOCK...

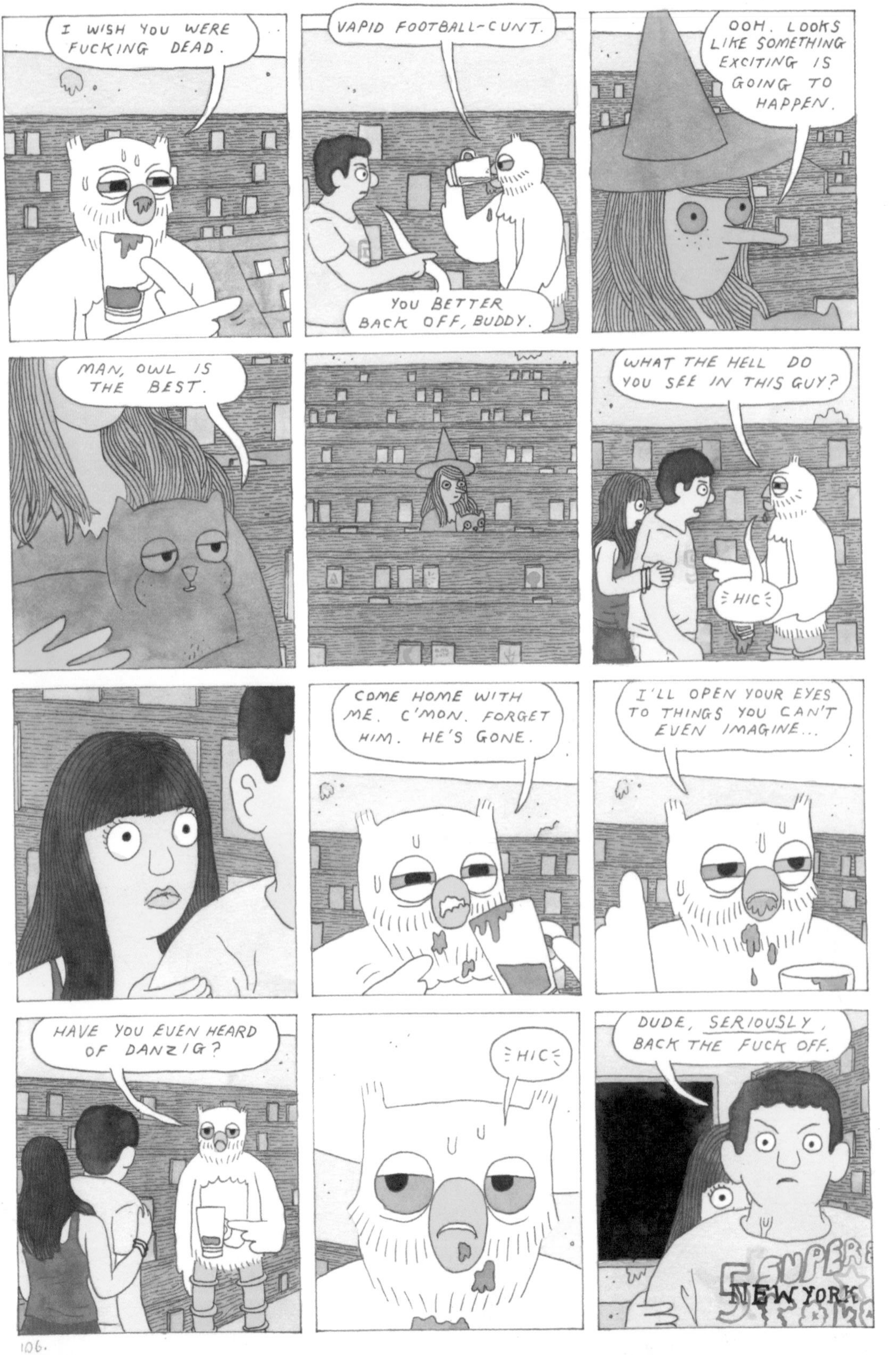
I WISH YOU WERE FUCKING DEAD.
VAPID FOOTBALL-CUNT.
YOU BETTER BACK OFF, BUDDY.
OOH. LOOKS LIKE SOMETHING EXCITING IS GOING TO HAPPEN.
MAN, OWL IS THE BEST.
WHAT THE HELL DO YOU SEE IN THIS GUY?
HIC
COME HOME WITH ME. C'MON. FORGET HIM. HE'S GONE.
I'LL OPEN YOUR EYES TO THINGS YOU CAN'T EVEN IMAGINE...
HAVE YOU EVEN HEARD OF DANZIG?
HIC
DUDE, SERIOUSLY, BACK THE FUCK OFF.
NEW YORK

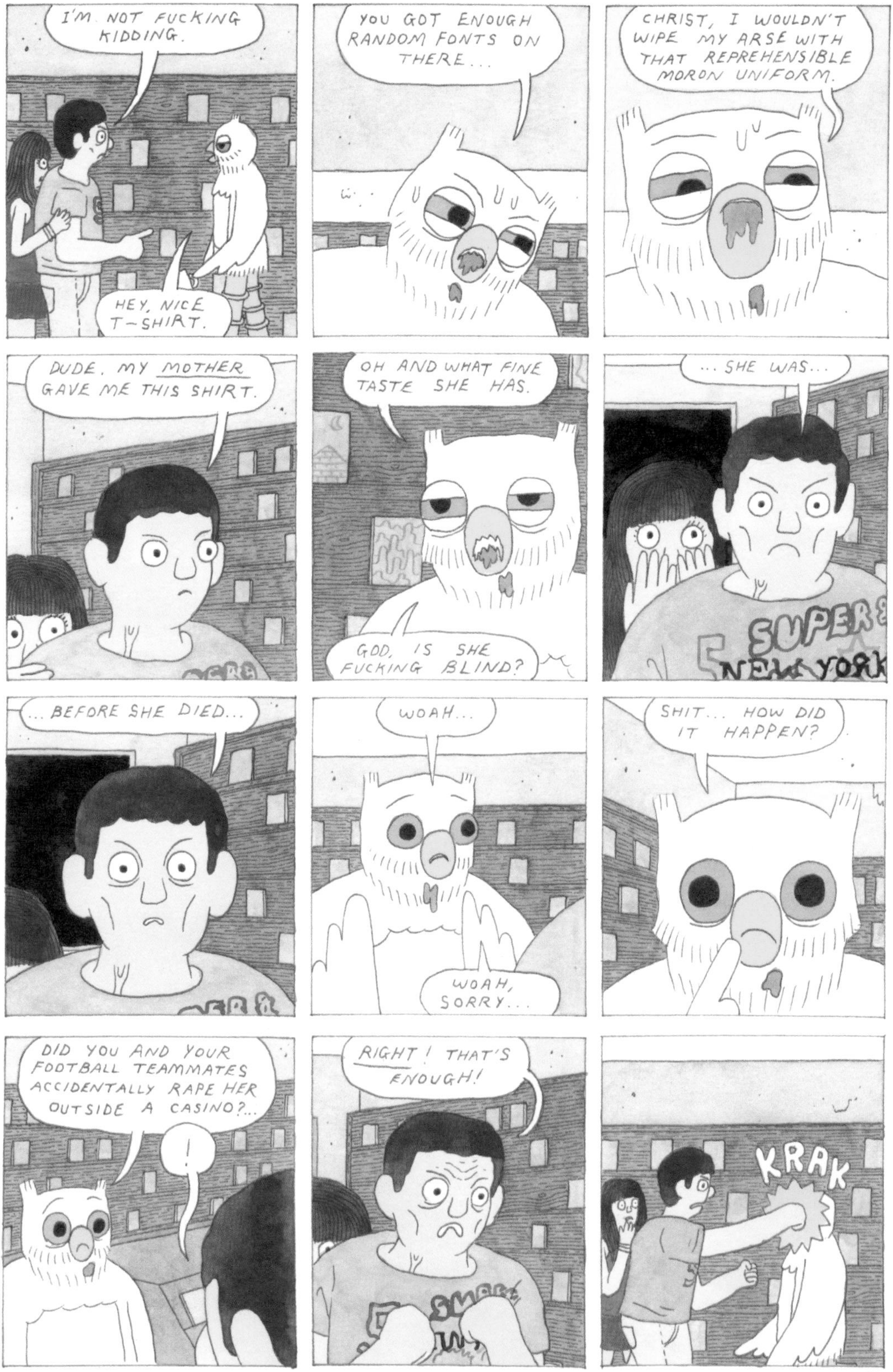
I'M NOT FUCKING KIDDING.
HEY, NICE T-SHIRT.
YOU GOT ENOUGH RANDOM FONTS ON THERE...
CHRIST, I WOULDN'T WIPE MY ARSE WITH THAT REPREHENSIBLE MORON UNIFORM.
DUDE. MY MOTHER GAVE ME THIS SHIRT.
OH AND WHAT FINE TASTE SHE HAS.
GOD, IS SHE FUCKING BLIND?
... SHE WAS...
SUPER
NEW YORK
... BEFORE SHE DIED...
WOAH...
WOAH, SORRY...
SHIT... HOW DID IT HAPPEN?
DID YOU AND YOUR FOOTBALL TEAMMATES ACCIDENTALLY RAPE HER OUTSIDE A CASINO?...
!
RIGHT! THAT'S ENOUGH!
KRAK

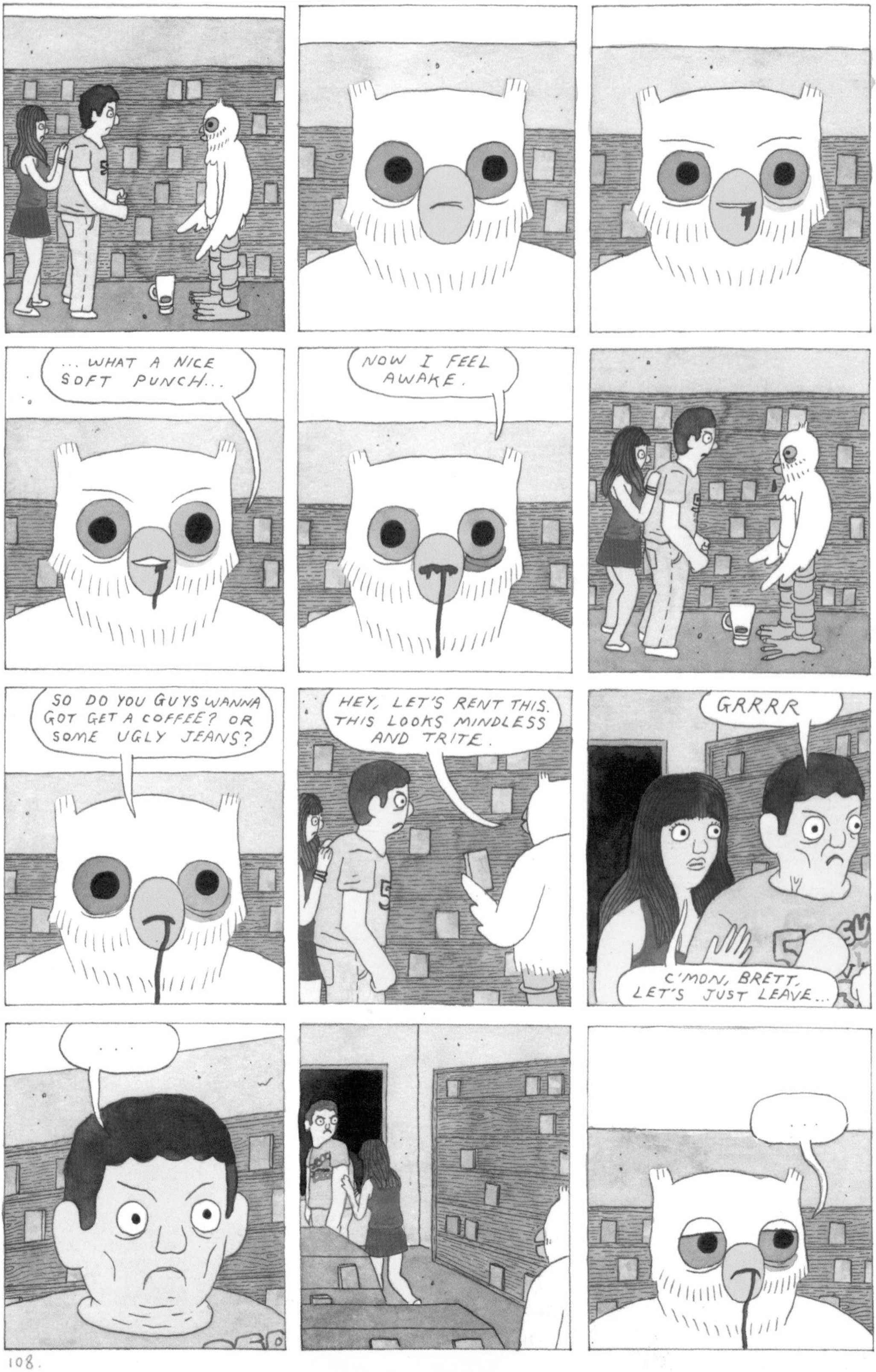
... WHAT A NICE SOFT PUNCH...
NOW I FEEL AWAKE.
SO DO YOU GUYS WANNA GOT GET A COFFEE? OR SOME UGLY JEANS?
HEY, LET'S RENT THIS. THIS LOOKS MINDLESS AND TRITE.
GRRRR
C'MON, BRETT, LET'S JUST LEAVE...
. . .
. . .

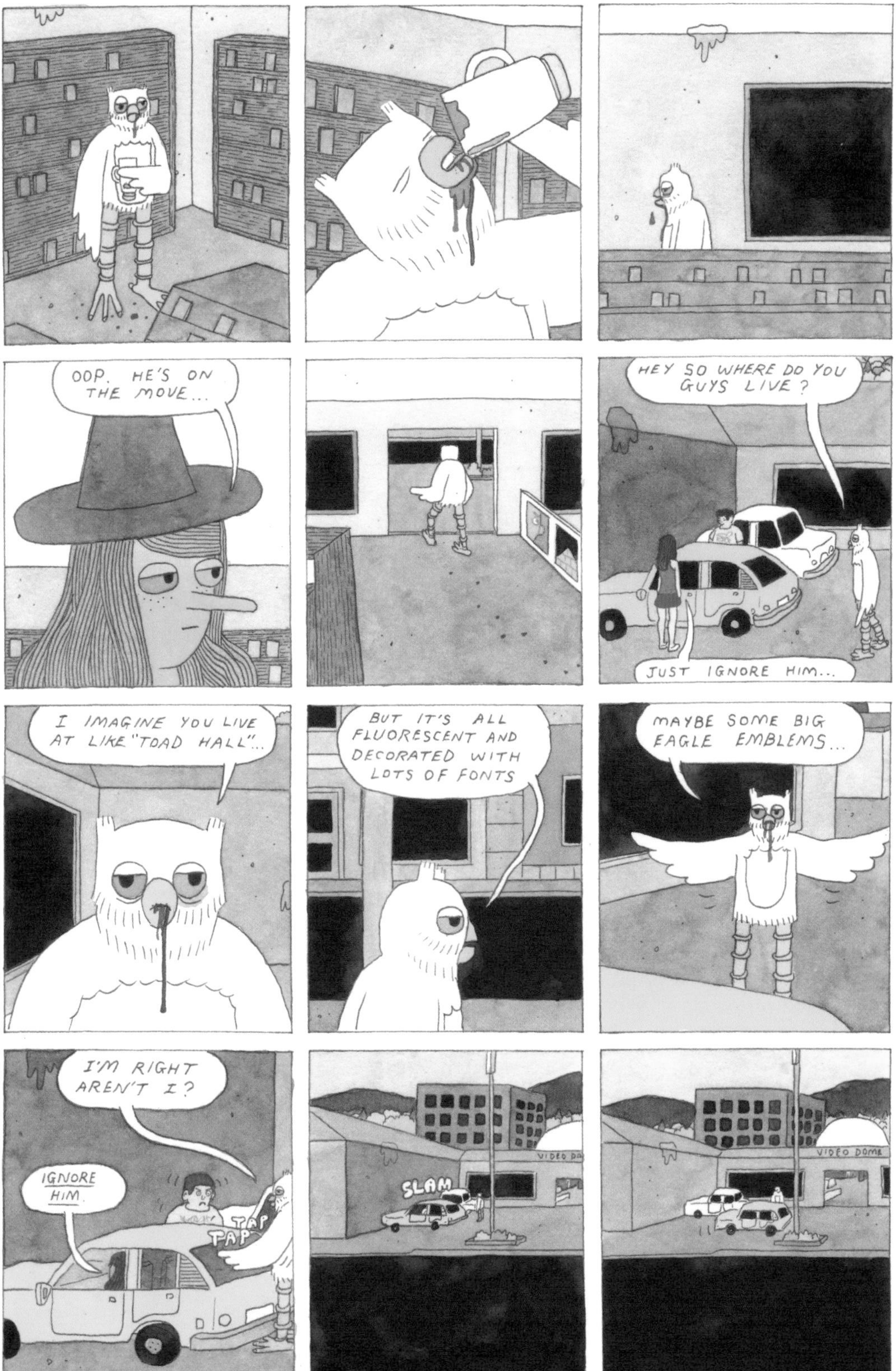
OOP. HE'S ON THE MOVE...
HEY SO WHERE DO YOU GUYS LIVE?
JUST IGNORE HIM...
I IMAGINE YOU LIVE AT LIKE "TOAD HALL"...
BUT IT'S ALL FLUORESCENT AND DECORATED WITH LOTS OF FONTS
MAYBE SOME BIG EAGLE EMBLEMS...
I'M RIGHT AREN'T I?
IGNORE HIM.
TAP
TAP
SLAM
VIDEO DOME

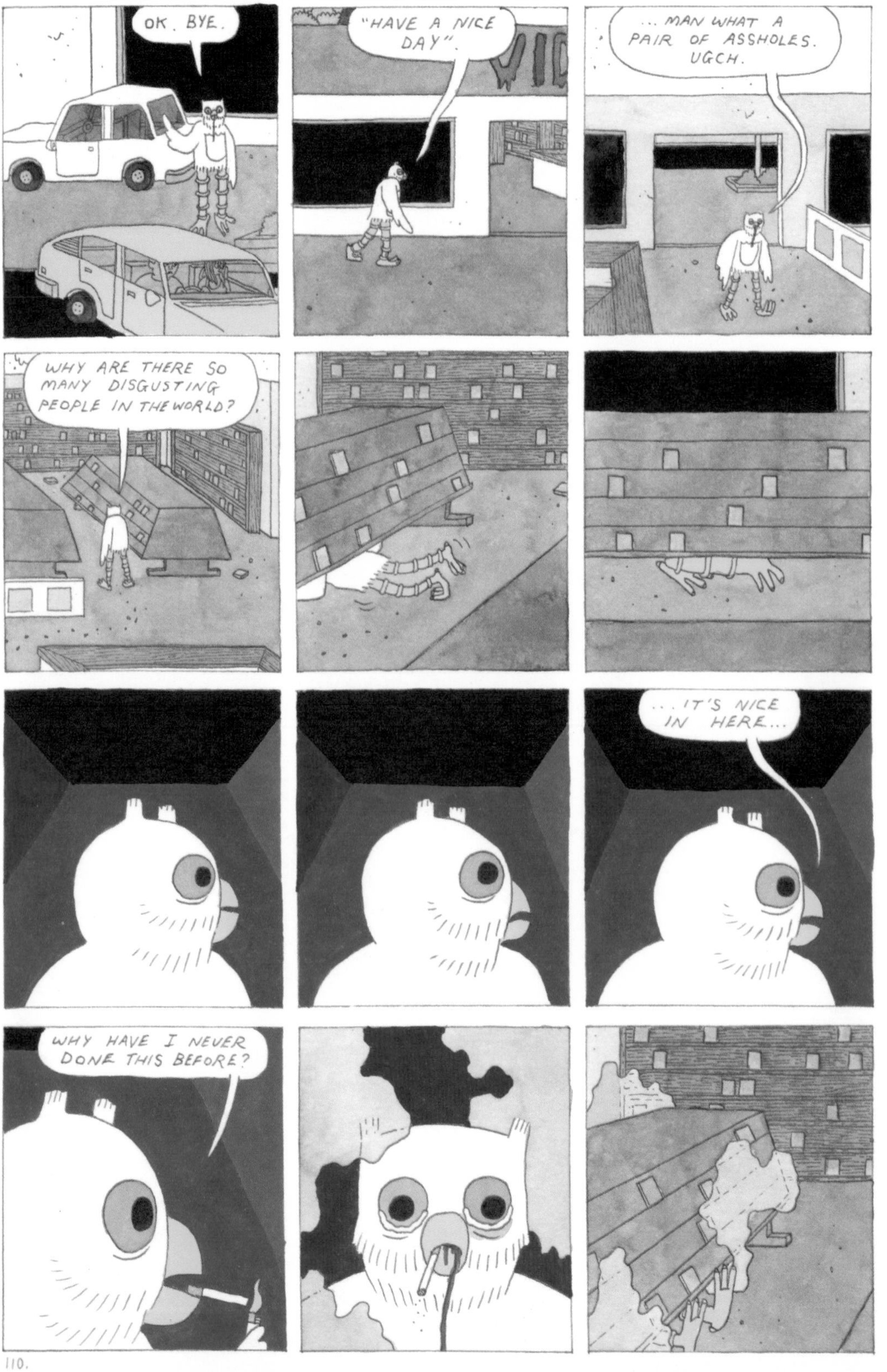
OK. BYE.
"HAVE A NICE DAY".
...MAN WHAT A PAIR OF ASSHOLES. UGCH.
WHY ARE THERE SO MANY DISGUSTING PEOPLE IN THE WORLD?
...IT'S NICE IN HERE...
WHY HAVE I NEVER DONE THIS BEFORE?

HEY, OWL, WHAT— CHA DOIN'?...

SNIFF

NOTHIN'... JUST SMOKING A CIGARETTE AND THINKING ABOUT THINGS...

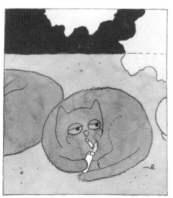

SOUNDS NICE...

...

YEAH... YEAH, I S'POSE SO.

YEAH... LIFE'S PRETTY GOOD RIGHT NOW.

...

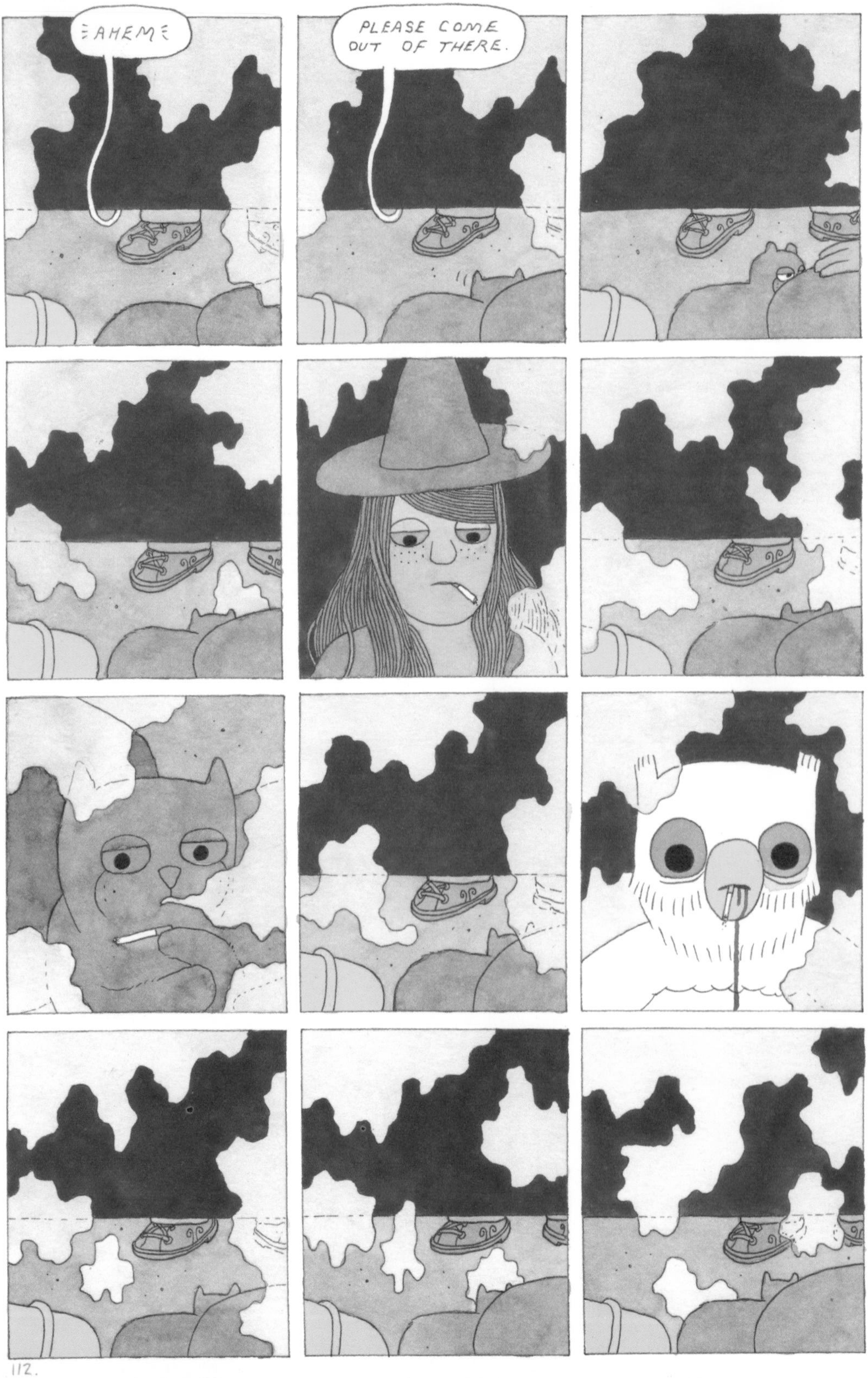
AHEM
PLEASE COME OUT OF THERE.

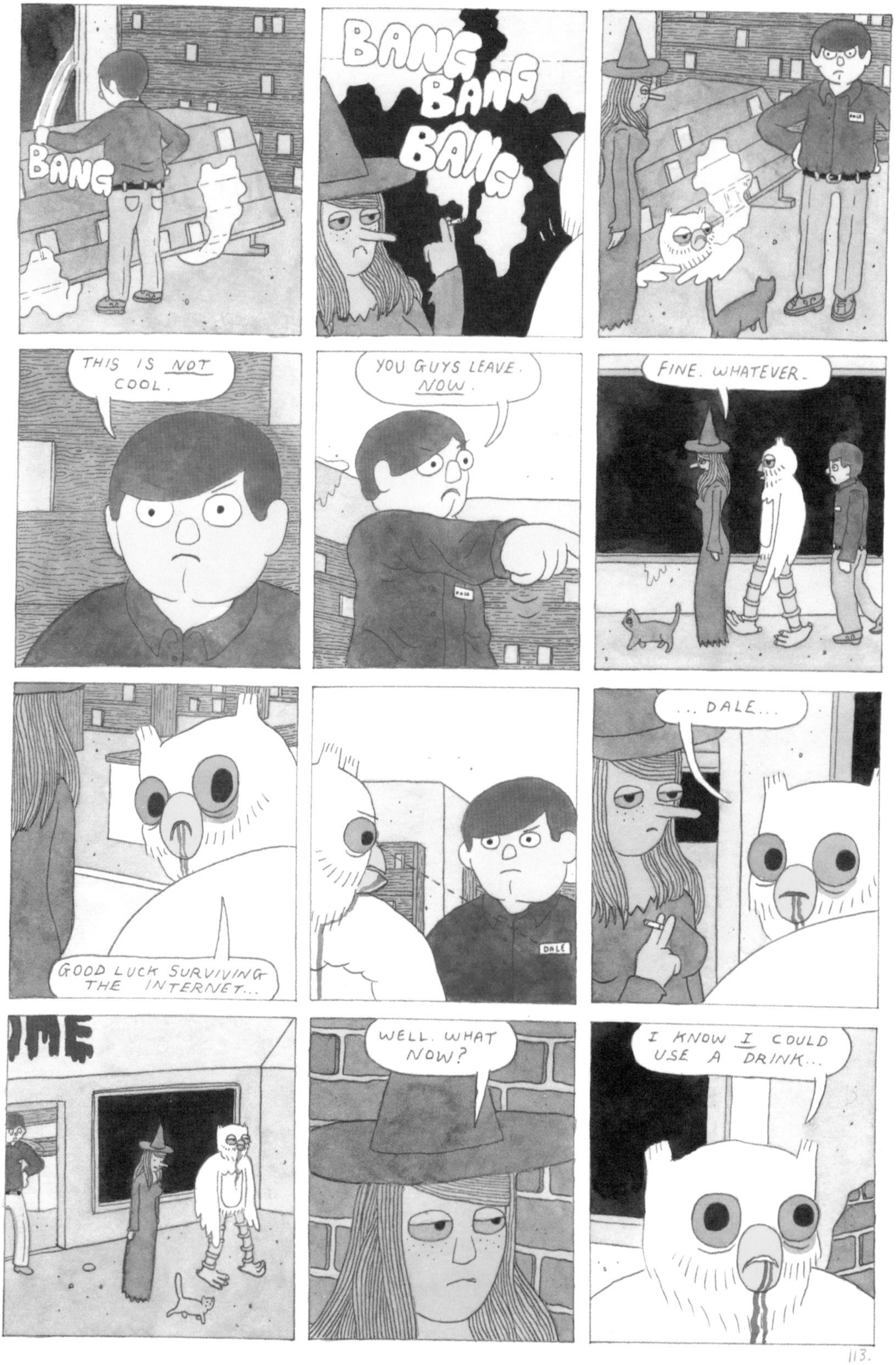
BANG
BANG
BANG
BANG
DALE
THIS IS NOT COOL.
YOU GUYS LEAVE. NOW.
DALE
FINE. WHATEVER.
GOOD LUCK SURVIVING THE INTERNET...
DALE
...DALE...
WELL. WHAT NOW?
I KNOW I COULD USE A DRINK...

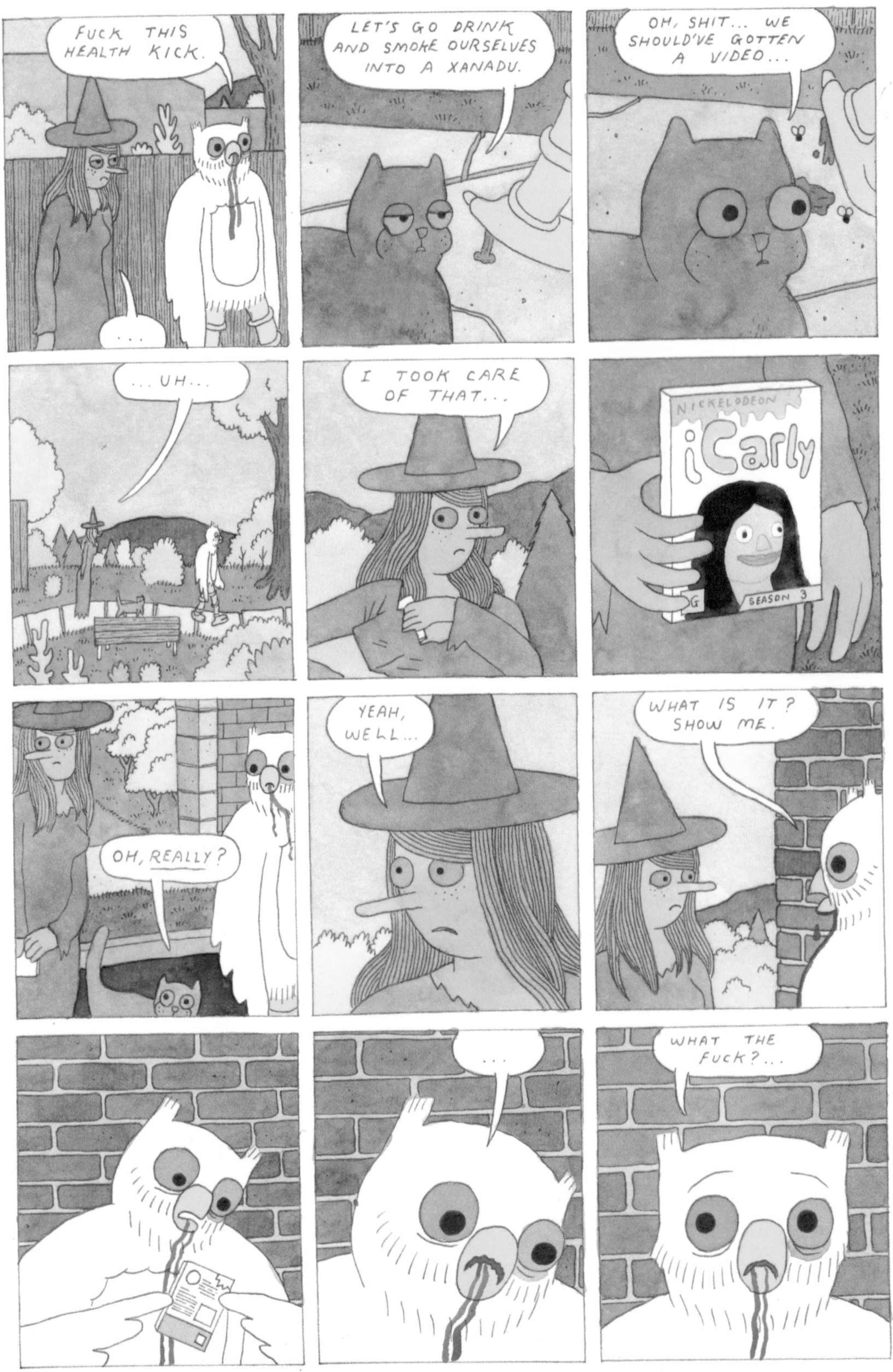
FUCK THIS HEALTH KICK.
...
LET'S GO DRINK AND SMOKE OURSELVES INTO A XANADU.
OH, SHIT... WE SHOULD'VE GOTTEN A VIDEO...
...UH...
I TOOK CARE OF THAT...
NICKELODEON
iCarly
G
SEASON 3
OH, REALLY?
YEAH, WELL...
WHAT IS IT? SHOW ME.
...
WHAT THE FUCK?...

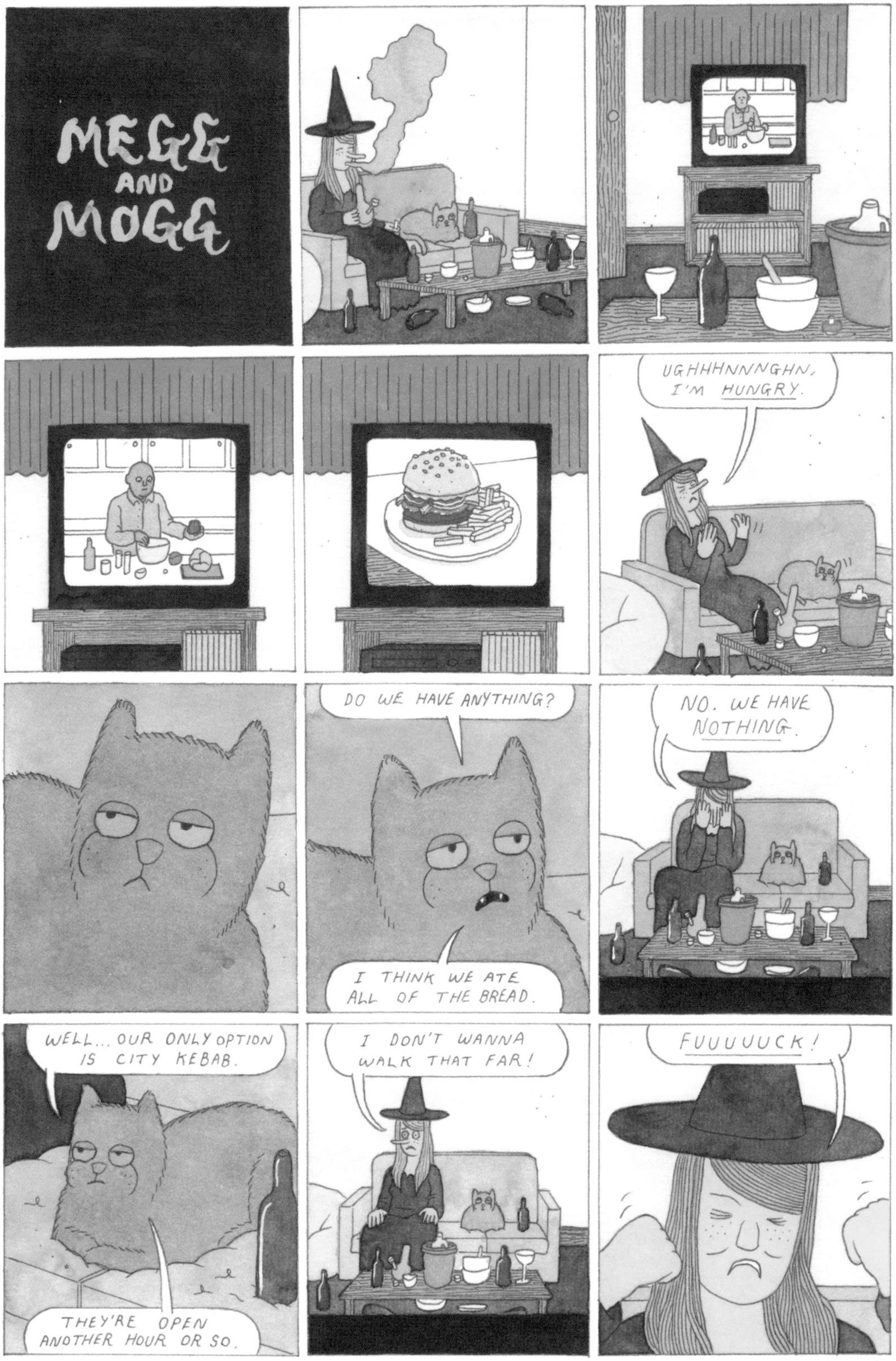
MEGG AND MOGG
UGHHHNNNGHN, I'M HUNGRY.
DO WE HAVE ANYTHING?
I THINK WE ATE ALL OF THE BREAD.
NO. WE HAVE NOTHING.
WELL... OUR ONLY OPTION IS CITY KEBAB.
THEY'RE OPEN ANOTHER HOUR OR SO.
I DON'T WANNA WALK THAT FAR!
FUUUUUCK!

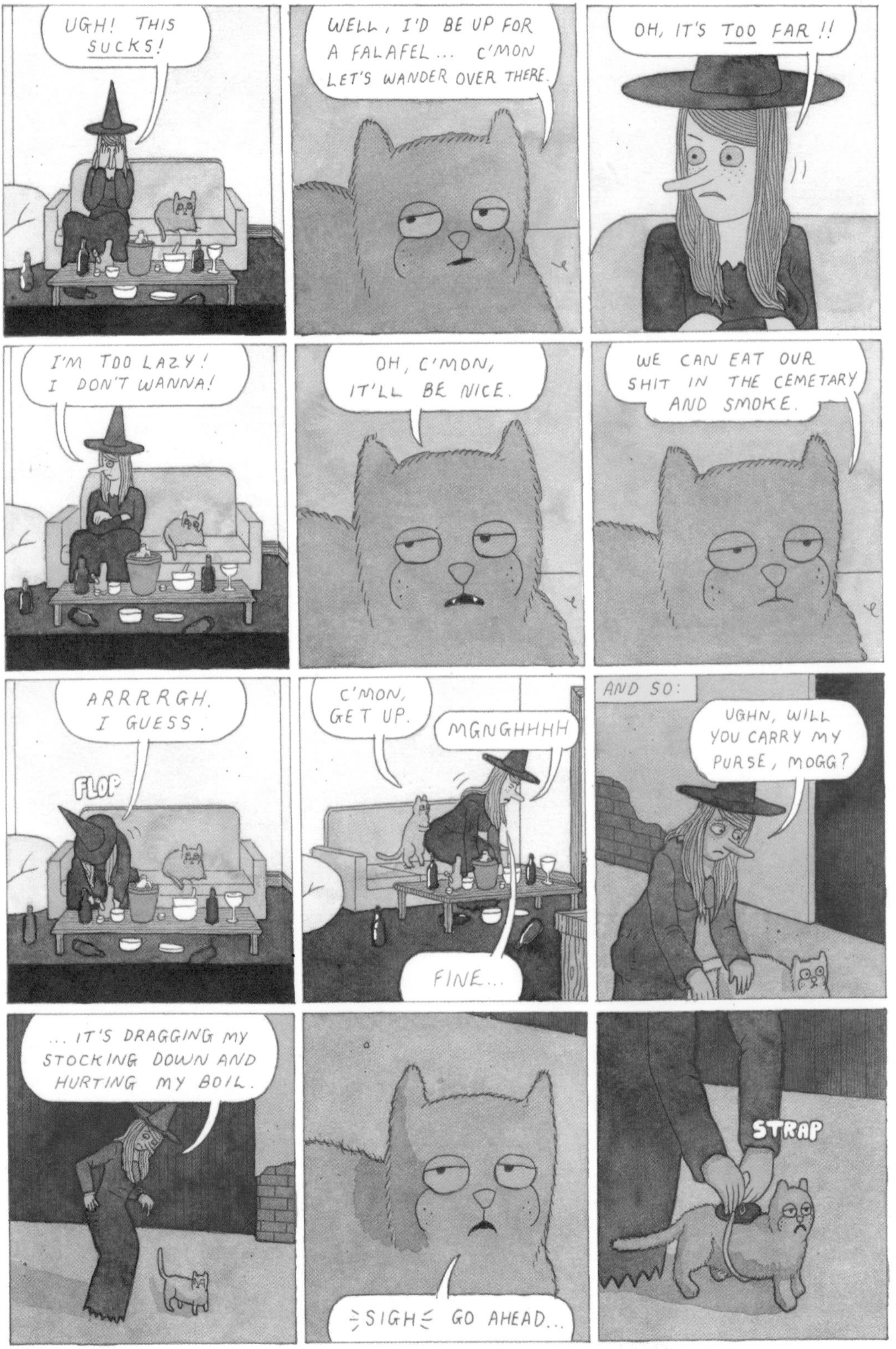
UGH! THIS SUCKS!
WELL, I'D BE UP FOR A FALAFEL... C'MON LET'S WANDER OVER THERE.
OH, IT'S TOO FAR!!
I'M TOO LAZY! I DON'T WANNA!
OH, C'MON, IT'LL BE NICE.
WE CAN EAT OUR SHIT IN THE CEMETARY AND SMOKE.
ARRRRGH. I GUESS.
FLOP
C'MON, GET UP.
MGNGHHHH
FINE...
AND SO:
UGHN, WILL YOU CARRY MY PURSE, MOGG?
... IT'S DRAGGING MY STOCKING DOWN AND HURTING MY BOIL.
SIGH GO AHEAD...
STRAP

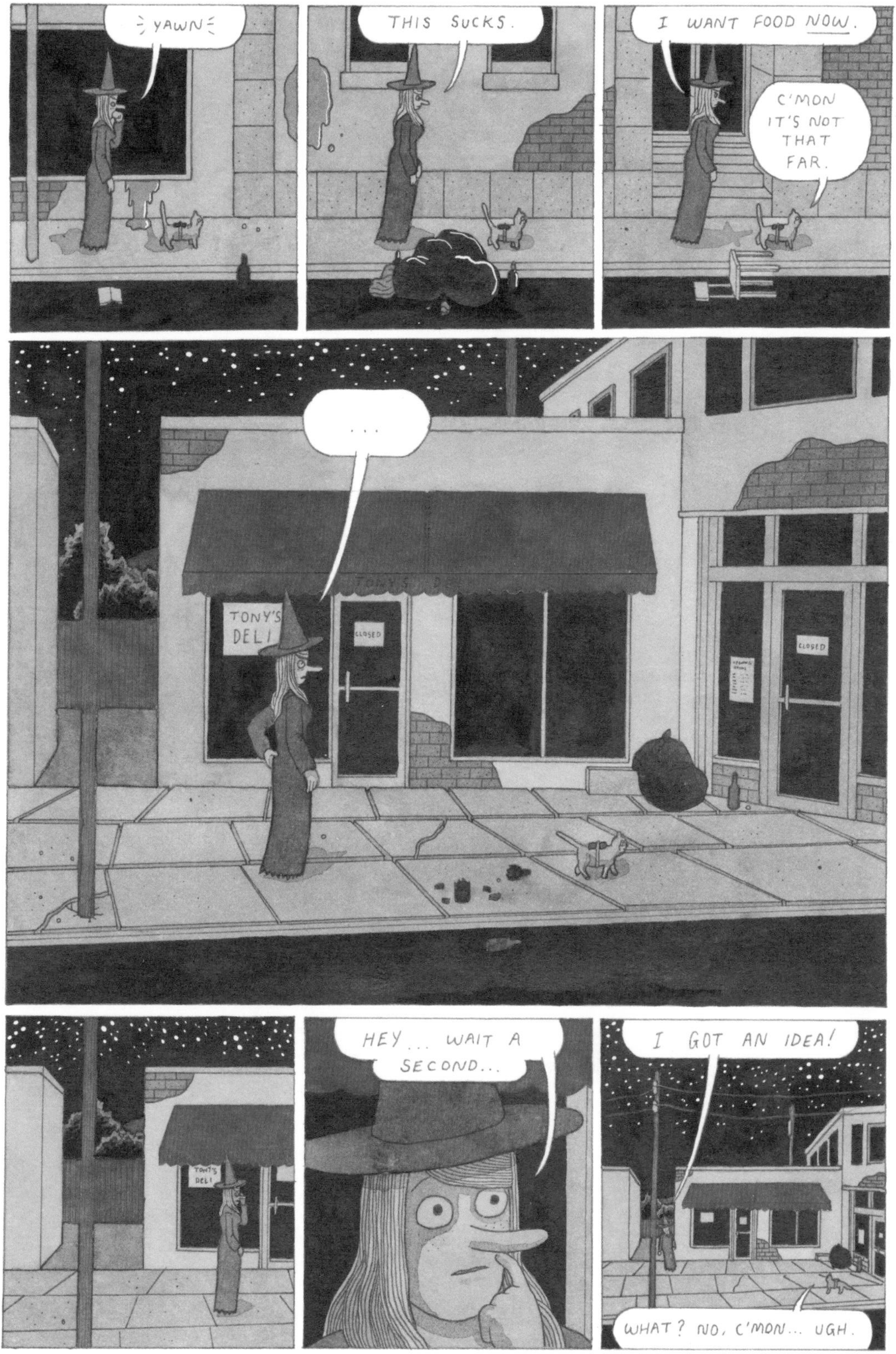
YAWN
THIS SUCKS.
I WANT FOOD NOW.
C'MON IT'S NOT THAT FAR.
TONY'S DELI
CLOSED
...
TONY'S DELI
CLOSED
HEY... WAIT A SECOND...
I GOT AN IDEA!
WHAT? NO, C'MON... UGH.

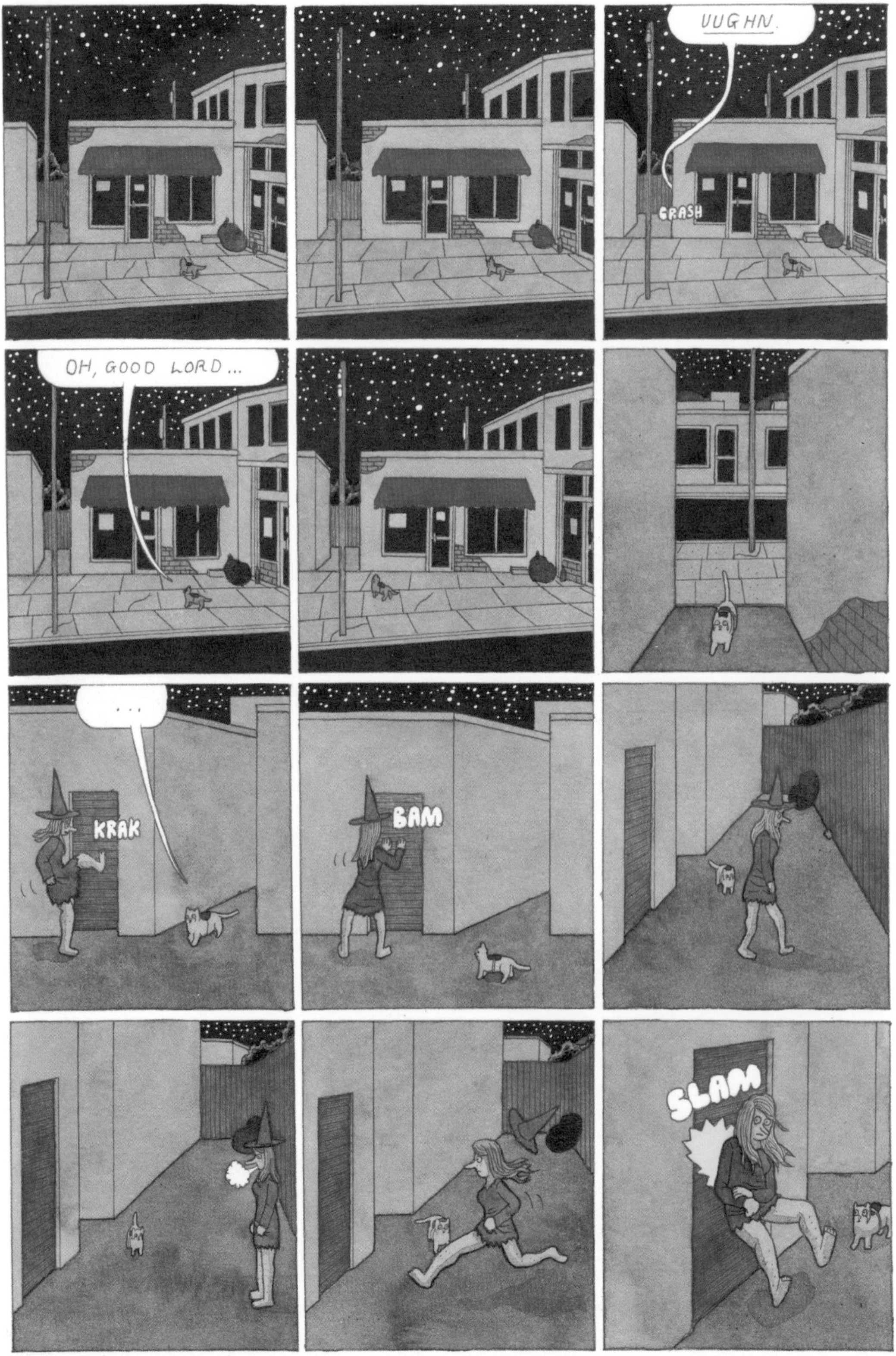
UUGHN.
CRASH
OH, GOOD LORD...
...
KRAK
BAM
SLAM

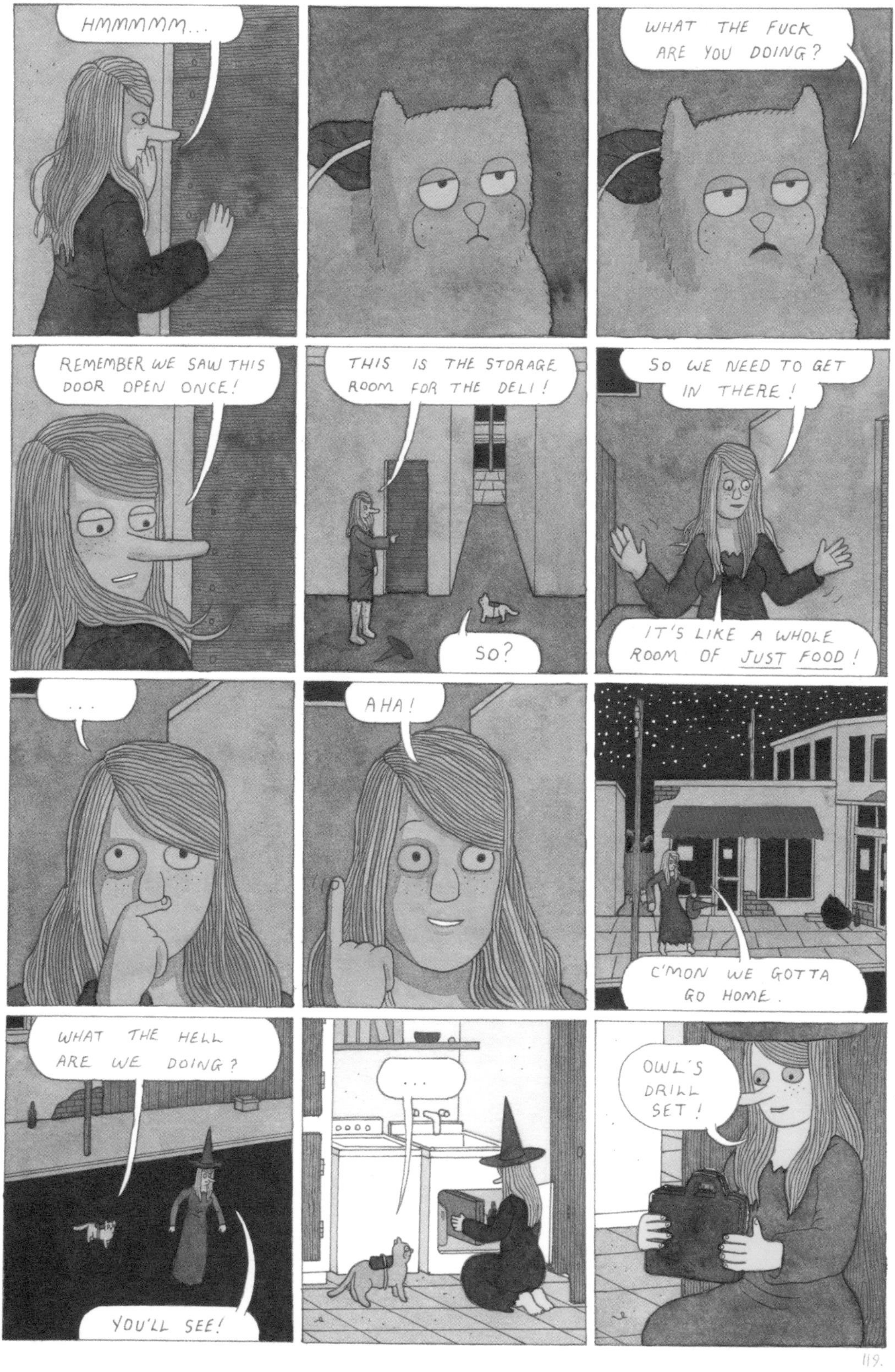
HMMMMM...
WHAT THE FUCK ARE YOU DOING?
REMEMBER WE SAW THIS DOOR OPEN ONCE!
THIS IS THE STORAGE ROOM FOR THE DELI!
SO?
SO WE NEED TO GET IN THERE!
IT'S LIKE A WHOLE ROOM OF JUST FOOD!
...
AHA!
C'MON WE GOTTA GO HOME.
WHAT THE HELL ARE WE DOING?
YOU'LL SEE!
...
OWL'S DRILL SET!

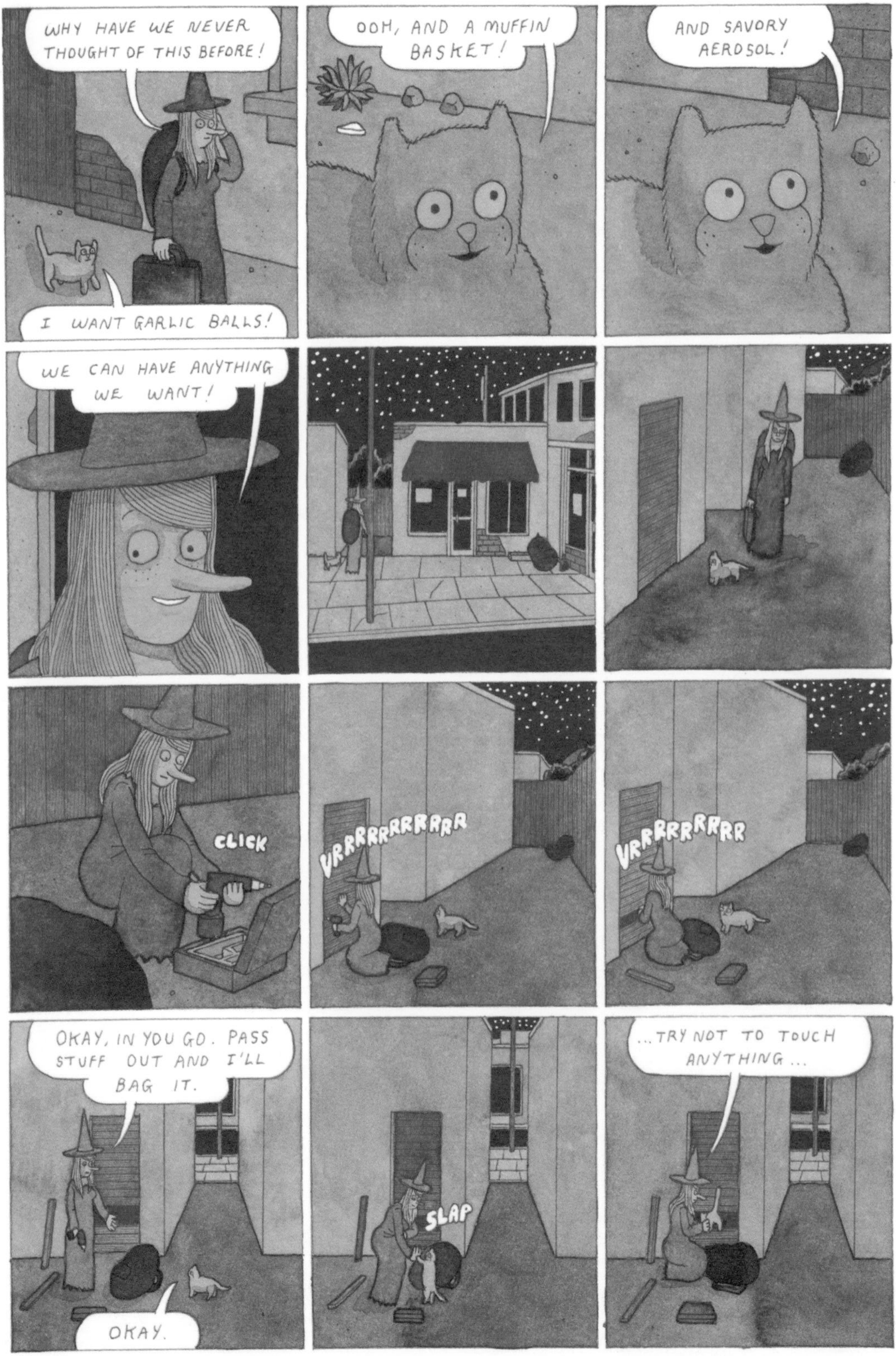
WHY HAVE WE NEVER THOUGHT OF THIS BEFORE!
I WANT GARLIC BALLS!
OOH, AND A MUFFIN BASKET!
AND SAVORY AEROSOL!
WE CAN HAVE ANYTHING WE WANT!
CLICK
VRRRRRRRRRRRR
VRRRRRRRRR
OKAY, IN YOU GO. PASS STUFF OUT AND I'LL BAG IT.
OKAY.
SLAP
...TRY NOT TO TOUCH ANYTHING...

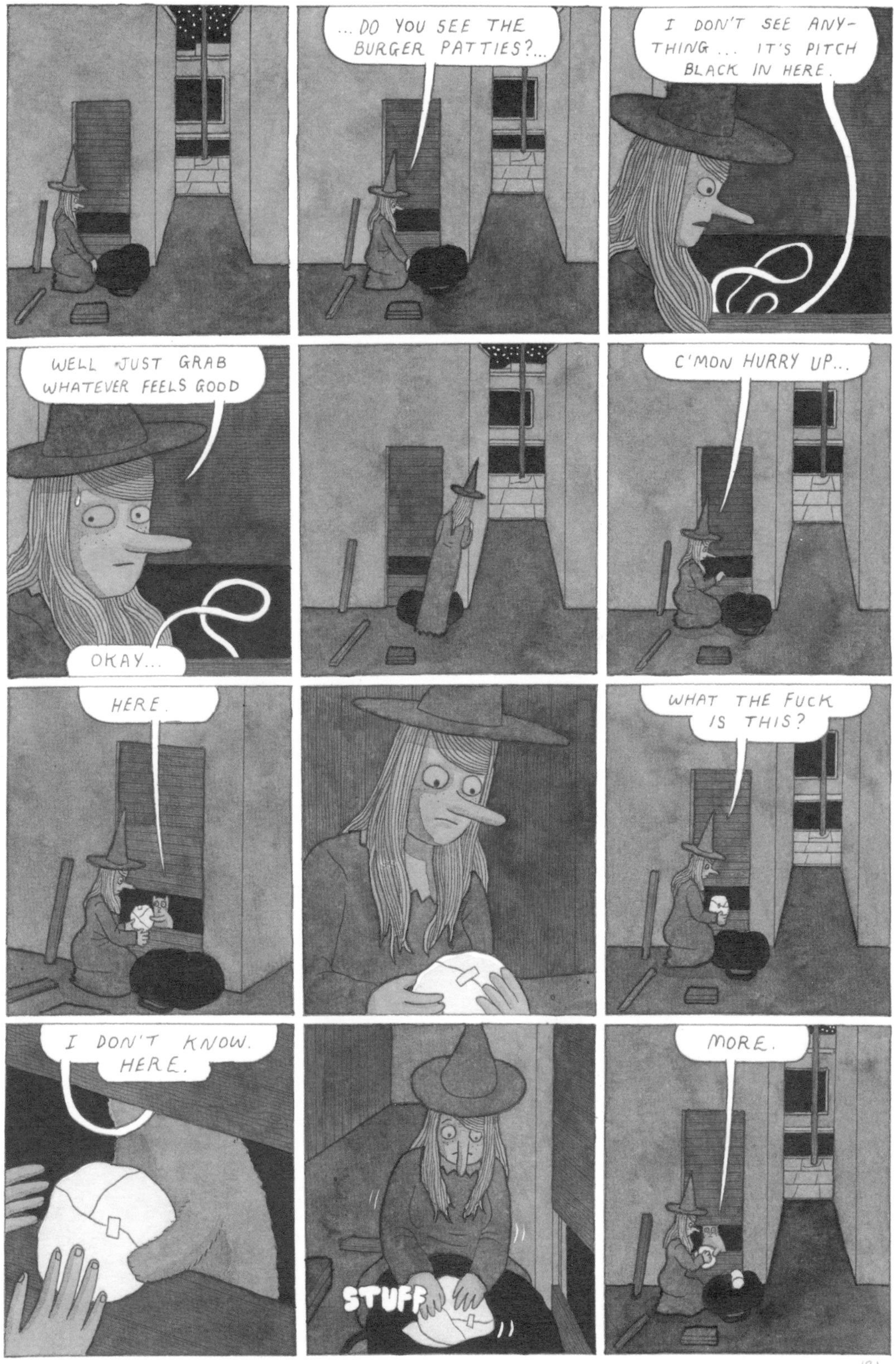
...DO YOU SEE THE BURGER PATTIES?...
I DON'T SEE ANY-THING... IT'S PITCH BLACK IN HERE.
WELL JUST GRAB WHATEVER FEELS GOOD
OKAY...
C'MON HURRY UP...
HERE.
WHAT THE FUCK IS THIS?
I DON'T KNOW. HERE.
STUFF
MORE.

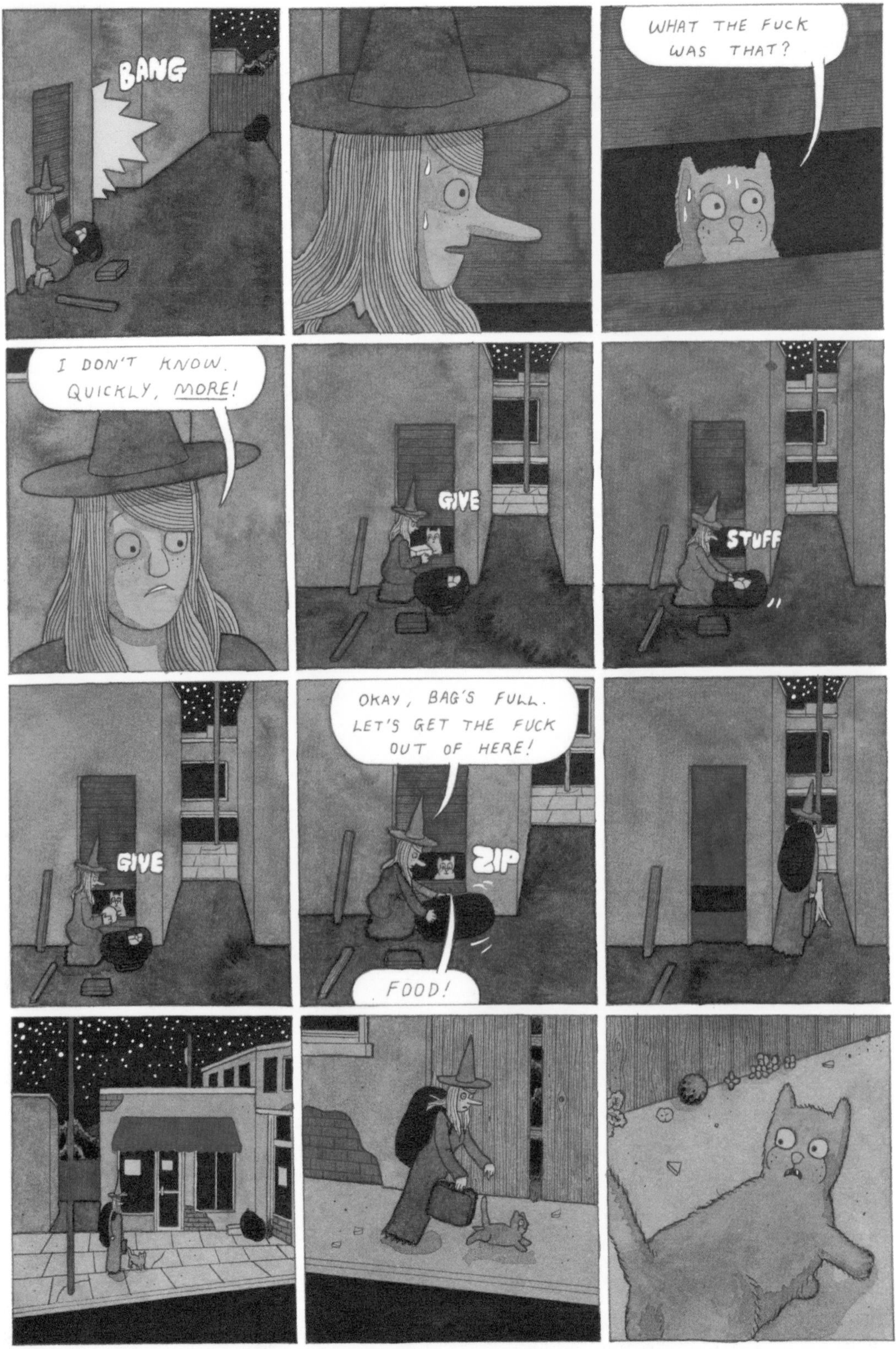

BANG
WHAT THE FUCK WAS THAT?
I DON'T KNOW. QUICKLY, MORE!
GIVE
STUFF
GIVE
OKAY, BAG'S FULL. LET'S GET THE FUCK OUT OF HERE!
ZIP
FOOD!

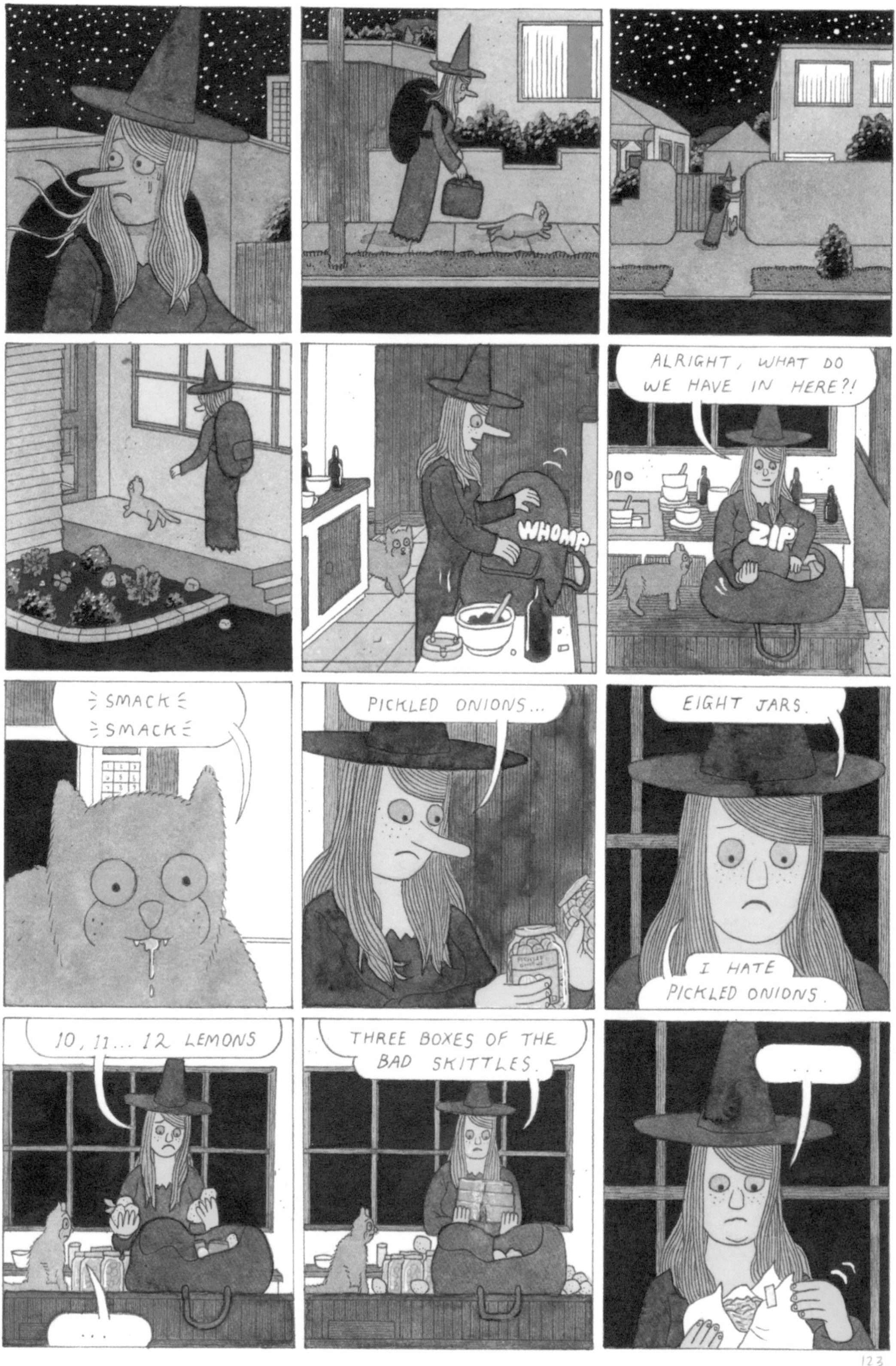
WHOMP
ALRIGHT, WHAT DO WE HAVE IN HERE?!
ZIP
SMACK SMACK
PICKLED ONIONS...
EIGHT JARS.
I HATE PICKLED ONIONS.
10, 11... 12 LEMONS
...
THREE BOXES OF THE BAD SKITTLES.
...

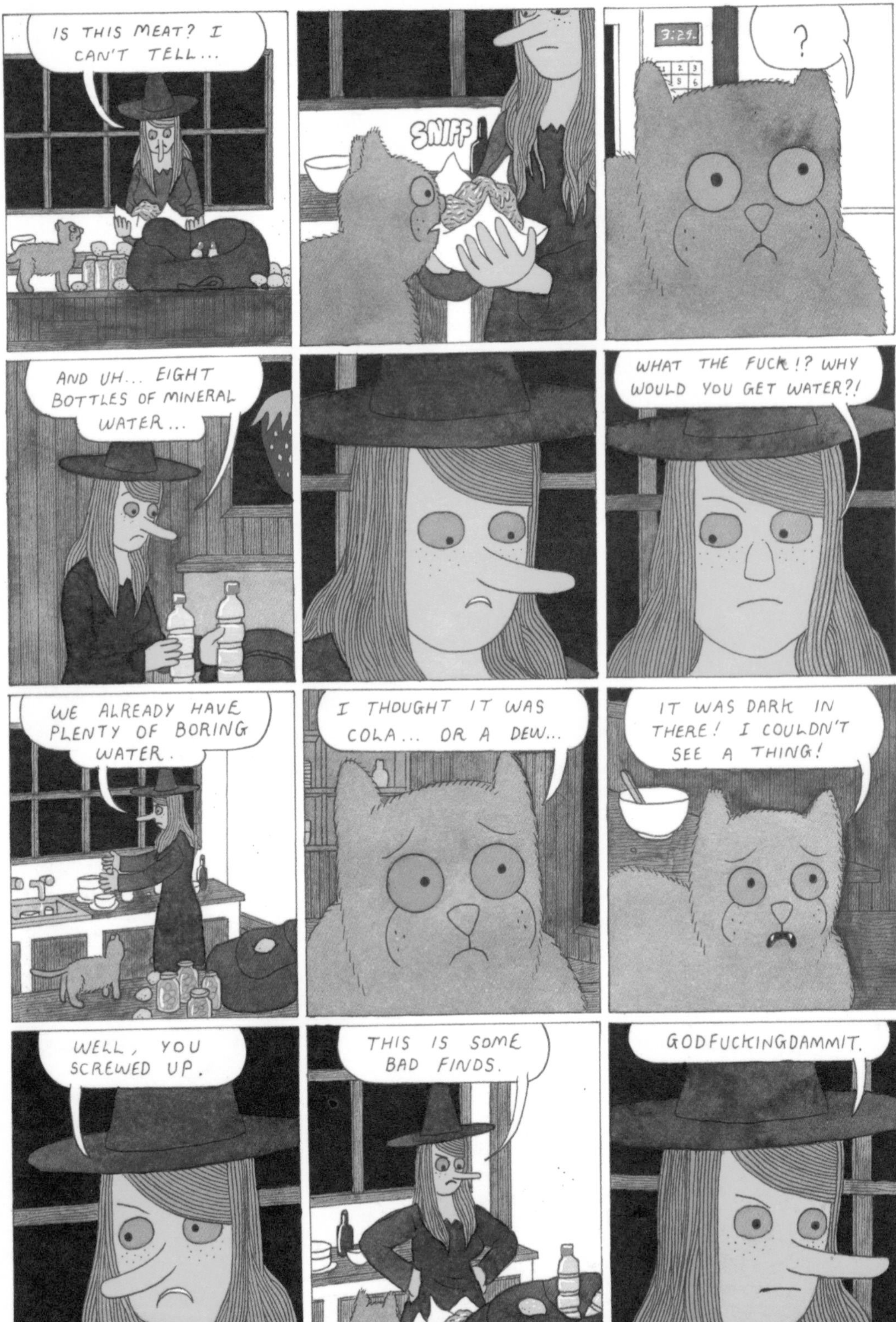
IS THIS MEAT? I CAN'T TELL...
SNIFF
?
AND UH... EIGHT BOTTLES OF MINERAL WATER...
WHAT THE FUCK!? WHY WOULD YOU GET WATER?!
WE ALREADY HAVE PLENTY OF BORING WATER.
I THOUGHT IT WAS COLA... OR A DEW...
IT WAS DARK IN THERE! I COULDN'T SEE A THING!
WELL, YOU SCREWED UP.
THIS IS SOME BAD FINDS.
GODFUCKINGDAMMIT.

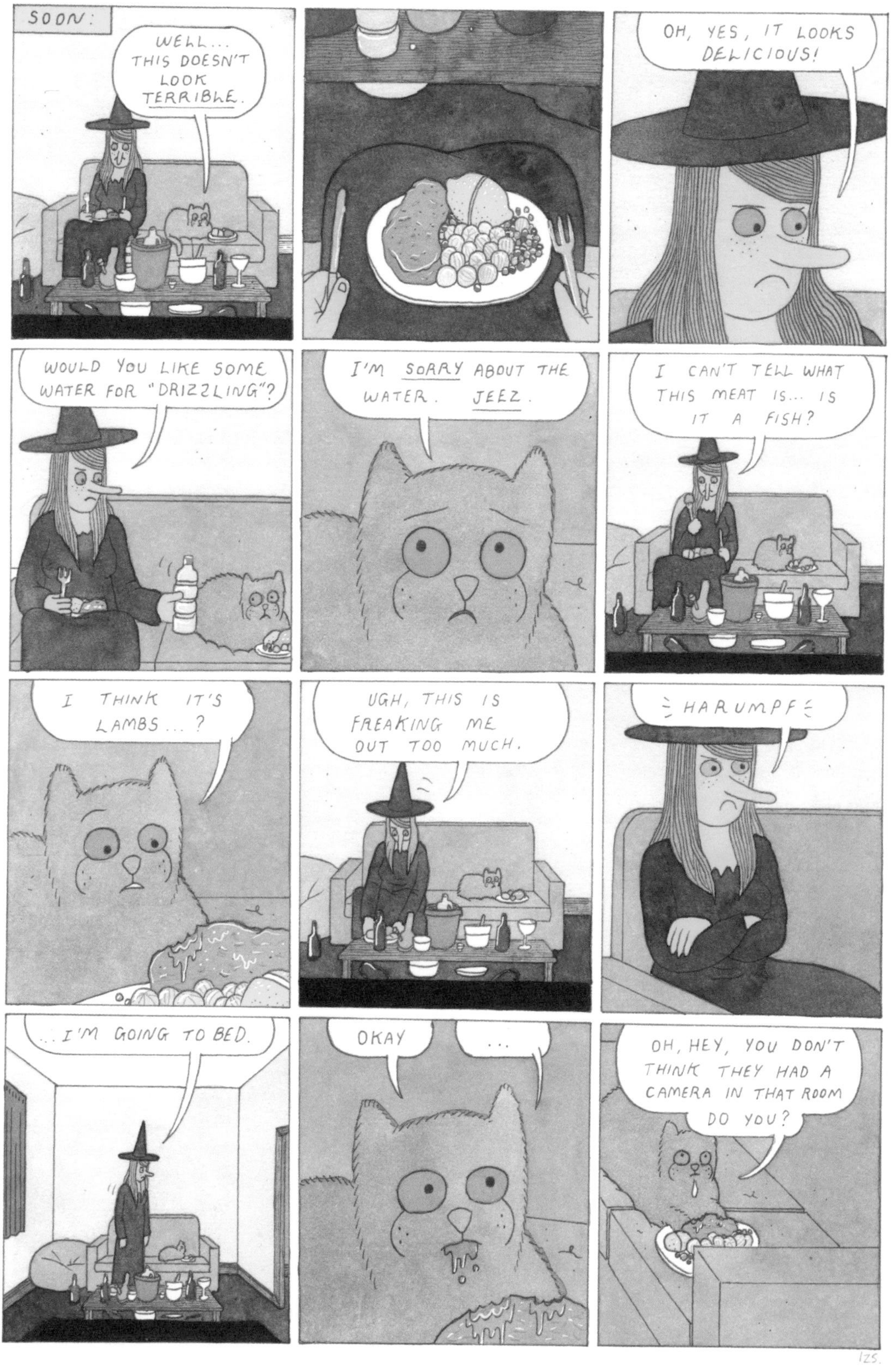
SOON:
WELL... THIS DOESN'T LOOK TERRIBLE.
OH, YES, IT LOOKS DELICIOUS!
WOULD YOU LIKE SOME WATER FOR "DRIZZLING"?
I'M SORRY ABOUT THE WATER. JEEZ.
I CAN'T TELL WHAT THIS MEAT IS... IS IT A FISH?
I THINK IT'S LAMBS...?
UGH, THIS IS FREAKING ME OUT TOO MUCH.
HARUMPF
...I'M GOING TO BED.
OKAY
...
OH, HEY, YOU DON'T THINK THEY HAD A CAMERA IN THAT ROOM DO YOU?

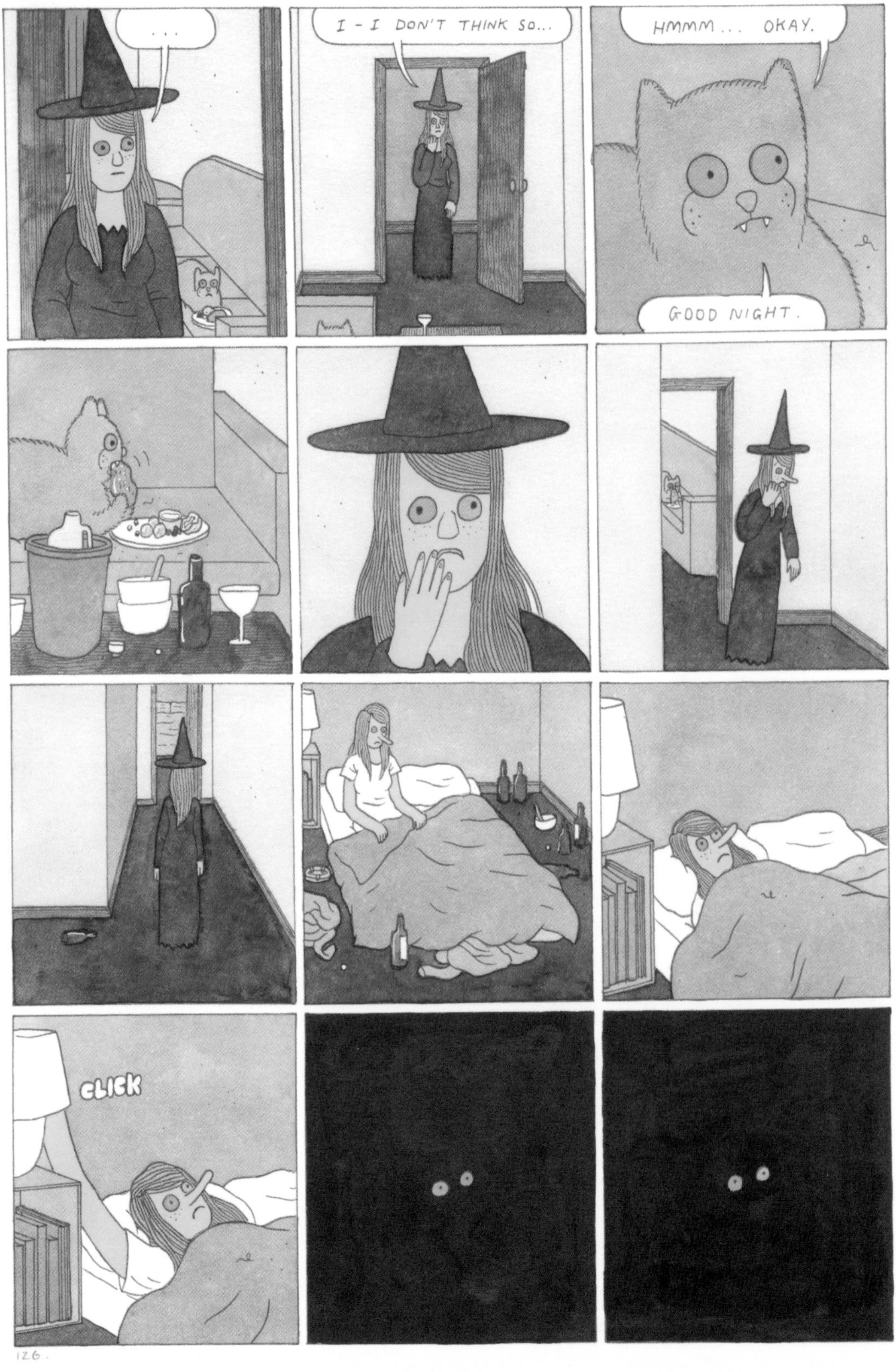
...
I - I DON'T THINK SO...
HMMM... OKAY.
GOOD NIGHT.
CLICK

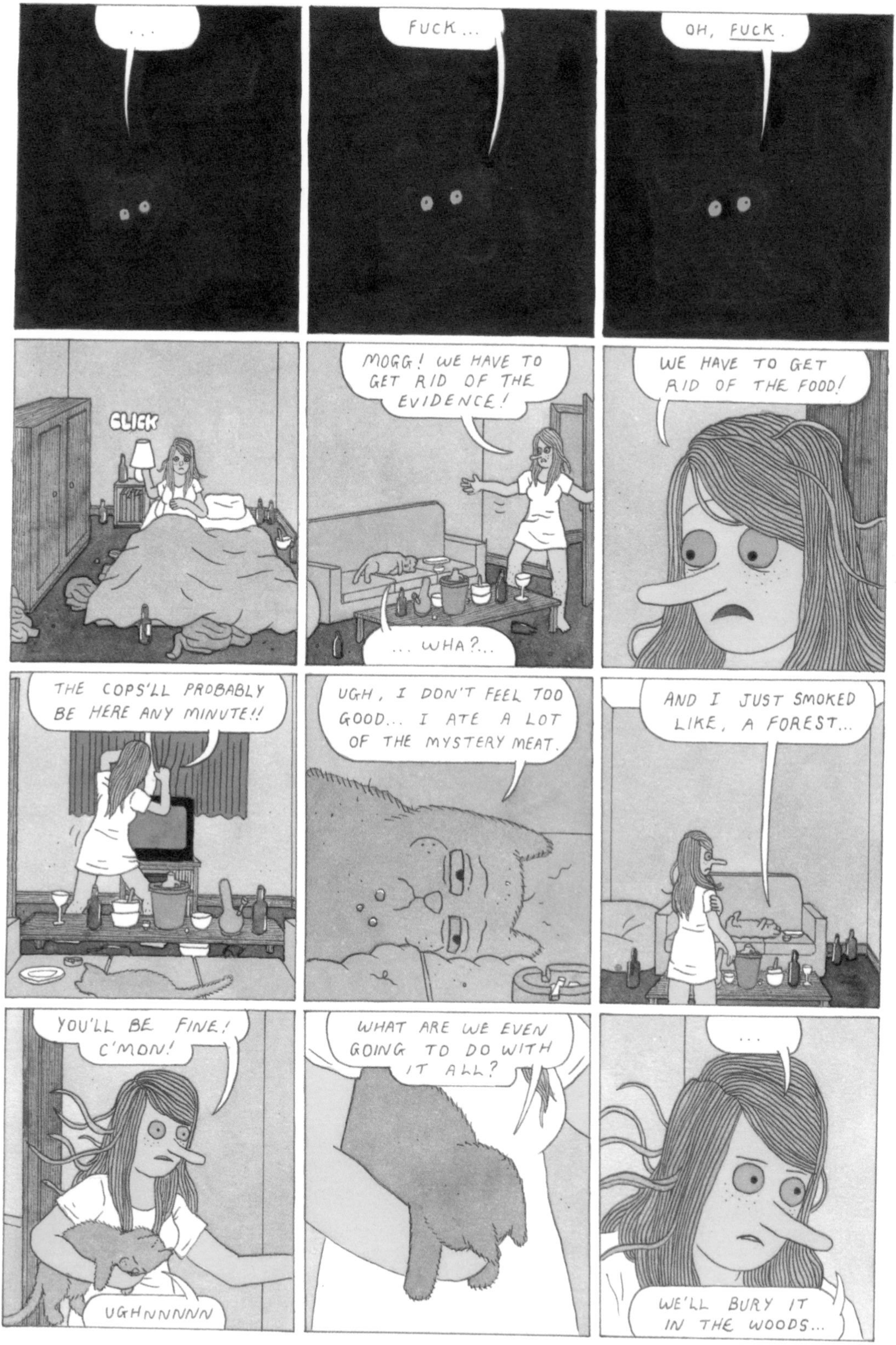
. . .
FUCK...
OH, FUCK.
CLICK
MOGG! WE HAVE TO GET RID OF THE EVIDENCE!
... WHA?...
WE HAVE TO GET RID OF THE FOOD!
THE COPS'LL PROBABLY BE HERE ANY MINUTE!!
UGH, I DON'T FEEL TOO GOOD... I ATE A LOT OF THE MYSTERY MEAT.
AND I JUST SMOKED LIKE, A FOREST...
YOU'LL BE FINE! C'MON!
UGHNNNNN
WHAT ARE WE EVEN GOING TO DO WITH IT ALL?
...
WE'LL BURY IT IN THE WOODS...

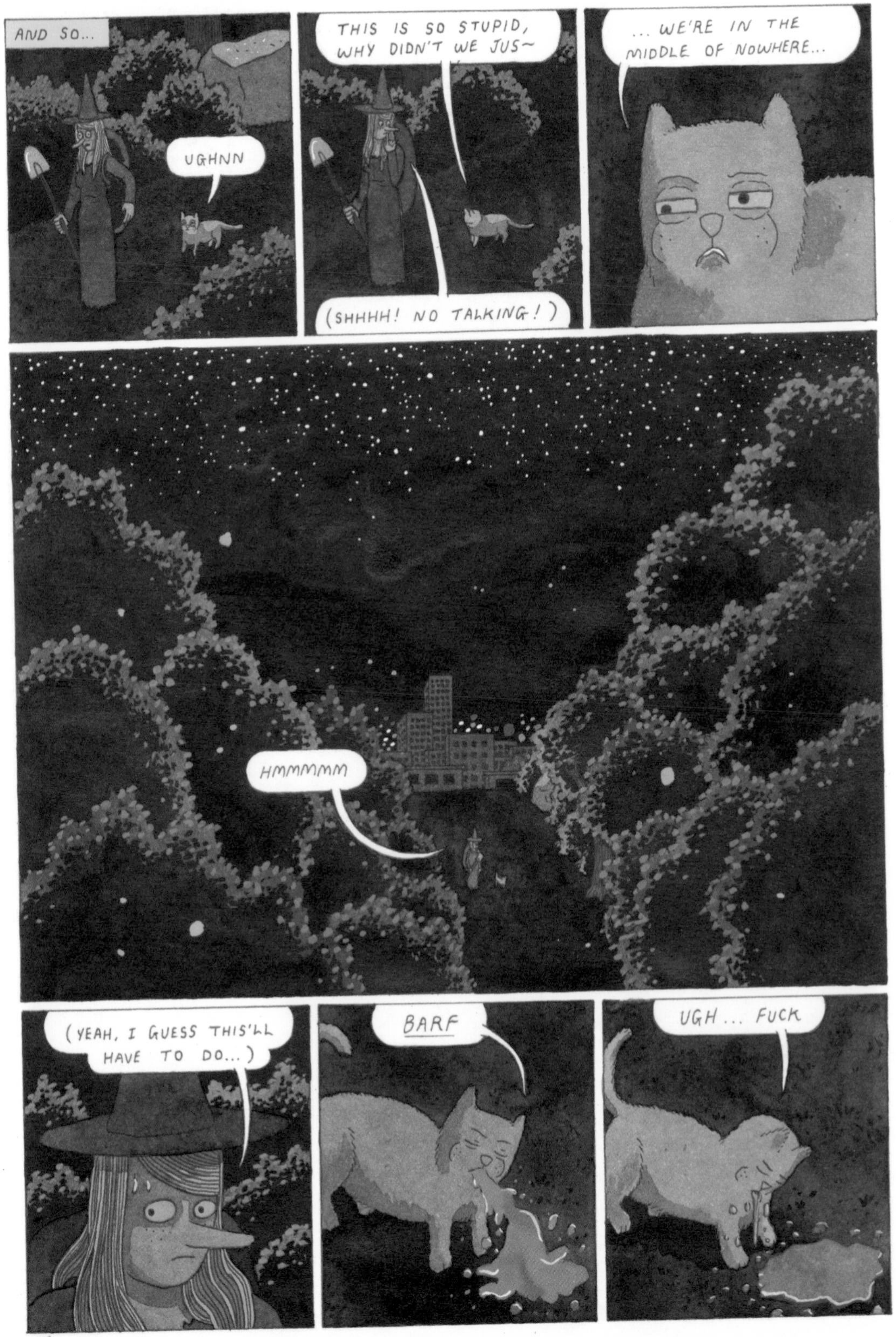
AND SO...
UGHNN
THIS IS SO STUPID, WHY DIDN'T WE JUS~
(SHHHH! NO TALKING!)
... WE'RE IN THE MIDDLE OF NOWHERE...
HMMMMM
(YEAH, I GUESS THIS'LL HAVE TO DO...)
BARF
UGH ... FUCK

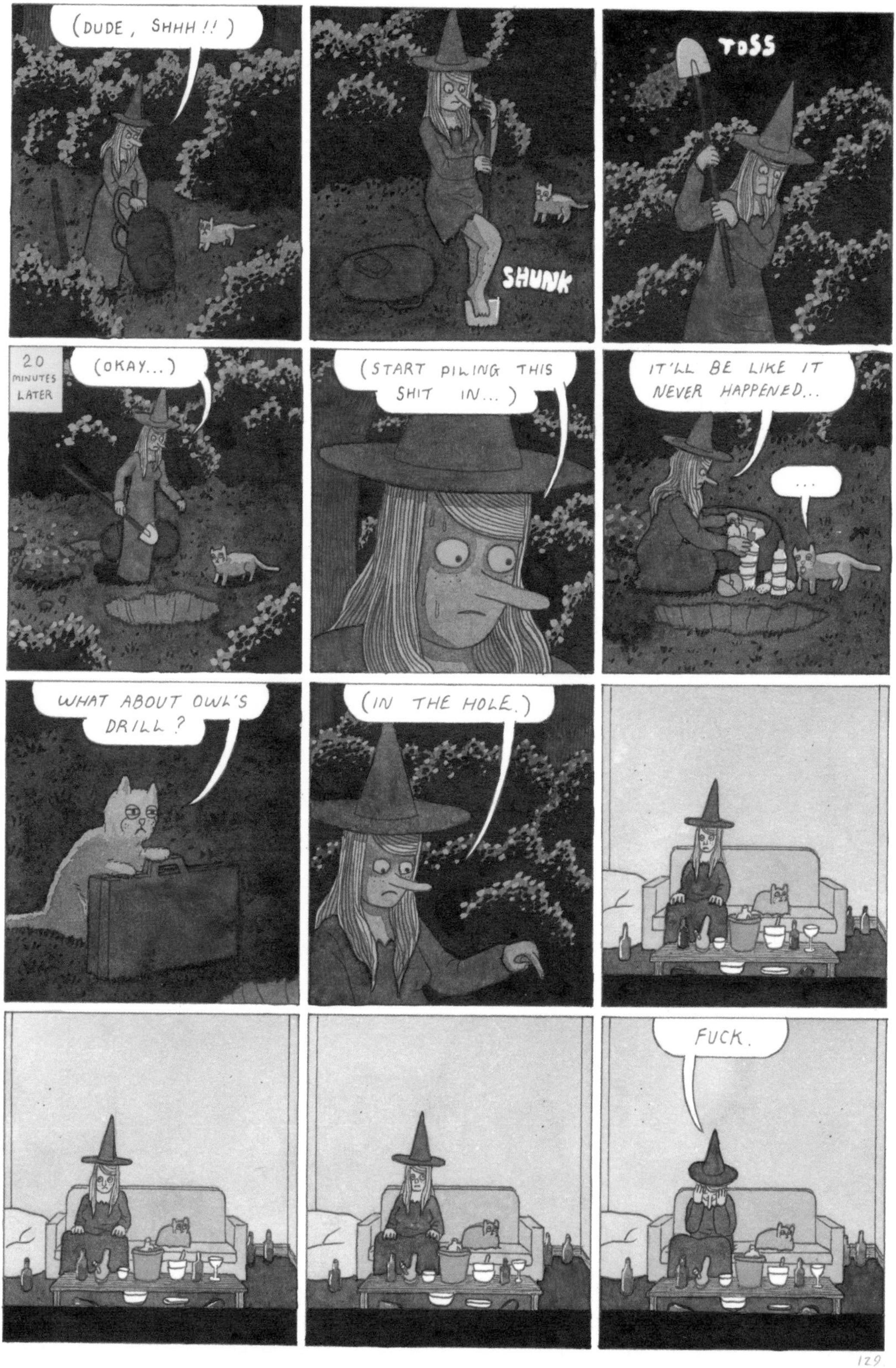
(DUDE, SHHH!!)
SHUNK
TOSS
20 MINUTES LATER
(OKAY...)
(START PILING THIS SHIT IN...)
IT'LL BE LIKE IT NEVER HAPPENED...
...
WHAT ABOUT OWL'S DRILL?
(IN THE HOLE.)
FUCK.

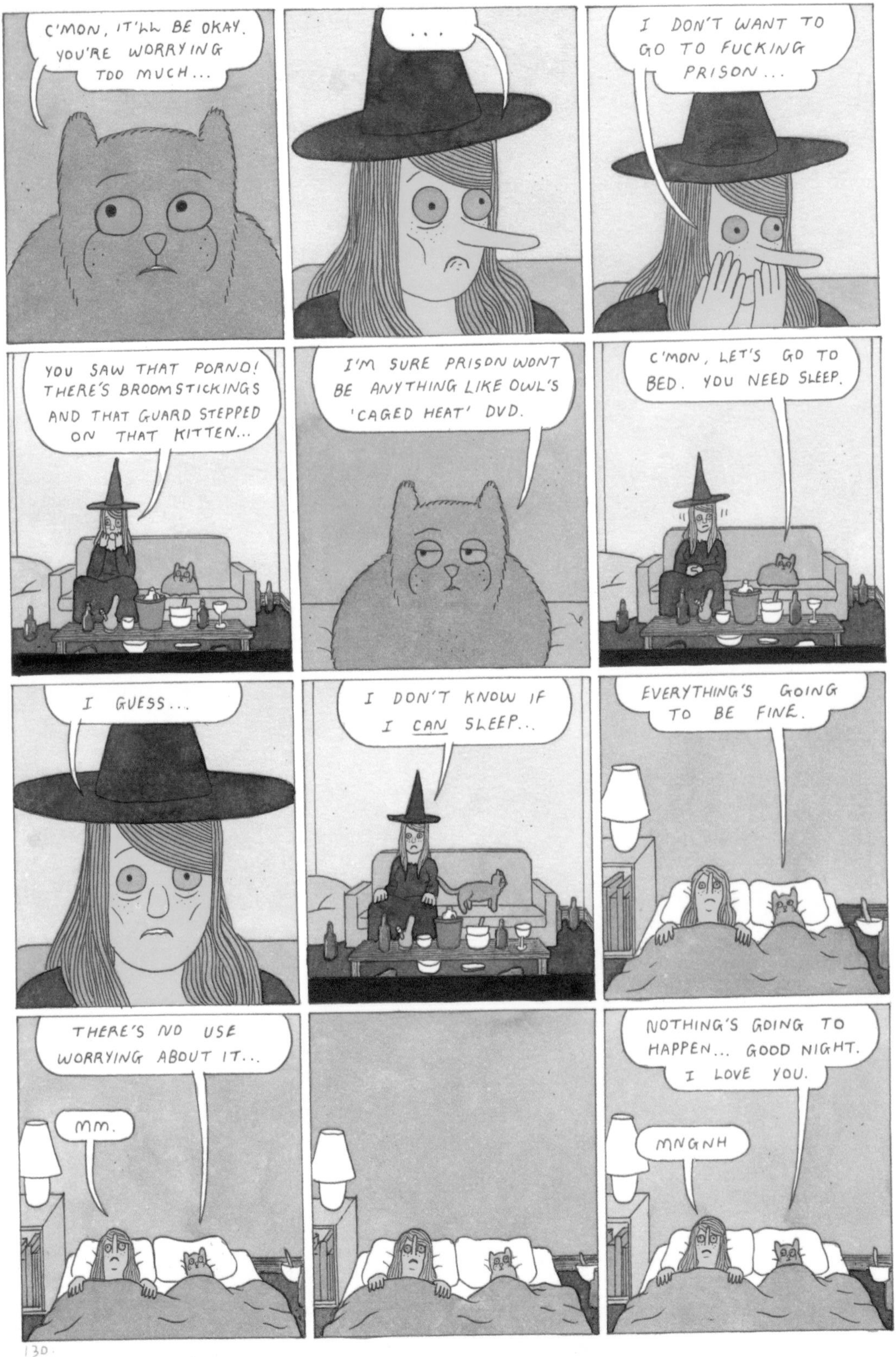
C'MON, IT'LL BE OKAY. YOU'RE WORRYING TOO MUCH...
...
I DON'T WANT TO GO TO FUCKING PRISON...
YOU SAW THAT PORNO! THERE'S BROOMSTICKINGS AND THAT GUARD STEPPED ON THAT KITTEN...
I'M SURE PRISON WONT BE ANYTHING LIKE OWL'S 'CAGED HEAT' DVD.
C'MON, LET'S GO TO BED. YOU NEED SLEEP.
I GUESS...
I DON'T KNOW IF I CAN SLEEP...
EVERYTHING'S GOING TO BE FINE.
THERE'S NO USE WORRYING ABOUT IT...
MM.
NOTHING'S GOING TO HAPPEN... GOOD NIGHT. I LOVE YOU.
MNGNH

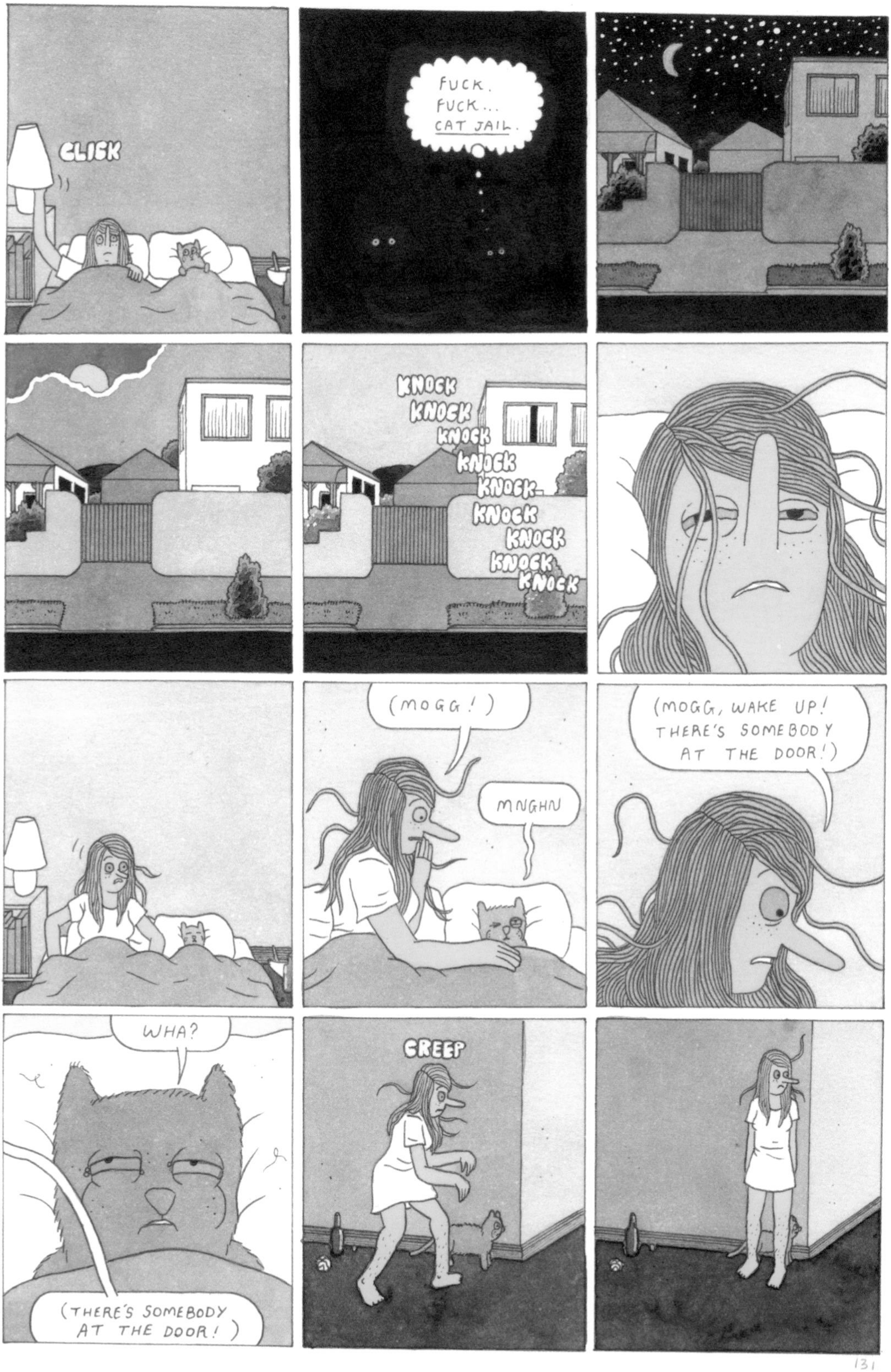
CLICK
FUCK.
FUCK...
CAT JAIL.
KNOCK
KNOCK
KNOCK
KNOCK
KNOCK
KNOCK
KNOCK
KNOCK
KNOCK
(MOGG!)
MNGHN
(MOGG, WAKE UP! THERE'S SOMEBODY AT THE DOOR!)
WHA?
(THERE'S SOMEBODY AT THE DOOR!)
CREEP

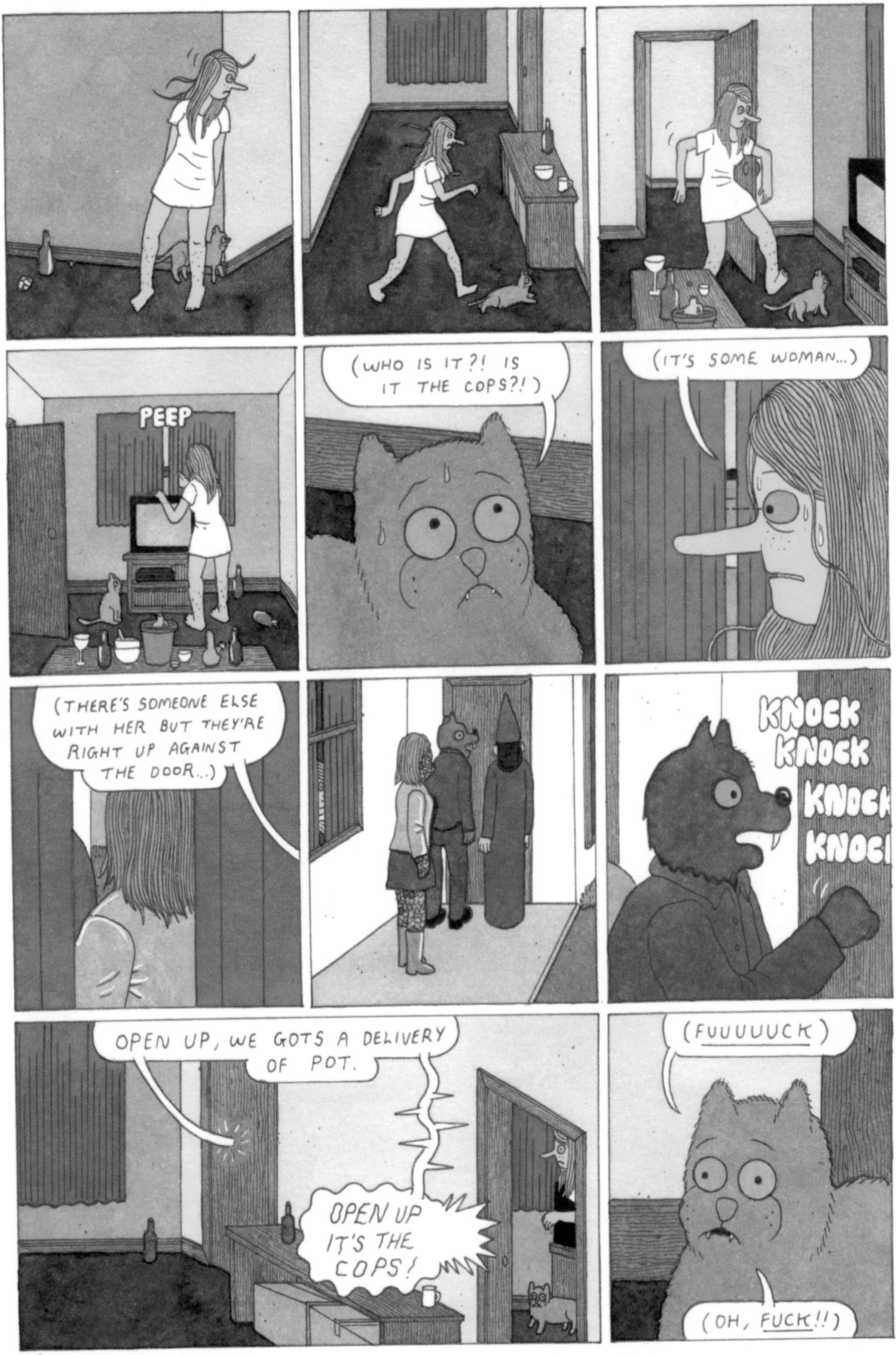
PEEP
(WHO IS IT?! IS IT THE COPS?!)
(IT'S SOME WOMAN...)
(THERE'S SOMEONE ELSE WITH HER BUT THEY'RE RIGHT UP AGAINST THE DOOR...)
KNOCK KNOCK KNOCK KNOCK
OPEN UP, WE GOTS A DELIVERY OF POT.
OPEN UP IT'S THE COPS!
(FUUUUUCK)
(OH, FUCK!!)

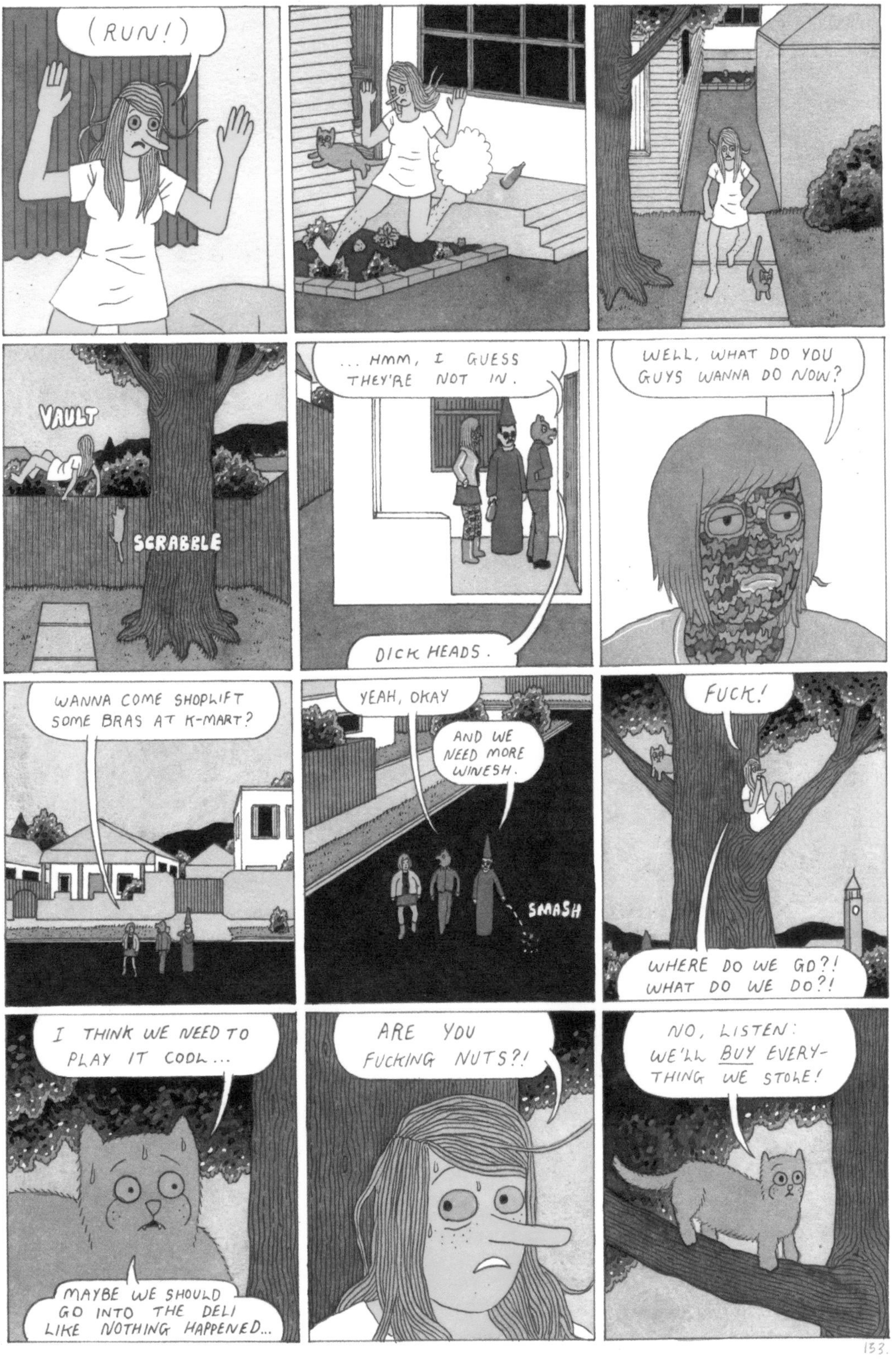
(RUN!)
VAULT
SCRABBLE
...HMM, I GUESS THEY'RE NOT IN.
DICK HEADS.
WELL, WHAT DO YOU GUYS WANNA DO NOW?
WANNA COME SHOPLIFT SOME BRAS AT K-MART?
YEAH, OKAY
AND WE NEED MORE WINESH.
SMASH
FUCK!
WHERE DO WE GO?! WHAT DO WE DO?!
I THINK WE NEED TO PLAY IT COOL...
MAYBE WE SHOULD GO INTO THE DELI LIKE NOTHING HAPPENED...
ARE YOU FUCKING NUTS?!
NO, LISTEN: WE'LL BUY EVERYTHING WE STOLE!

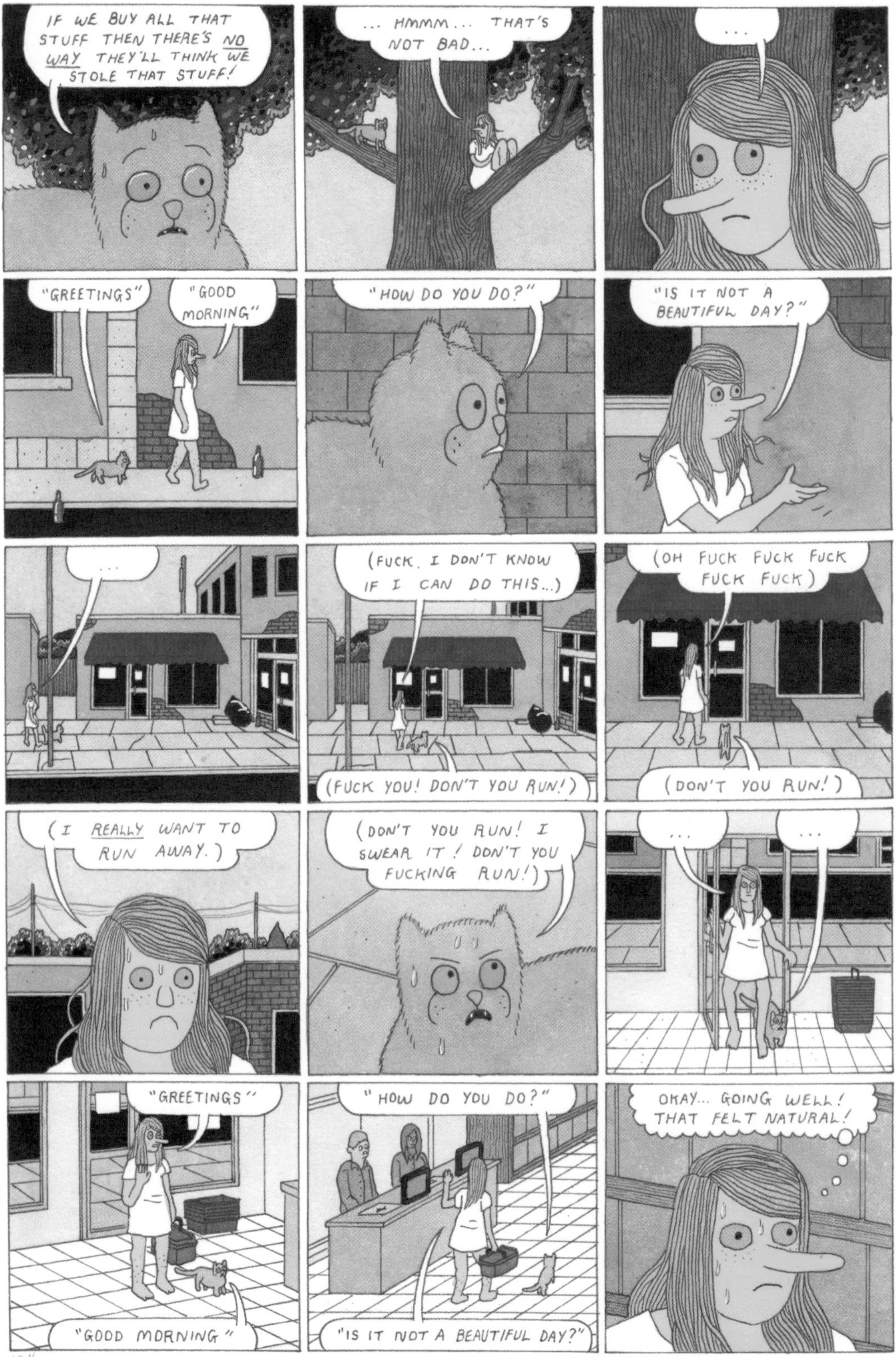
IF WE BUY ALL THAT STUFF THEN THERE'S NO WAY THEY'LL THINK WE STOLE THAT STUFF!
... HMMM... THAT'S NOT BAD...
...
"GREETINGS"
"GOOD MORNING"
"HOW DO YOU DO?"
"IS IT NOT A BEAUTIFUL DAY?"
...
(FUCK. I DON'T KNOW IF I CAN DO THIS...)
(FUCK YOU! DON'T YOU RUN!)
(OH FUCK FUCK FUCK FUCK FUCK)
(DON'T YOU RUN!)
(I REALLY WANT TO RUN AWAY.)
(DON'T YOU RUN! I SWEAR IT! DON'T YOU FUCKING RUN!)
...
...
"GREETINGS"
"GOOD MORNING"
"HOW DO YOU DO?"
"IS IT NOT A BEAUTIFUL DAY?"
OKAY... GOING WELL! THAT FELT NATURAL!

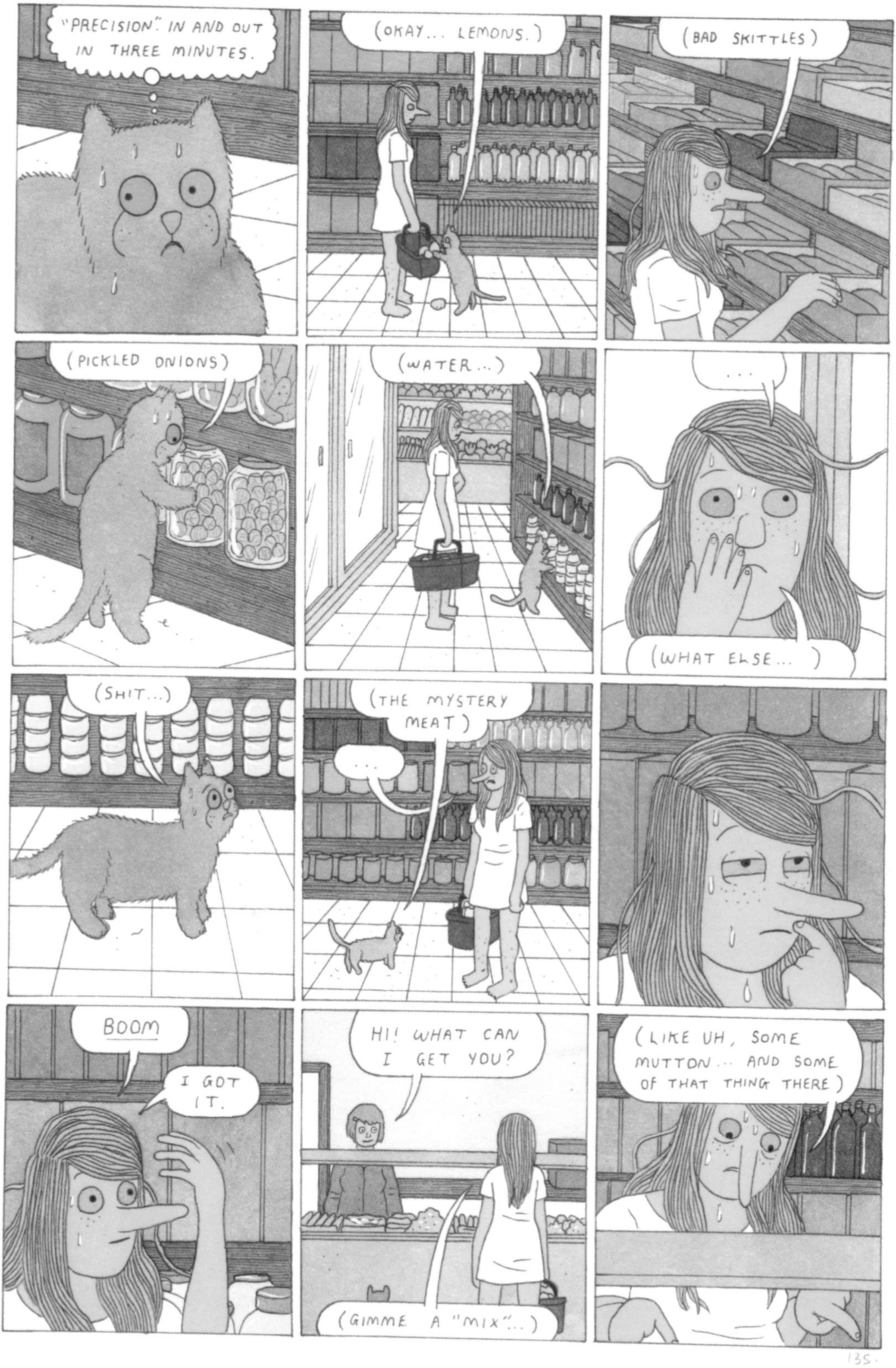
"PRECISION". IN AND OUT IN THREE MINUTES.
(OKAY... LEMONS.)
(BAD SKITTLES)
(PICKLED ONIONS)
(WATER...)
...
(WHAT ELSE...)
(SHIT...)
(THE MYSTERY MEAT)
...
BOOM
I GOT IT.
HI! WHAT CAN I GET YOU?
(GIMME A "MIX"...)
(LIKE UH, SOME MUTTON... AND SOME OF THAT THING THERE)

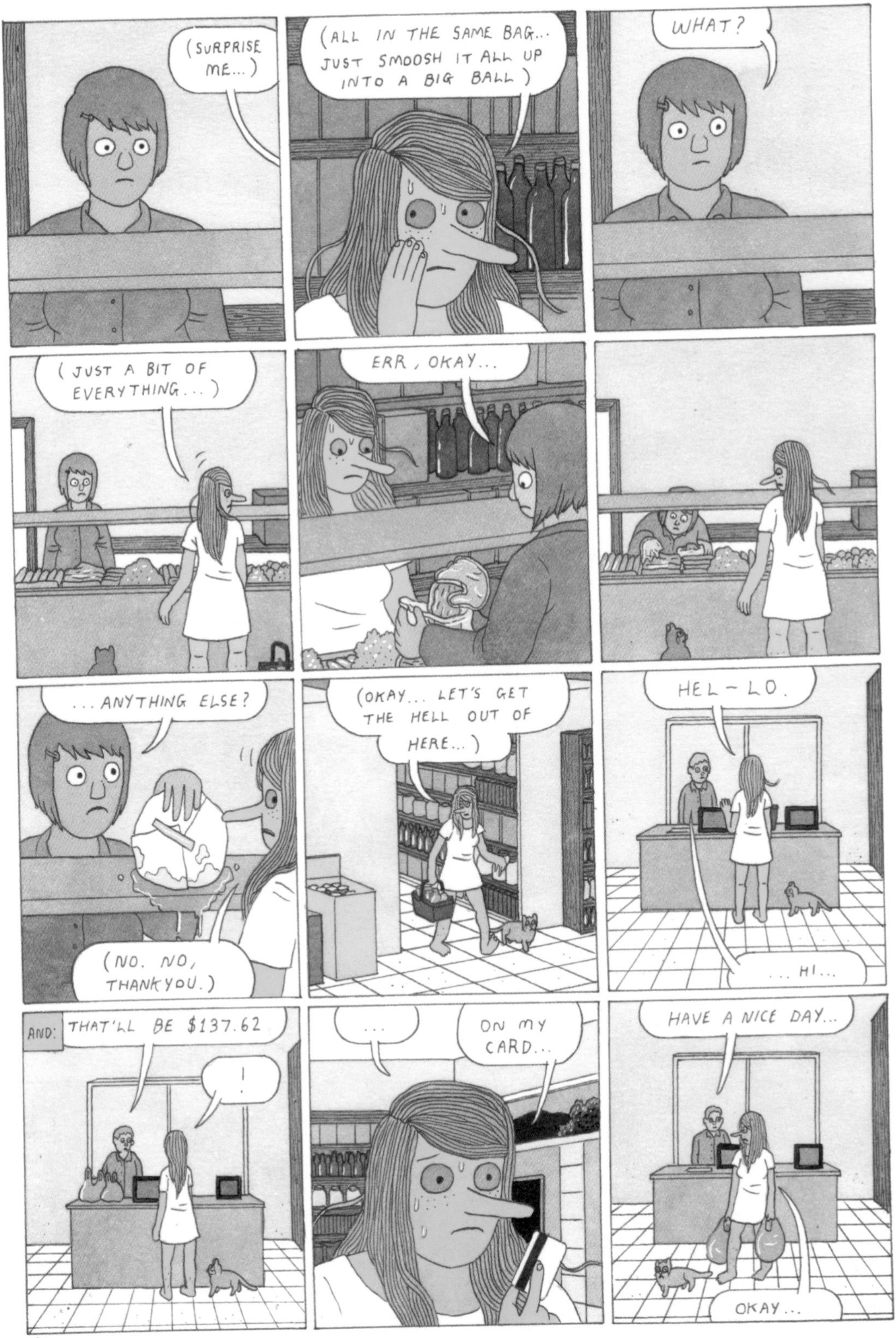
(SURPRISE ME...)
(ALL IN THE SAME BAG... JUST SMOOSH IT ALL UP INTO A BIG BALL)
WHAT?
(JUST A BIT OF EVERYTHING...)
ERR, OKAY...
...ANYTHING ELSE?
(NO. NO, THANKYOU.)
(OKAY... LET'S GET THE HELL OUT OF HERE...)
HEL-LO.
...HI...
AND: THAT'LL BE $137.62
!
...
ON MY CARD...
HAVE A NICE DAY...
OKAY...

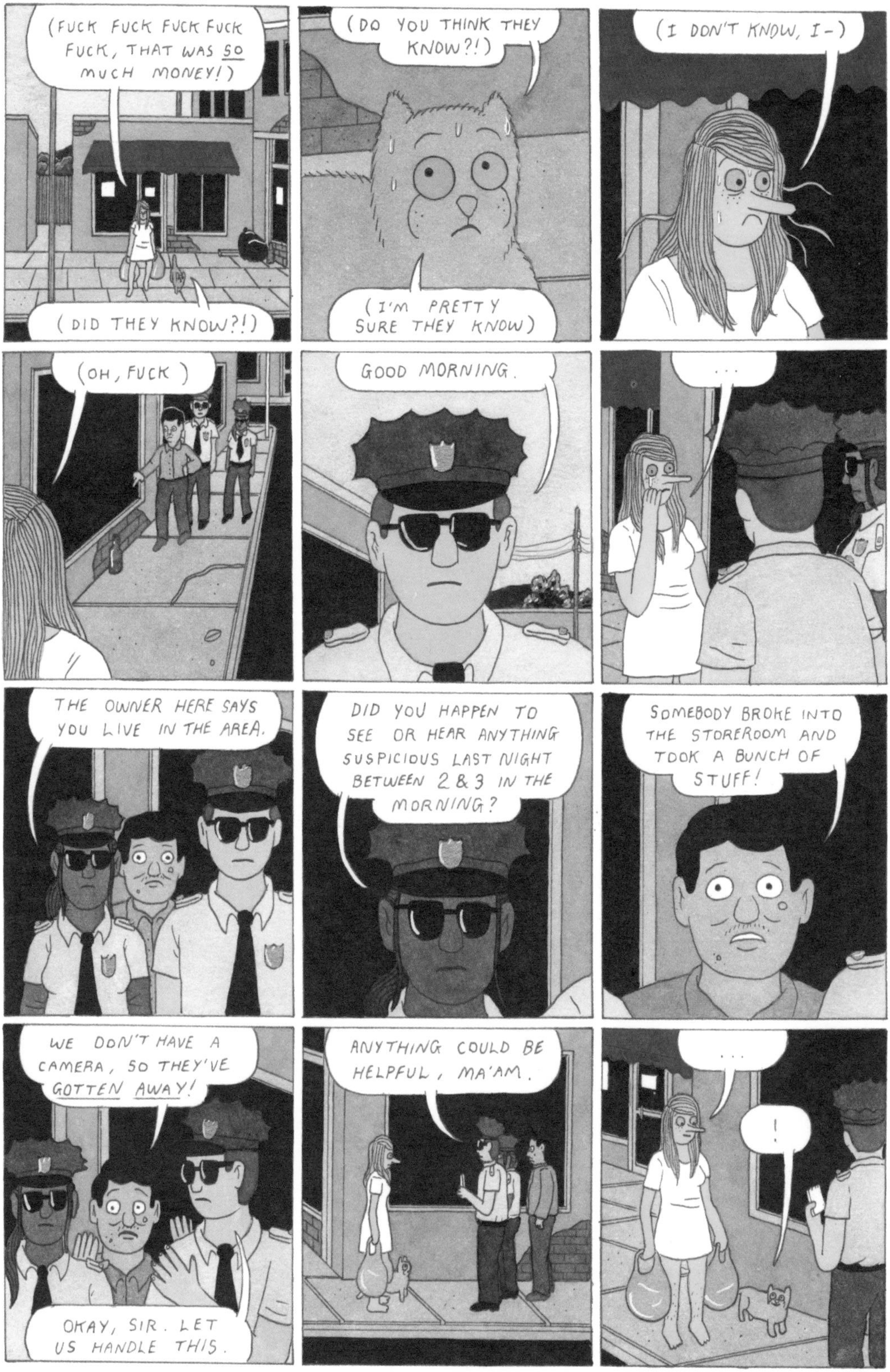
(FUCK FUCK FUCK FUCK FUCK, THAT WAS SO MUCH MONEY!)
(DID THEY KNOW?!)
(DO YOU THINK THEY KNOW?!)
(I'M PRETTY SURE THEY KNOW)
(I DON'T KNOW, I-)
(OH, FUCK)
GOOD MORNING.
...
THE OWNER HERE SAYS YOU LIVE IN THE AREA.
DID YOU HAPPEN TO SEE OR HEAR ANYTHING SUSPICIOUS LAST NIGHT BETWEEN 2 & 3 IN THE MORNING?
SOMEBODY BROKE INTO THE STOREROOM AND TOOK A BUNCH OF STUFF!
WE DON'T HAVE A CAMERA, SO THEY'VE GOTTEN AWAY!
OKAY, SIR. LET US HANDLE THIS.
ANYTHING COULD BE HELPFUL, MA'AM.
...
!

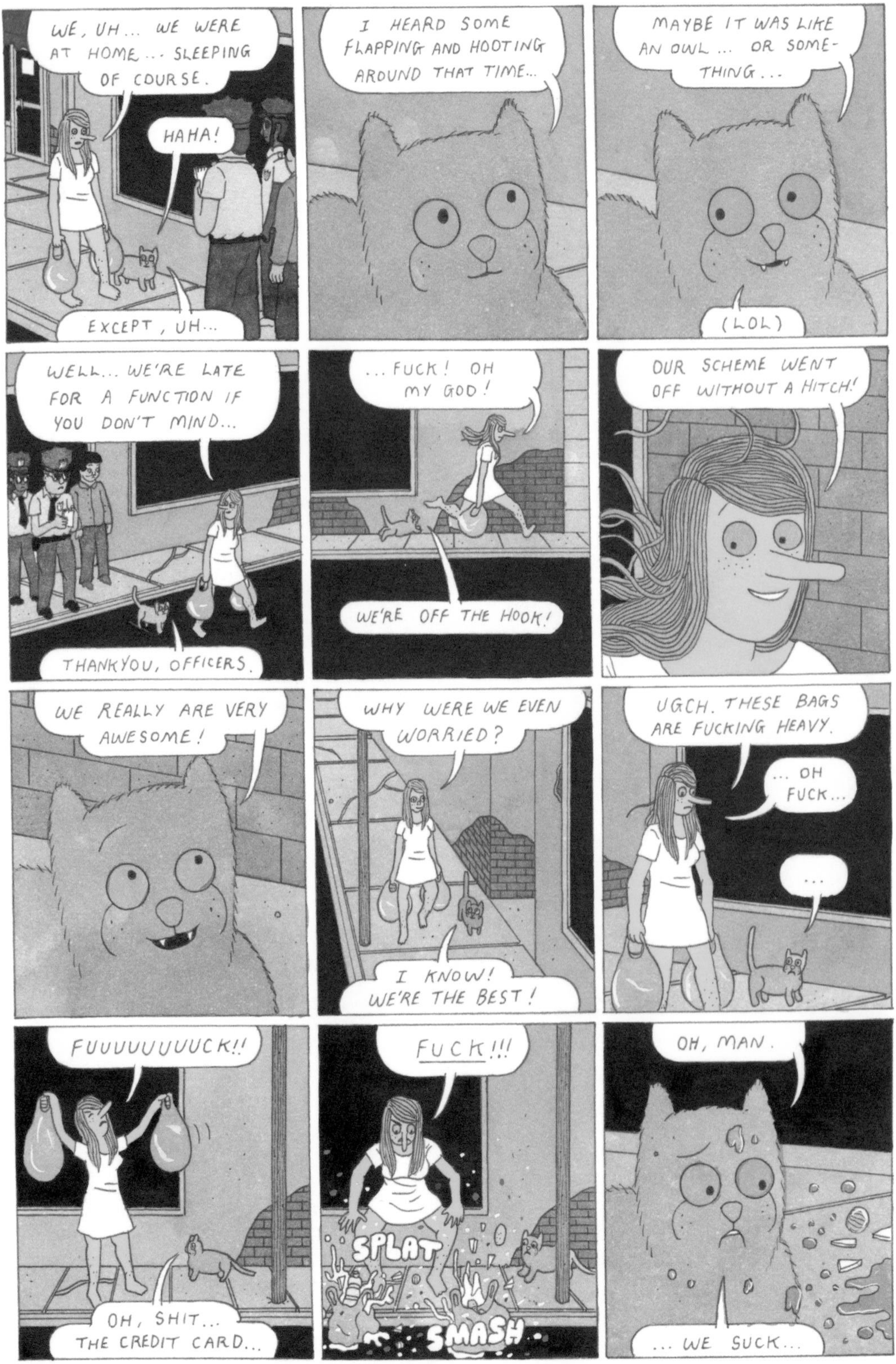
WE, UH... WE WERE AT HOME... SLEEPING OF COURSE.
HAHA!
EXCEPT, UH...
I HEARD SOME FLAPPING AND HOOTING AROUND THAT TIME...
MAYBE IT WAS LIKE AN OWL... OR SOME-THING...
(LOL)
WELL... WE'RE LATE FOR A FUNCTION IF YOU DON'T MIND...
THANKYOU, OFFICERS.
...FUCK! OH MY GOD!
WE'RE OFF THE HOOK!
OUR SCHEME WENT OFF WITHOUT A HITCH!
WE REALLY ARE VERY AWESOME!
WHY WERE WE EVEN WORRIED?
I KNOW! WE'RE THE BEST!
UGCH. THESE BAGS ARE FUCKING HEAVY.
...OH FUCK...
...
FUUUUUUUCK!!
OH, SHIT... THE CREDIT CARD...
FUCK!!!
SPLAT
SMASH
OH, MAN.
...WE SUCK...

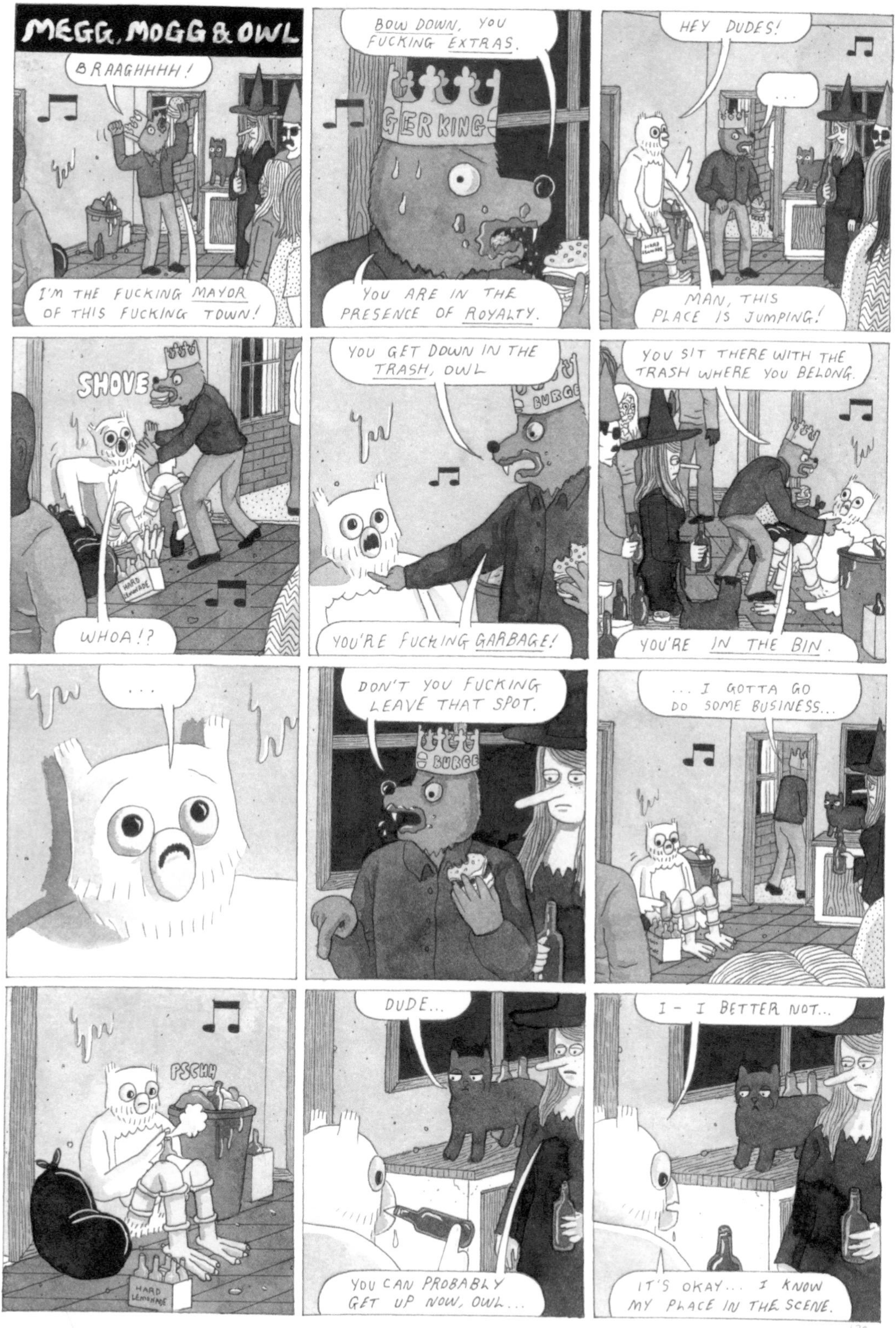
MEGG, MOGG & OWL
BRAAGHHHH!
I'M THE FUCKING MAYOR OF THIS FUCKING TOWN!
BOW DOWN, YOU FUCKING EXTRAS.
GER KING
YOU ARE IN THE PRESENCE OF ROYALTY.
HEY DUDES!
...
MAN, THIS PLACE IS JUMPING!
SHOVE
WHOA!?
HARD LEMONADE
YOU GET DOWN IN THE TRASH, OWL
BURGE
YOU'RE FUCKING GARBAGE!
YOU SIT THERE WITH THE TRASH WHERE YOU BELONG.
YOU'RE IN THE BIN.
...
DON'T YOU FUCKING LEAVE THAT SPOT.
BURGE
... I GOTTA GO DO SOME BUSINESS...
PSCHH
HARD LEMONADE
DUDE...
YOU CAN PROBABLY GET UP NOW, OWL...
I- I BETTER NOT...
IT'S OKAY... I KNOW MY PLACE IN THE SCENE.

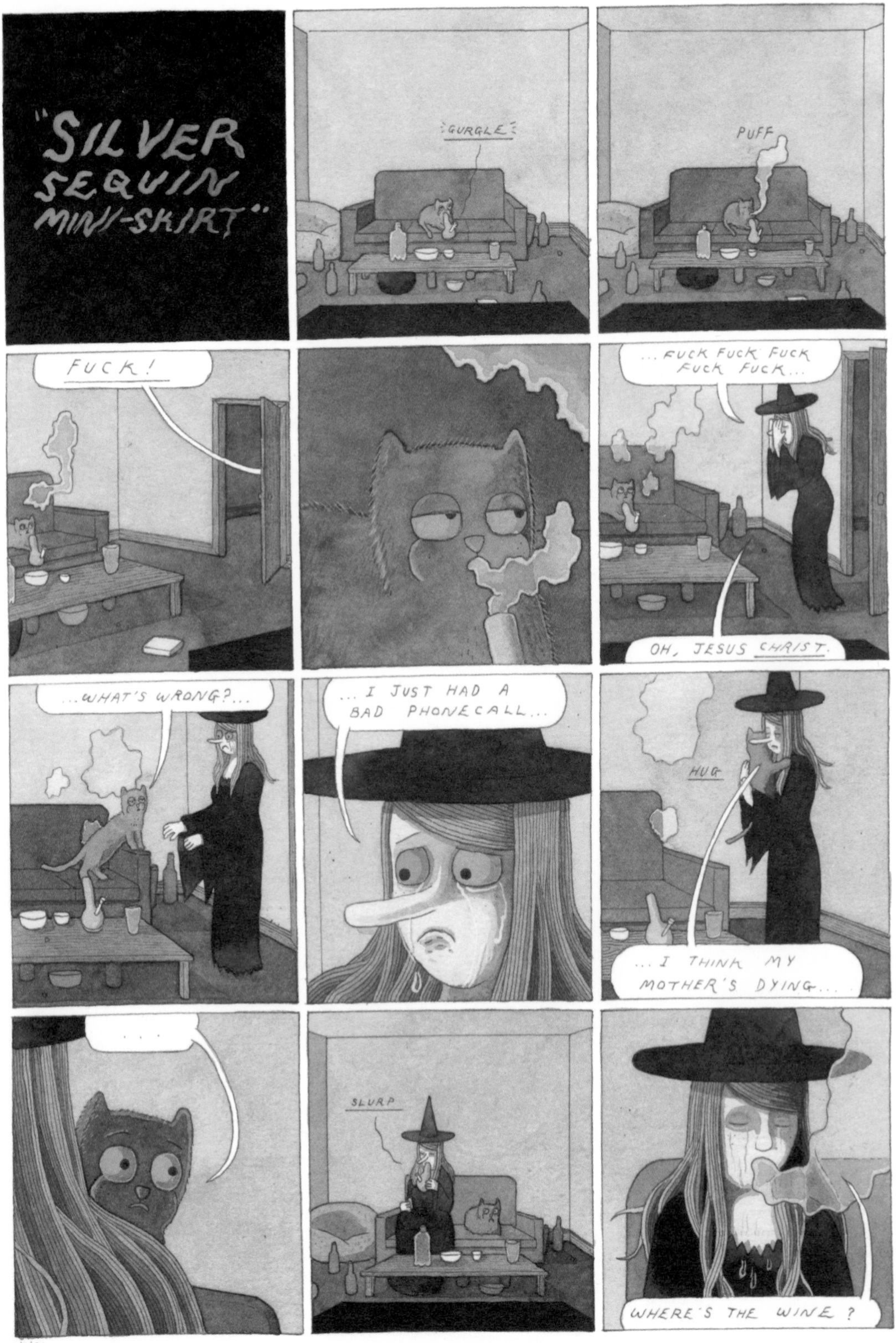
"SILVER SEQUIN MINI-SKIRT"
GURGLE
PUFF
FUCK!
...FUCK FUCK FUCK FUCK FUCK...
OH, JESUS CHRIST.
...WHAT'S WRONG?...
...I JUST HAD A BAD PHONECALL...
HUG
...I THINK MY MOTHER'S DYING...
. . .
SLURP
WHERE'S THE WINE?

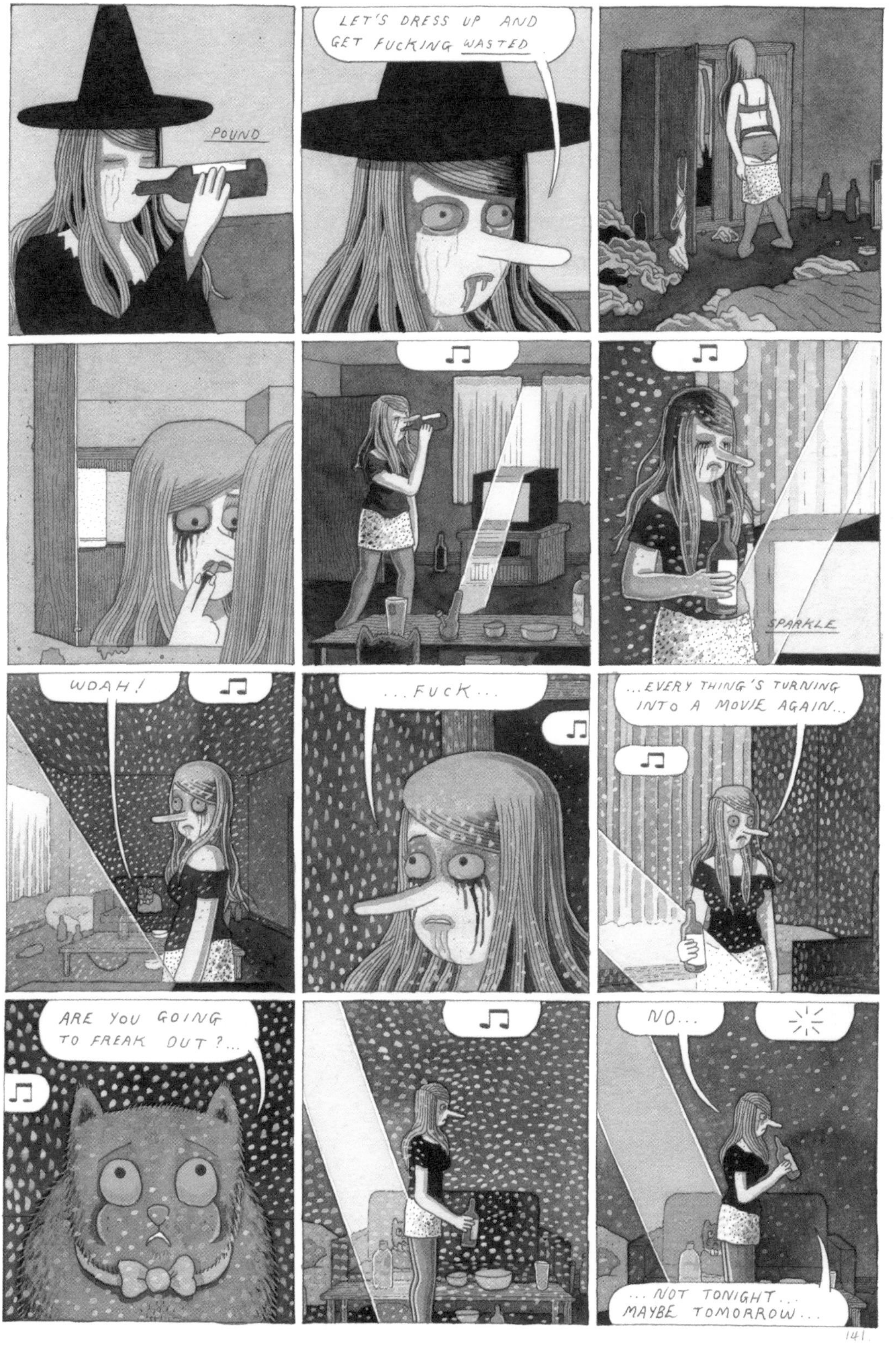
POUND
LET'S DRESS UP AND GET FUCKING WASTED
♫
♫
SPARKLE
WOAH!
♫
...FUCK...
♫
...EVERY THING'S TURNING INTO A MOVIE AGAIN...
♫
ARE YOU GOING TO FREAK OUT?...
♫
♫
NO...
...NOT TONIGHT... MAYBE TOMORROW...

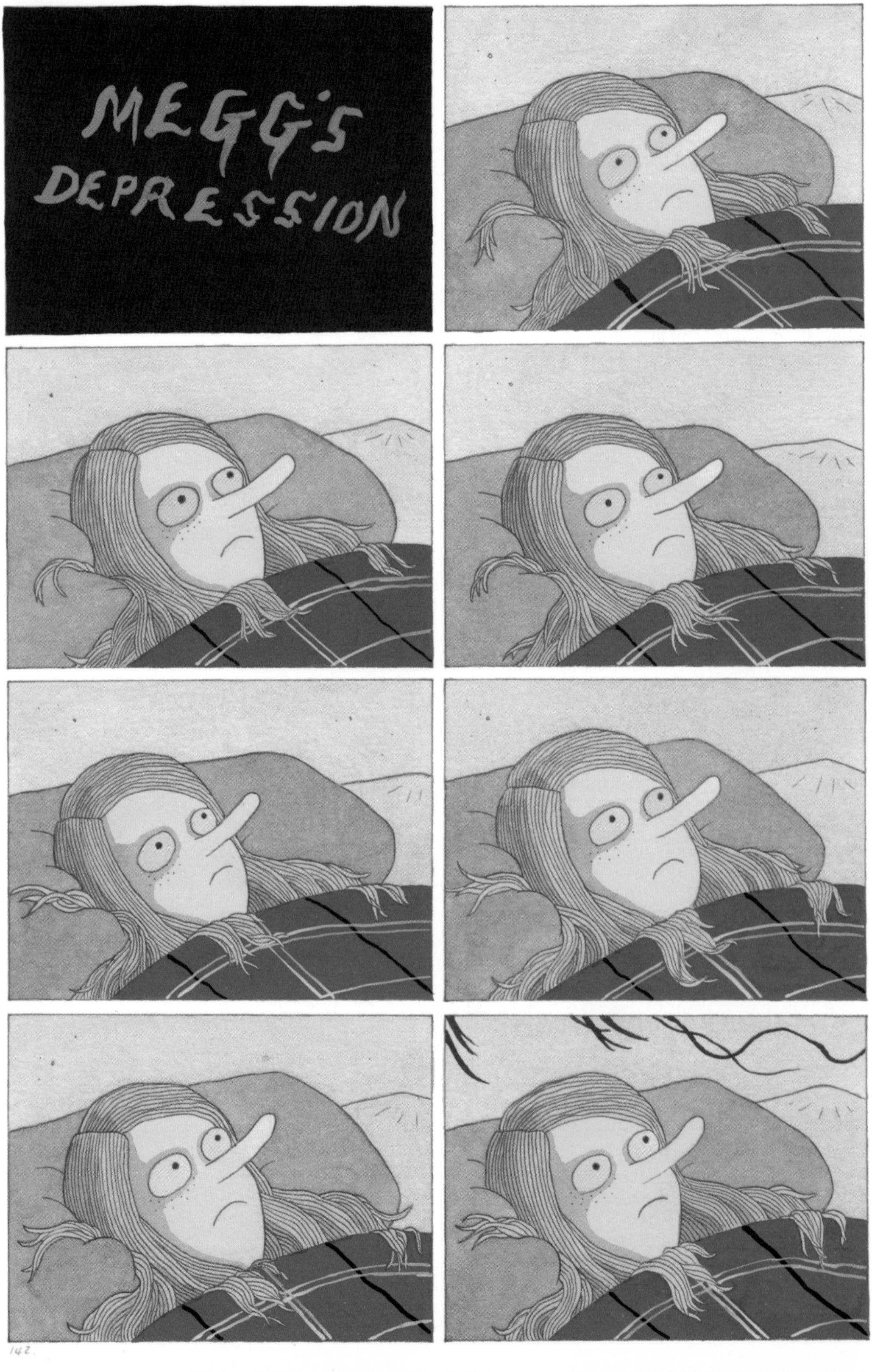
MEGG'S
DEPRESSION

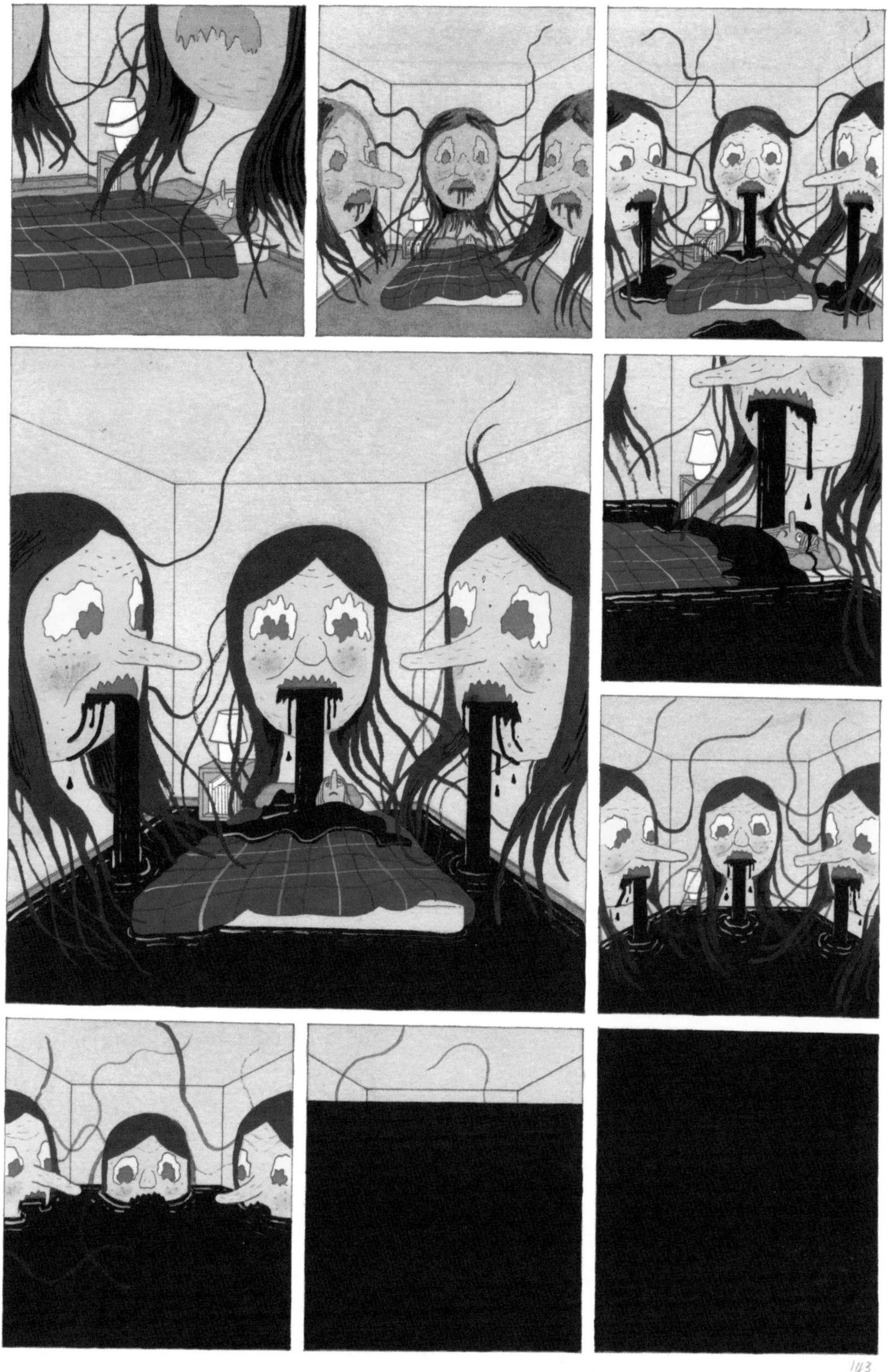

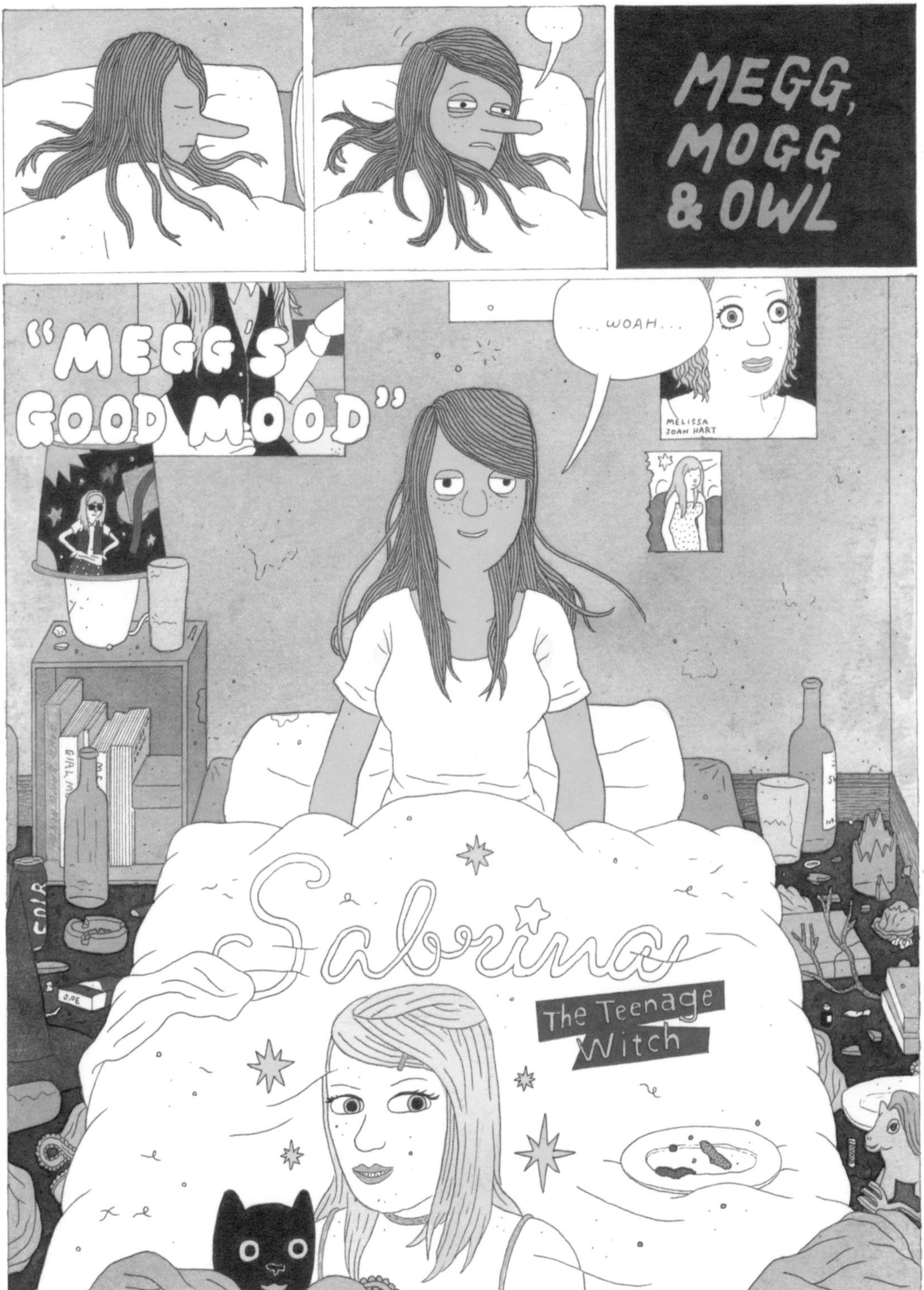
...
MEGG, MOGG & OWL
"MEGG'S GOOD MOOD"
... WOAH ...
MELISSA JOAN HART
Sabrina
The Teenage Witch

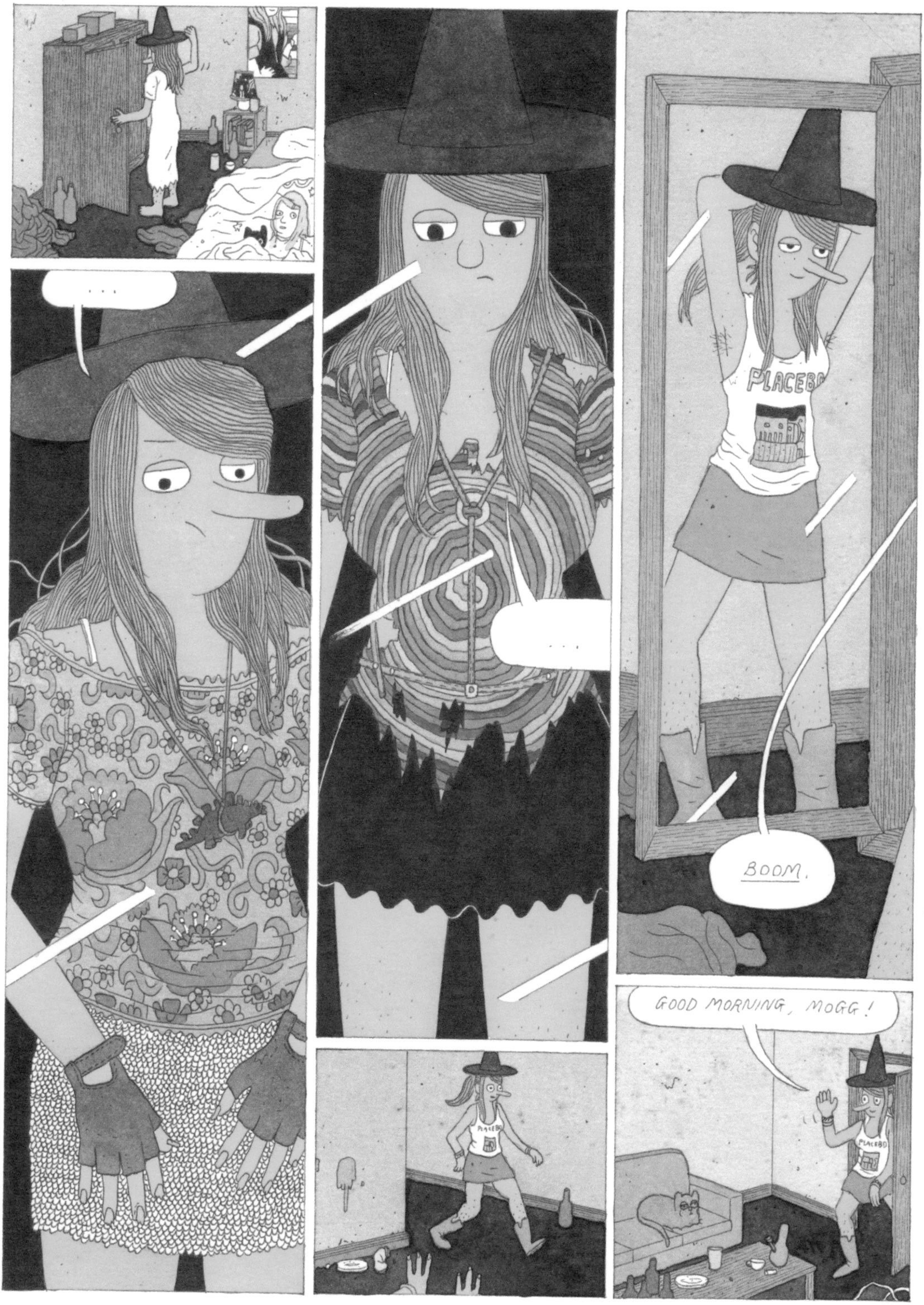
. . .
. . .
PLACEBO
BOOM.
GOOD MORNING, MOGG!

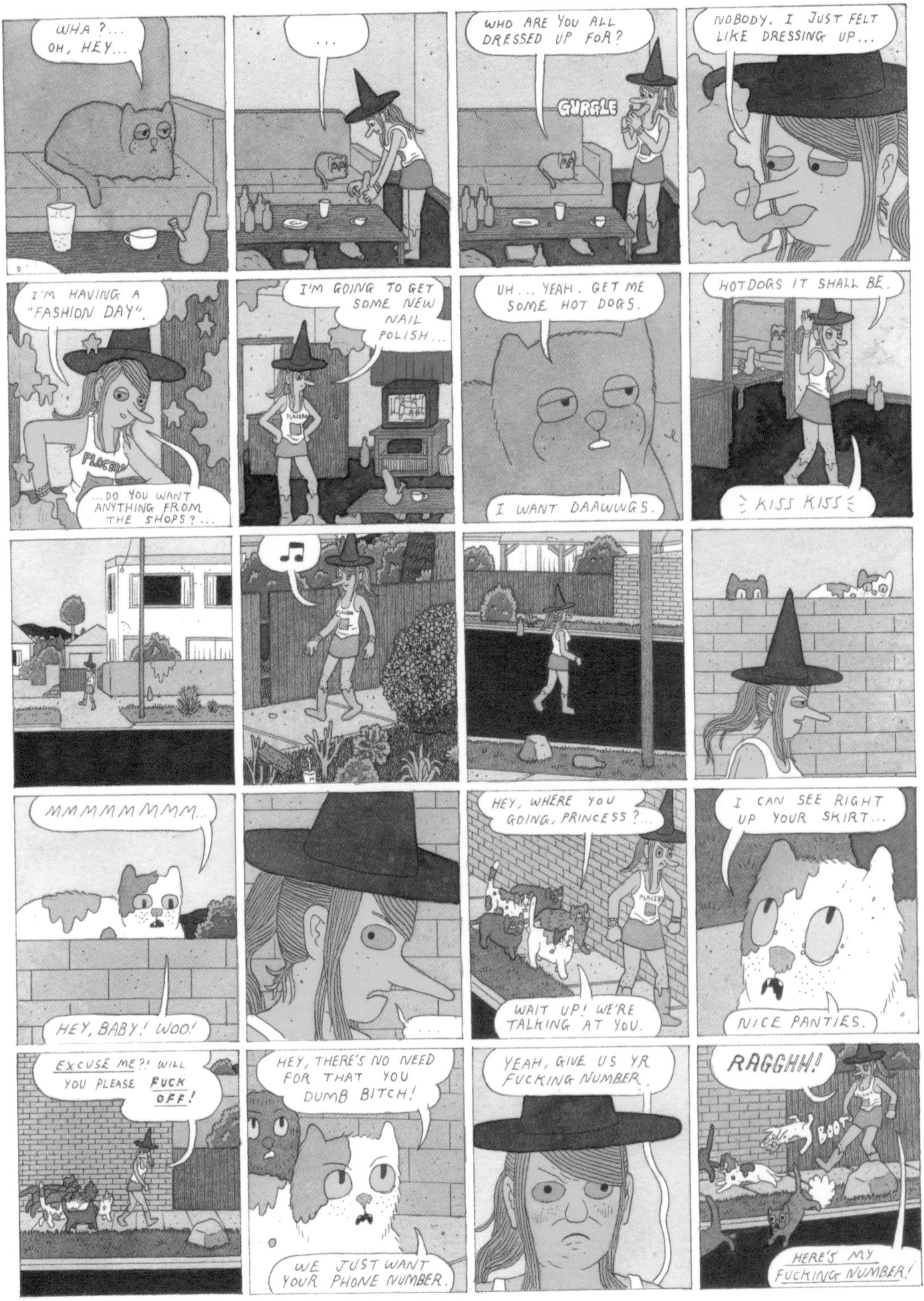
WHA ?...
OH, HEY...
...
WHO ARE YOU ALL DRESSED UP FOR?
GURGLE
NOBODY. I JUST FELT LIKE DRESSING UP...
I'M HAVING A "FASHION DAY".
...DO YOU WANT ANYTHING FROM THE SHOPS?...
I'M GOING TO GET SOME NEW NAIL POLISH...
UH... YEAH. GET ME SOME HOT DOGS.
I WANT DAAWWGS.
HOTDOGS IT SHALL BE.
KISS KISS
MMMMMMMM...
HEY, BABY! WOO!
...
HEY, WHERE YOU GOING, PRINCESS?...
WAIT UP! WE'RE TALKING AT YOU.
I CAN SEE RIGHT UP YOUR SKIRT...
NICE PANTIES.
EXCUSE ME?! WILL YOU PLEASE FUCK OFF!
HEY, THERE'S NO NEED FOR THAT YOU DUMB BITCH!
WE JUST WANT YOUR PHONE NUMBER.
YEAH, GIVE US YR FUCKING NUMBER.
RAGGHH!
BOOT
HERE'S MY FUCKING NUMBER!

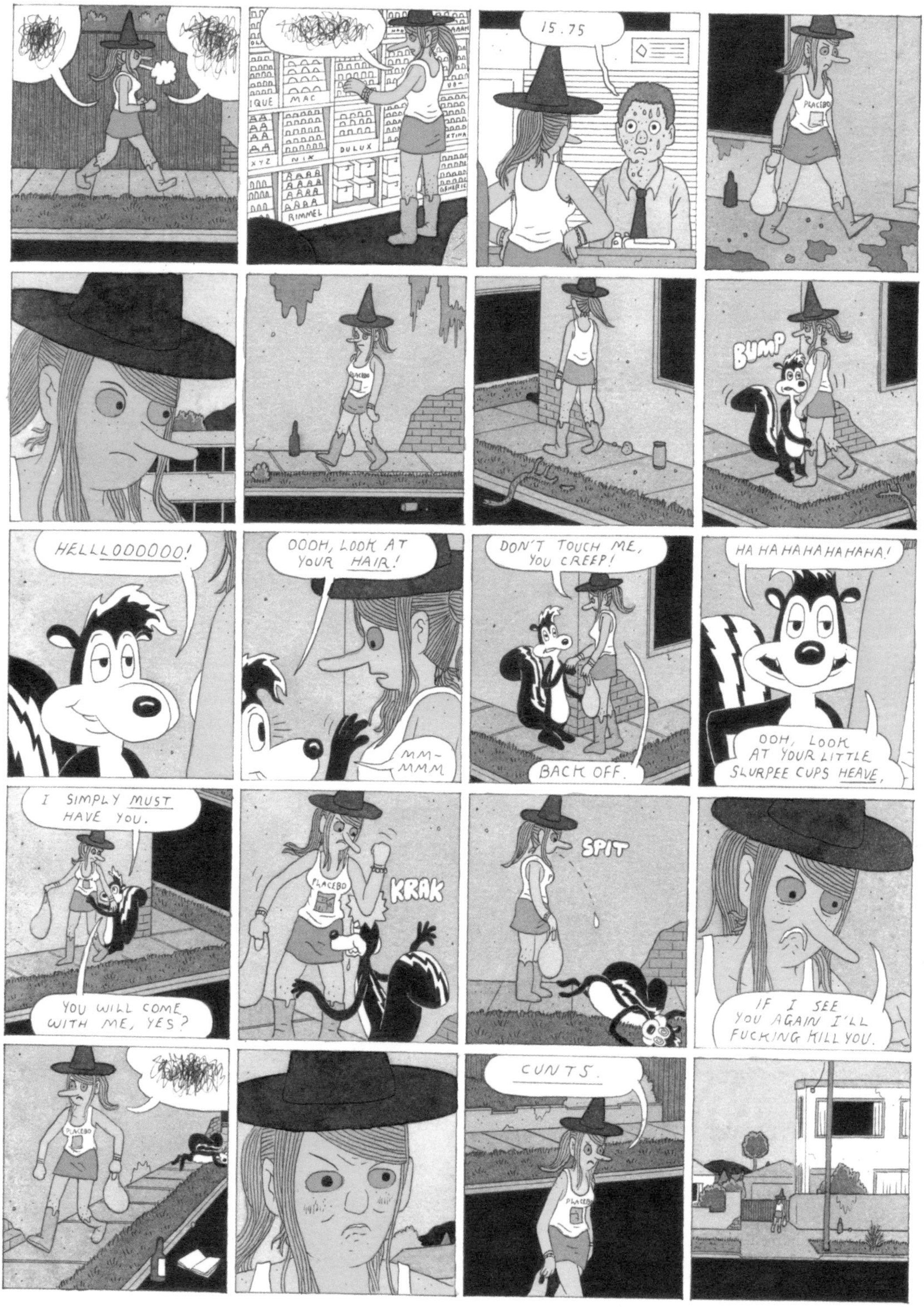
IQUE
MAC
DULUX
XYZ
NIX
RIMMEL
GENERIC
15.75
PLACEBO
BUMP
HELLLOOOOOO!
OOOH, LOOK AT YOUR HAIR!
MM-MMM
DON'T TOUCH ME, YOU CREEP!
BACK OFF.
HA HA HA HA HA HA HA HA!
OOH, LOOK AT YOUR LITTLE SLURPEE CUPS HEAVE,
I SIMPLY MUST HAVE YOU.
YOU WILL COME WITH ME, YES?
PLACEBO
KRAK
SPIT
IF I SEE YOU AGAIN I'LL FUCKING KILL YOU.
PLACEBO
CUNTS.
PLACEBO

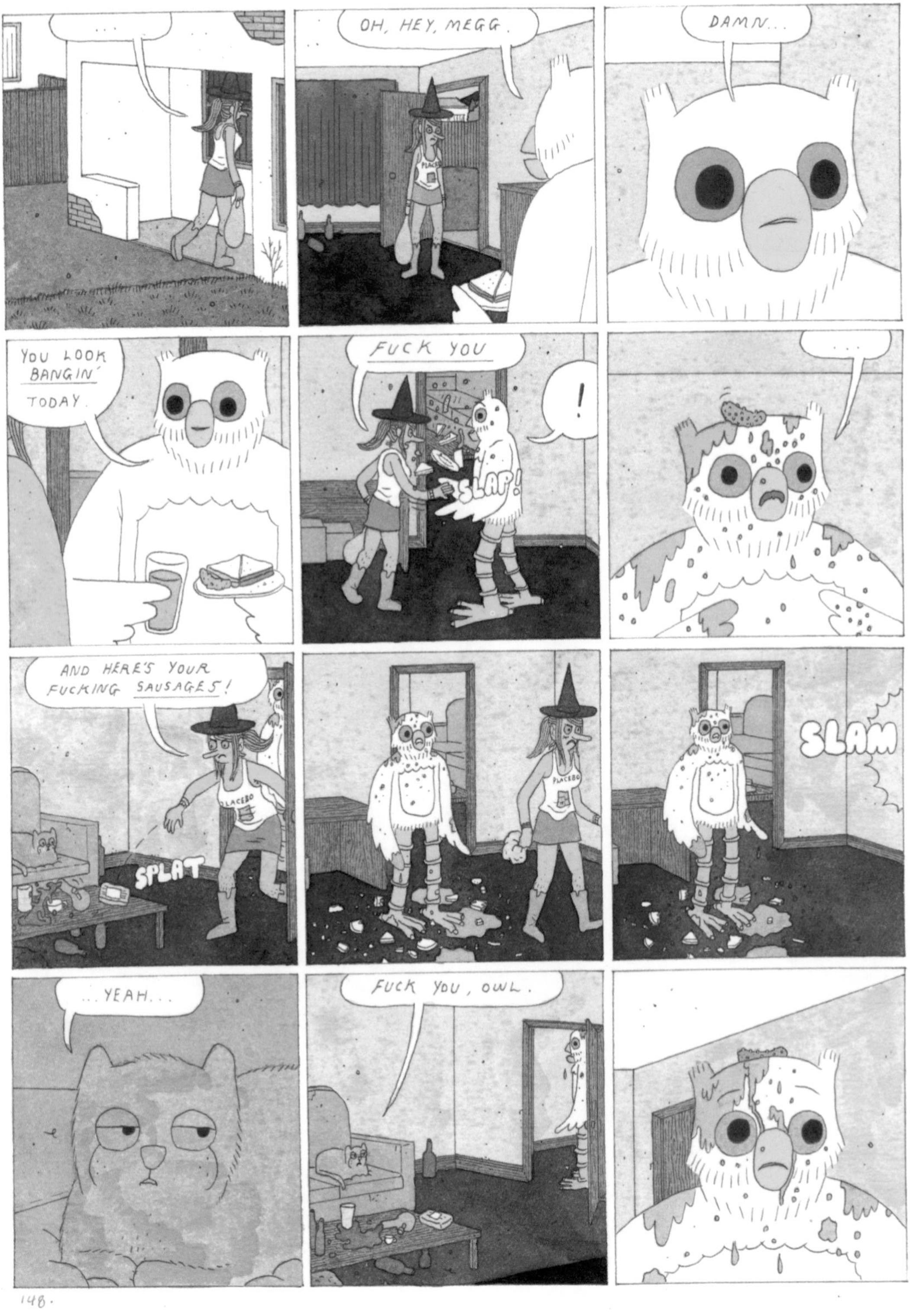
...
OH, HEY, MEGG.
DAMN...
YOU LOOK BANGIN' TODAY.
FUCK YOU
!
SLAP!
...
AND HERE'S YOUR FUCKING SAUSAGES!
SPLAT
PLACEBO
SLAM
...YEAH...
FUCK YOU, OWL.

MMO! BAD BRAINS

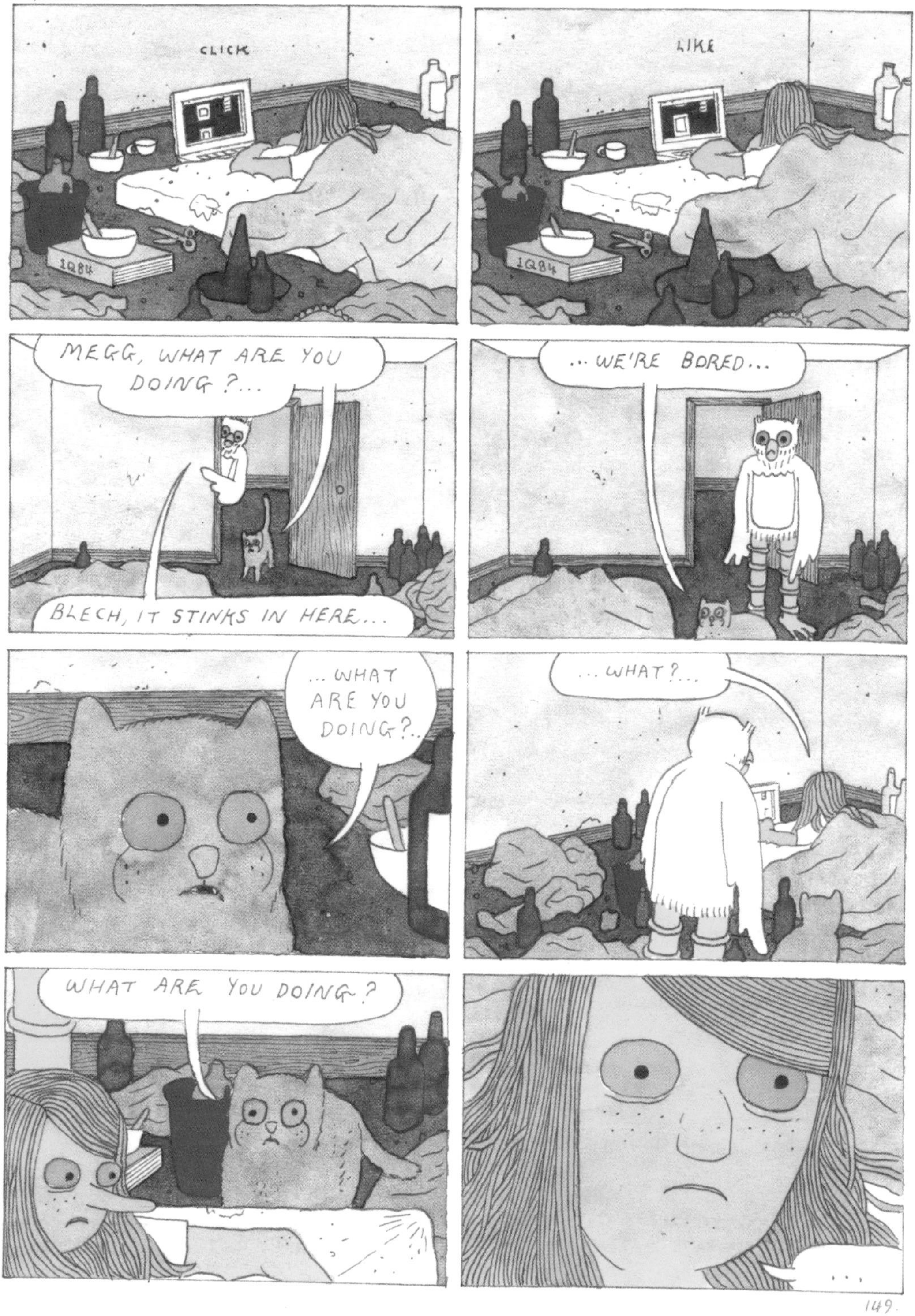
CLICK
1Q84
LIKE
1Q84
MEGG, WHAT ARE YOU DOING?...
BLECH, IT STINKS IN HERE...
...WE'RE BORED...
...WHAT ARE YOU DOING?...
...WHAT?...
WHAT ARE YOU DOING?
...

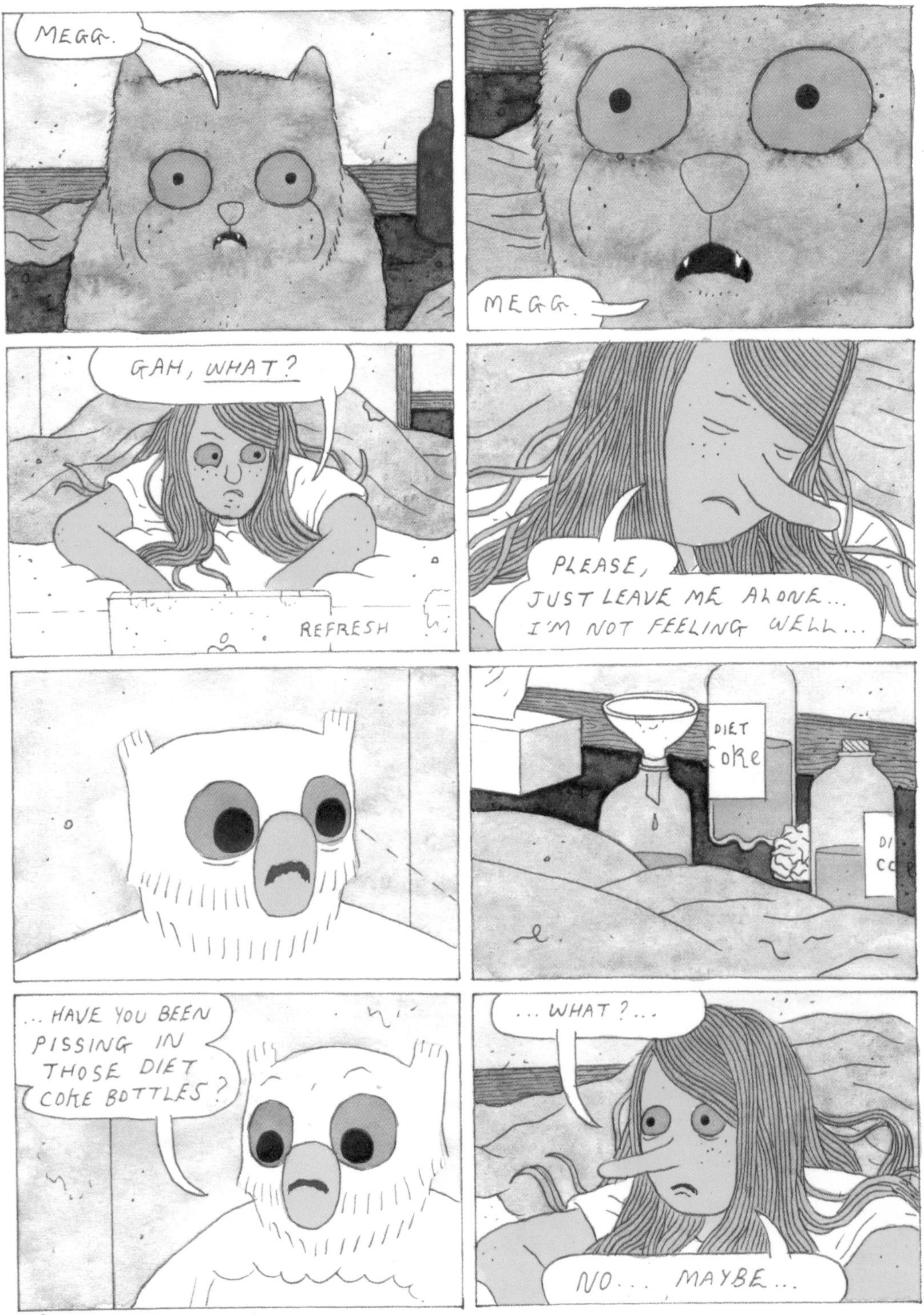
MEGG.
MEGG.
GAH, WHAT?
REFRESH
PLEASE, JUST LEAVE ME ALONE... I'M NOT FEELING WELL...
DIET COKE
... HAVE YOU BEEN PISSING IN THOSE DIET COKE BOTTLES?
... WHAT?...
NO... MAYBE...

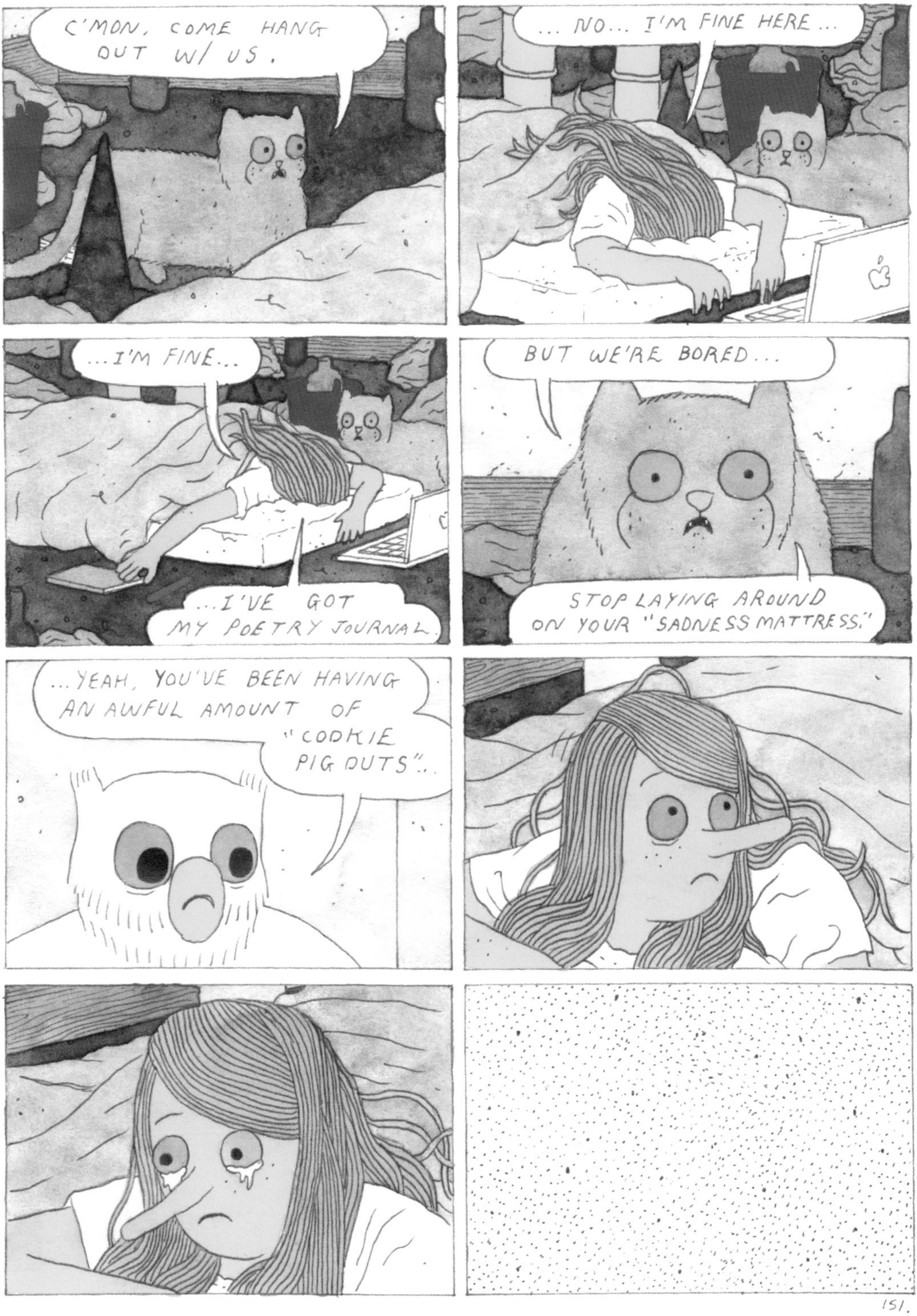
C'MON, COME HANG OUT W/ US.
... NO... I'M FINE HERE...
...I'M FINE...
...I'VE GOT MY POETRY JOURNAL.
BUT WE'RE BORED...
STOP LAYING AROUND ON YOUR "SADNESS MATTRESS."
...YEAH, YOU'VE BEEN HAVING AN AWFUL AMOUNT OF "COOKIE PIG OUTS"...

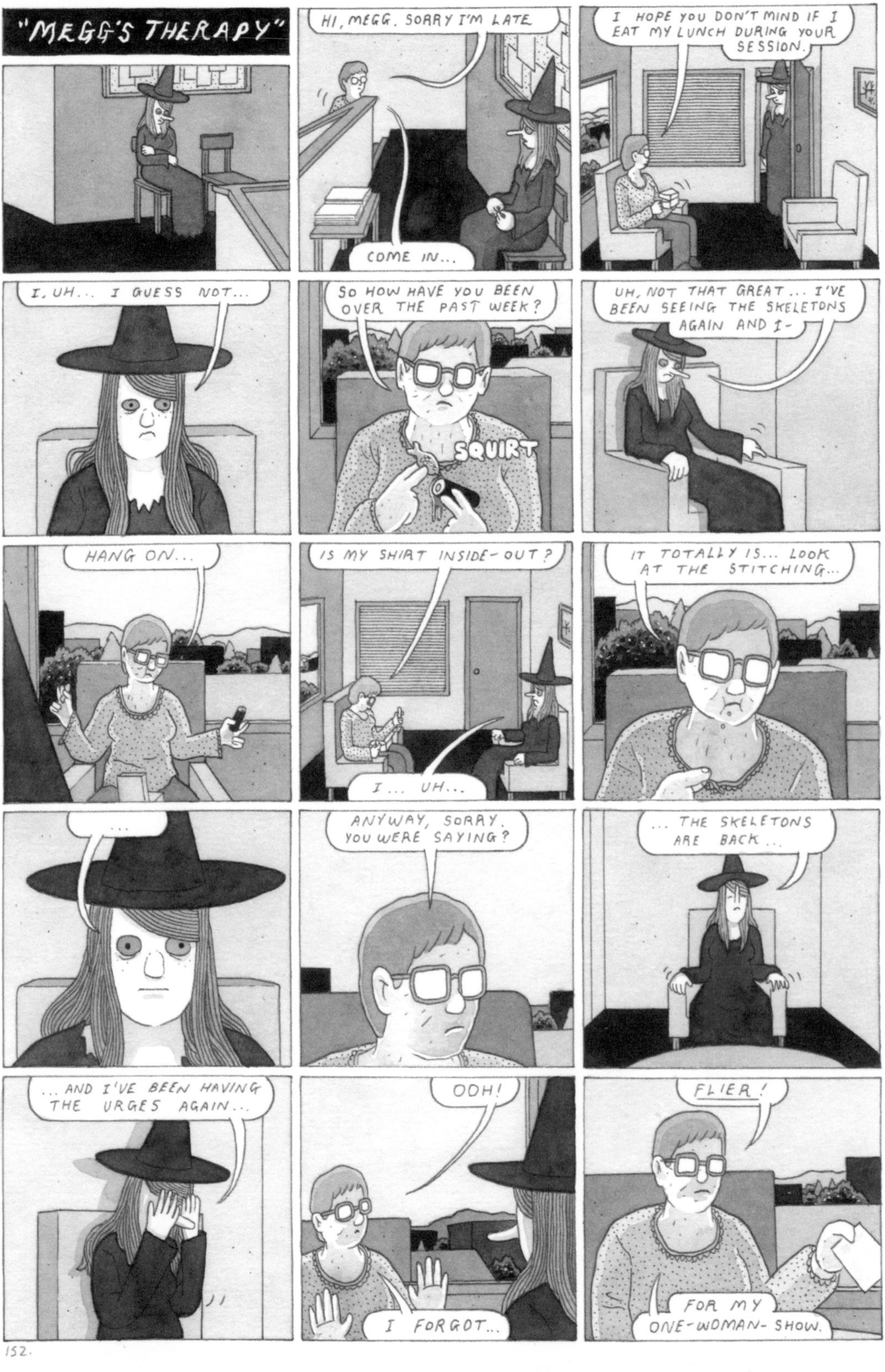
"MEGG'S THERAPY"
HI, MEGG. SORRY I'M LATE
COME IN...
I HOPE YOU DON'T MIND IF I EAT MY LUNCH DURING YOUR SESSION.
I, UH... I GUESS NOT...
SO HOW HAVE YOU BEEN OVER THE PAST WEEK?
SQUIRT
UH, NOT THAT GREAT... I'VE BEEN SEEING THE SKELETONS AGAIN AND I-
HANG ON...
IS MY SHIRT INSIDE-OUT?
I... UH...
IT TOTALLY IS... LOOK AT THE STITCHING...
...
ANYWAY, SORRY. YOU WERE SAYING?
... THE SKELETONS ARE BACK...
... AND I'VE BEEN HAVING THE URGES AGAIN...
OOH!
I FORGOT...
FLIER!
FOR MY ONE-WOMAN-SHOW.

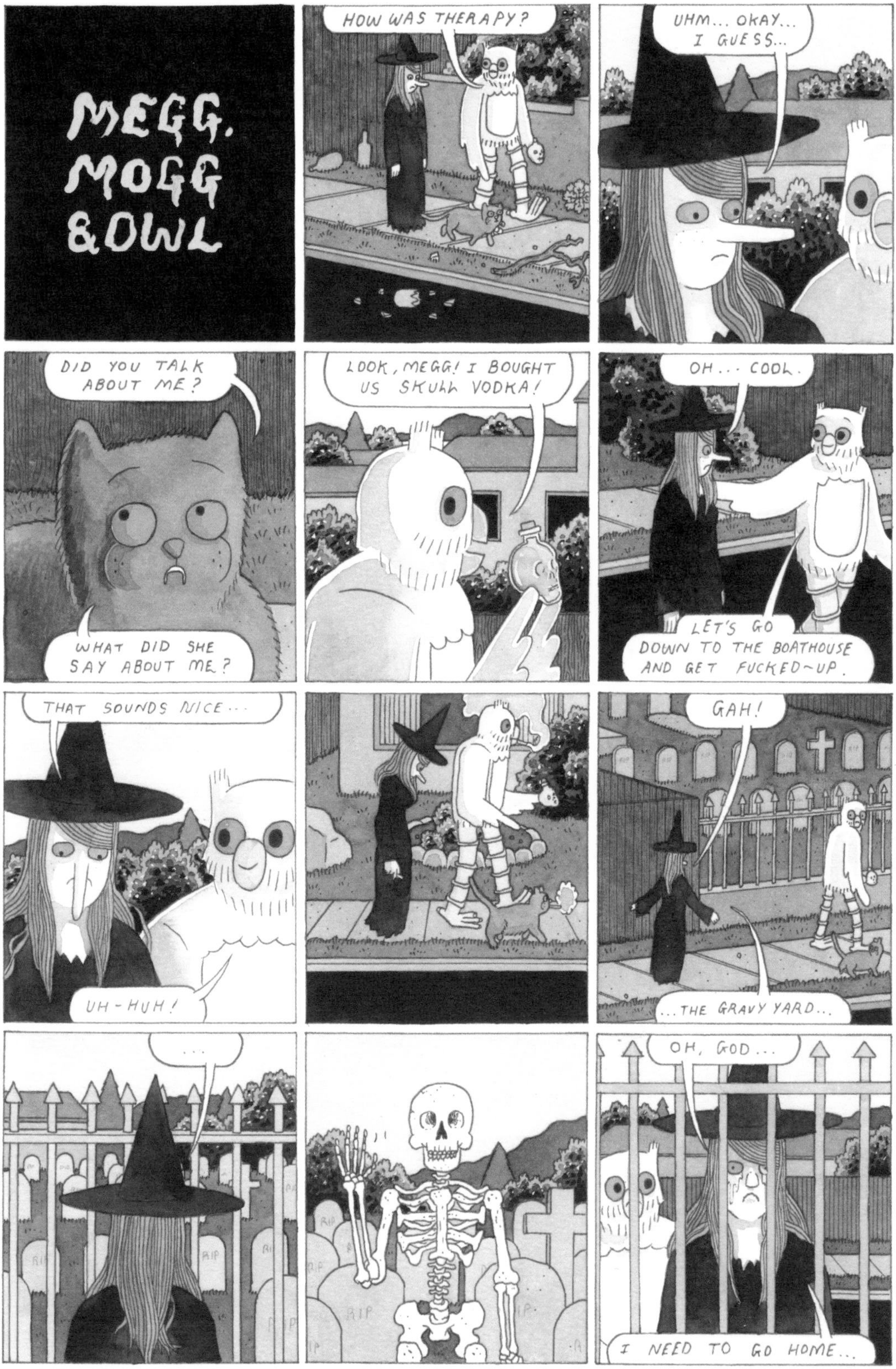
MEGG, MOGG & OWL
HOW WAS THERAPY?
UHM... OKAY... I GUESS...
DID YOU TALK ABOUT ME?
WHAT DID SHE SAY ABOUT ME?
LOOK, MEGG! I BOUGHT US SKULL VODKA!
OH... COOL.
LET'S GO DOWN TO THE BOATHOUSE AND GET FUCKED-UP.
THAT SOUNDS NICE...
UH-HUH!
GAH!
...THE GRAVY YARD...
...
OH, GOD...
I NEED TO GO HOME...

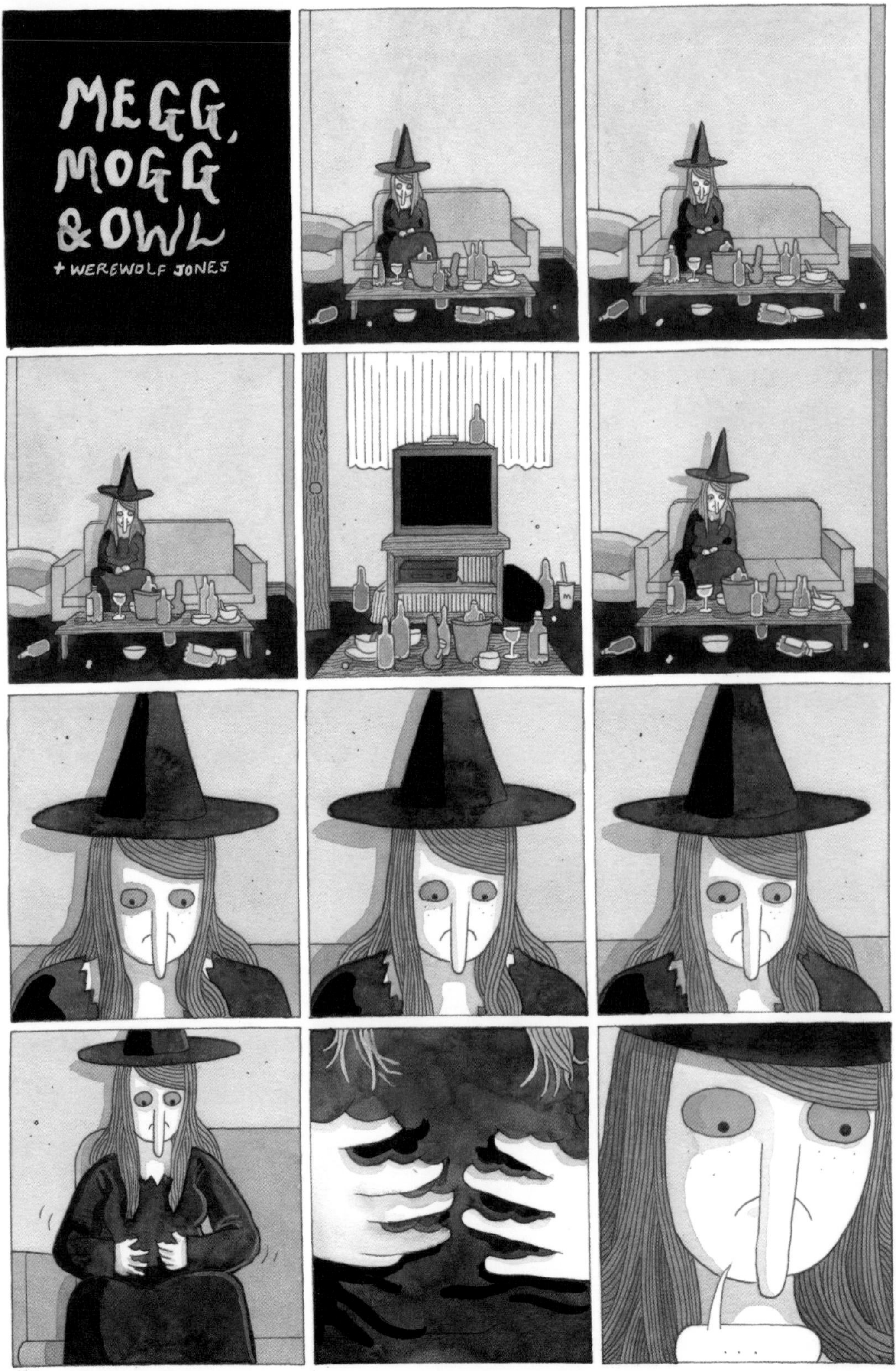
MEGG, MOGG & OWL
+ WEREWOLF JONES
. . .

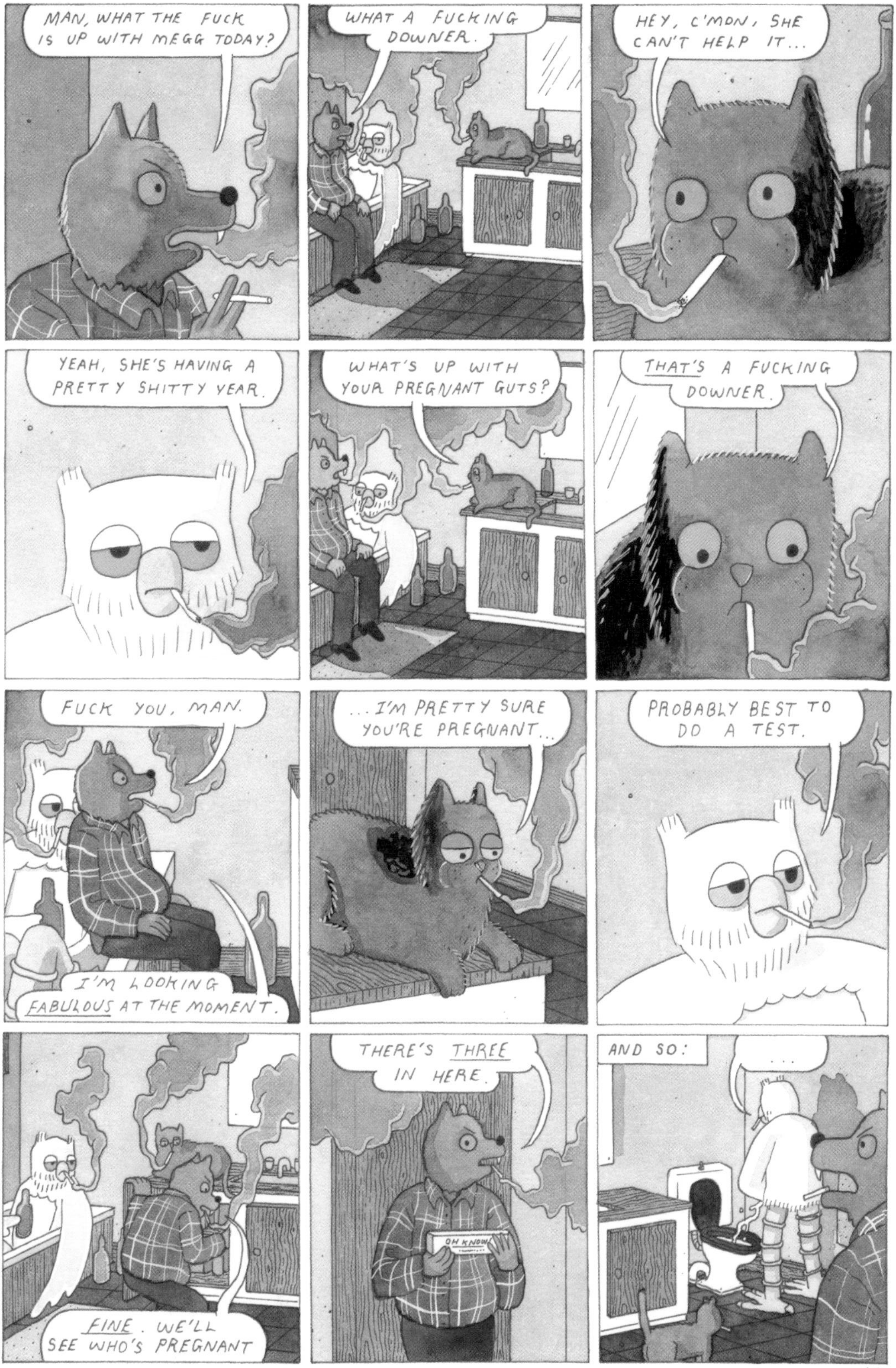
MAN, WHAT THE FUCK IS UP WITH MEGG TODAY?
WHAT A FUCKING DOWNER.
HEY, C'MON, SHE CAN'T HELP IT...
YEAH, SHE'S HAVING A PRETTY SHITTY YEAR.
WHAT'S UP WITH YOUR PREGNANT GUTS?
THAT'S A FUCKING DOWNER.
FUCK YOU, MAN.
I'M LOOKING FABULOUS AT THE MOMENT.
...I'M PRETTY SURE YOU'RE PREGNANT...
PROBABLY BEST TO DO A TEST.
FINE. WE'LL SEE WHO'S PREGNANT
THERE'S THREE IN HERE.
OH KNOW!
AND SO:
...

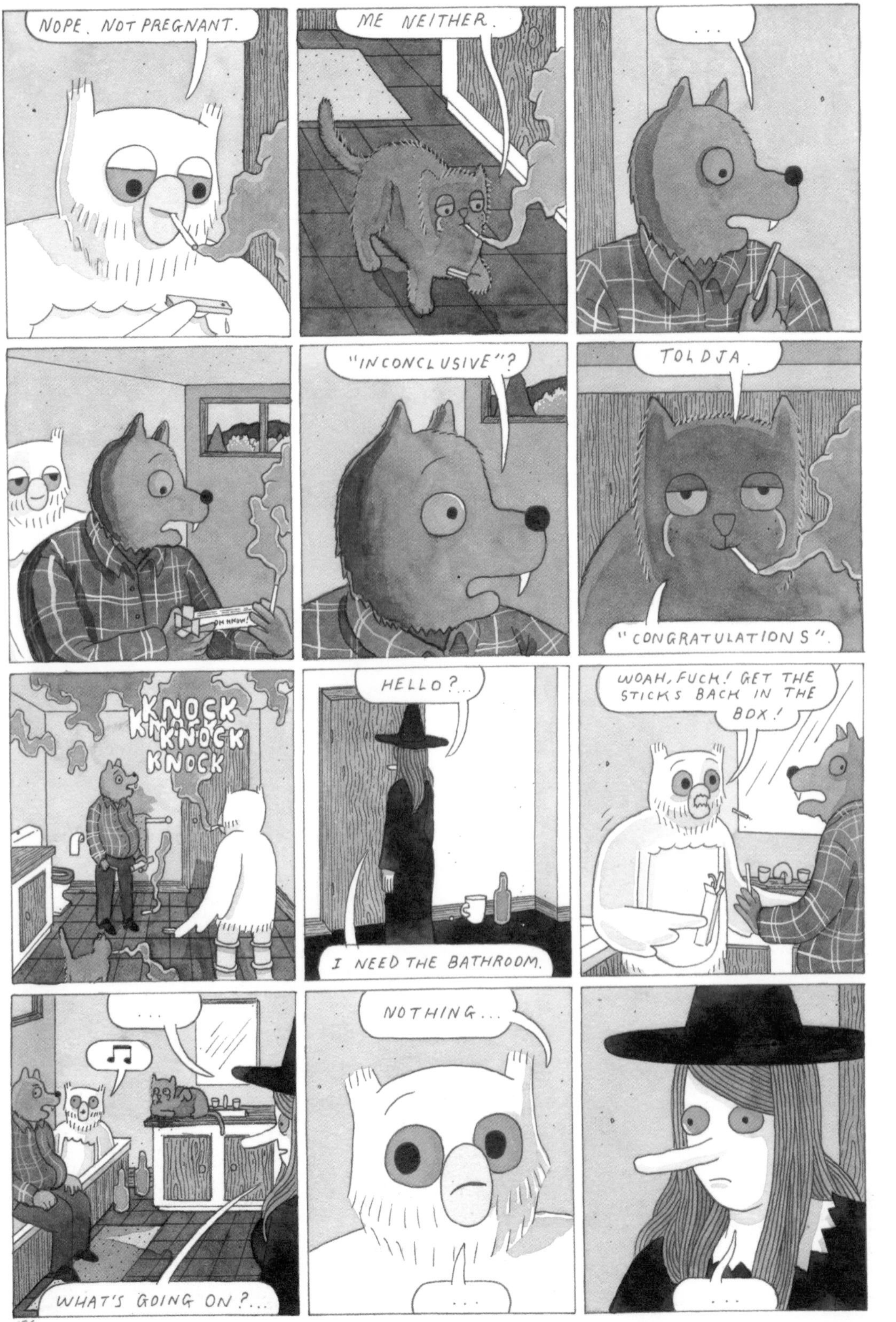
NOPE. NOT PREGNANT.
ME NEITHER.
...
"INCONCLUSIVE"?
TOLDJA.
"CONGRATULATIONS".
KNOCK
KNOCK
KNOCK
HELLO?...
I NEED THE BATHROOM.
WOAH, FUCK! GET THE STICKS BACK IN THE BOX!
...
♫
WHAT'S GOING ON?...
NOTHING...
...
...

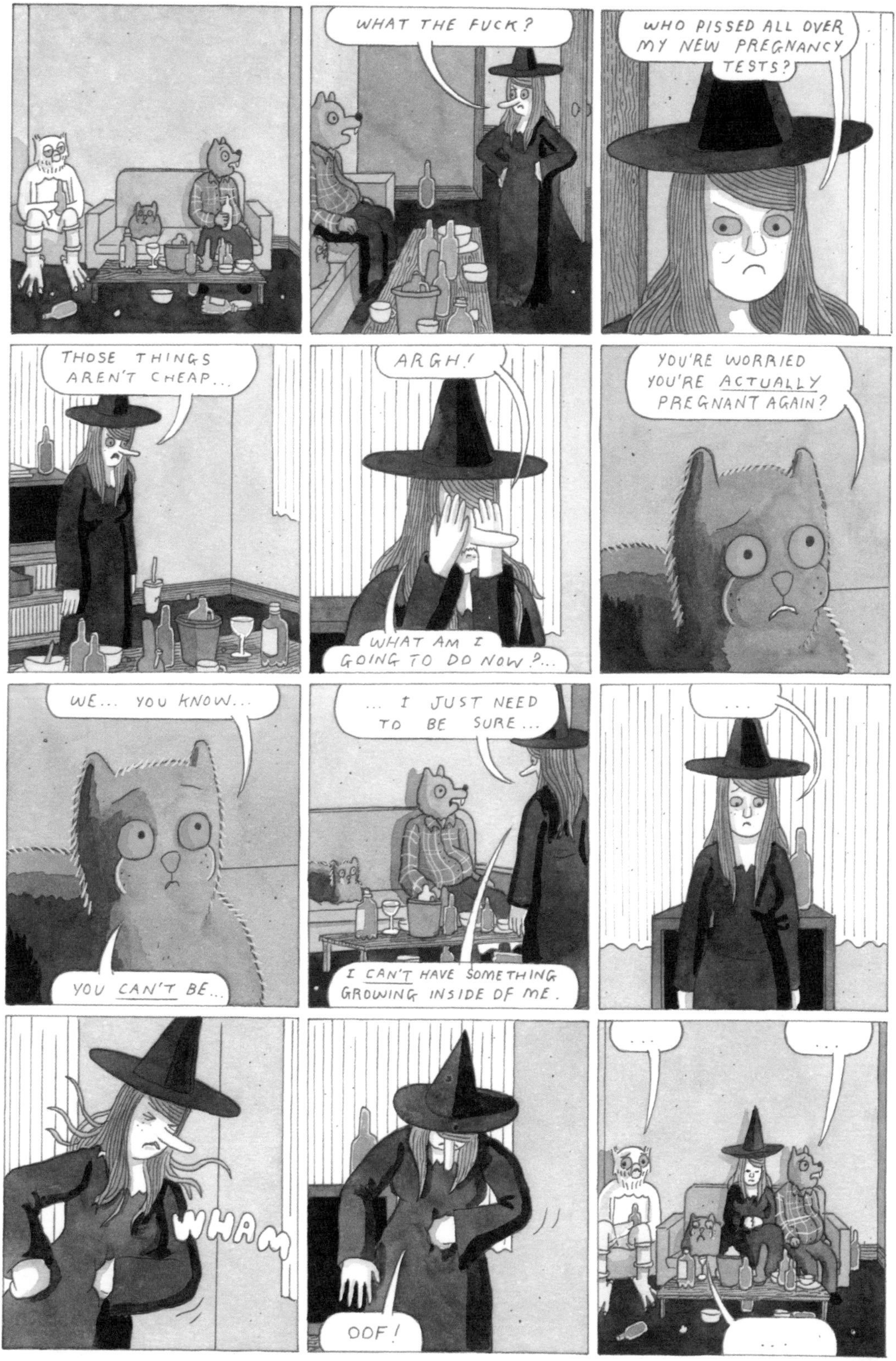
WHAT THE FUCK?
WHO PISSED ALL OVER MY NEW PREGNANCY TESTS?
THOSE THINGS AREN'T CHEAP...
ARGH!
WHAT AM I GOING TO DO NOW?...
YOU'RE WORRIED YOU'RE ACTUALLY PREGNANT AGAIN?
WE... YOU KNOW...
YOU CAN'T BE...
... I JUST NEED TO BE SURE...
I CAN'T HAVE SOMETHING GROWING INSIDE OF ME.
...
WHAM
OOF!
...
...
...

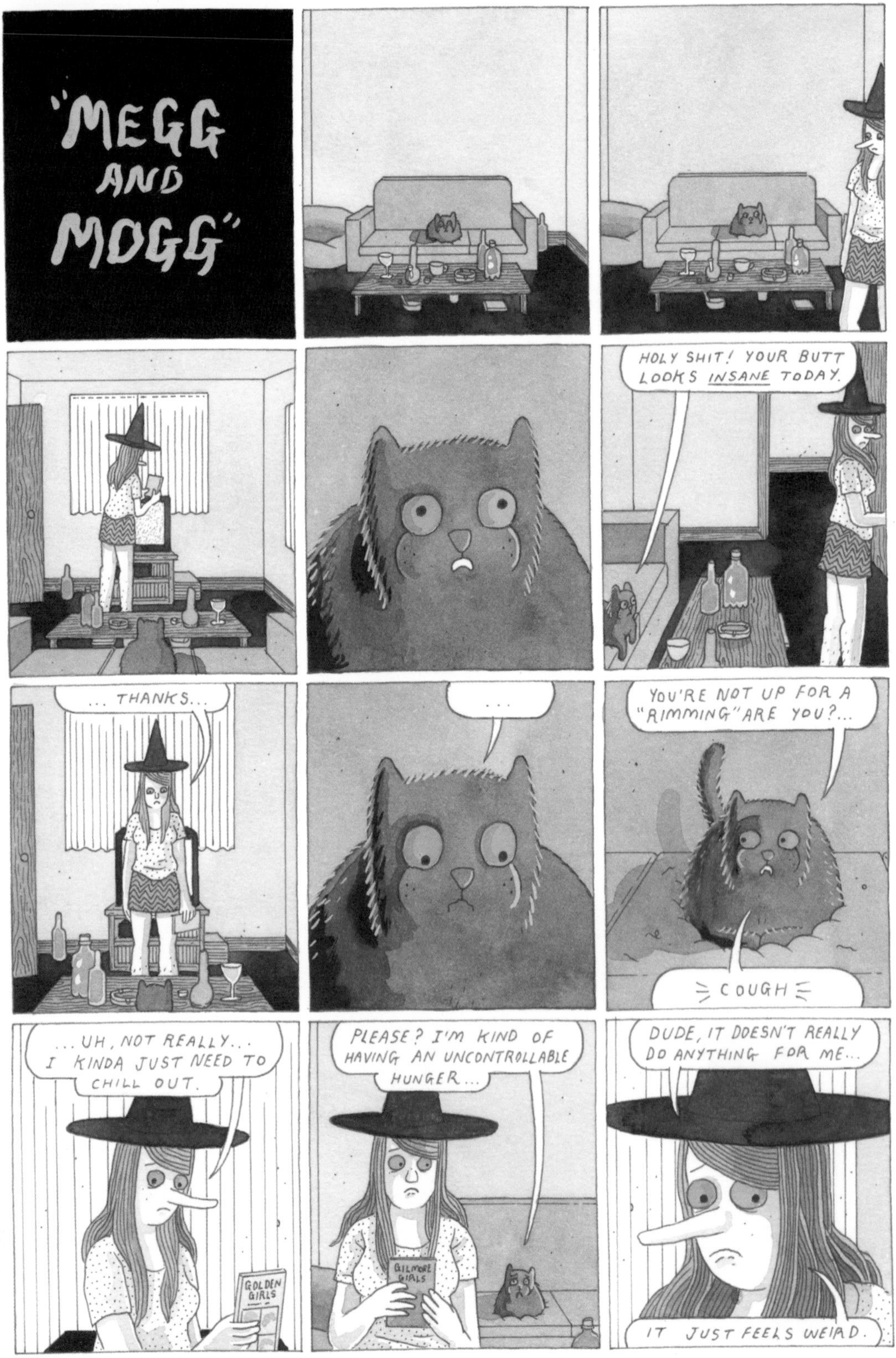
"MEGG AND MOGG"
HOLY SHIT! YOUR BUTT LOOKS INSANE TODAY.
... THANKS...
...
YOU'RE NOT UP FOR A "RIMMING" ARE YOU?...
COUGH
...UH, NOT REALLY... I KINDA JUST NEED TO CHILL OUT.
GOLDEN GIRLS
PLEASE? I'M KIND OF HAVING AN UNCONTROLLABLE HUNGER...
GILMORE GIRLS
DUDE, IT DOESN'T REALLY DO ANYTHING FOR ME...
IT JUST FEELS WEIRD.

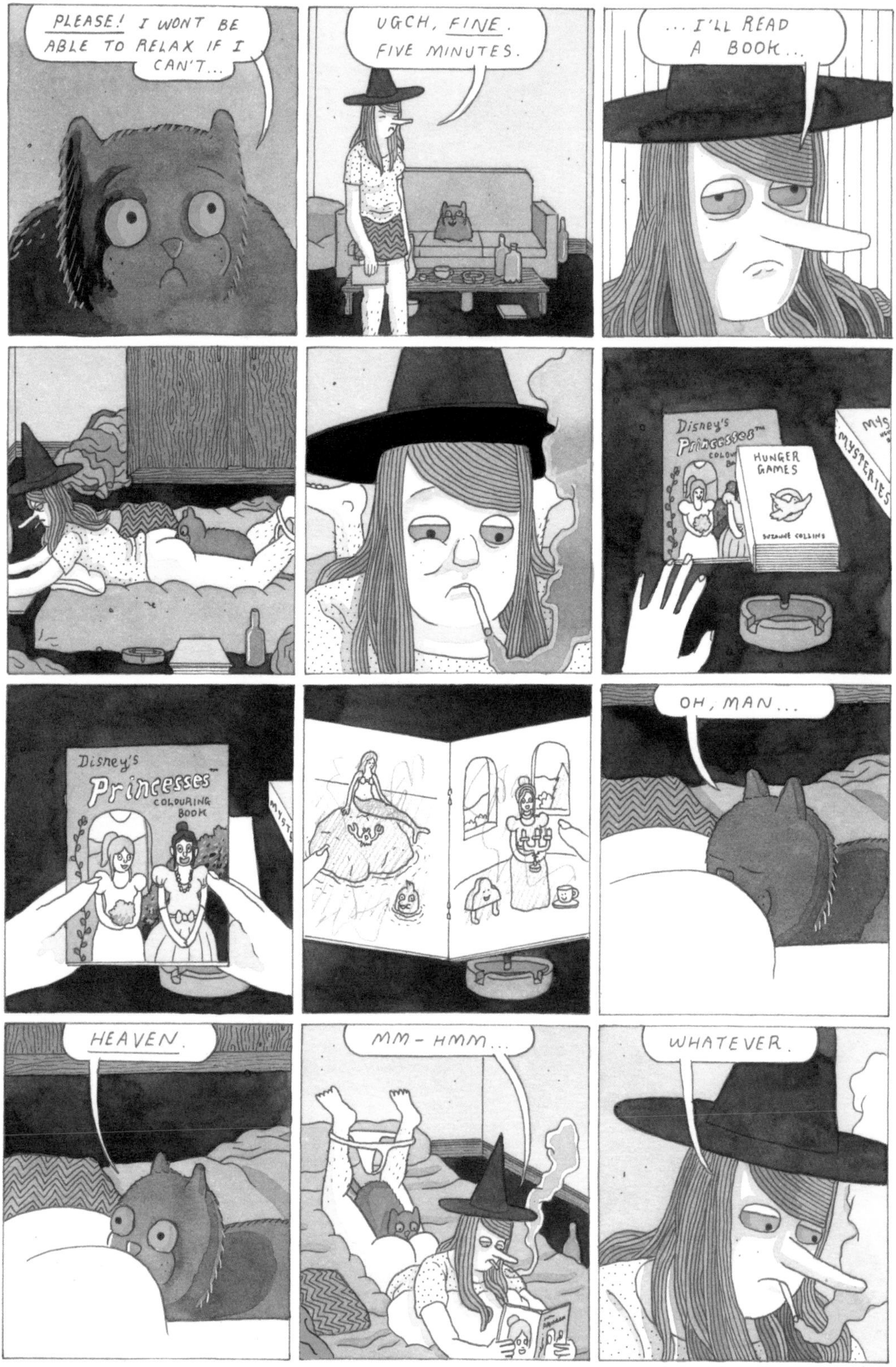
PLEASE! I WONT BE ABLE TO RELAX IF I CAN'T...
UGCH, FINE. FIVE MINUTES.
... I'LL READ A BOOK...
HUNGER GAMES
SUZANNE COLLINS
MYSTERIES
Disney's Princesses™ COLOURING BOOK
OH, MAN...
HEAVEN.
MM-HMM...
WHATEVER.

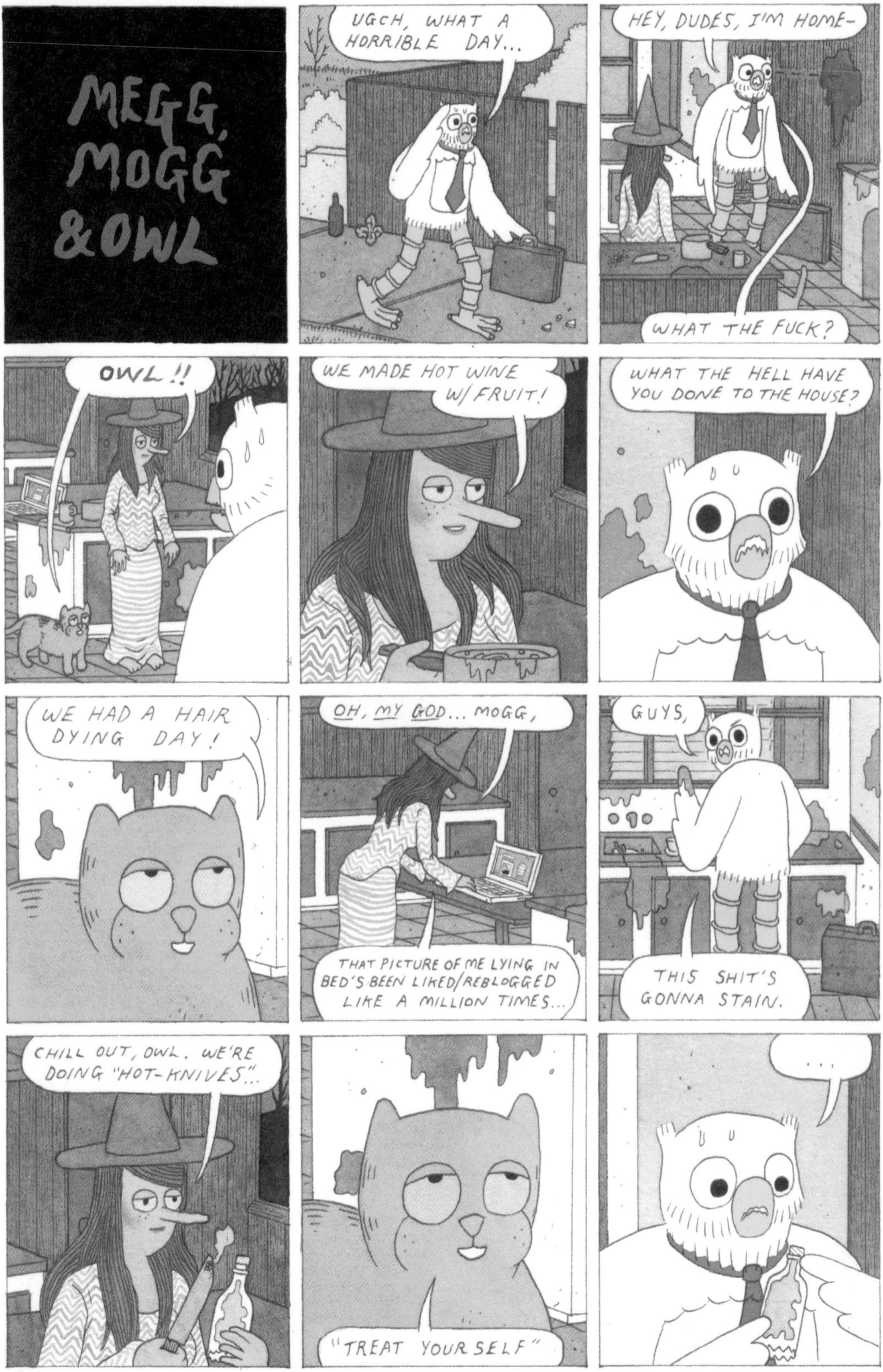
MEGG, MOGG & OWL
UGCH, WHAT A HORRIBLE DAY...
HEY, DUDES, I'M HOME-
WHAT THE FUCK?
OWL!!
WE MADE HOT WINE W/ FRUIT!
WHAT THE HELL HAVE YOU DONE TO THE HOUSE?
WE HAD A HAIR DYING DAY!
OH, MY GOD... MOGG,
THAT PICTURE OF ME LYING IN BED'S BEEN LIKED/REBLOGGED LIKE A MILLION TIMES...
GUYS,
THIS SHIT'S GONNA STAIN.
CHILL OUT, OWL. WE'RE DOING "HOT-KNIVES"...
"TREAT YOURSELF"
...

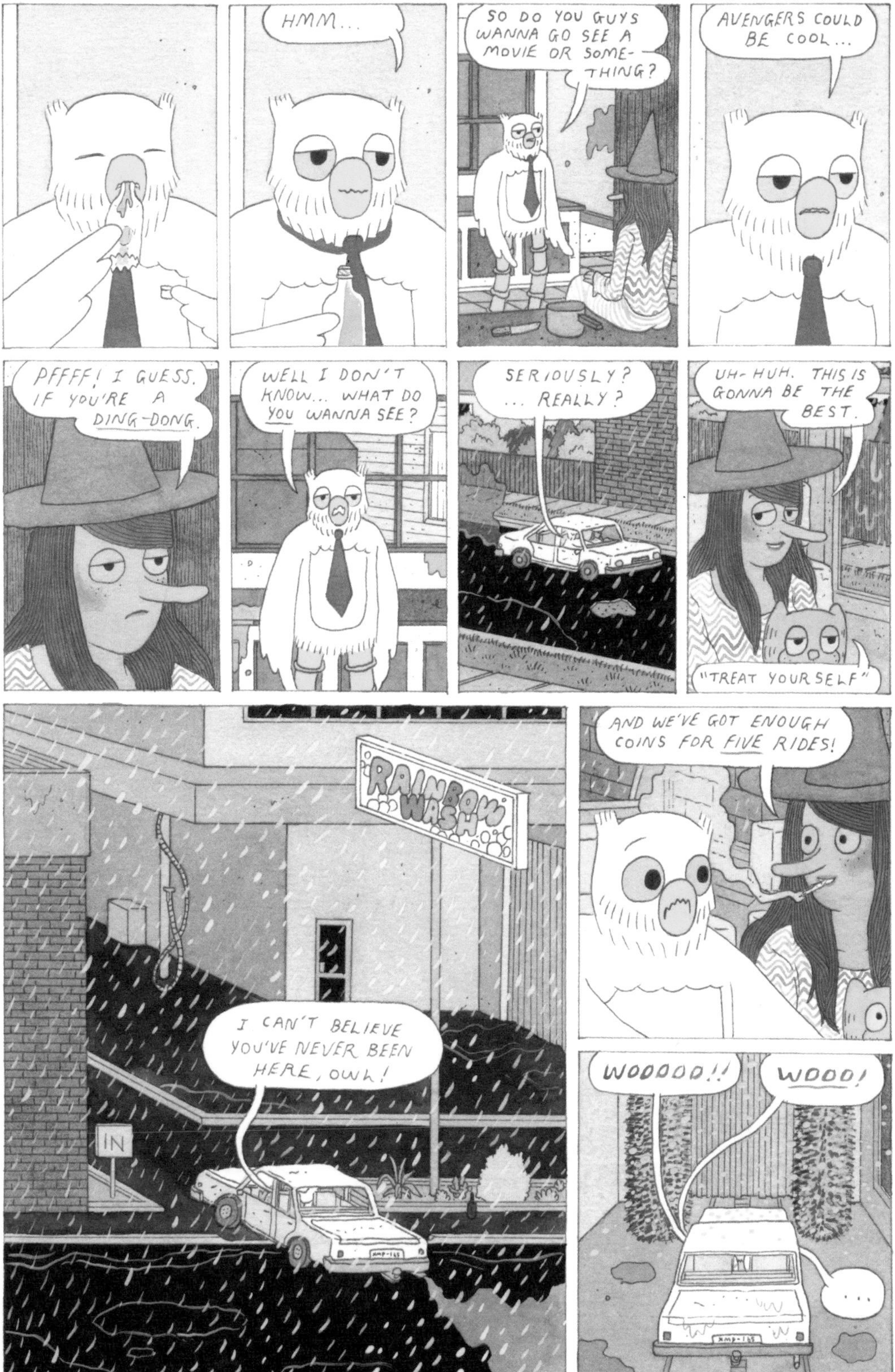
HMM...
SO DO YOU GUYS WANNA GO SEE A MOVIE OR SOME-THING?
AVENGERS COULD BE COOL...
PFFFF! I GUESS. IF YOU'RE A DING-DONG.
WELL I DON'T KNOW... WHAT DO YOU WANNA SEE?
SERIOUSLY? ... REALLY?
UH-HUH. THIS IS GONNA BE THE BEST.
"TREAT YOURSELF"
RAINBOW WASH
IN
I CAN'T BELIEVE YOU'VE NEVER BEEN HERE, OWL!
AND WE'VE GOT ENOUGH COINS FOR FIVE RIDES!
WOOOOO!!
WOOO!
...

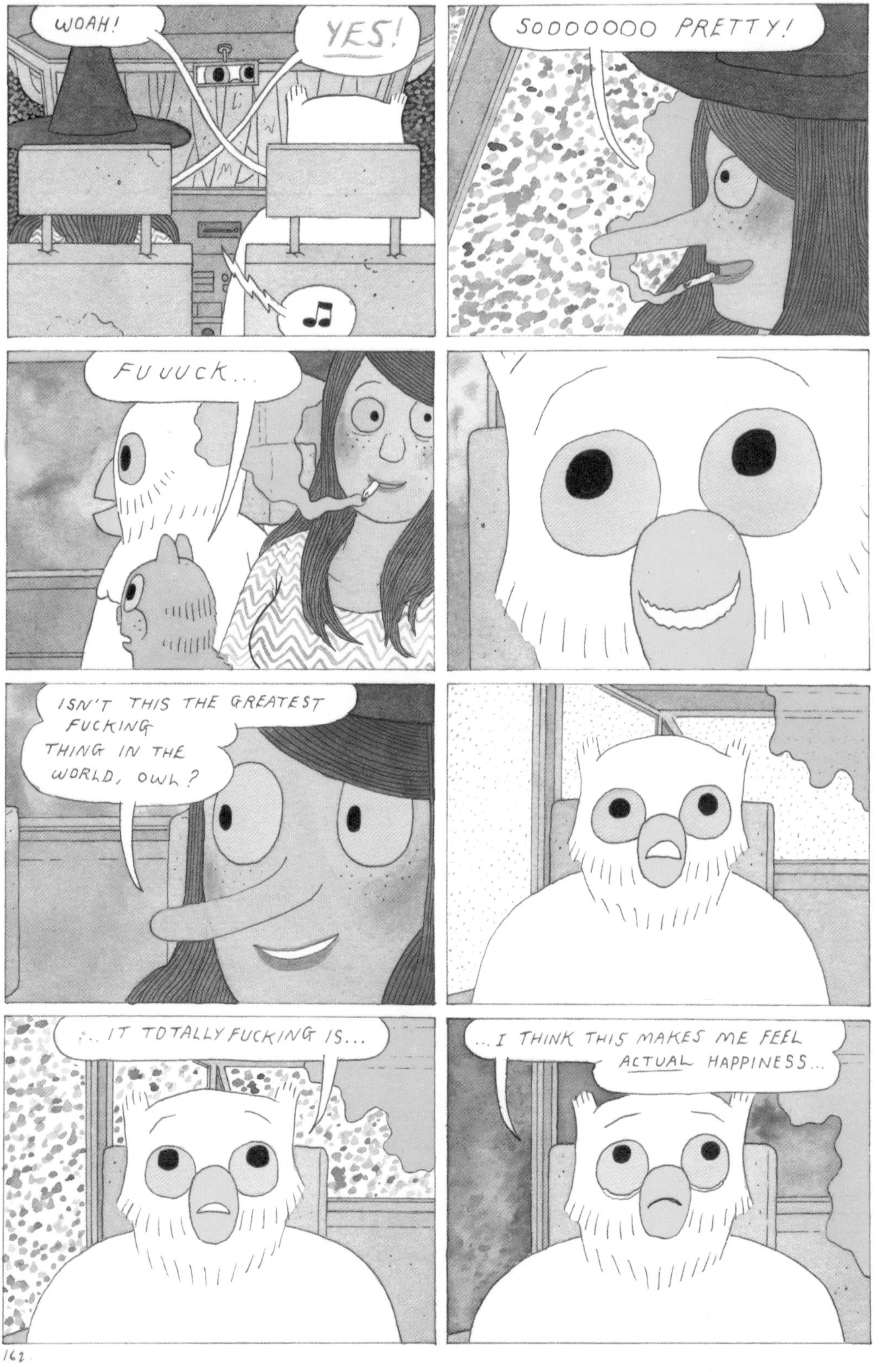
WOAH!
YES!
SOOOOOOO PRETTY!
FUUUCK...
ISN'T THIS THE GREATEST FUCKING THING IN THE WORLD, OWL?
...IT TOTALLY FUCKING IS...
...I THINK THIS MAKES ME FEEL ACTUAL HAPPINESS...

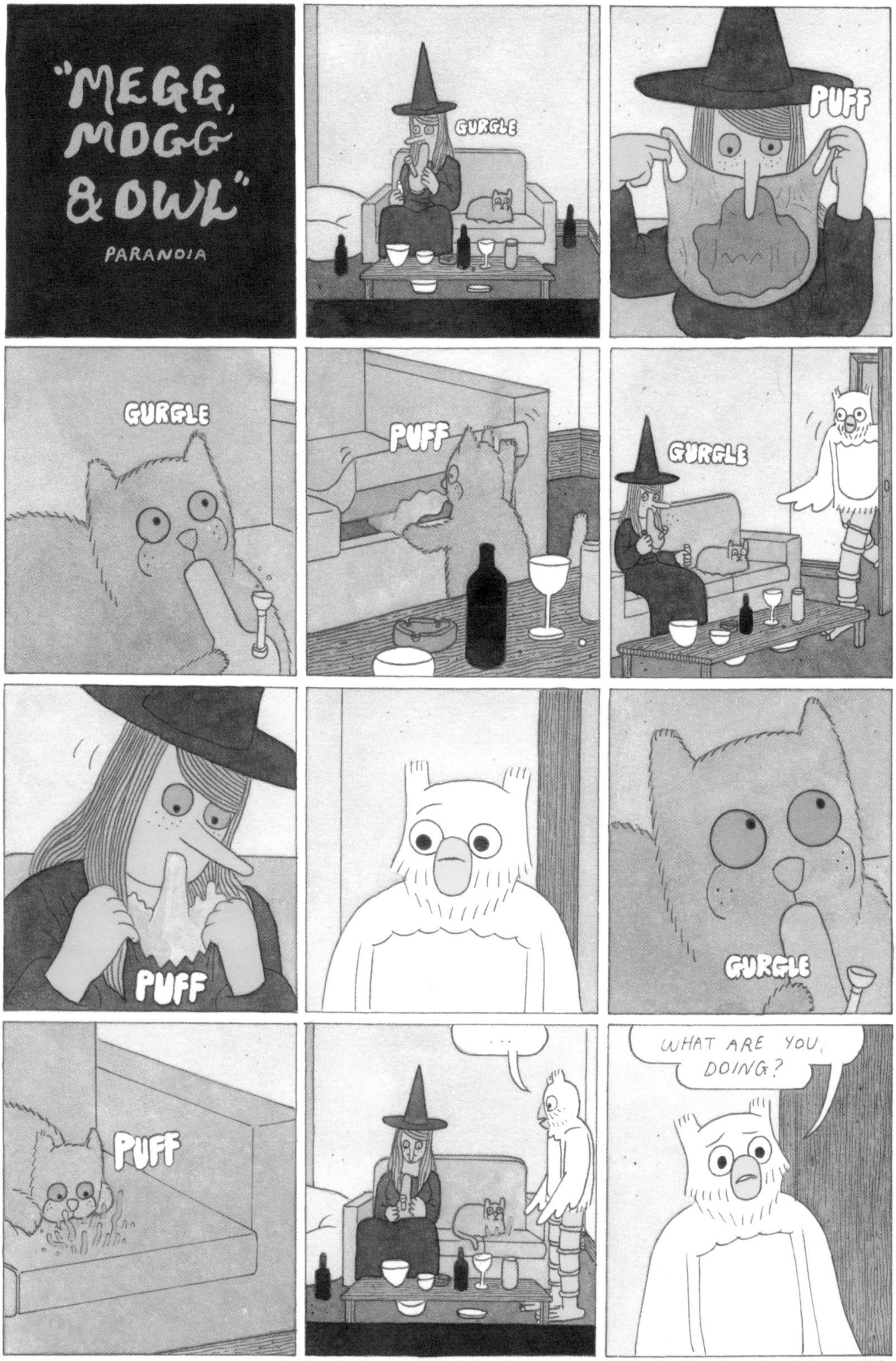
"MEGG, MOGG & OWL"
PARANOIA
GURGLE
PUFF
GURGLE
PUFF
GURGLE
PUFF
GURGLE
PUFF
...
WHAT ARE YOU DOING?

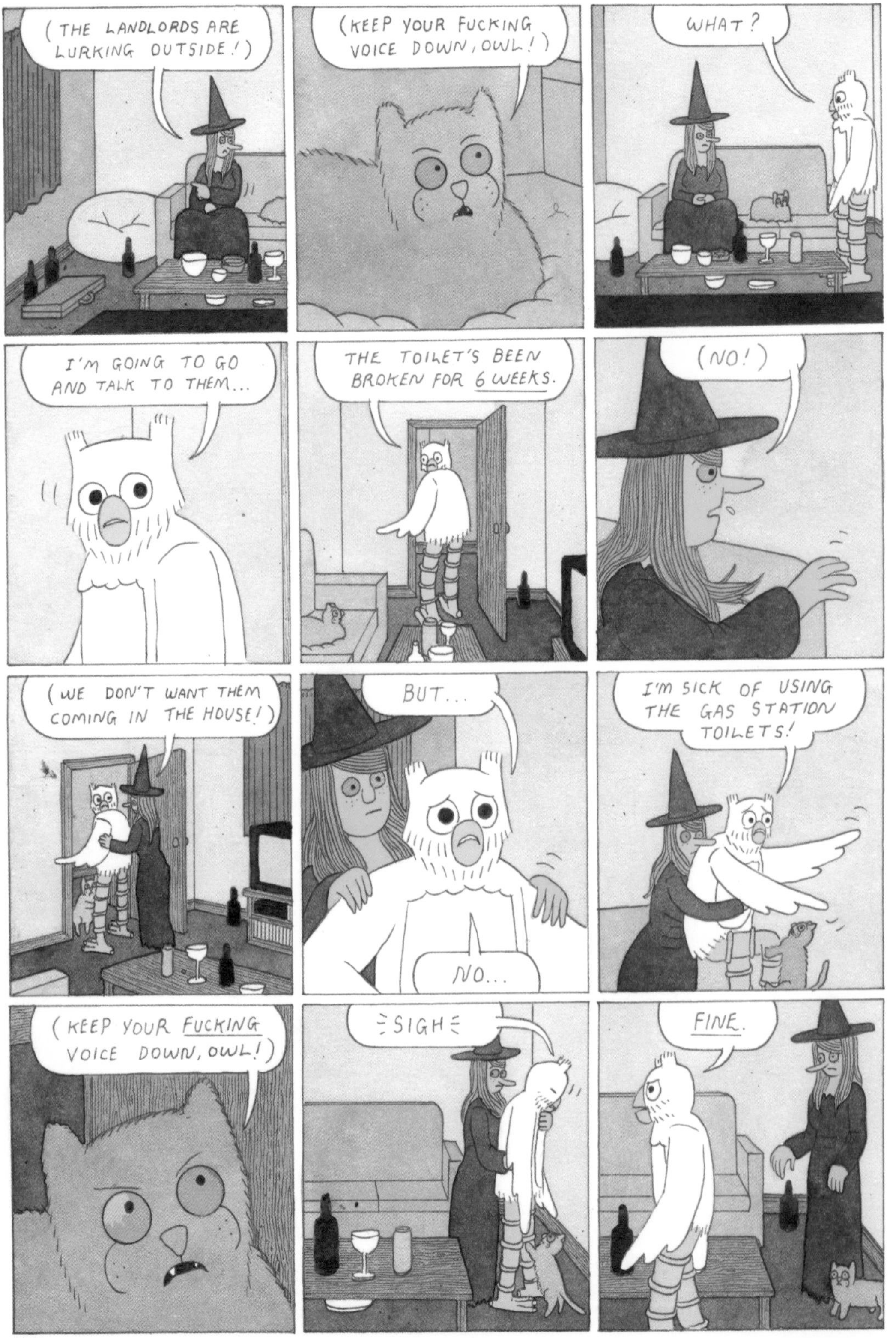
(THE LANDLORDS ARE LURKING OUTSIDE!)
(KEEP YOUR FUCKING VOICE DOWN, OWL!)
WHAT?
I'M GOING TO GO AND TALK TO THEM...
THE TOILET'S BEEN BROKEN FOR 6 WEEKS.
(NO!)
(WE DON'T WANT THEM COMING IN THE HOUSE!)
BUT...
NO...
I'M SICK OF USING THE GAS STATION TOILETS!
(KEEP YOUR FUCKING VOICE DOWN, OWL!)
SIGH
FINE.

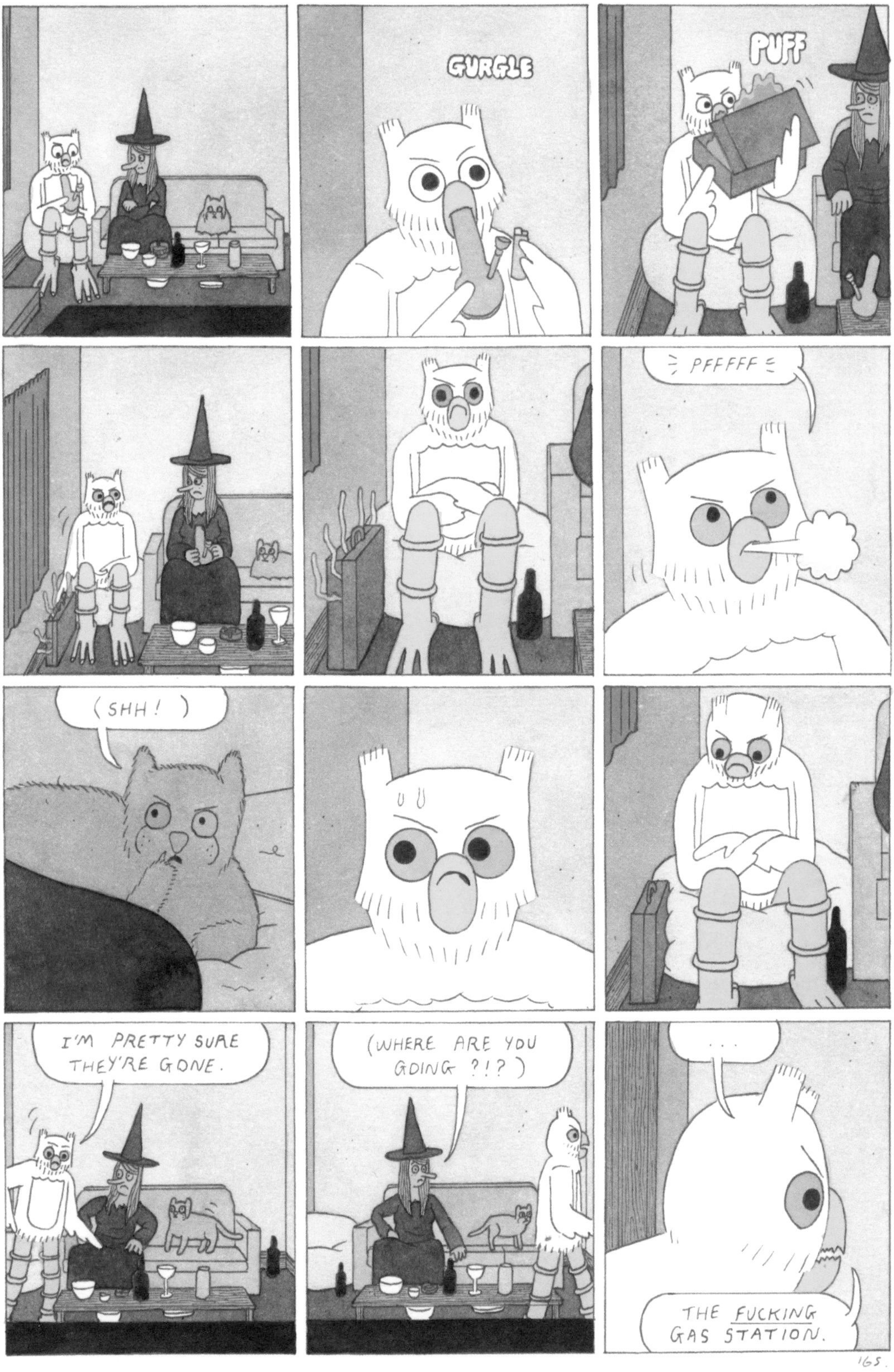
GURGLE
PUFF
PFFFFF
(SHH!)
I'M PRETTY SURE THEY'RE GONE.
(WHERE ARE YOU GOING ?!?)
. . .
THE FUCKING GAS STATION.

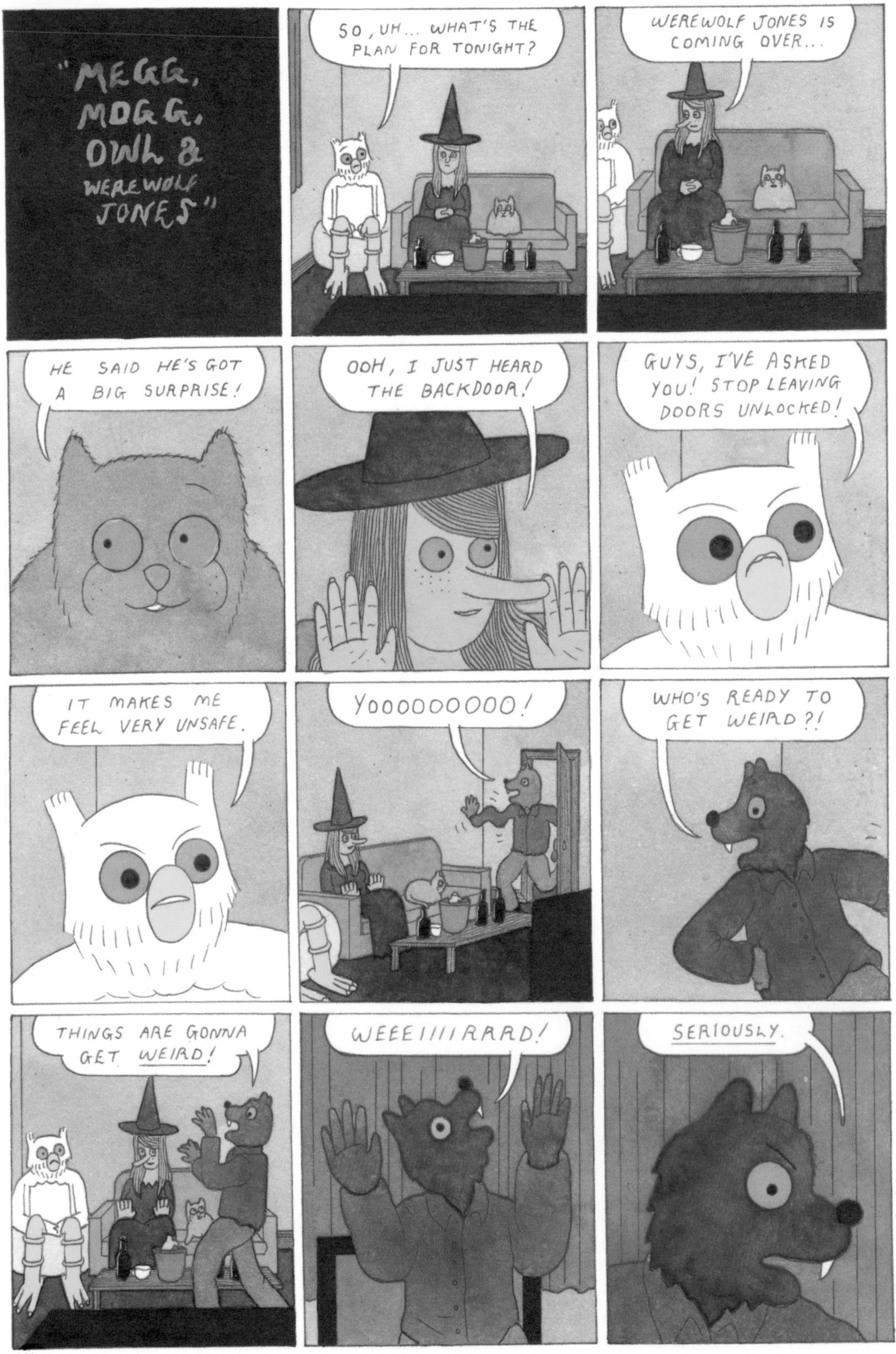
"MEGG, MOGG, OWL & WEREWOLF JONES"
SO, UH... WHAT'S THE PLAN FOR TONIGHT?
WEREWOLF JONES IS COMING OVER...
HE SAID HE'S GOT A BIG SURPRISE!
OOH, I JUST HEARD THE BACKDOOR!
GUYS, I'VE ASKED YOU! STOP LEAVING DOORS UNLOCKED!
IT MAKES ME FEEL VERY UNSAFE.
YOOOOOOOOO!
WHO'S READY TO GET WEIRD?!
THINGS ARE GONNA GET WEIRD!
WEEEIIIIRRRD!
SERIOUSLY.

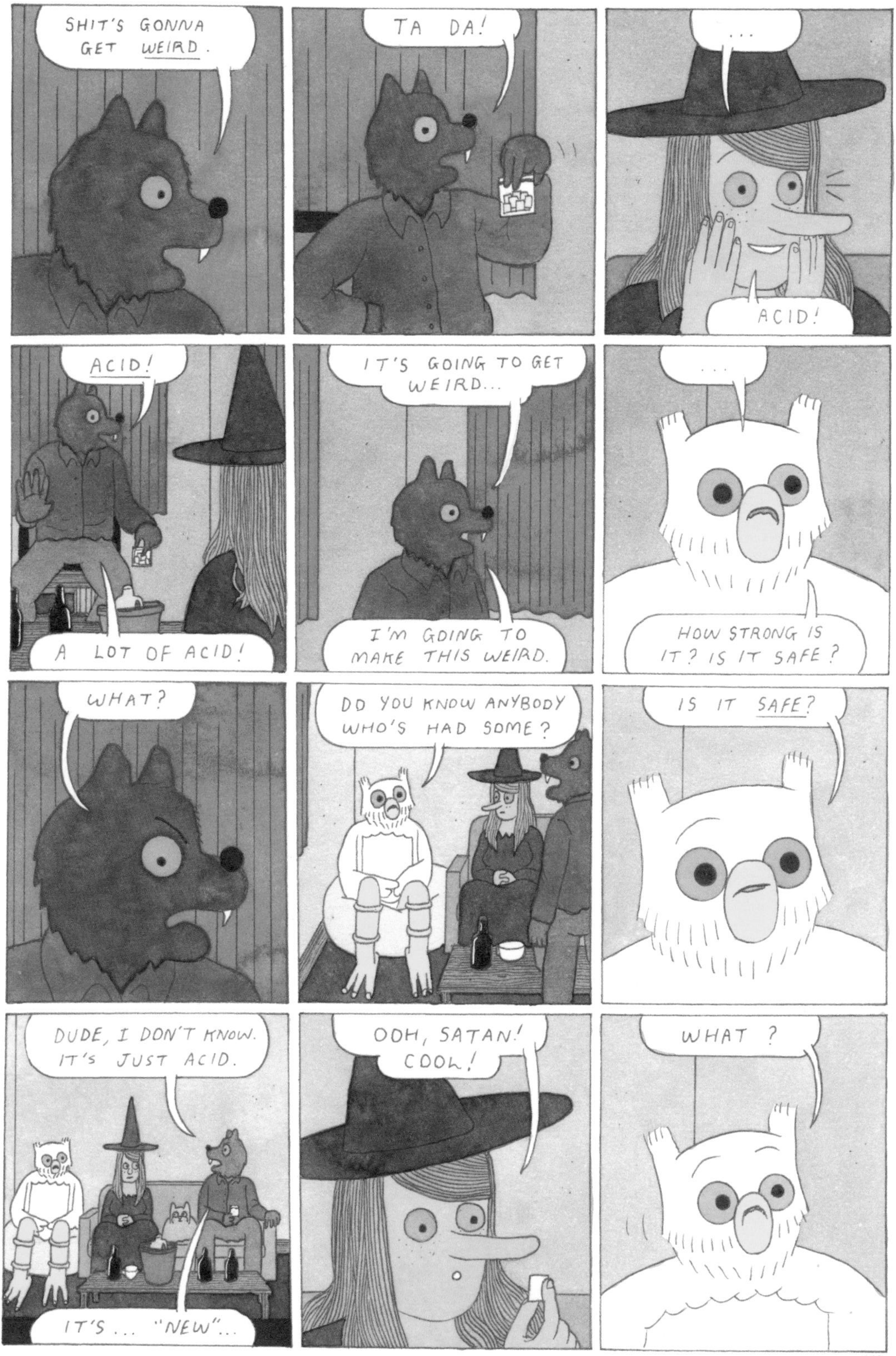
SHIT'S GONNA GET WEIRD.
TA DA!
...
ACID!
ACID!
A LOT OF ACID!
IT'S GOING TO GET WEIRD...
I'M GOING TO MAKE THIS WEIRD.
...
HOW STRONG IS IT? IS IT SAFE?
WHAT?
DO YOU KNOW ANYBODY WHO'S HAD SOME?
IS IT SAFE?
DUDE, I DON'T KNOW. IT'S JUST ACID.
IT'S... "NEW"...
OOH, SATAN! COOL!
WHAT ?

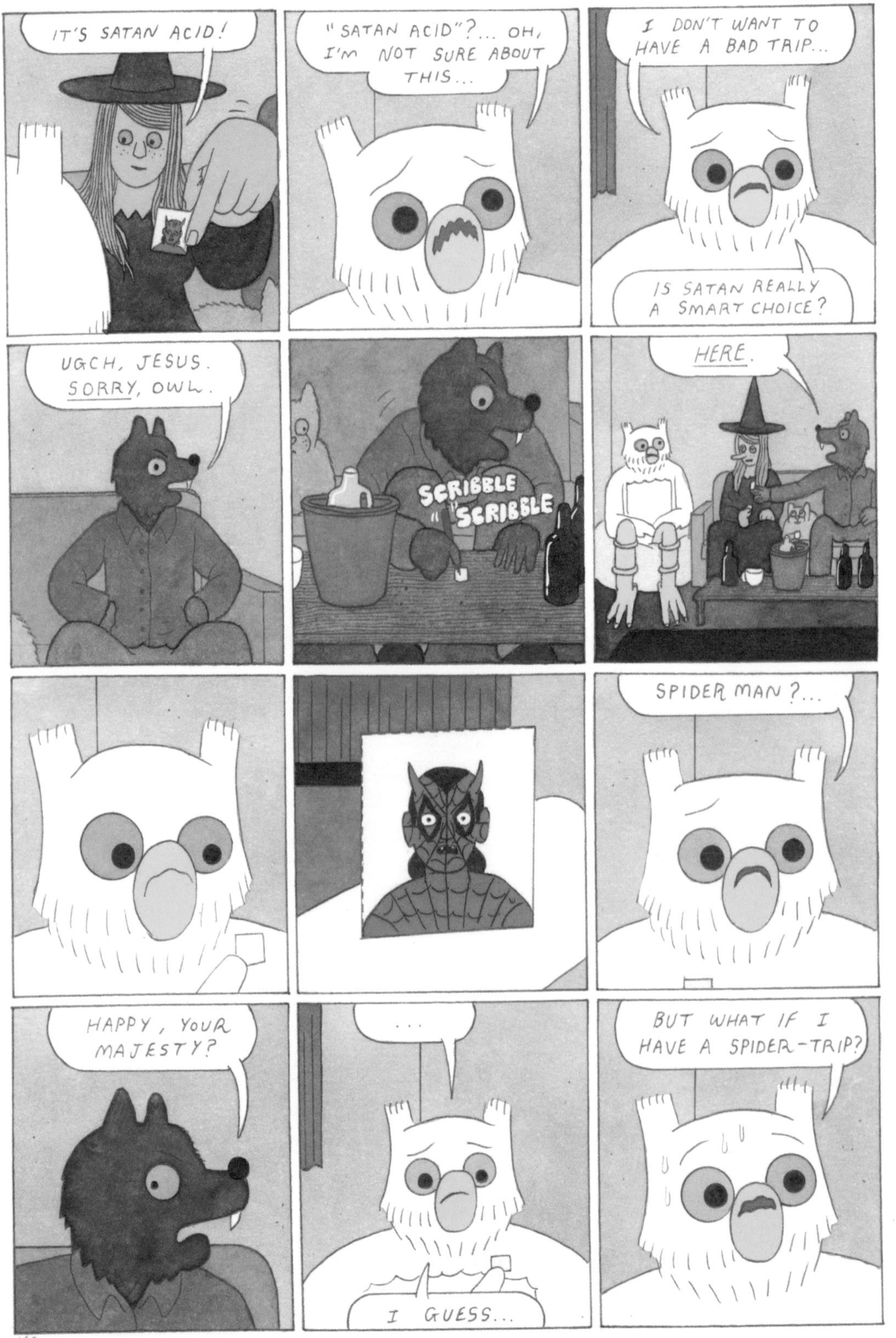
IT'S SATAN ACID!
"SATAN ACID"?... OH, I'M NOT SURE ABOUT THIS...
I DON'T WANT TO HAVE A BAD TRIP...
IS SATAN REALLY A SMART CHOICE?
UGCH, JESUS. SORRY, OWL.
SCRIBBLE SCRIBBLE
HERE.
SPIDER MAN?...
HAPPY, YOUR MAJESTY?
...
I GUESS...
BUT WHAT IF I HAVE A SPIDER-TRIP?

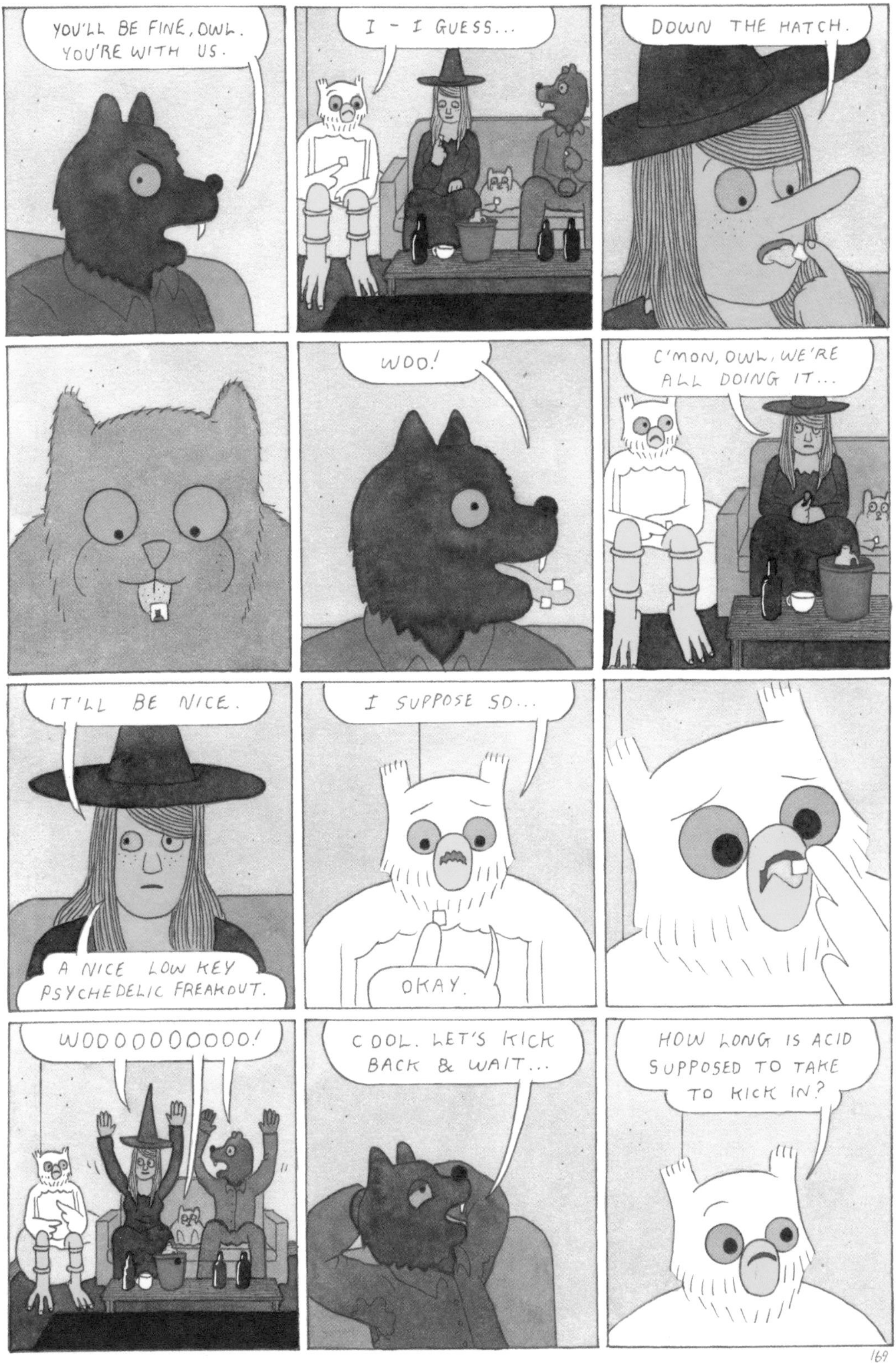
YOU'LL BE FINE, OWL. YOU'RE WITH US.
I - I GUESS...
DOWN THE HATCH.
WOO!
C'MON, OWL, WE'RE ALL DOING IT...
IT'LL BE NICE.
A NICE LOW KEY PSYCHEDELIC FREAKOUT.
I SUPPOSE SO...
OKAY.
WOOOOOOOOOO!
COOL. LET'S KICK BACK & WAIT...
HOW LONG IS ACID SUPPOSED TO TAKE TO KICK IN?

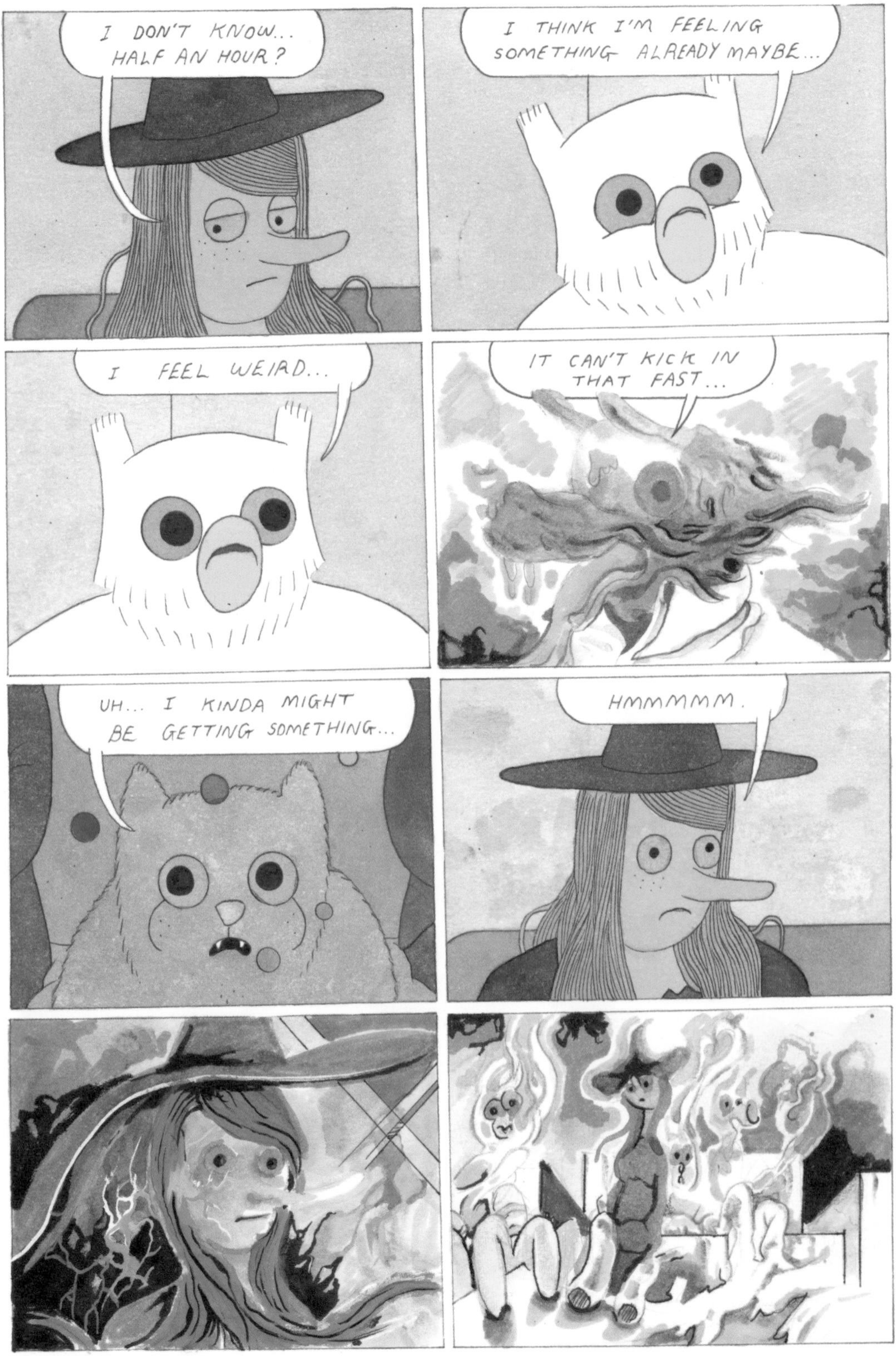
I DON'T KNOW...
HALF AN HOUR?
I THINK I'M FEELING
SOMETHING ALREADY MAYBE...
I FEEL WEIRD...
IT CAN'T KICK IN
THAT FAST...
UH... I KINDA MIGHT
BE GETTING SOMETHING...
HMMMMM.

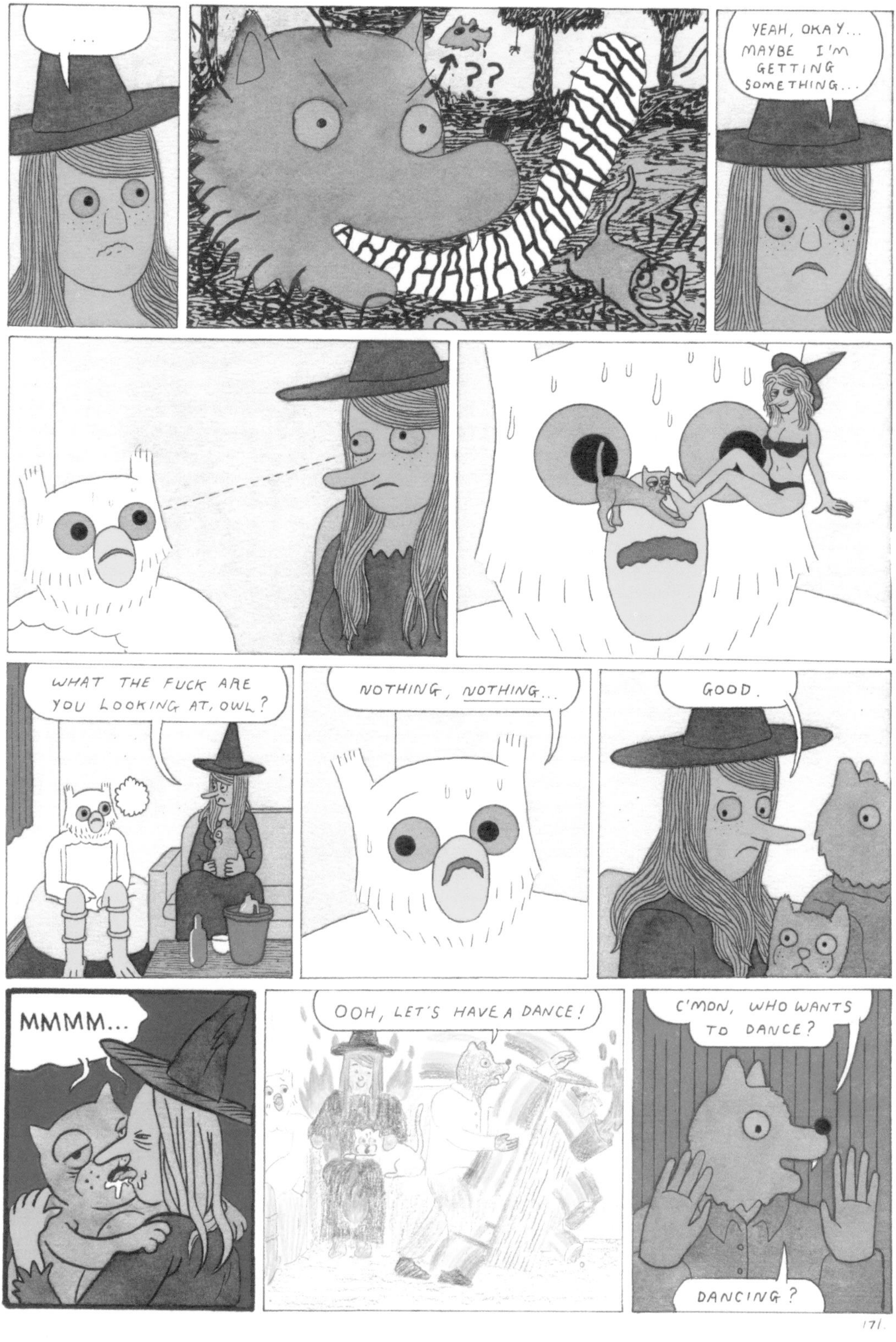

...
??
AHAHAHAHAHAHAHA
YEAH, OKAY... MAYBE I'M GETTING SOMETHING...
WHAT THE FUCK ARE YOU LOOKING AT, OWL?
NOTHING, NOTHING...
GOOD.
MMMM...
OOH, LET'S HAVE A DANCE!
C'MON, WHO WANTS TO DANCE?
DANCING?

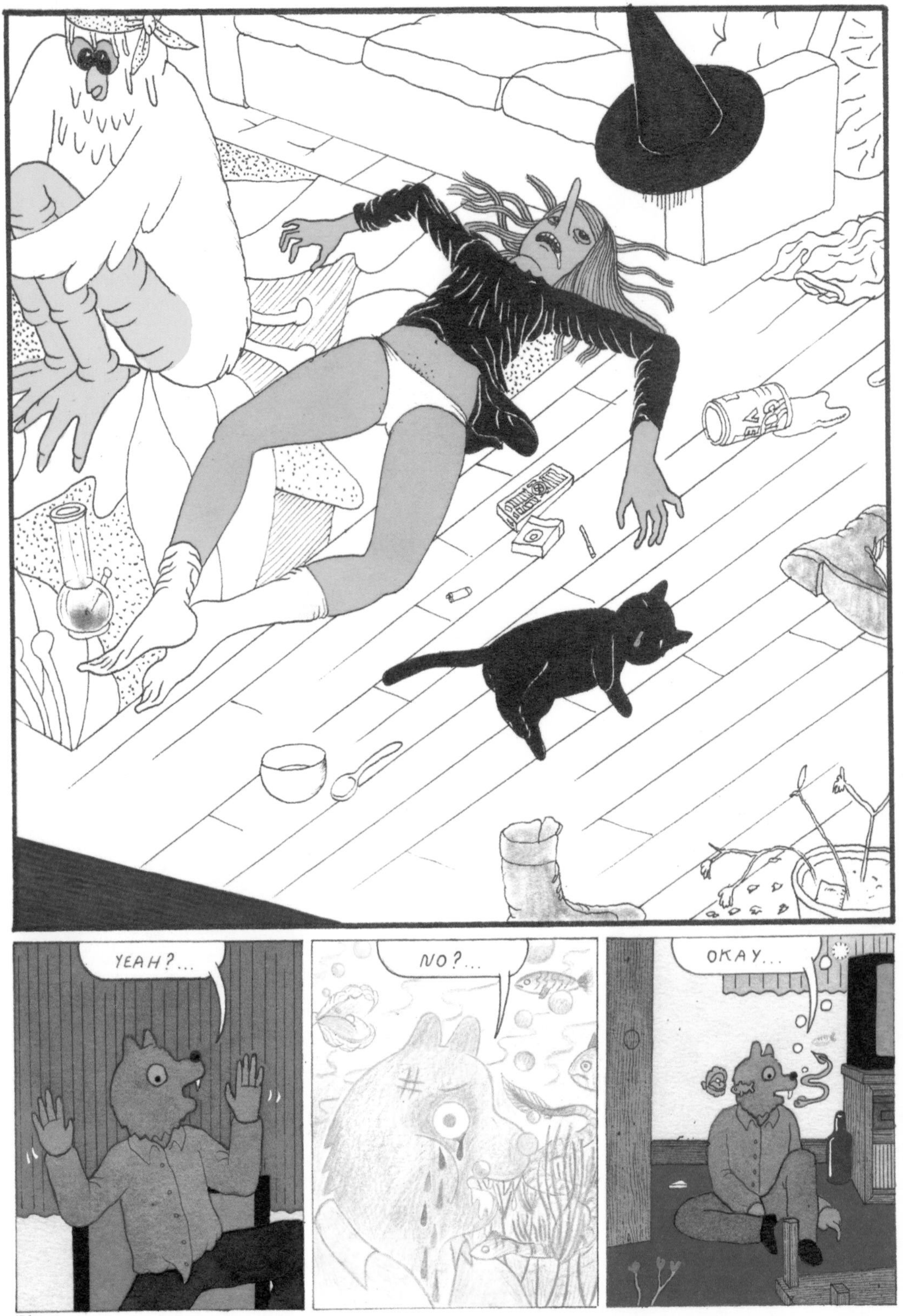
YEAH?...
NO?...
OKAY...

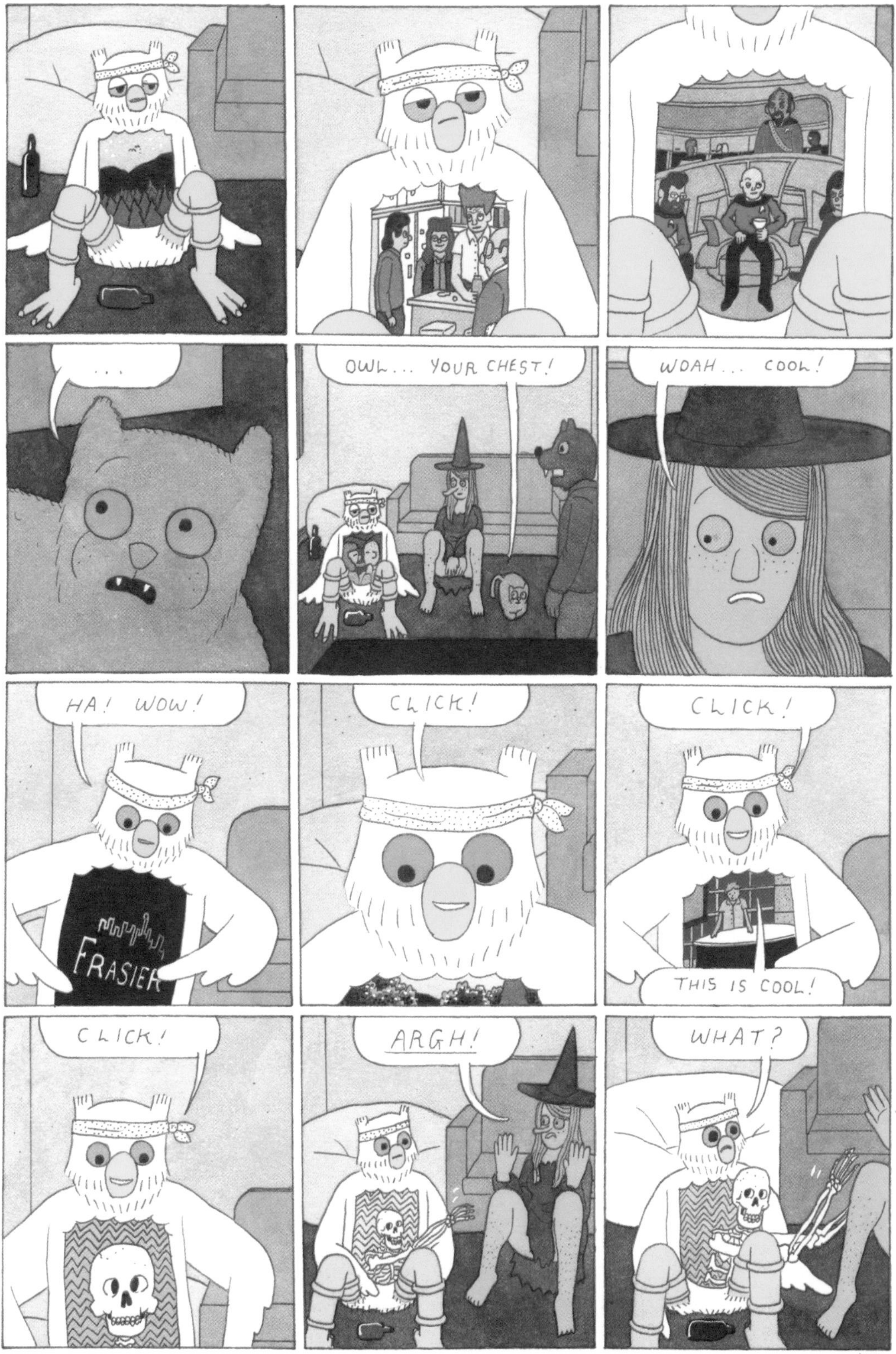
. . .
OWL... YOUR CHEST!
WOAH... COOL!
HA! WOW!
FRASIER
CLICK!
CLICK!
THIS IS COOL!
CLICK!
ARGH!
WHAT?

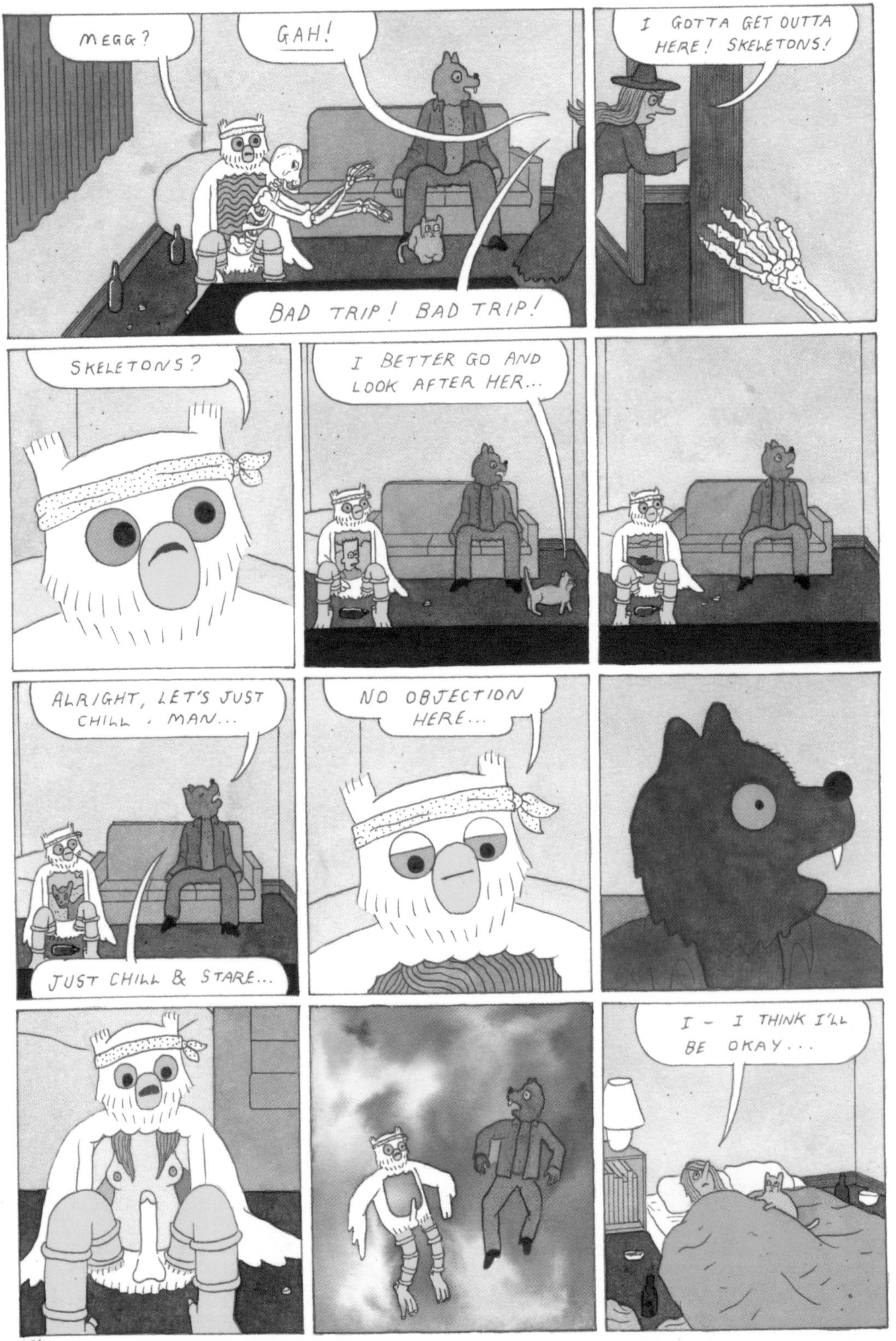
MEGG?
GAH!
BAD TRIP! BAD TRIP!
I GOTTA GET OUTTA HERE! SKELETONS!
SKELETONS?
I BETTER GO AND LOOK AFTER HER...
ALRIGHT, LET'S JUST CHILL, MAN...
JUST CHILL & STARE...
NO OBJECTION HERE...
I - I THINK I'LL BE OKAY...

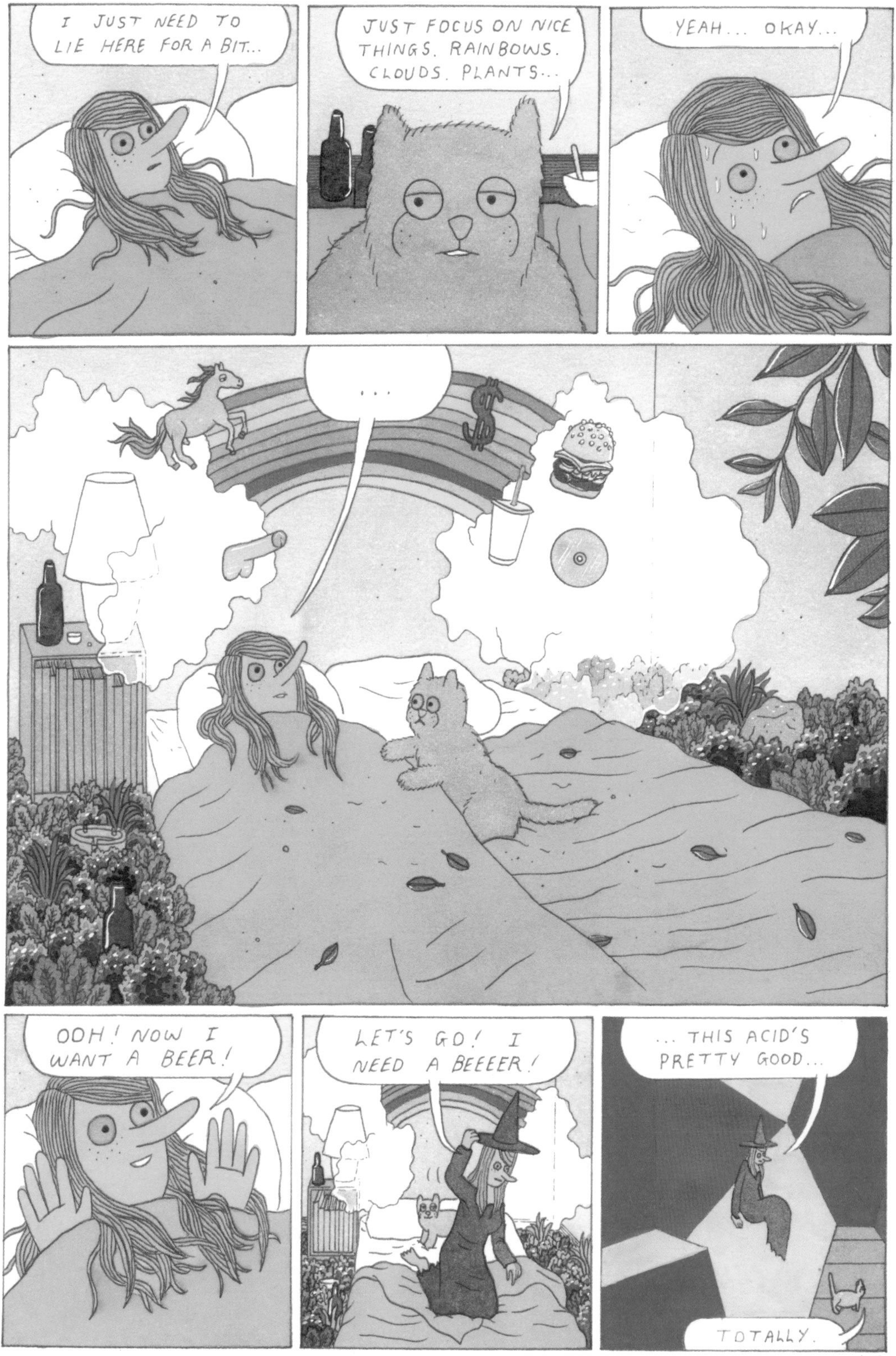
I JUST NEED TO LIE HERE FOR A BIT...
JUST FOCUS ON NICE THINGS. RAINBOWS. CLOUDS. PLANTS...
YEAH... OKAY...
...
OOH! NOW I WANT A BEER!
LET'S GO! I NEED A BEEEER!
... THIS ACID'S PRETTY GOOD...
TOTALLY.

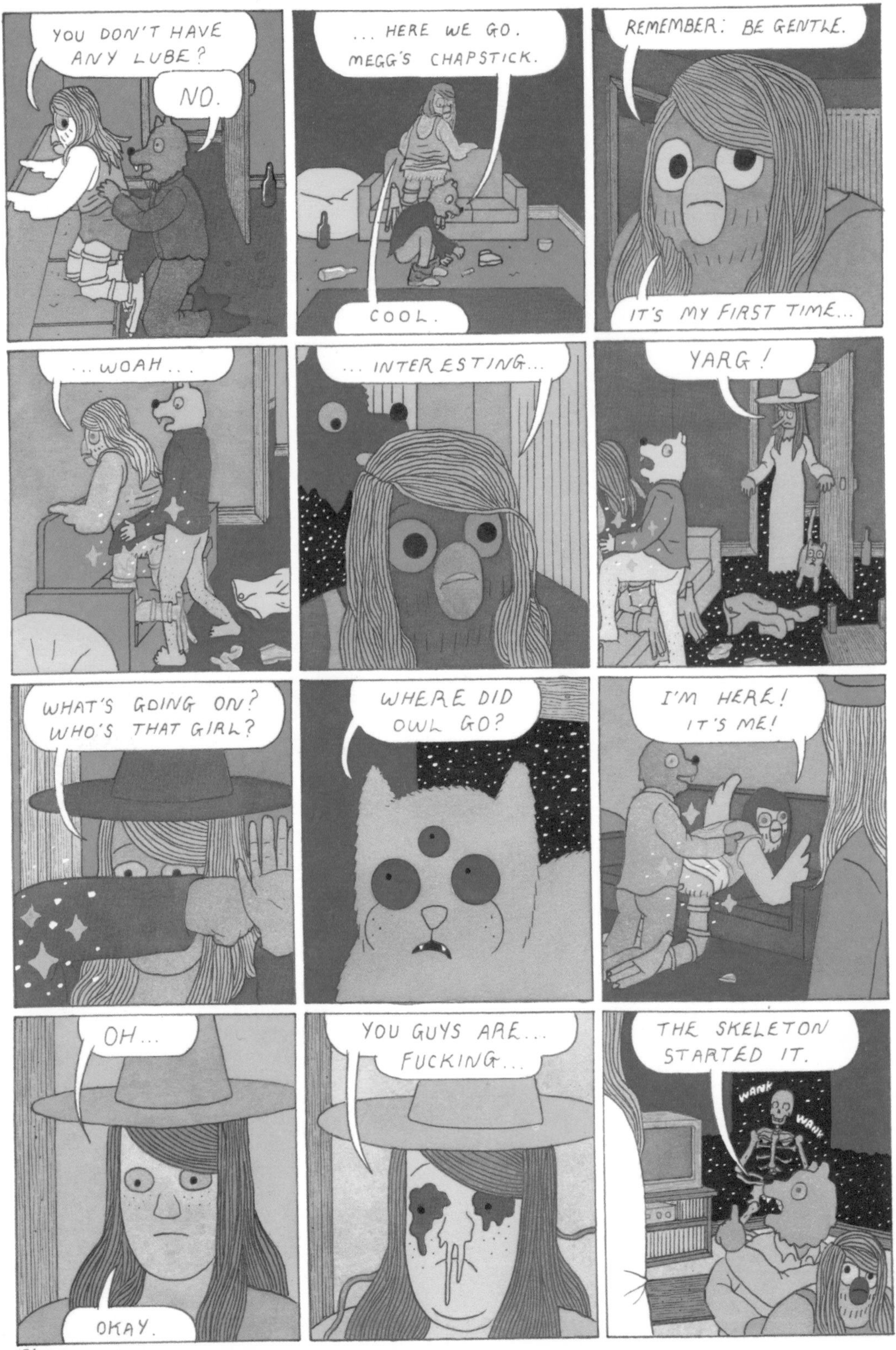
YOU DON'T HAVE ANY LUBE?
NO.
... HERE WE GO. MEGG'S CHAPSTICK.
COOL.
REMEMBER: BE GENTLE.
IT'S MY FIRST TIME...
... WOAH ...
... INTERESTING...
YARG!
WHAT'S GOING ON? WHO'S THAT GIRL?
WHERE DID OWL GO?
I'M HERE! IT'S ME!
OH...
OKAY.
YOU GUYS ARE... FUCKING...
THE SKELETON STARTED IT.
WANK
WANK

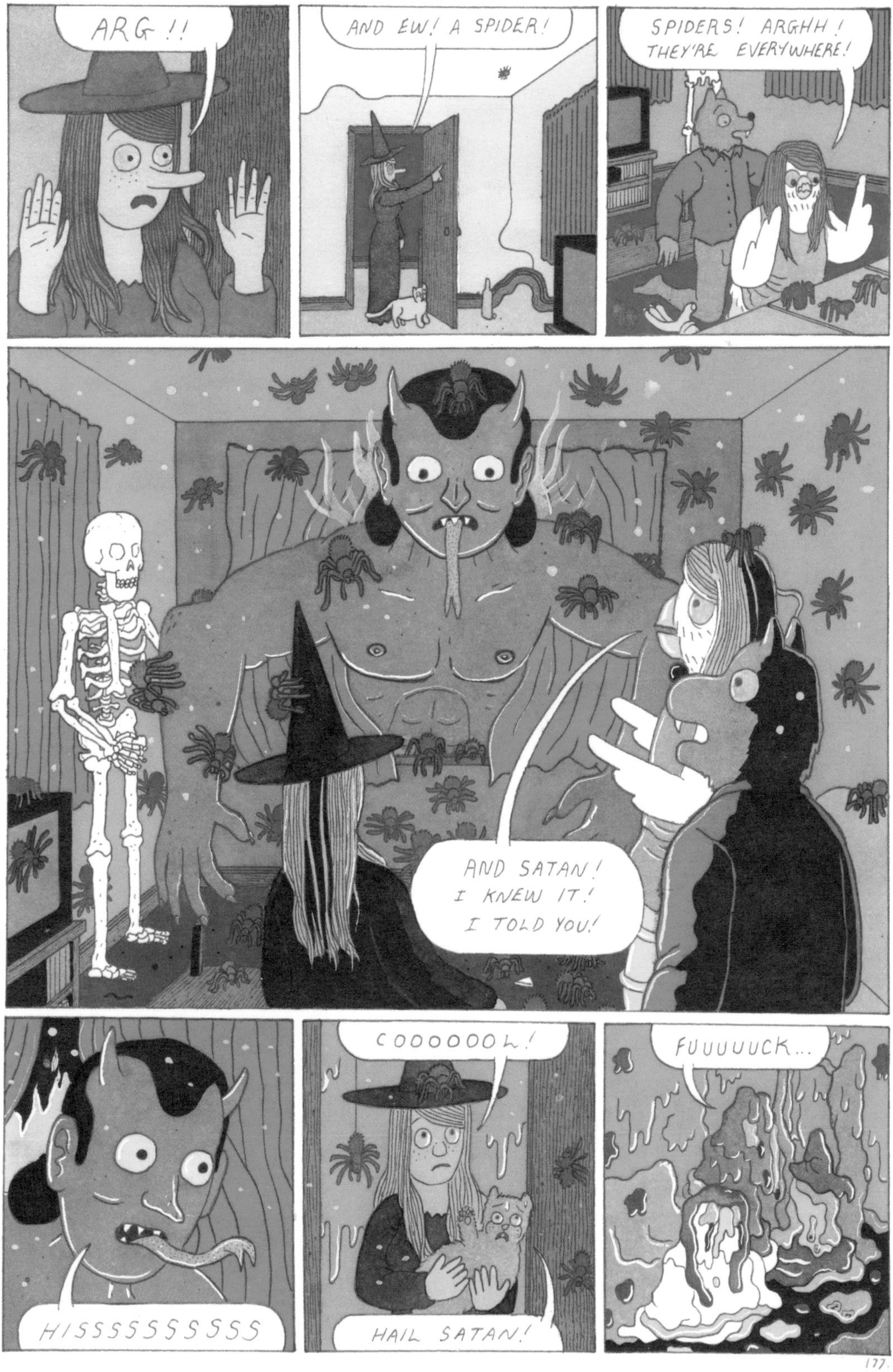
ARG!!
AND EW! A SPIDER!
SPIDERS! ARGHH! THEY'RE EVERYWHERE!
AND SATAN! I KNEW IT! I TOLD YOU!
HISSSSSSSSSS
COOOOOOL!
HAIL SATAN!
FUUUUUCK...

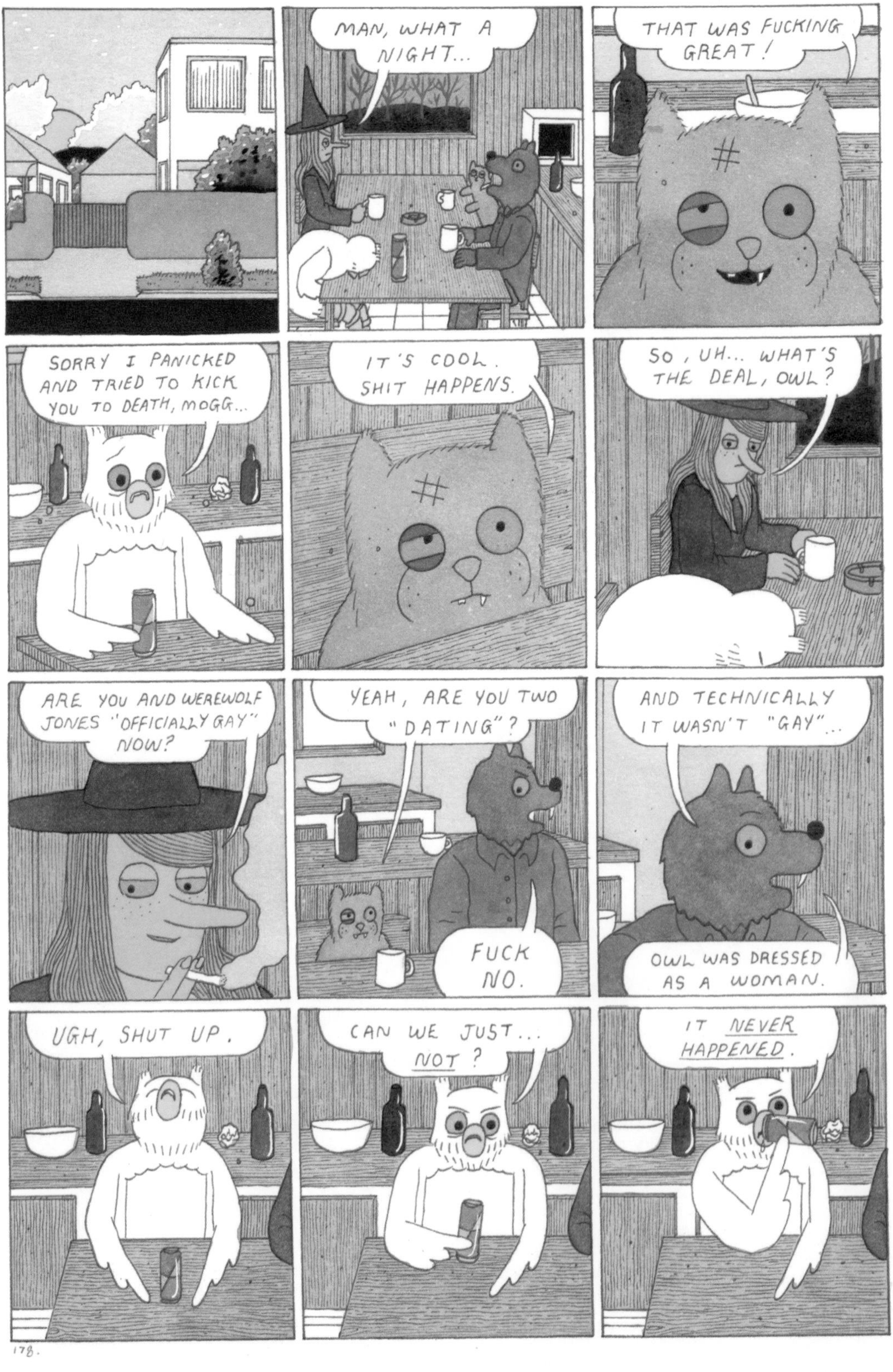
MAN, WHAT A NIGHT...
THAT WAS FUCKING GREAT!
SORRY I PANICKED AND TRIED TO KICK YOU TO DEATH, MOGG...
IT'S COOL. SHIT HAPPENS.
SO, UH... WHAT'S THE DEAL, OWL?
ARE YOU AND WEREWOLF JONES "OFFICIALLY GAY" NOW?
YEAH, ARE YOU TWO "DATING"?
FUCK NO.
AND TECHNICALLY IT WASN'T "GAY"...
OWL WAS DRESSED AS A WOMAN.
UGH, SHUT UP.
CAN WE JUST... NOT?
IT NEVER HAPPENED.

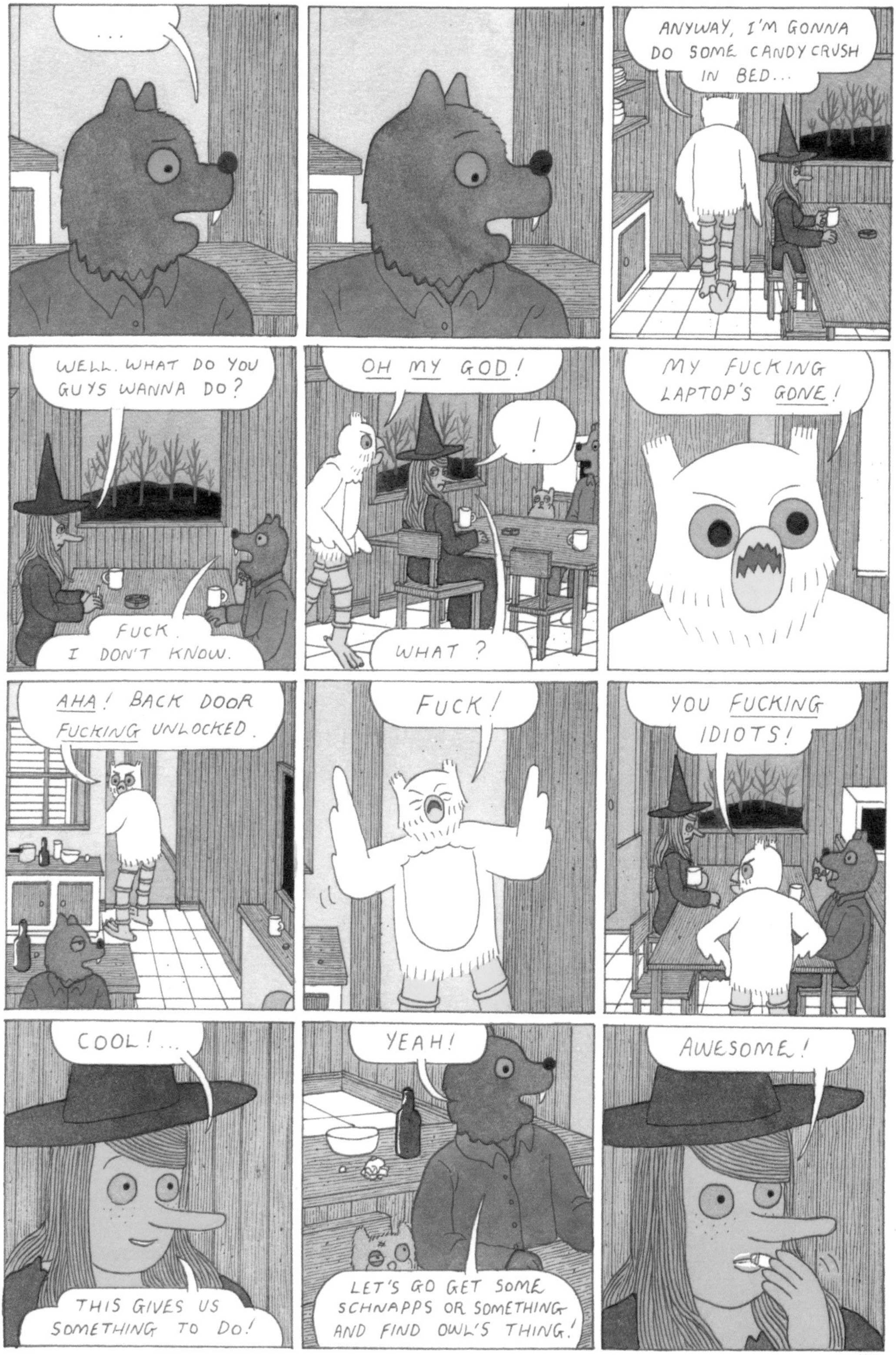
...
ANYWAY, I'M GONNA DO SOME CANDY CRUSH IN BED...
WELL. WHAT DO YOU GUYS WANNA DO?
FUCK. I DON'T KNOW.
OH MY GOD!
!
WHAT?
MY FUCKING LAPTOP'S GONE!
AHA! BACK DOOR FUCKING UNLOCKED.
FUCK!
YOU FUCKING IDIOTS!
COOL!...
THIS GIVES US SOMETHING TO DO!
YEAH!
LET'S GO GET SOME SCHNAPPS OR SOMETHING AND FIND OWL'S THING!
AWESOME!

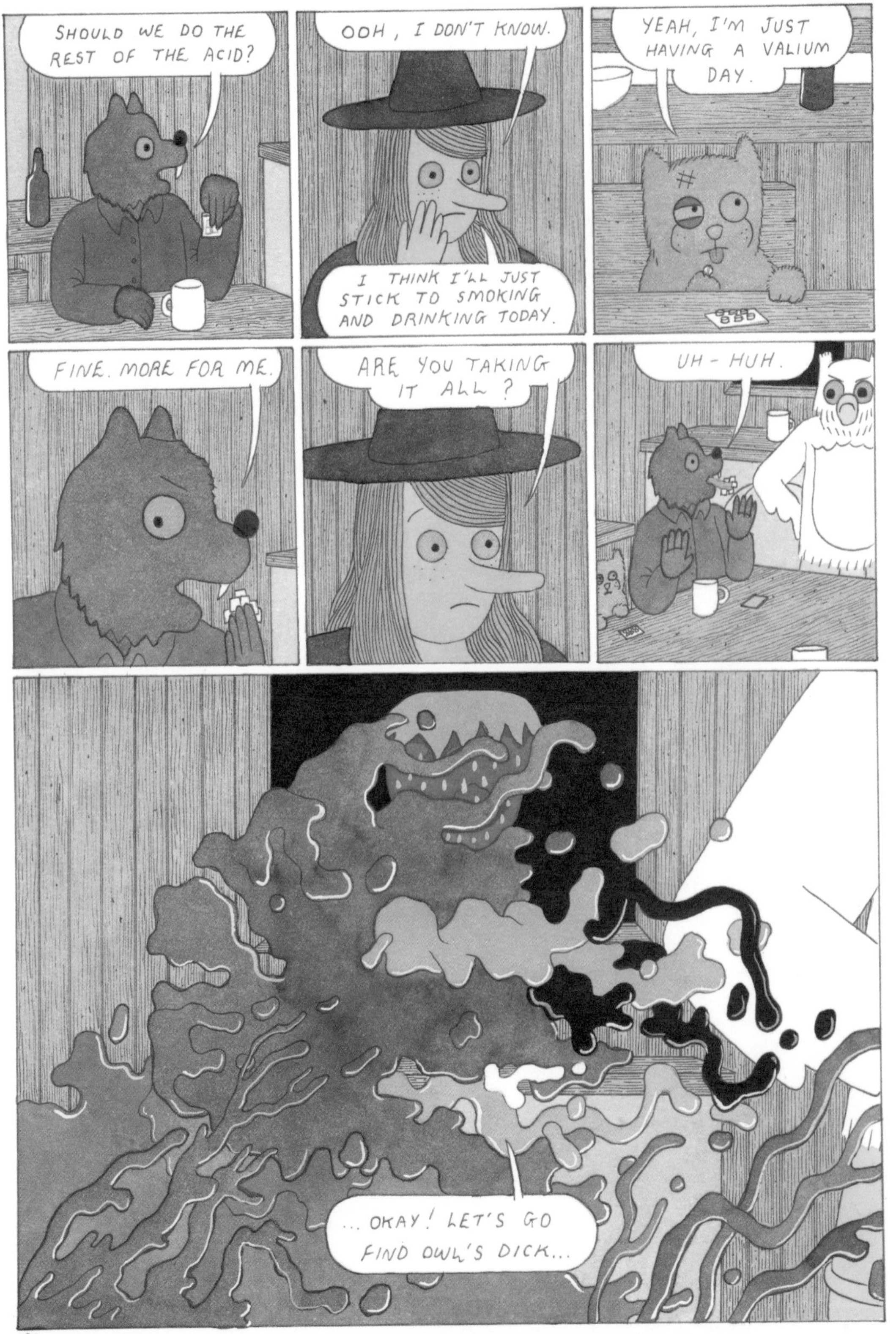
SHOULD WE DO THE REST OF THE ACID?
OOH, I DON'T KNOW.
I THINK I'LL JUST STICK TO SMOKING AND DRINKING TODAY.
YEAH, I'M JUST HAVING A VALIUM DAY.
FINE. MORE FOR ME.
ARE YOU TAKING IT ALL?
UH-HUH.
...OKAY! LET'S GO FIND OWL'S DICK...

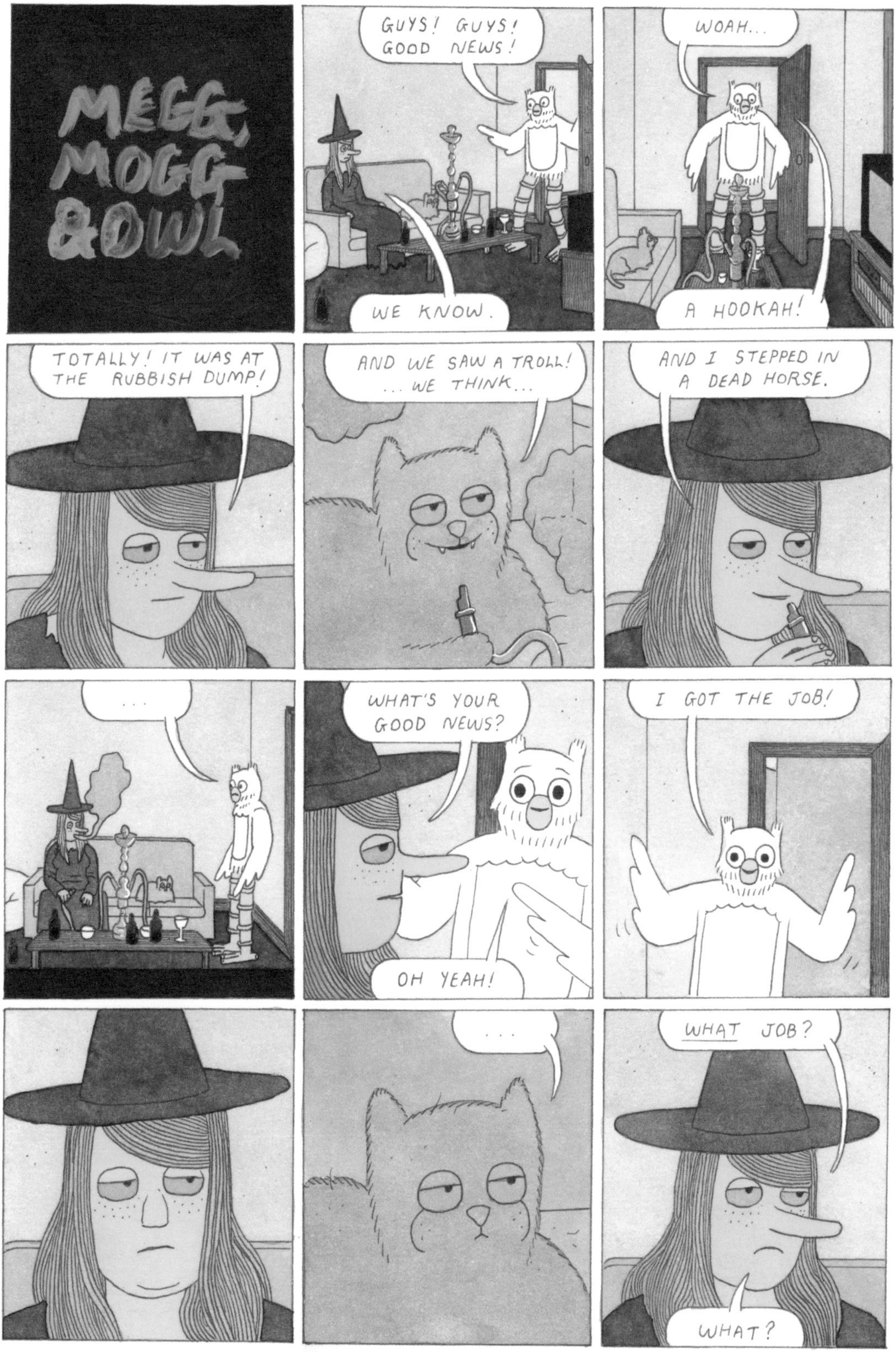
MEGG, MOGG & OWL
GUYS! GUYS! GOOD NEWS!
WE KNOW.
WOAH...
A HOOKAH!
TOTALLY! IT WAS AT THE RUBBISH DUMP!
AND WE SAW A TROLL! ... WE THINK...
AND I STEPPED IN A DEAD HORSE.
...
WHAT'S YOUR GOOD NEWS?
OH YEAH!
I GOT THE JOB!
...
WHAT JOB?
WHAT?

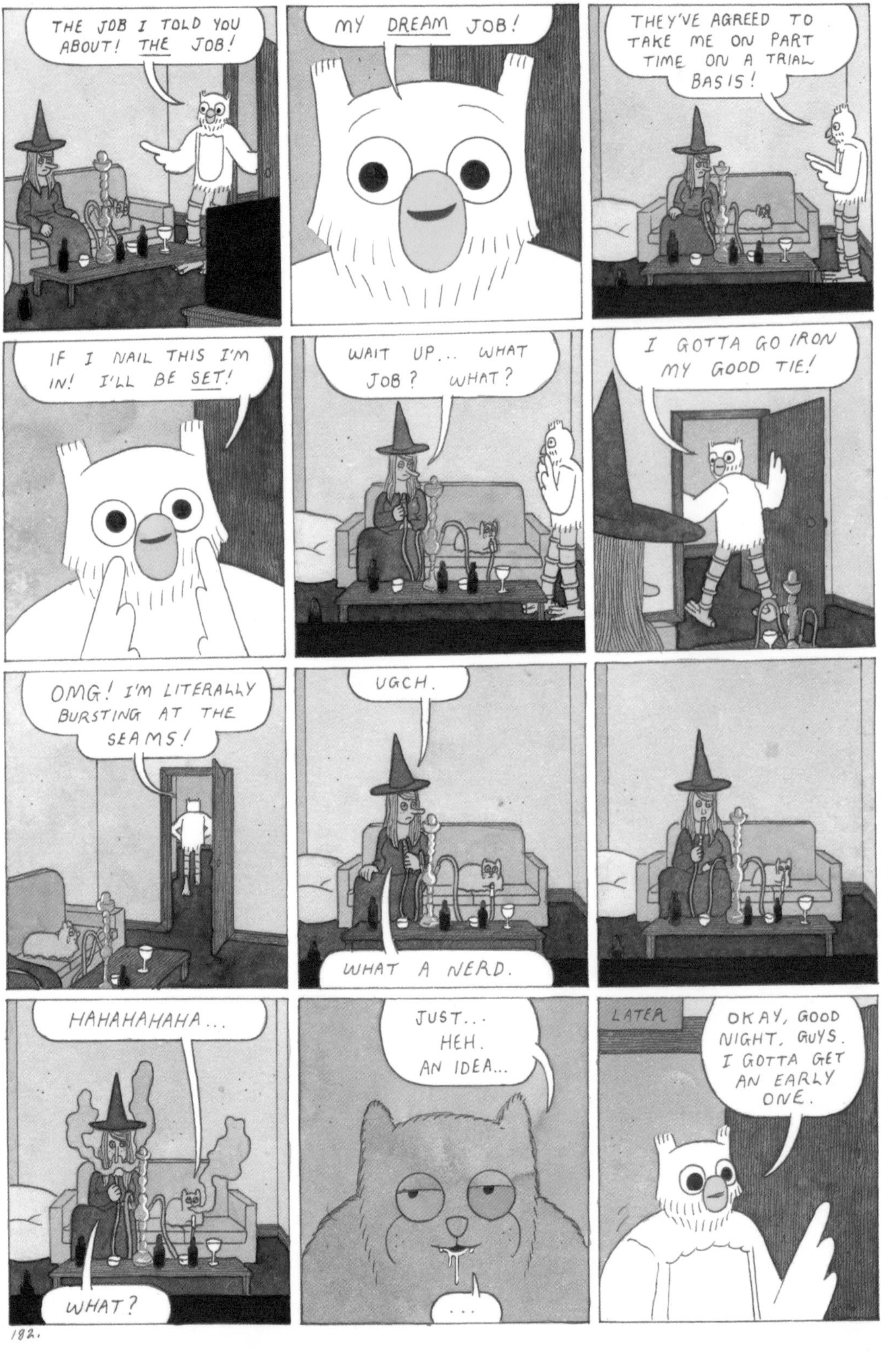
THE JOB I TOLD YOU ABOUT! THE JOB!
MY DREAM JOB!
THEY'VE AGREED TO TAKE ME ON PART TIME ON A TRIAL BASIS!
IF I NAIL THIS I'M IN! I'LL BE SET!
WAIT UP... WHAT JOB? WHAT?
I GOTTA GO IRON MY GOOD TIE!
OMG! I'M LITERALLY BURSTING AT THE SEAMS!
UGCH.
WHAT A NERD.
HAHAHAHAHA...
WHAT?
JUST... HEH. AN IDEA...
...
LATER
OKAY, GOOD NIGHT, GUYS. I GOTTA GET AN EARLY ONE.

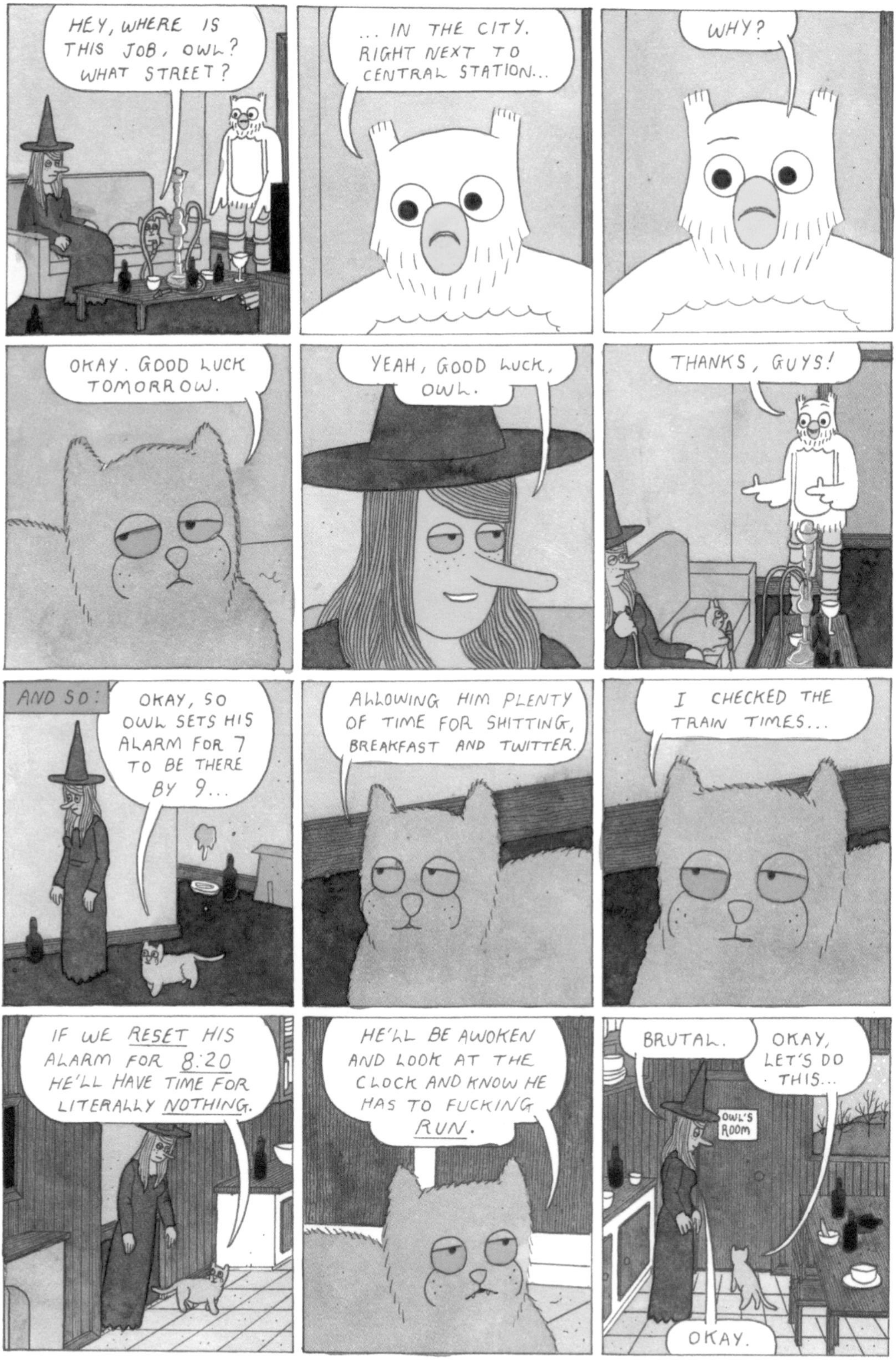

HEY, WHERE IS THIS JOB, OWL? WHAT STREET?
... IN THE CITY. RIGHT NEXT TO CENTRAL STATION...
WHY?
OKAY. GOOD LUCK TOMORROW.
YEAH, GOOD LUCK, OWL.
THANKS, GUYS!
AND SO:
OKAY, SO OWL SETS HIS ALARM FOR 7 TO BE THERE BY 9...
ALLOWING HIM PLENTY OF TIME FOR SHITTING, BREAKFAST AND TWITTER.
I CHECKED THE TRAIN TIMES...
IF WE RESET HIS ALARM FOR 8:20 HE'LL HAVE TIME FOR LITERALLY NOTHING.
HE'LL BE AWOKEN AND LOOK AT THE CLOCK AND KNOW HE HAS TO FUCKING RUN.
BRUTAL.
OKAY, LET'S DO THIS...
OWL'S ROOM
OKAY.

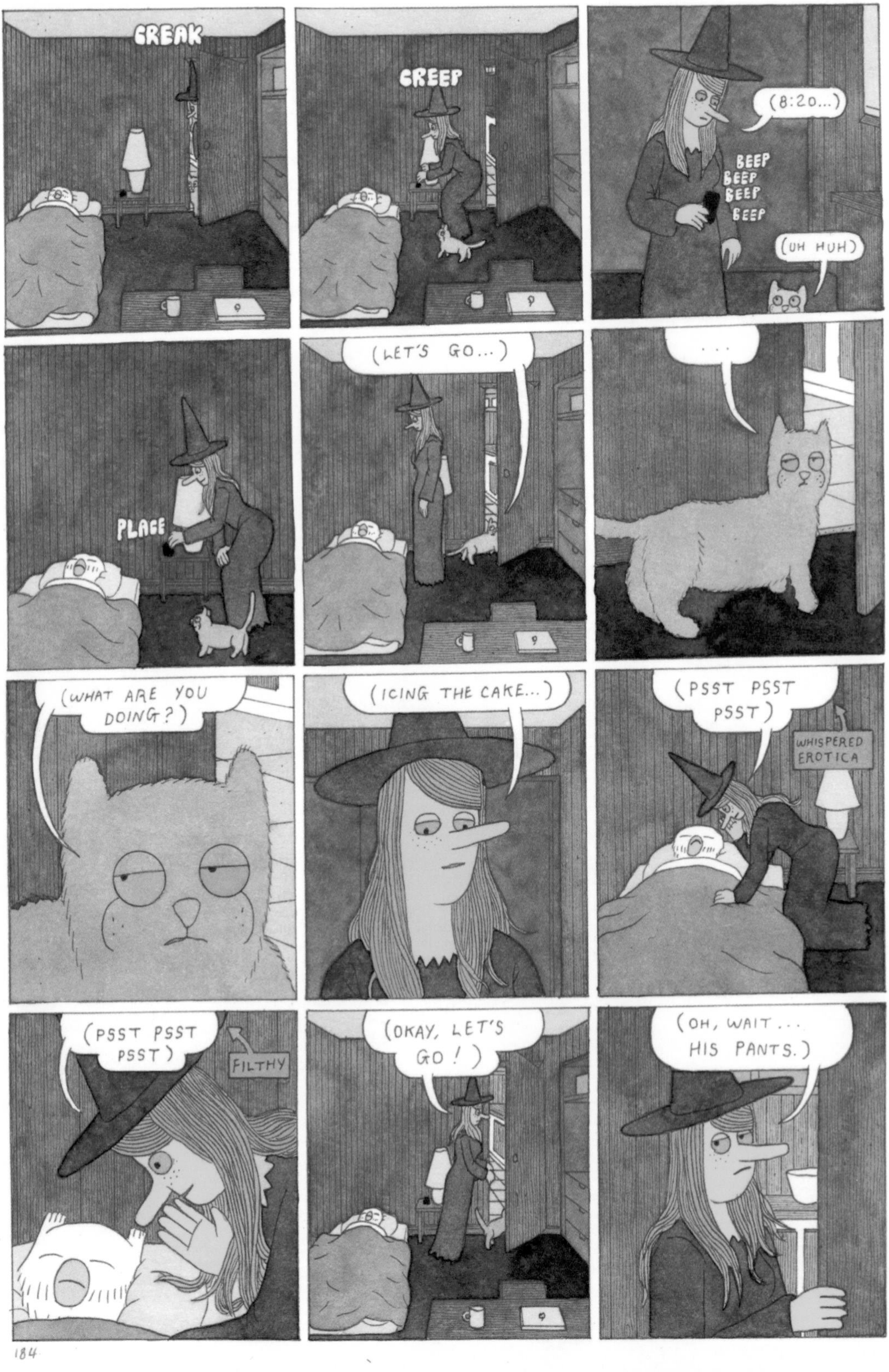
CREAK
CREEP
(8:20...)
BEEP BEEP BEEP BEEP
(UH HUH)
PLACE
(LET'S GO...)
...
(WHAT ARE YOU DOING?)
(ICING THE CAKE...)
(PSST PSST PSST)
WHISPERED EROTICA
(PSST PSST PSST)
FILTHY
(OKAY, LET'S GO!)
(OH, WAIT... HIS PANTS.)

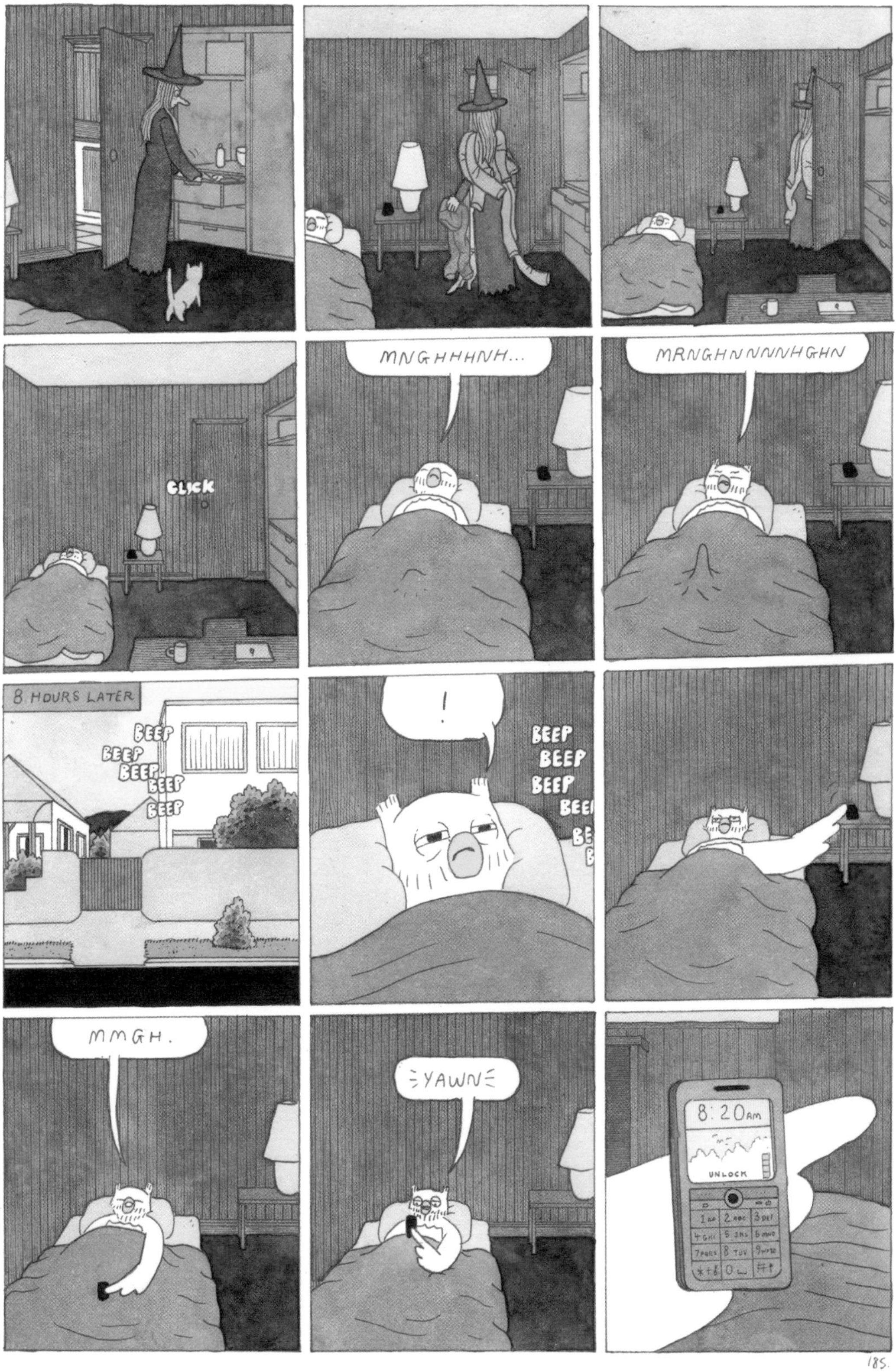
CLICK
MNGHHHNH...
MRNGHNNNNHGHN
8 HOURS LATER
BEEP
BEEP
BEEP
BEEP
BEEP
!
BEEP
BEEP
BEEP
MMGH.
YAWN
8:20AM
UNLOCK

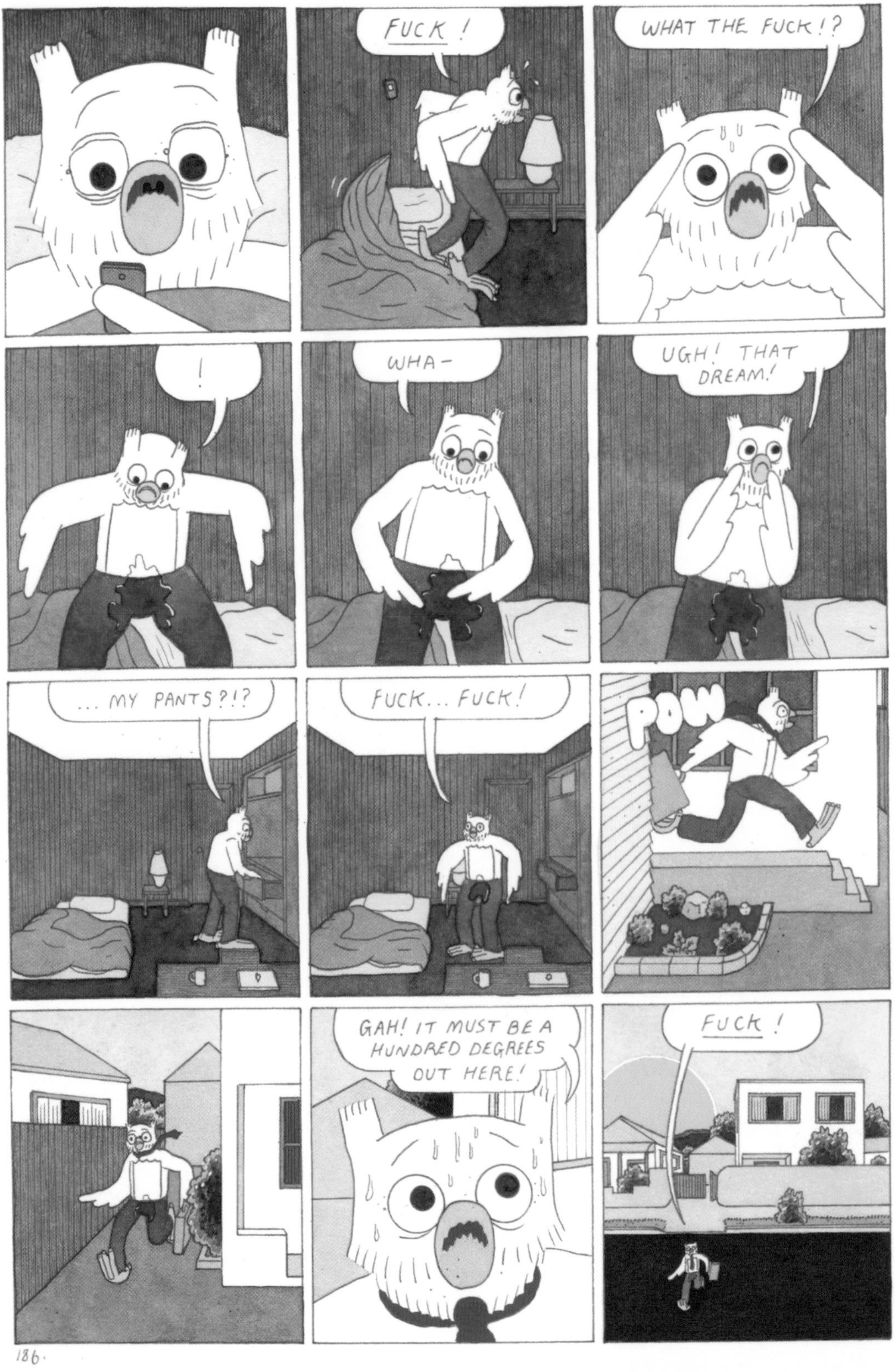
FUCK!
WHAT THE FUCK!?
!
WHA-
UGH! THAT DREAM!
... MY PANTS?!?
FUCK... FUCK!
POW
GAH! IT MUST BE A HUNDRED DEGREES OUT HERE!
FUCK!

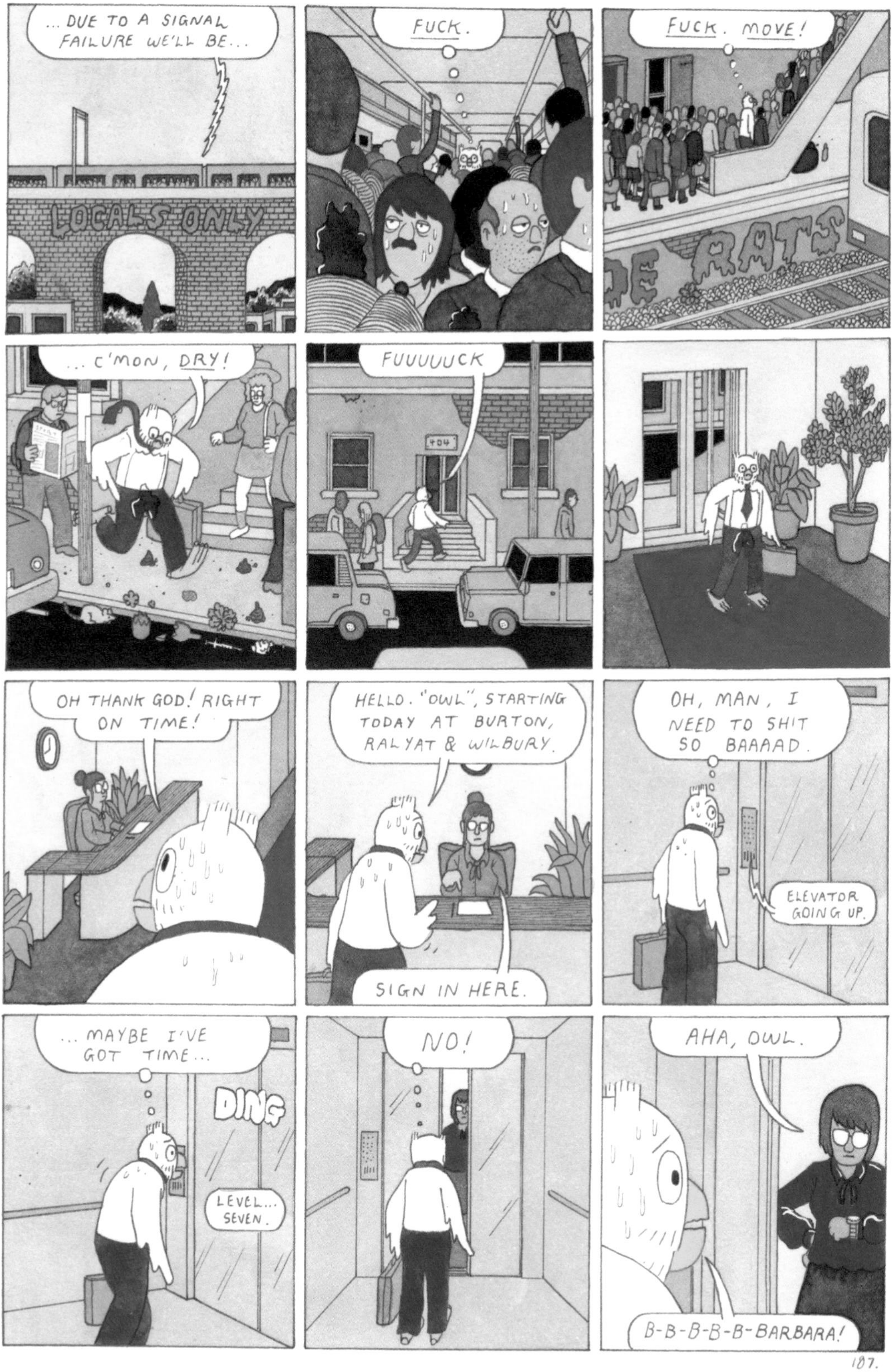

... DUE TO A SIGNAL FAILURE WE'LL BE...
LOCALS ONLY
FUCK.
FUCK. MOVE!
RATS
... C'MON, DRY!
FUUUUUCK
404
OH THANK GOD! RIGHT ON TIME!
HELLO. "OWL", STARTING TODAY AT BURTON, RALYAT & WILBURY.
SIGN IN HERE.
OH, MAN, I NEED TO SHIT SO BAAAAD.
ELEVATOR GOING UP.
... MAYBE I'VE GOT TIME...
DING
LEVEL... SEVEN.
NO!
AHA, OWL.
B-B-B-B-B-BARBARA!

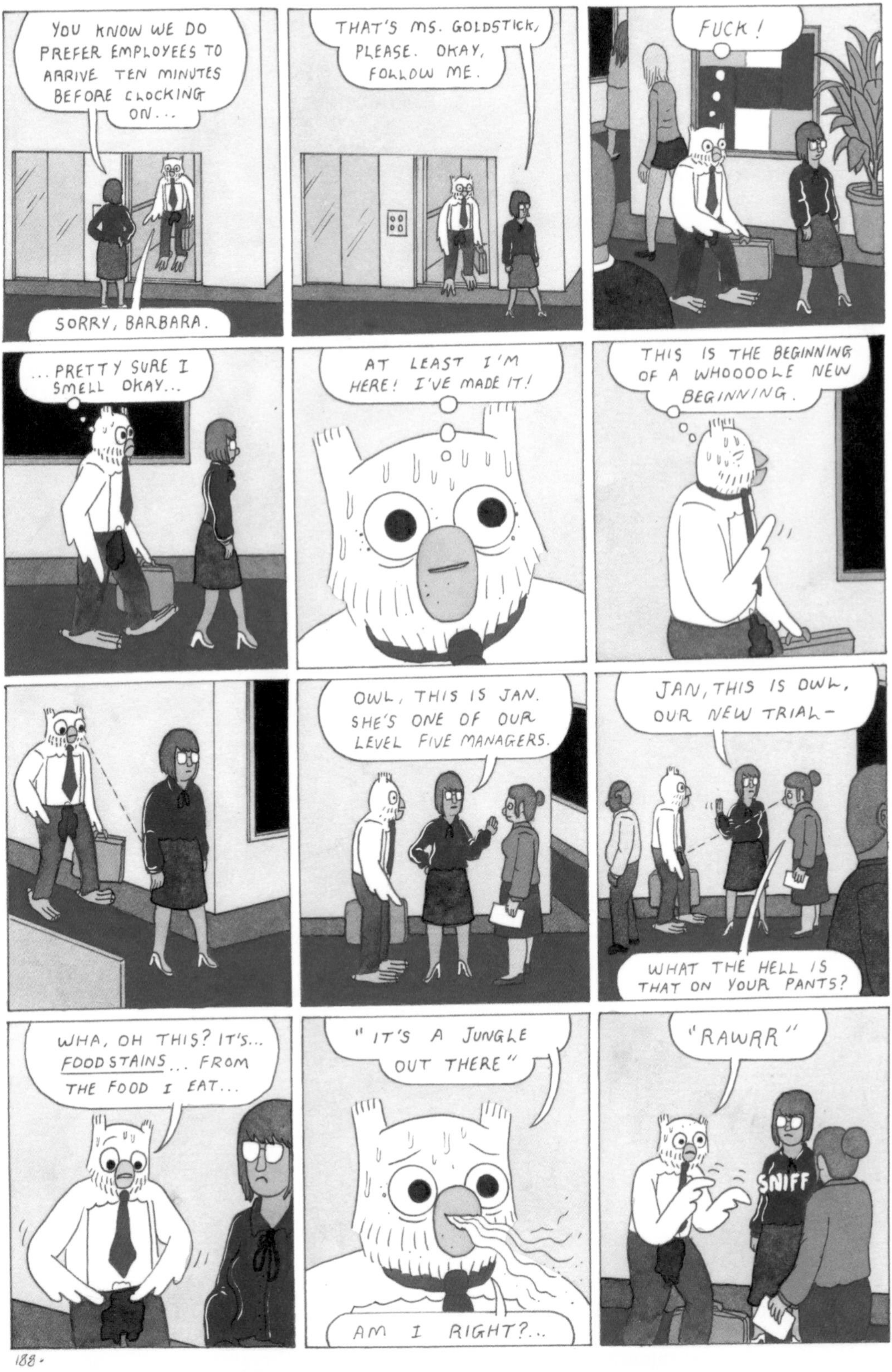
YOU KNOW WE DO PREFER EMPLOYEES TO ARRIVE TEN MINUTES BEFORE CLOCKING ON...
SORRY, BARBARA.
THAT'S MS. GOLDSTICK, PLEASE. OKAY, FOLLOW ME.
FUCK!
...PRETTY SURE I SMELL OKAY...
AT LEAST I'M HERE! I'VE MADE IT!
THIS IS THE BEGINNING OF A WHOOOOLE NEW BEGINNING.
OWL, THIS IS JAN. SHE'S ONE OF OUR LEVEL FIVE MANAGERS.
JAN, THIS IS OWL, OUR NEW TRIAL-
WHAT THE HELL IS THAT ON YOUR PANTS?
WHA, OH THIS? IT'S... FOOD STAINS... FROM THE FOOD I EAT...
" IT'S A JUNGLE OUT THERE "
AM I RIGHT?...
"RAWRR"
SNIFF

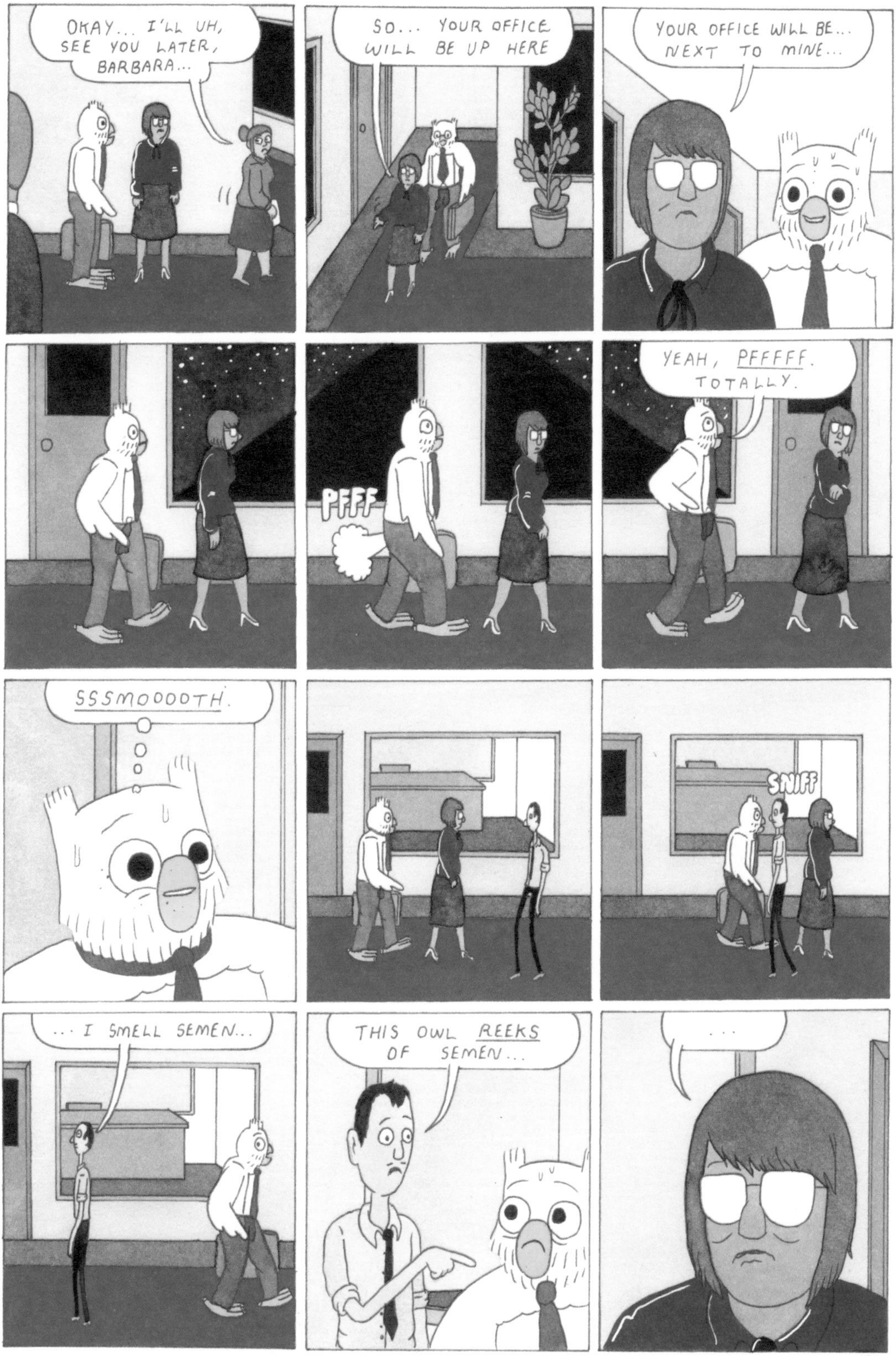
OKAY... I'LL UH, SEE YOU LATER, BARBARA...
SO... YOUR OFFICE WILL BE UP HERE
YOUR OFFICE WILL BE... NEXT TO MINE...
PFFF
YEAH, PFFFFF. TOTALLY.
SSSMOOOOTH.
SNIFF
... I SMELL SEMEN...
THIS OWL REEKS OF SEMEN...
...

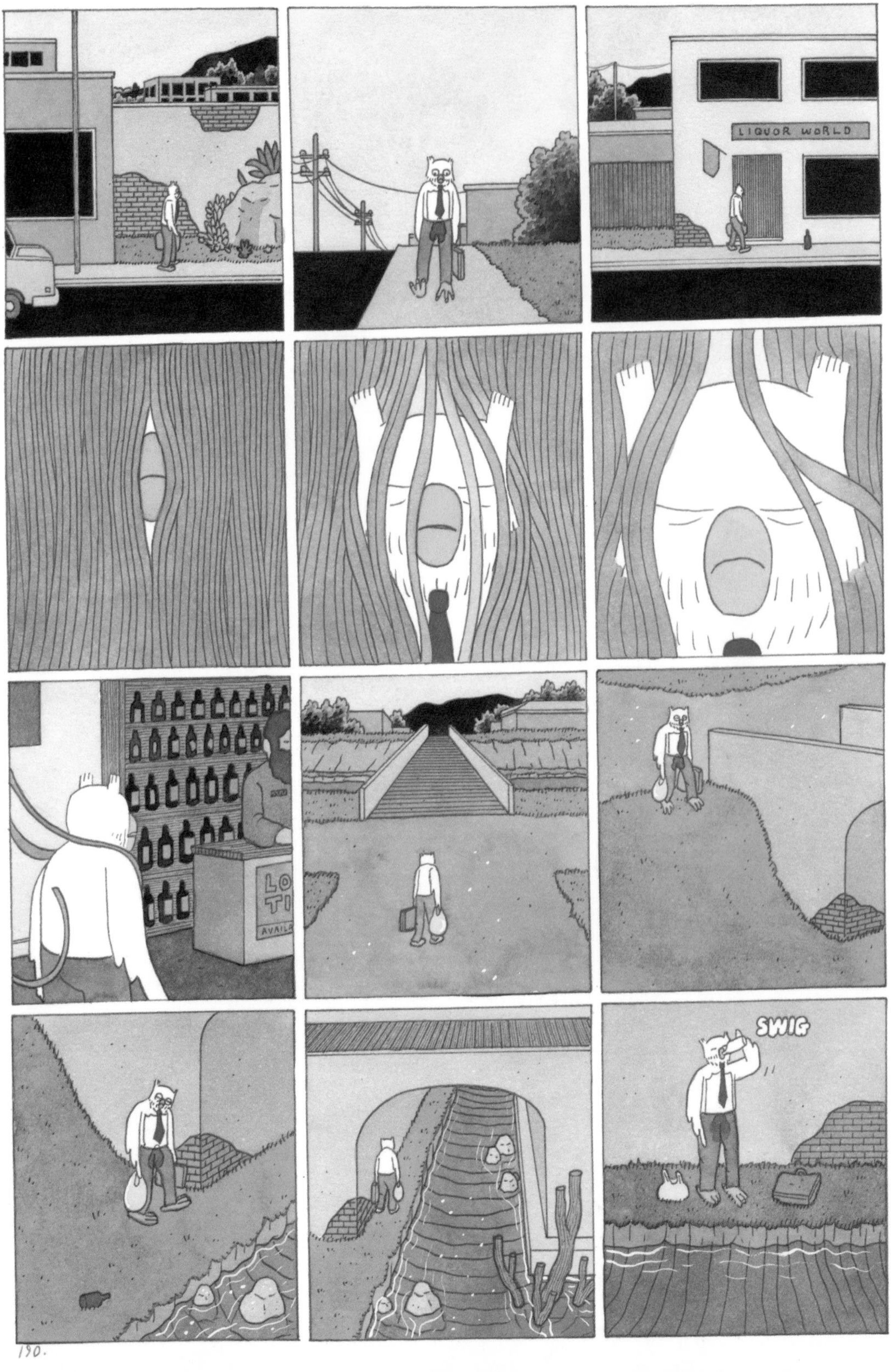
LIQUOR WORLD
SWIG

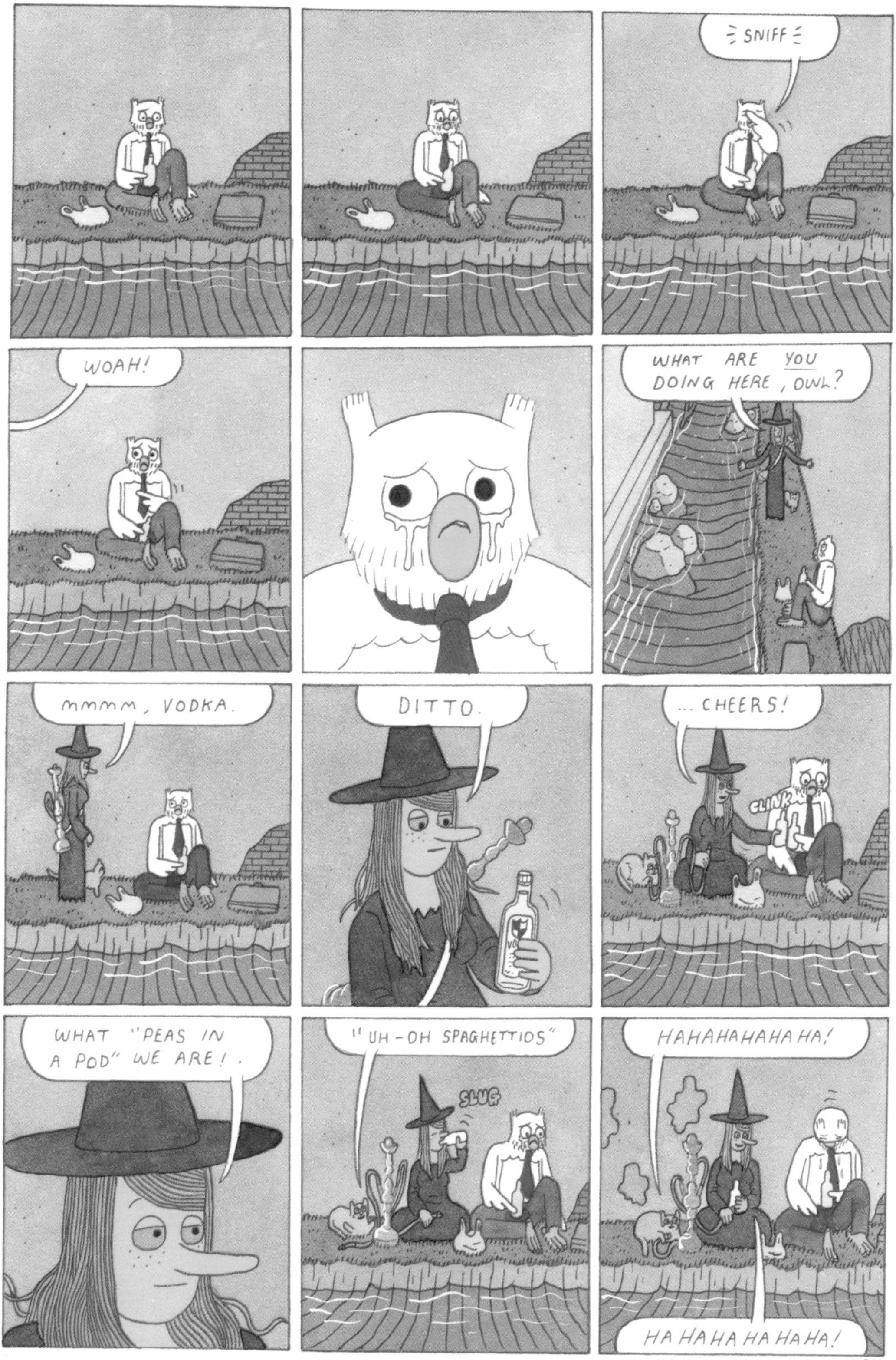
SNIFF
WOAH!
WHAT ARE YOU DOING HERE, OWL?
mmmm, VODKA.
DITTO.
... CHEERS!
CLINK
WHAT "PEAS IN A POD" WE ARE!.
"UH-OH SPAGHETTIOS"
SLUG
HAHAHAHAHAHA!
HA HAHA HA HAHA!

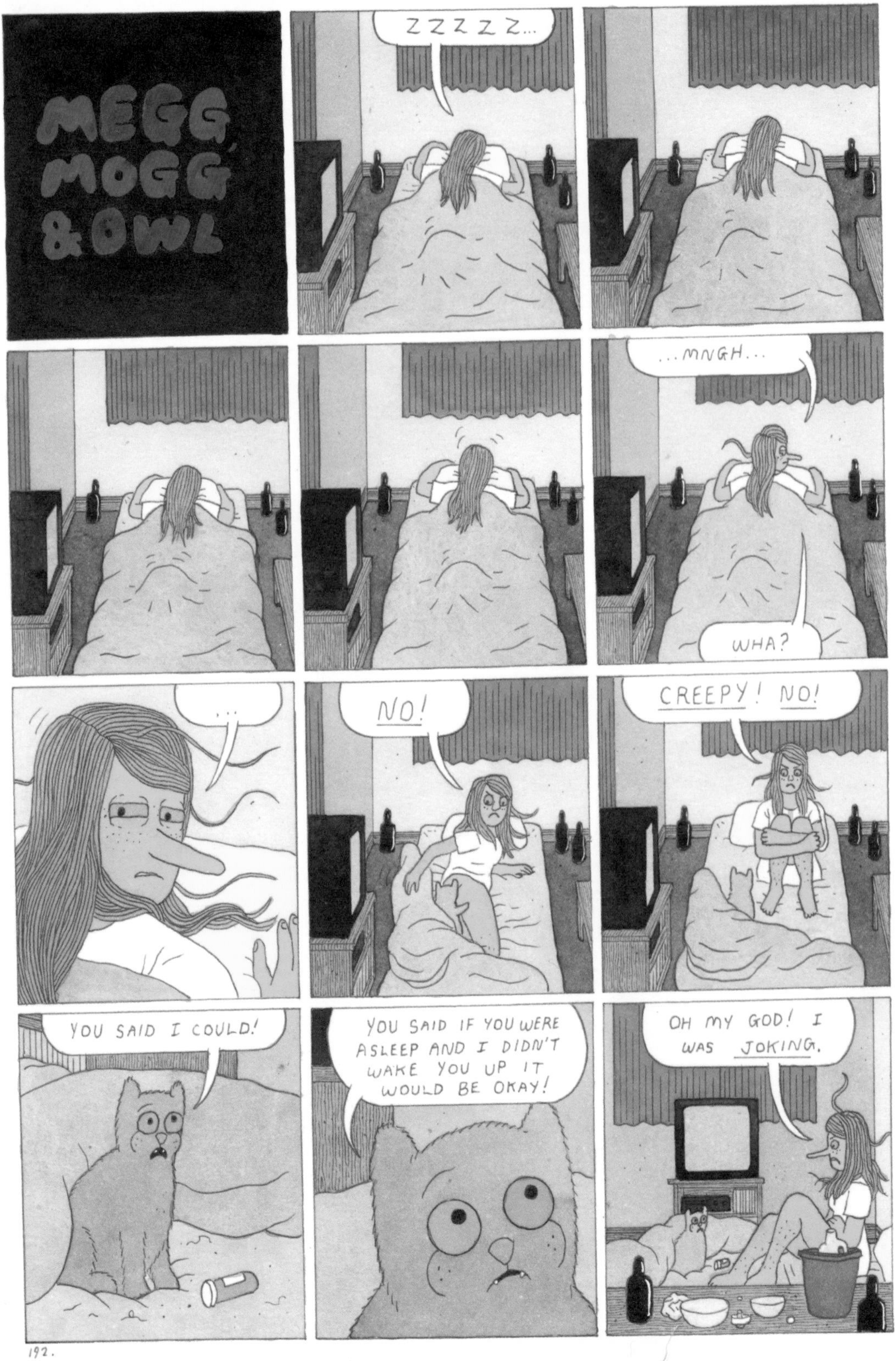
MEGG, MOGG & OWL
ZZZZZ...
...MNGH...
WHA?
...
NO!
CREEPY! NO!
YOU SAID I COULD!
YOU SAID IF YOU WERE ASLEEP AND I DIDN'T WAKE YOU UP IT WOULD BE OKAY!
OH MY GOD! I WAS JOKING.

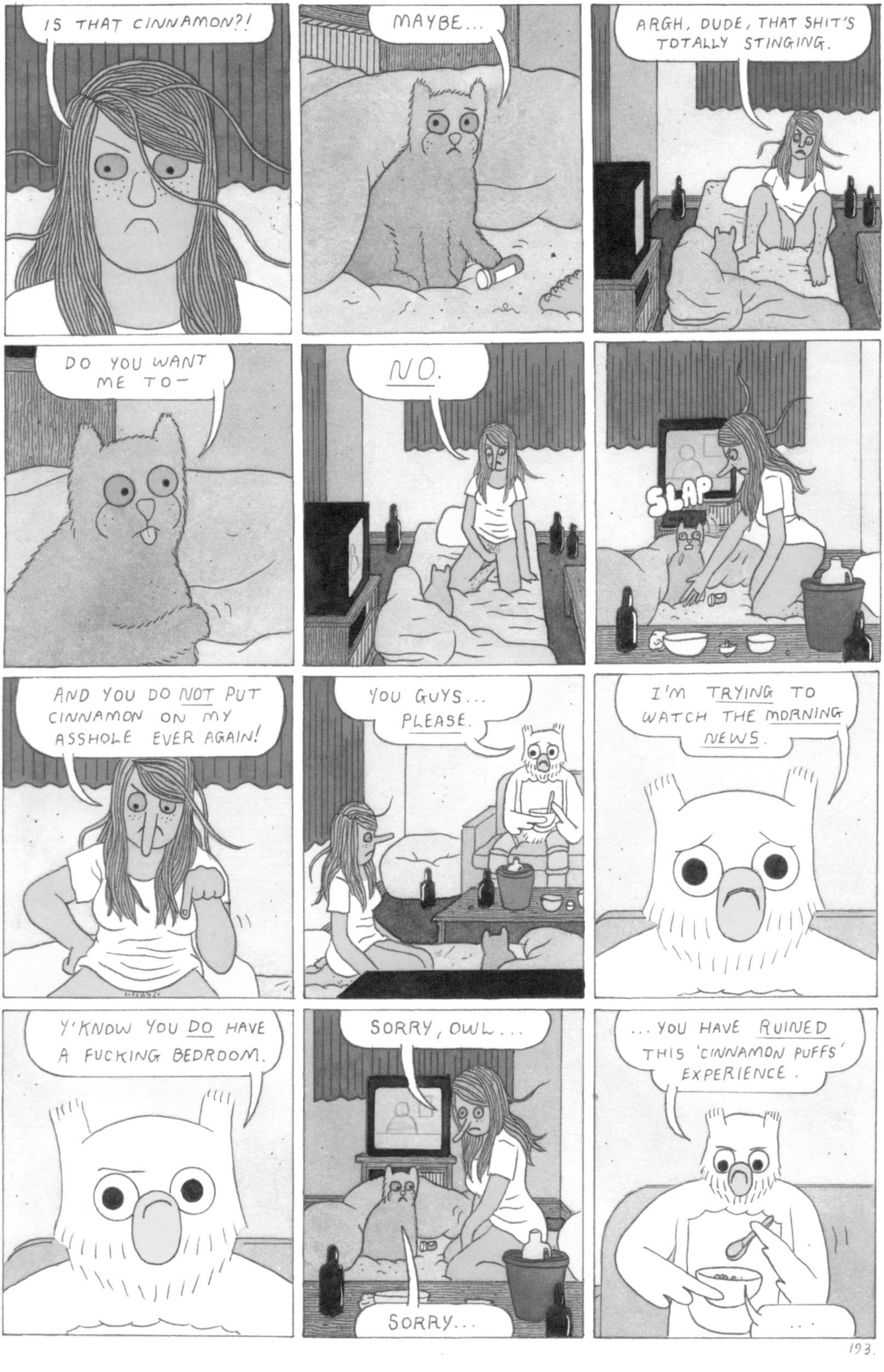
IS THAT CINNAMON?!
MAYBE...
ARGH, DUDE, THAT SHIT'S TOTALLY STINGING.
DO YOU WANT ME TO-
NO.
SLAP
AND YOU DO NOT PUT CINNAMON ON MY ASSHOLE EVER AGAIN!
YOU GUYS... PLEASE.
I'M TRYING TO WATCH THE MORNING NEWS.
Y'KNOW YOU DO HAVE A FUCKING BEDROOM.
SORRY, OWL...
SORRY...
...YOU HAVE RUINED THIS 'CINNAMON PUFFS' EXPERIENCE.
...

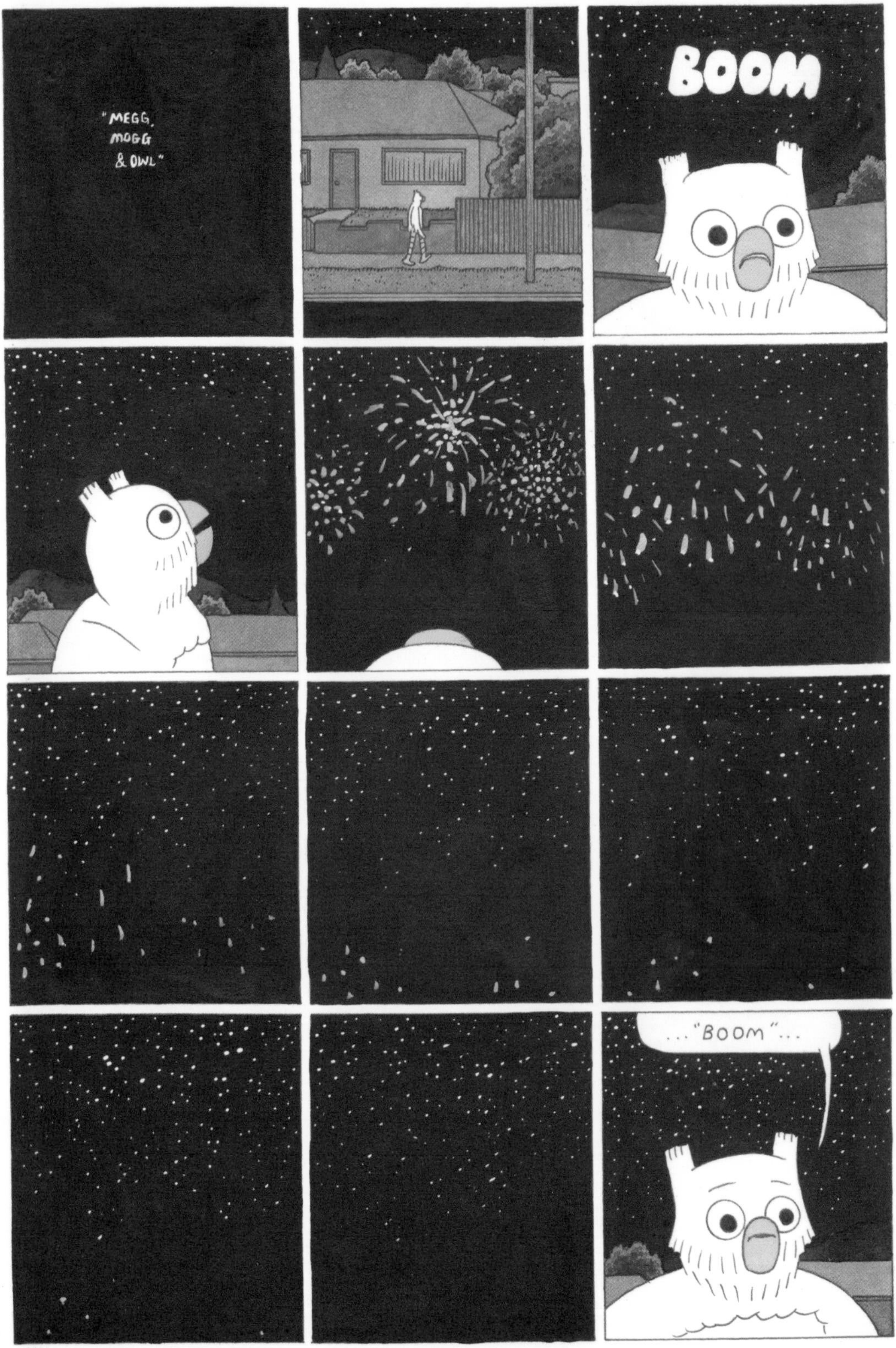
"MEGG, MOGG & OWL"
BOOM
..."BOOM"...

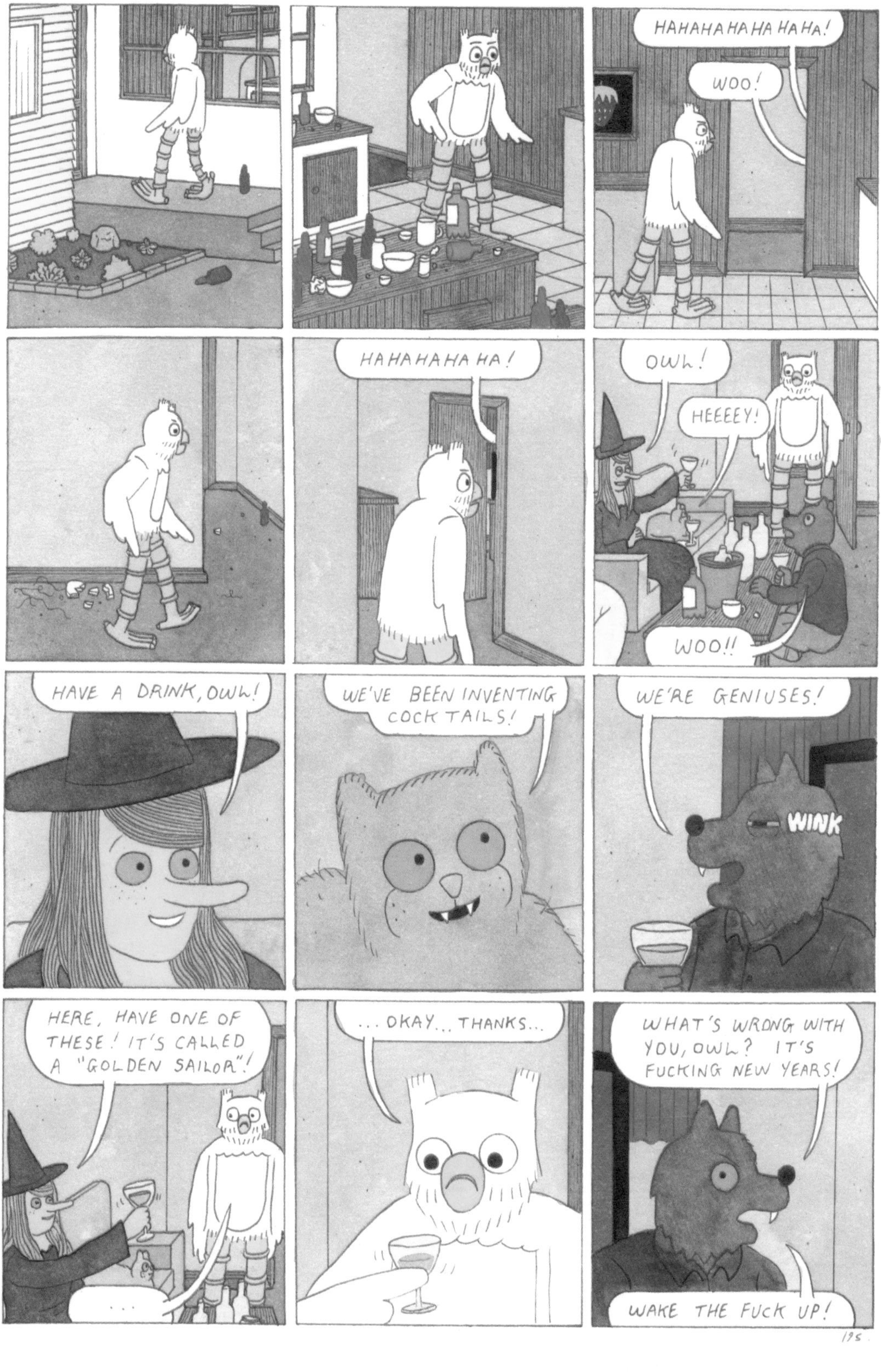
HAHAHAHAHAHAHAHA!
WOO!
HAHAHAHAHA HA!
OWL!
HEEEEY!
WOO!!
HAVE A DRINK, OWL!
WE'VE BEEN INVENTING COCKTAILS!
WE'RE GENIUSES!
WINK
HERE, HAVE ONE OF THESE! IT'S CALLED A "GOLDEN SAILOR"!
...
... OKAY... THANKS...
WHAT'S WRONG WITH YOU, OWL? IT'S FUCKING NEW YEARS!
WAKE THE FUCK UP!

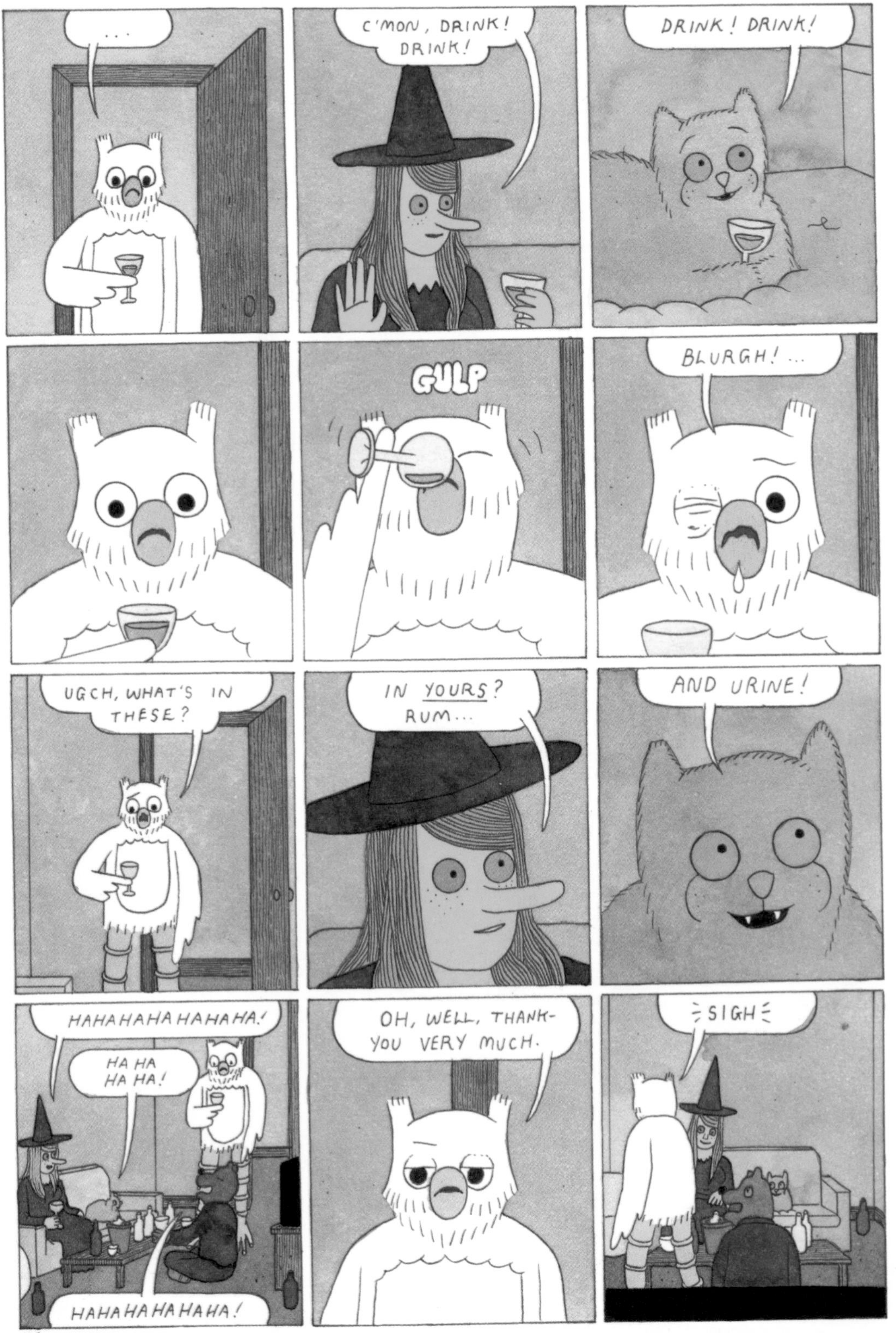
...
C'MON, DRINK! DRINK!
DRINK! DRINK!
GULP
BLURGH! ...
UGCH, WHAT'S IN THESE?
IN YOURS? RUM...
AND URINE!
HAHAHAHAHAHAHA!
HA HA HA HA!
HAHAHAHAHAHA!
OH, WELL, THANK-YOU VERY MUCH.
SIGH

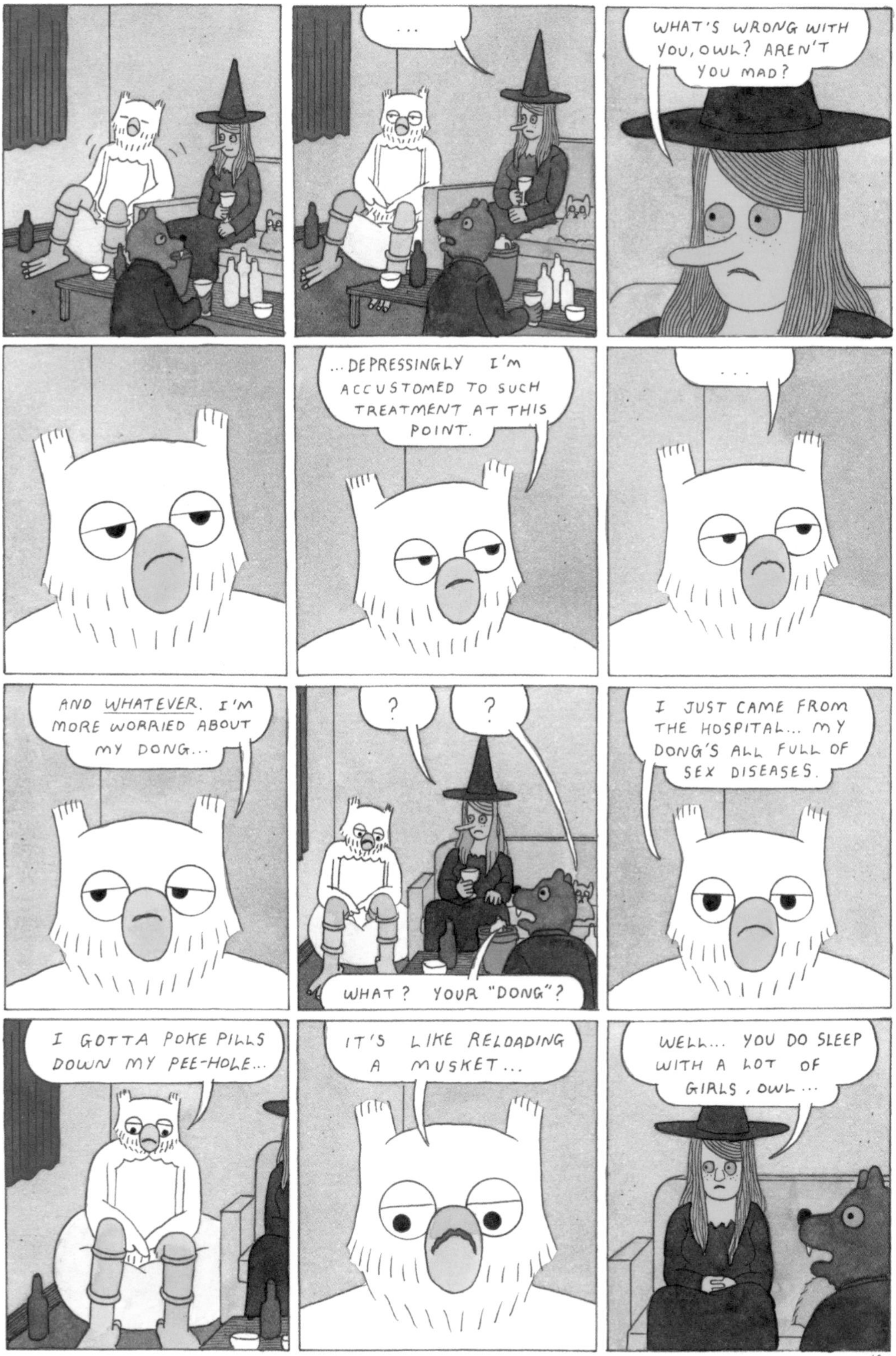

...
WHAT'S WRONG WITH YOU, OWL? AREN'T YOU MAD?
...DEPRESSINGLY I'M ACCUSTOMED TO SUCH TREATMENT AT THIS POINT.
...
AND WHATEVER. I'M MORE WORRIED ABOUT MY DONG...
?
?
WHAT? YOUR "DONG"?
I JUST CAME FROM THE HOSPITAL... MY DONG'S ALL FULL OF SEX DISEASES.
I GOTTA POKE PILLS DOWN MY PEE-HOLE...
IT'S LIKE RELOADING A MUSKET...
WELL... YOU DO SLEEP WITH A LOT OF GIRLS, OWL...

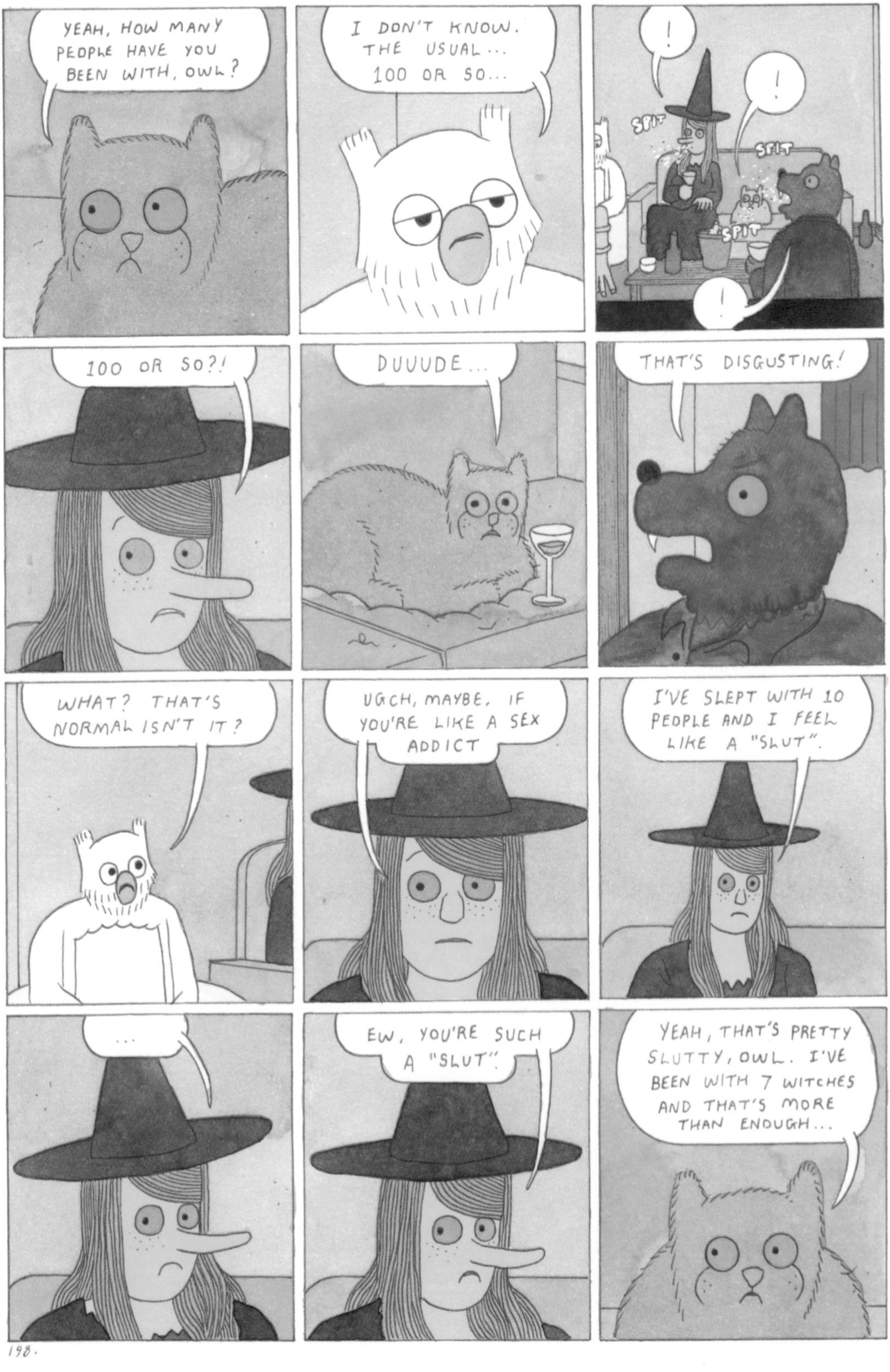
YEAH, HOW MANY PEOPLE HAVE YOU BEEN WITH, OWL?
I DON'T KNOW. THE USUAL... 100 OR SO...
!
!
SPIT
SPIT
SPIT
!
100 OR SO?!
DUUUDE...
THAT'S DISGUSTING!
WHAT? THAT'S NORMAL ISN'T IT?
UGCH, MAYBE, IF YOU'RE LIKE A SEX ADDICT
I'VE SLEPT WITH 10 PEOPLE AND I FEEL LIKE A "SLUT".
...
EW, YOU'RE SUCH A "SLUT".
YEAH, THAT'S PRETTY SLUTTY, OWL. I'VE BEEN WITH 7 WITCHES AND THAT'S MORE THAN ENOUGH...

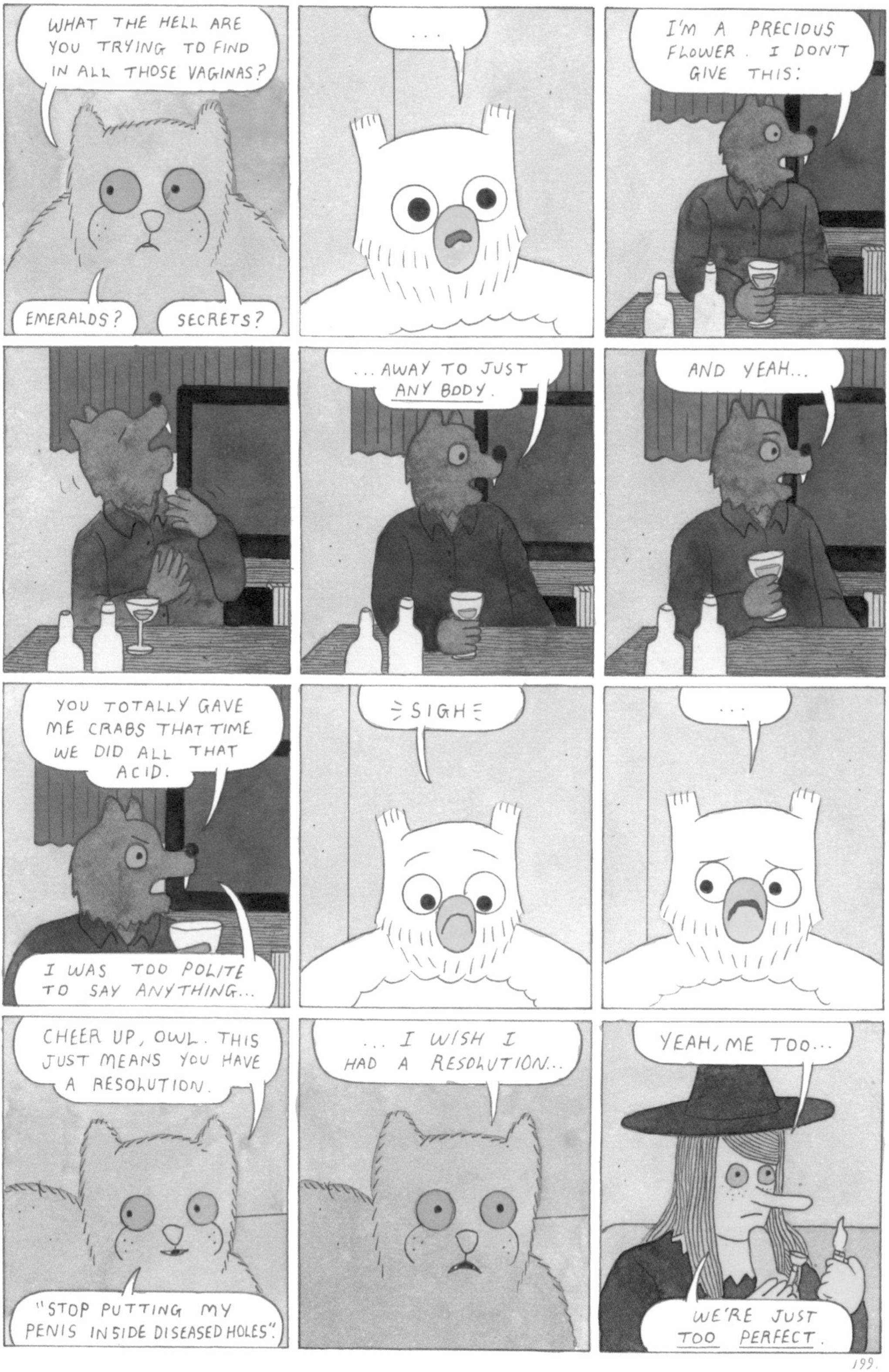
WHAT THE HELL ARE YOU TRYING TO FIND IN ALL THOSE VAGINAS?
EMERALDS?
SECRETS?
...
I'M A PRECIOUS FLOWER. I DON'T GIVE THIS:
...AWAY TO JUST ANY BODY.
AND YEAH...
YOU TOTALLY GAVE ME CRABS THAT TIME WE DID ALL THAT ACID.
I WAS TOO POLITE TO SAY ANYTHING...
SIGH
...
CHEER UP, OWL. THIS JUST MEANS YOU HAVE A RESOLUTION.
"STOP PUTTING MY PENIS INSIDE DISEASED HOLES".
...I WISH I HAD A RESOLUTION...
YEAH, ME TOO...
WE'RE JUST TOO PERFECT.

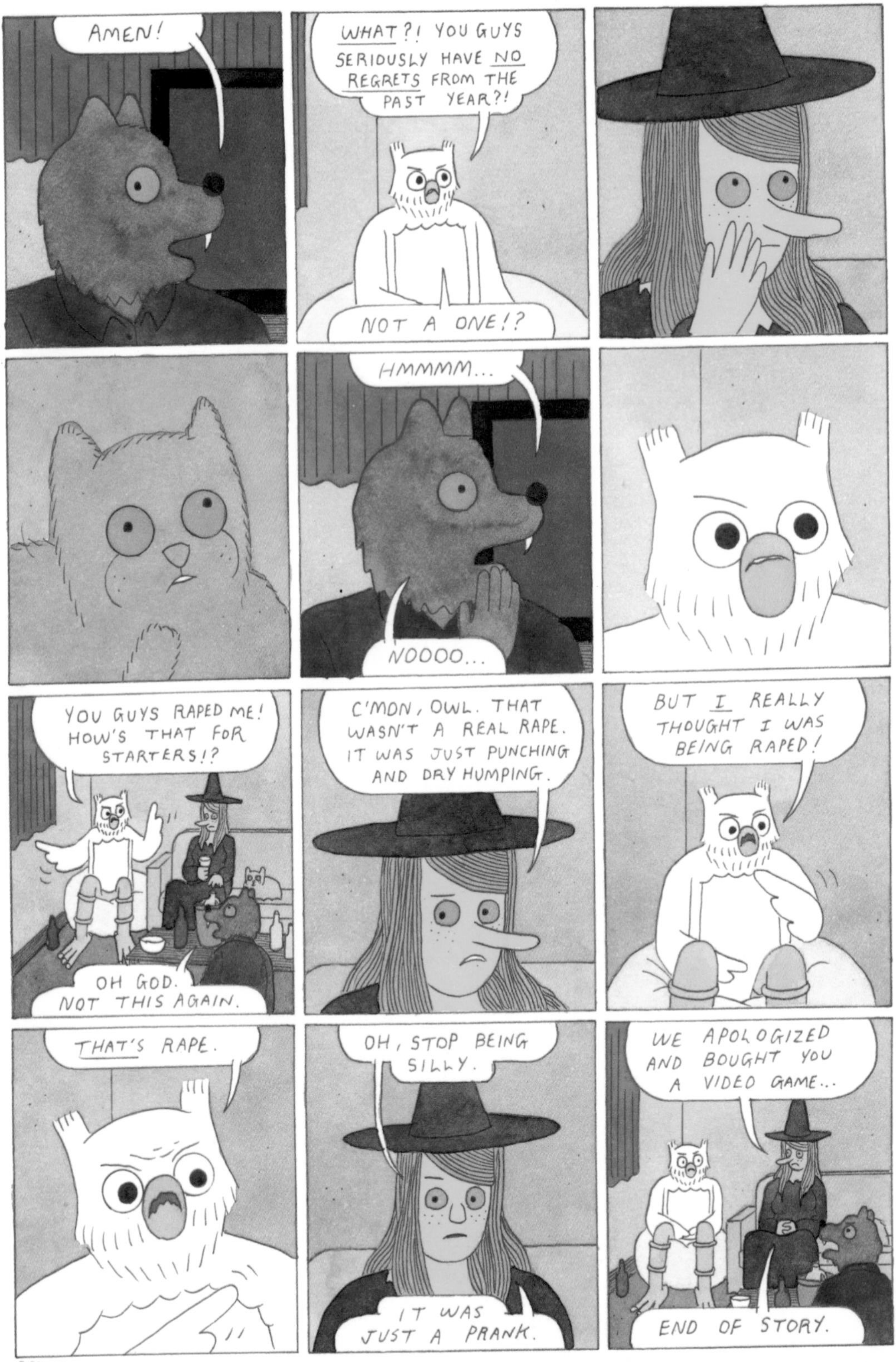
AMEN!
WHAT?! YOU GUYS SERIOUSLY HAVE NO REGRETS FROM THE PAST YEAR?!
NOT A ONE!?
HMMMM...
NOOOO...
YOU GUYS RAPED ME! HOW'S THAT FOR STARTERS!?
OH GOD. NOT THIS AGAIN.
C'MON, OWL. THAT WASN'T A REAL RAPE. IT WAS JUST PUNCHING AND DRY HUMPING.
BUT I REALLY THOUGHT I WAS BEING RAPED!
THAT'S RAPE.
OH, STOP BEING SILLY.
IT WAS JUST A PRANK.
WE APOLOGIZED AND BOUGHT YOU A VIDEO GAME...
END OF STORY.

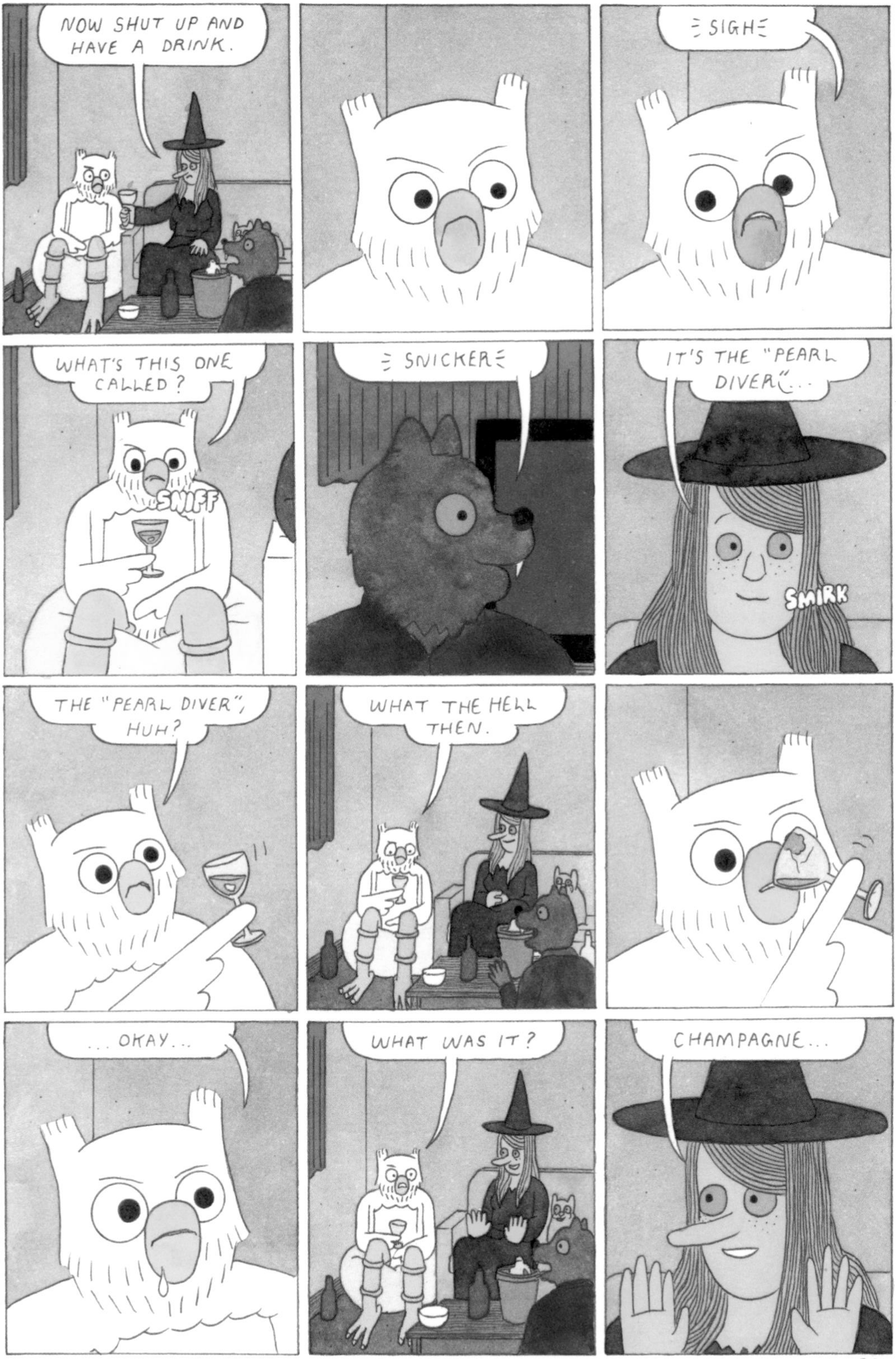
NOW SHUT UP AND HAVE A DRINK.
SIGH
WHAT'S THIS ONE CALLED?
SNIFF
SNICKER
IT'S THE "PEARL DIVER"...
SMIRK
THE "PEARL DIVER", HUH?
WHAT THE HELL THEN.
... OKAY...
WHAT WAS IT?
CHAMPAGNE...

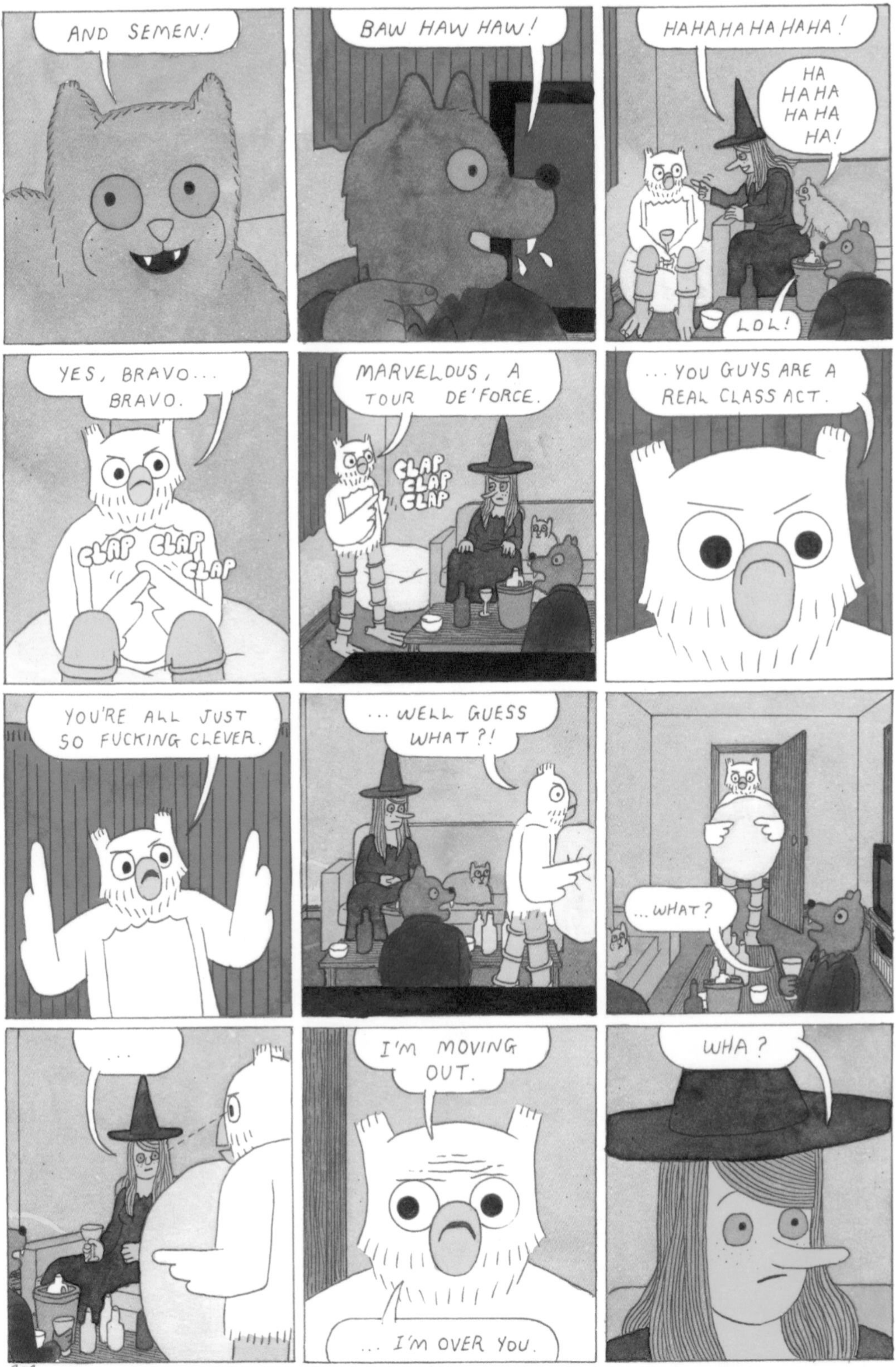
AND SEMEN!
BAW HAW HAW!
HAHAHAHAHAHA!
HA HAHA HAHA HA!
LOL!
YES, BRAVO... BRAVO.
CLAP CLAP CLAP
MARVELOUS, A TOUR DE'FORCE.
CLAP CLAP CLAP
...YOU GUYS ARE A REAL CLASS ACT.
YOU'RE ALL JUST SO FUCKING CLEVER.
...WELL GUESS WHAT?!
...WHAT?
...
I'M MOVING OUT.
... I'M OVER YOU.
WHA?

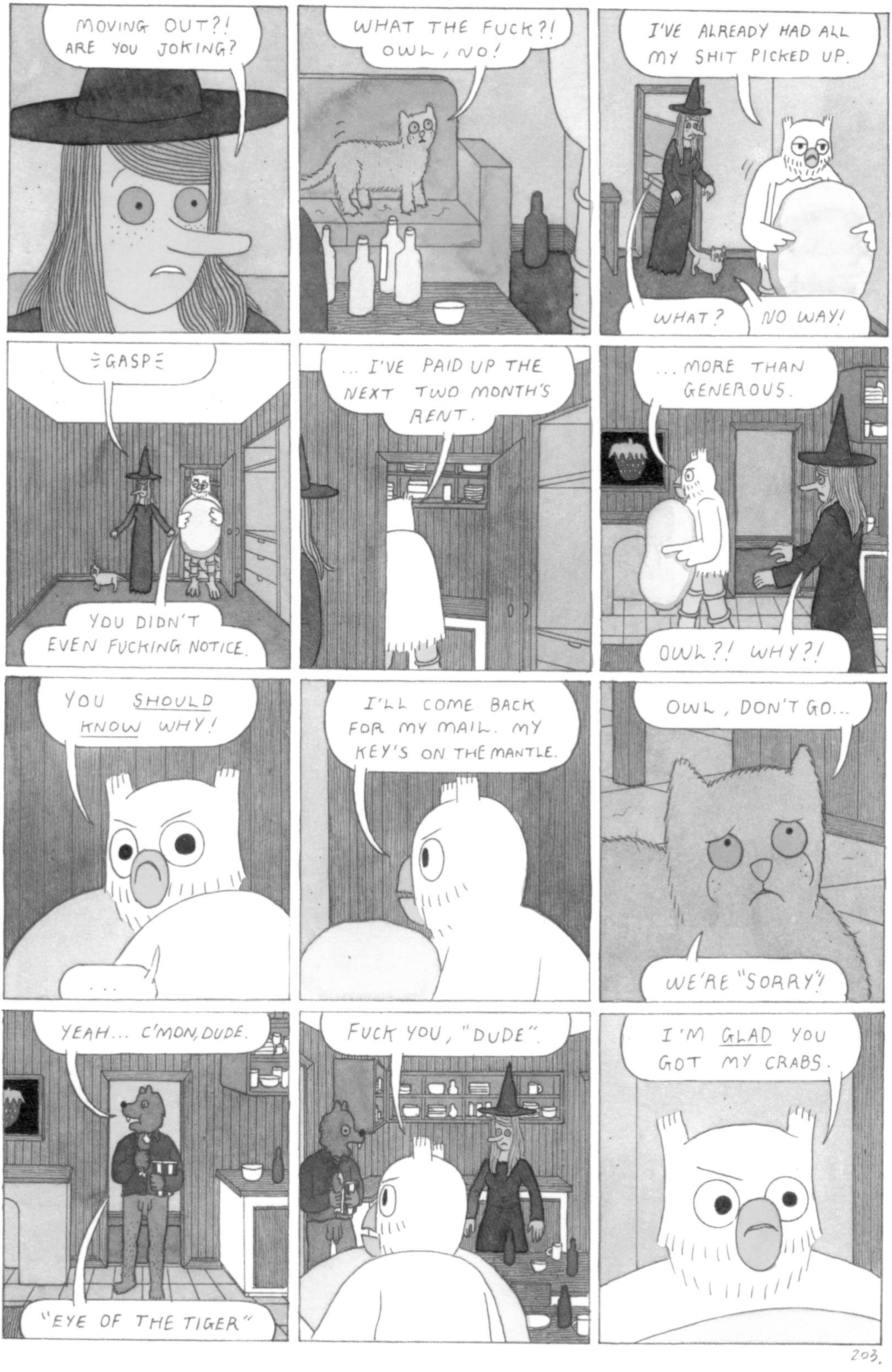
MOVING OUT?! ARE YOU JOKING?
WHAT THE FUCK?! OWL, NO!
I'VE ALREADY HAD ALL MY SHIT PICKED UP.
WHAT?
NO WAY!
GASP
YOU DIDN'T EVEN FUCKING NOTICE.
... I'VE PAID UP THE NEXT TWO MONTH'S RENT.
... MORE THAN GENEROUS.
OWL?! WHY?!
YOU SHOULD KNOW WHY!
...
I'LL COME BACK FOR MY MAIL. MY KEY'S ON THE MANTLE.
OWL, DON'T GO...
WE'RE "SORRY"!
YEAH... C'MON, DUDE.
"EYE OF THE TIGER"
FUCK YOU, "DUDE".
I'M GLAD YOU GOT MY CRABS.

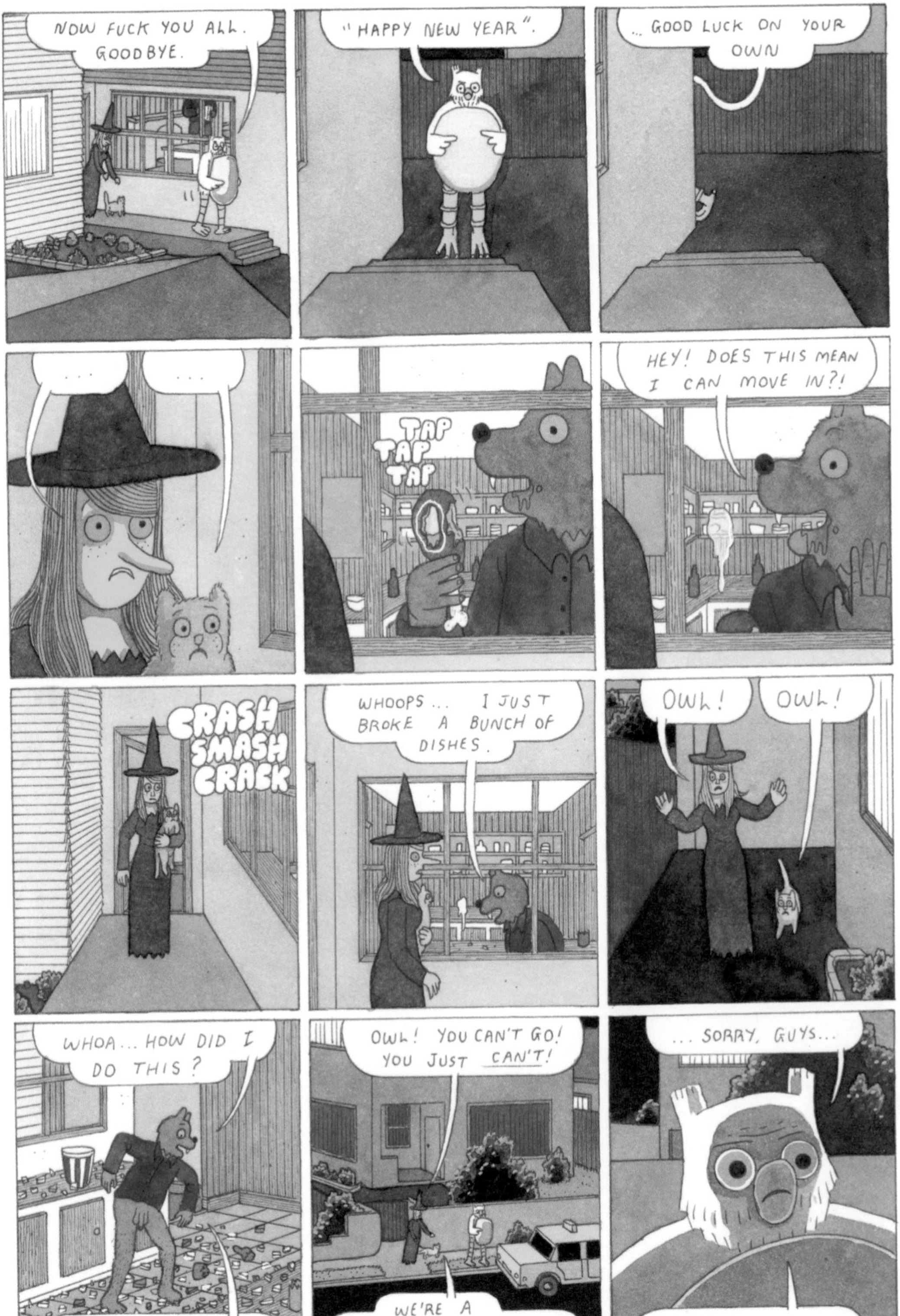
NOW FUCK YOU ALL. GOODBYE.
"HAPPY NEW YEAR".
... GOOD LUCK ON YOUR OWN
...
...
TAP TAP TAP
HEY! DOES THIS MEAN I CAN MOVE IN?!
CRASH SMASH CRACK
WHOOPS... I JUST BROKE A BUNCH OF DISHES.
OWL!
OWL!
WHOA... HOW DID I DO THIS?
UH-OH. BARE FEET...
OWL! YOU CAN'T GO! YOU JUST CAN'T!
WE'RE A THREE PERSON COUPLE!
... SORRY, GUYS...
I HAVE TO DO THIS.

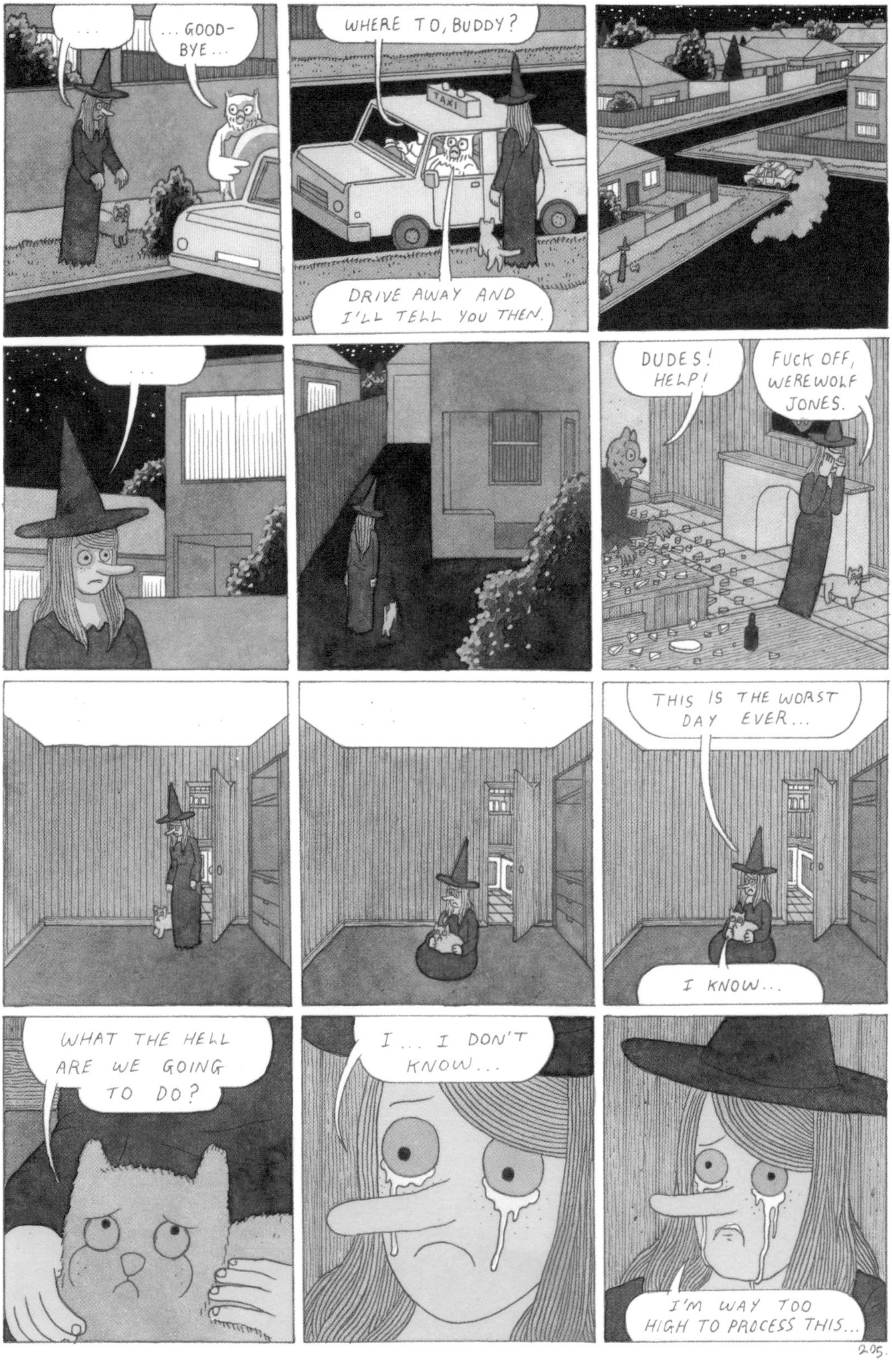
...
... GOOD-BYE ...
WHERE TO, BUDDY?
DRIVE AWAY AND I'LL TELL YOU THEN.
TAXI
...
DUDES! HELP!
FUCK OFF, WEREWOLF JONES.
THIS IS THE WORST DAY EVER...
I KNOW...
WHAT THE HELL ARE WE GOING TO DO?
I ... I DON'T KNOW...
I'M WAY TOO HIGH TO PROCESS THIS...

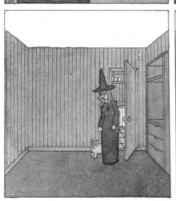

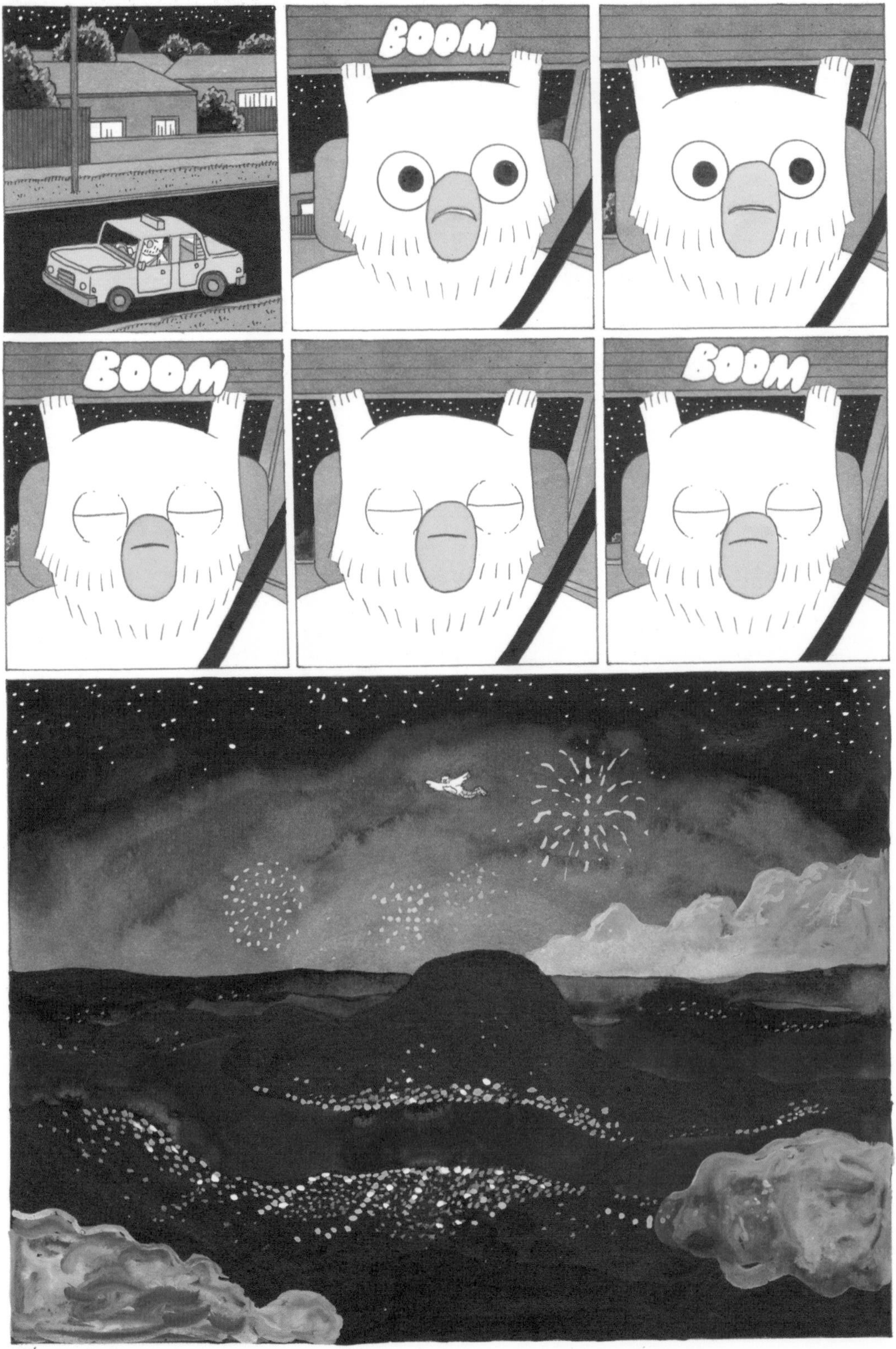
BOOM
BOOM
BOOM

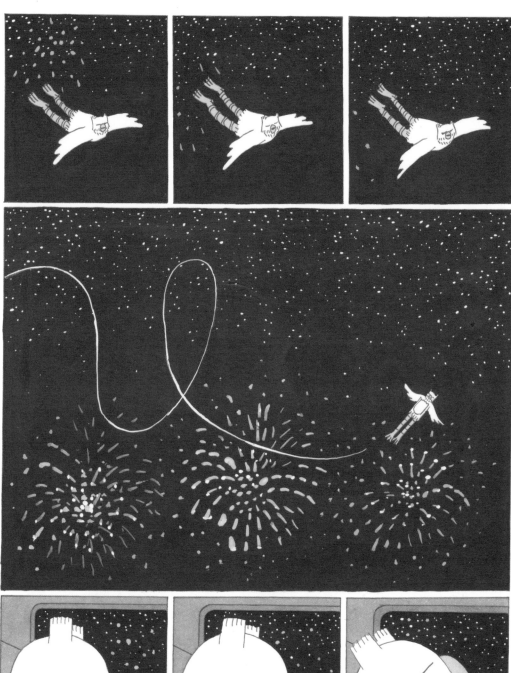

207.

MEGAHEX WAS DRAWN BY SIMON HANSELMANN
JANUARY 2009 - MARCH 2014

RICHMOND UPON THAMES, UNITED KINGDOM.
EAGLEMONT, VICTORIA.
THE NATIONAL GALLERY OF VICTORIA.
LAUNCESTON, TASMANIA.
BRUNSWICK EAST, VICTORIA.

PORTIONS OF THIS MATERIAL PREVIOUSLY APPEARED IN KUS,
SMOKE SIGNAL, GANGBANG BONG, MINI COMICS & ONLINE.

FEB-MARCH 2014 ASSISTANTS/"INTERNS":
KATIE PARRISH, MARC PEARSON, GREGORY MACKAY.
("ASSISTANTS" ARE PAID $100 + A BOOK FOR 2-3 AFTERNOONS
OF GENERAL WATERCOLOURING ASSISTANCE.)

"ACID" GUESTS:
MICHAEL HAWKINS, MICKEY Z, MATT FURIE, SAMMY HARKHAM,
HTML FLOWERS, JONNY NEGRON. THANKYOU MARC PEARSON
FOR COMPUTER ASSISTANCE.

CREDITS.

OTHER "MEGG AND MOGG"
PUBLICATIONS:

- ST. OWL'S BAY
- WIFE ZONE
- HECHIZO TOTAL (SPANISH)
- MAXIMAL SPLEEN (FRENCH)

WEBSITES:
GIRLMOUNTAIN.TUMBLR.COM
FANTAGRAPHICS.COM

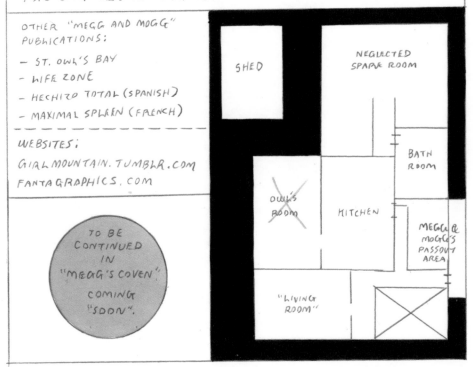

SHED

NEGLECTED
SPARE ROOM

BATH
ROOM

OWL'S
ROOM

KITCHEN

MEGG &
MOGG'S
PASSOUT
AREA

TO BE
CONTINUED
IN
"MEGG'S COVEN"
COMING
"SOON".

"LIVING
ROOM"

FANTAGRAPHICS BOOKS WOULD LIKE TO THANK:
RANDALL BETHUNE, BIG PLANET COMICS, BLACK HOOK PRESS JAPAN,
NICK CAPETILLO, KEVIN CZAPIEWSKI, JOHN DIBELLO, JUAN MANUEL
DOMINGUEZ, MATHIEU DOUBLET, DAN EVANS III, THOMAS EYKEMANS,
SCOTT FRITSCH-HAMMES, COCO AND EDDIE GORODETSKY, KAREN GREEN,
TED HAYCRAFT, EDUARDO TAKEO "LIZARHEO" IGARASHI, NEVDON
JAMGOCHIAN, ANDY HOOPMANS, PHILIP NEL, VANESSA PALACIOS,
KURT SAYENGA, ANNA WISE ROSYGAARD SCHMIDT, CHRISTIAN
SCHREMSER, SECRET HEADQUARTERS, PAUL VAN DIJKEN, MUNGO
VAN KRIMPEN-HALL, JASON AARON WONG, THOMAS ZIMMERMANN.

SIMON HANSELMANN WOULD LIKE TO THANK:

JACQ COHEN, ERIC REYNOLDS, GARY GROTH, KIM THOMPSON,
JEN VAUGHN, PAUL BARESH, FRANK SANTORO, HTML FLOWERS,
KATIE PARRISH, MARC PEARSON, GREGORY MACKAY, MICKEY Z,
JONNY NEGRON, SAMMY HARKHAM, MATT FURIE, MICHAEL
HAWKINS, KAREN CONRAD, TYLER MINDER, ICHIBOD, MICHAEL
FIKARIS, LASHNA TUSCHEWSKI, GHOST PATROL, DAVID MAHLER,
LEIGH RIGOZZI, BECKETT ROZENTALS, JESSICA PINNEY, MICHAEL
FISHER, ARI DYBAL, THEMBI SODDELL, SAM DUNSCOMBE, CLAIRE
TITLEY, CHRISTOPHER TIPTON, RAJINDER SINGH SANGHERA, SIMON
BARNARD, DAN CROSS (FOR THE NAME "WEREWOLF JONES"), PATRICK
CROSS, ANDREW HARPER, KARL VON BAMBERGER, JULIAN TRAHLE,
ELIZABETH ROSE JAMES, RONNIE SCOTT, KUKE RANDALL, FRANK
DAFT, JESSE CLARK, GRAHAM HOLBEINS, STICKY INSTITUTE,
EDIE FAKE, ANNIE KOYAMA, CESAR SANCHEZ, MANUEL DONADA,
DAMIEN FILLIATRE, MICHAEL RENAUD, IT'S NICE THAT, NICKY
MINUS, GENEVIÈVE CASTREE, BLAISE LARMEE, ADELAIDE SHORT,
PHIL ELVERUM, GABE FOWLER, LESLIE STEIN, INES ESTRADA,
GINETTE LAPALME, LALA ALBERT, MICHAEL DEFORGE, PATRICK
KYLE, RYAN SANDS, ALVIN BUENAVENTURA, NICK GAZIN,
ALEXANDRA ZSIGMOND, LISA HANAWALT, SEAN T. COLLINS,
MIA SCHWARTZ, FLORENT RUPPERT, HUGH FROST, LEON SADLER,
DASH SHAW, JMKE, MATT GROENING, COMICS WORM BOOK,
MACK PAULY, SAM ALDEN, JASON LEIVIAN, JOR MESSHER,
ANTOINE COSSE, TOM OLDHAM, SIMON HACKING, DAN NADEL,
STEPHANIE HURTADO, ZACH HAZARD VAUPEN, ROBIN McCONNELL,
HUS, JORDAN CRANE, TUMBLR FOLLOWERS, RED BULL, CIGARETTES.

THE END.

SIMON HANSELMANN WAS BORN IN 1981 IN
LAUNCESTON, TASMANIA. HIS WORK HAS APP-
EARED IN VICE, THE BELIEVER, THE PITCHFORK
REVIEW AND THE NEW YORK TIMES. CURR-
ENTLY HE LIVES IN MELBOURNE, AUSTRALIA
IN A SMALL ROOM FULL OF BOOKS & DRESSES.

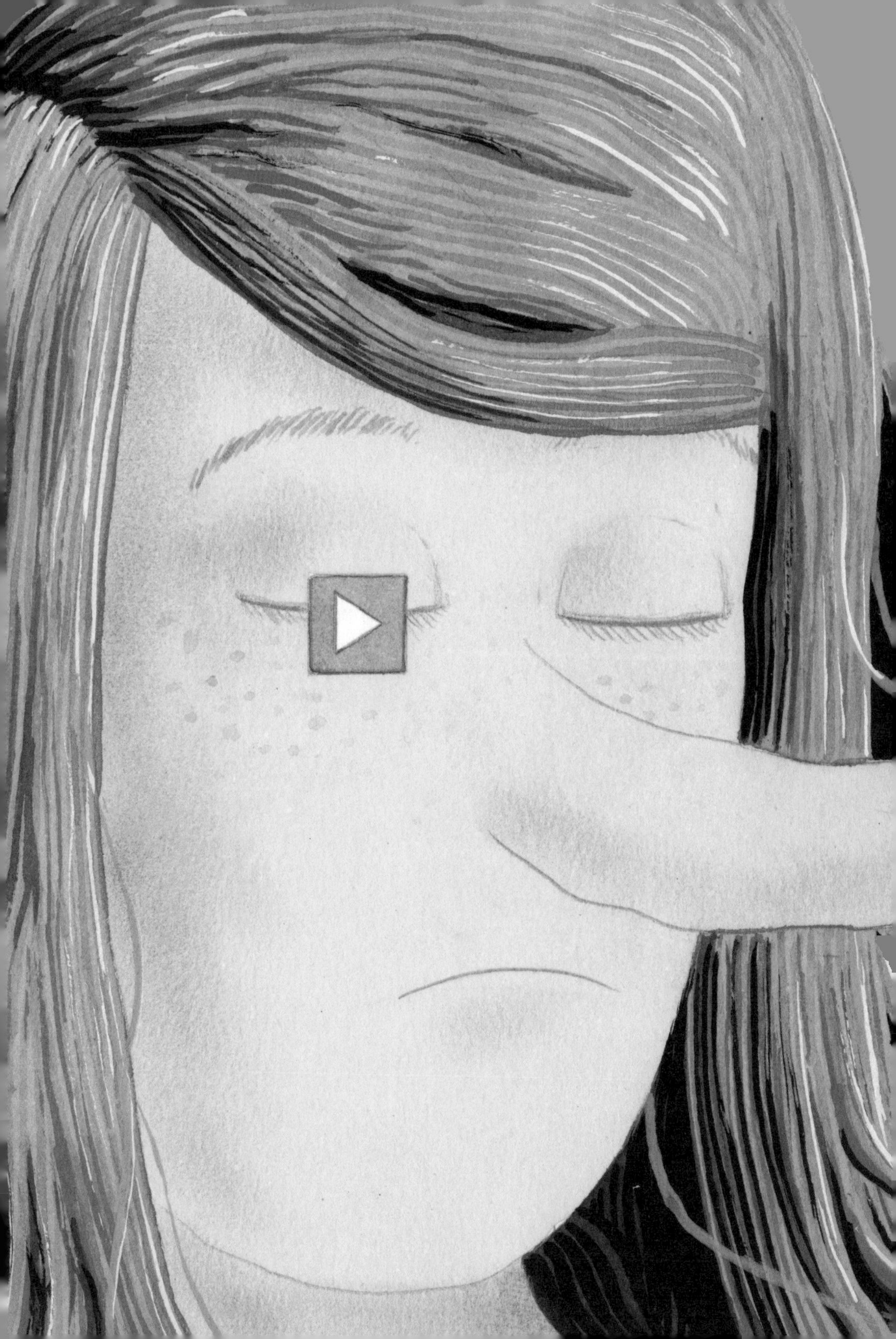

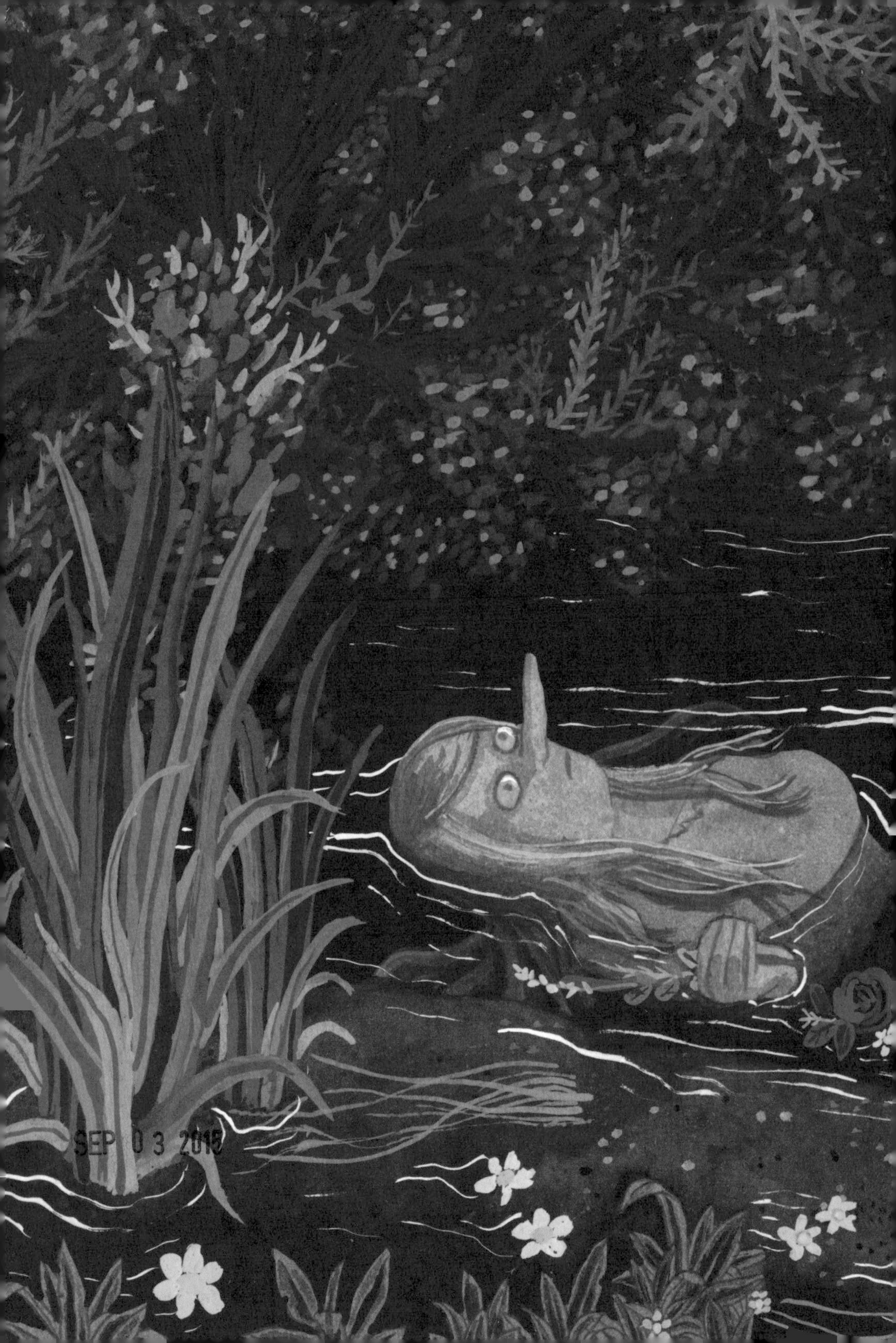